The Economic Impact of New Firms in Post-Socialist Countries

The Economic Impact of New Firms in Post-Socialist Countries

Bottom-up Transformation in Eastern Europe

Edited by
Horst Brezinski
and
Michael Fritsch

Technical University
Bergakademie Freiberg, Germany

European Association for Comparative Economic Studies

Edward Elgar
Cheltenham, UK • Brookfield, US

Published by
Edward Elgar Publishing Limited
8 Lansdown Place
Cheltenham
Glos GL50 2HU
UK

Edward Elgar Publishing Company
Old Post Road
Brookfield
Vermont 05036
US

British Library Cataloguing in Publication Data

Economic Impact of New Firms in
Post-socialist Countries: Bottom-up
Transformation in Eastern Europe
I. Brezinski, Horst II. Fritsch, Michael
338.0947

Library of Congress Cataloguing in Publication Data

The economic impact of new firms in post-socialist countries : bottom
-up transformation in Eastern Europe / edited by Horst Brezinski and
Michael Fritsch.
Includes indexes.
1. Small business—Europe, Eastern—Congresses. 2. Small
business—Former Soviet republics—Congresses. 3. Entrepreneurship–
–Europe, Eastern—Congresses. 4. Entrepreneurship—Former Soviet
republics—Congresses. I. Brezinski, Horst Dieter, 1947–
II. Fritsch, Michael.
HD2346.E92E36 1996 95–30783
330.947'086—dc20 CIP

ISBN 1 85898 121 2

Printed and bound in Great Britain by
Hartnolls Limited, Bodmin, Cornwall

Contents

List of tables vii

List of figures ix

Contributors xi

Foreword xiii

1 Introduction: the scope for bottom-up transformation in post-socialist countries 1
Horst Brezinski and *Michael Fritsch*

2 The role of entrepreneurship in economic systems: developed market and post-socialist economies 7
Paul D. Reynolds

3 A dynamic evolutionary perspective on transformation 35
Michael Keren

4 Entrepreneurship in Eastern Europe: a critical view 52
Sergio Arzeni

5 Small businesses in Russia 59
Alexander J. Chepurenko and *Alexander V. Vilensky*

6 The development of science parks and new technology-based firms in Russia 72
Stephen Batstone and *Paul Westhead*

7 Big problems of small businesses in Estonia 94
Karel Haav

8 Private economy in an etatist environment: the case of Romania 107
Gábor Hunya

9 The small private firms in Bulgaria and the impact of the economic reform on their growth and future 116
Tatiana Houbenova-Delissivkova and *Plamen Puchev*

10 The nature and performance of small firms in Bulgaria 131
Derek C. Jones

11 Small firms in South East Europe: the importance of initial conditions 151
Will Bartlett and *Paul Hoggett*

12 Poland and the Czech Republic: Privatization from above versus privatization from below or mass privatization versus generic private enterprise building 175
Krzysztof J. Ners

13 The entrepreneurial sector and its role in industrial transformation in East Germany and Poland 189
Hans-Peter Brunner

14 Small entrepreneurs in the society of employees 217
Richard Růžička

15 How to become an entrepreneur in East Germany: conditions, steps and effects of the constitution of new entrepreneurs 227
Michael Thomas

16 Businesses founded in East Germany: economic activity and capital investment 233
Thomas Hinz and *Rolf Ziegler*

17 The bottom-up strategy to transformation: summary and policy conclusions 253
Horst Brezinski and *Michael Fritsch*

Author Index 263

Subject Index 269

List of tables

2.1 Sources of job creation (per cent) 10
2.2 Correlation of firm births with job growth in following period: US 1976-88 11
2.3 Firm birth rates and variation by country 16
2.4 Overview of major results 18
2.5 Entrepreneurial process transition proportion and new effects 25
2.6 New firms, start-up teams, birth rates and marriage rates 27

5.1 Definitions of small businesses by sector 59
5.2 Industrial small enterprises in the Russian industry (end 1991) 61
5.3 Small enterprises created in 1992 62

7.1 Foreign trade of the Republic of Estonia (million Estonian kroon) 96
7.2 The structure of Estonian foreign trade (in per cent) 97
7.3 Estonia's foreign trade partners (in per cent) 97
7.4 Number of firms in Estonia 98
7.5 Ownership of Estonian enterprises (as of January 1993) 99
7.6 Overview on main problems facing entrepreneurs in Estonia 103

8.1 Share of the private sector in the economy (per cent) 110
8.2 Number of firms in the Romanian economy 111

9.1 Distribution of Bulgarian private firms according to the number of employees 125

10.1 Property forms in large manufacturing sample (per cent) 135
10.2 Descriptive statistics: Bulgarian small firms: 1991 142
10.3 Comparisons of small firms in different post socialist economies 144
10.4 Performance indicators by size and ownership 146

11.1 Employment in small firms in Slovenia and Macedonia 1988 158
11.2 Evolution of new forms of economic unit introduced in 1982 in Hungary 159
11.3 Firm size distribution - industrial firms Slovenia, Bulgaria and Macedonia 1989/90 160
11.4 GDP growth rates (per cent) 161
11.5 Unemployment rates (per cent) 162
11.6a Share of new small firms in Slovenia 163
11.6b The growth of new firms in Macedonia 163
11.7 Share of new small firms in Hungary 164

11.8 Legal form of ownership of the enterprise sector in Bulgaria and Hungary, 1991 . . . 166
11.9 Sector distribution of registered small firms in Hungary and Bulgaria, 1992 (per cent) . . . 167
11.A1 Changing structure of enterprise, Macadonia (per cent) . . . 173
11.A2 Changing structure of enterprise, Slovenia (per cent) . . . 173
11.A3 Changing structure of enterprise, Hungary (per cent) . . . 174
11.A4 Changing structure of enterprise, Bulgaria (per cent) . . . 174

13.1 Size distribution of industrial firms in Poland and East Germany compared with West Germany . . . 190
13.2 Sectoral distribution of firms, East Germany (per cent) . . . 193
13.3 Industry structure in East Germany . . . 196
13.4 Changes in stock of firms with Treuhand, 1991-1992 (all sectors) . . . 197
13.5 Transformation rates by Treuhand (per cent change) . . . 199
13.6a Poland: industrial enterprise population . . . 202
13.6b Poland: industrial enterprise population . . . 205
13.6c Poland: industrial enterprise population . . . 207
13.7 Poland: value added in industry . . . 208

14.1 Structure of employment in 1980 . . . 218
14.2 Structure of property (per cent) . . . 219
14.3 Obstacles to enterprise development (per cent; the rest no answer) . . . 223
14.4 Origins of the financing of enterprise investment . . . 224

16.1a Economic activity of registered firms in the region of Leipzig . . . 239
16.1b Organizational basic patterns of new firms in the regions of Leipzig and Munich (per cent) . . . 240
16.2 Determinants of start-up capital of newly founded firms in the regions of Leipzig and Munich (organizational variables) . . . 242
16.3 Determinants of start-up capital of newly founded firms (organizational and personal variables) . . . 244
16.4a Share of personal capital (per cent) . . . 247
16.4b Sources of outside capital (per cent) . . . 248
16.A1 Means of variables used in regression . . . 250

List of figures

2.1 Entrepreneurial process transitions 20
2.2 Prevalence of nascent entrepreneurs in Wisconsin: selected comparisons . 22

3.A1 Panel a; delta = 0.05, high (G+N) sensitivity 49
3.A2 Panel b; delta = 0.1, high (G+N) sensitivity 49
3.A3 Panel c; delta = 0.2, high (G+N) sensitivity 50
3.A4 Panel a; delta = 0.05, low (G+N) sensitivity 50
3.A5 Panel b; delta = 0.1, low (G+N) sensitivity 51
3.A6 Panel c; delta = 0.2, low (G+N) sensitivity 51

5.1 Legal forms of private enterprises according to the Law on Privatization (1986-1988) 63
5.2 Legal forms of private enterprises in industry (1989-1991) 63
5.3 Legal forms of private enterprises in trade and services in 1992 64
5.4 Legal forms of start-ups (since 1991) 64
5.A1 Sources of initial capital of Russian small business owners 70
5.A2 Priorities of economic reform in the opinion of Russian small business owners 71

6.1 MSU science park model of the innovation process 82

9.1 Number of registered small private firms in Bulgaria in 1989-92 123
9.2 Spheres of activity of Bulgarian small private firms (in per cent) 124
9.3 Critical private firms' attitude against institutions and infrastructure 128

14.1 Structure of employment 217
14.2 Change in the structure of employment 218
14.3 Instruments of financing enterprises 224
14.4 Motives to start enterprises 225

16.1 Start-up capital of newly founded firms 241
16.2 Personal capital of newly founded firms 247

Contributors

Sergio Arzeni, *Organization for Economic Co-operation and Development, Paris, France.*

Will Bartlett, *University of Bristol, UK.*

Stephen Batstone, *University of Warwick, UK.*

Horst Brezinski, *Technical University Bergakademie Freiberg, Germany.*

Hans-Peter Brunner, *Friedrich Schiller University Jena, Germany.*

Alexander J. Chepurenko, *Russian Independent Institute for Social and Nationalities Problems, Moscow, Russia.*

Michael Fritsch, *Technical University Bergakademie Freiberg, Germany.*

Karel Haav, *Free Enterprise Institute, Tallinn, Estonia.*

Thomas Hinz, *Ludwig-Maximilians University Munich, Germany.*

Paul Hoggett, *University of Bristol, UK.*

Tatiana Houbenova-Delissivkova, *Institute of Economics, Bulgarian Academy of Sciences, Sofia, Bulgaria.*

Gábor Hunya, *The Vienna Institute for Comparative Economic Studies, Austria.*

Derek C. Jones, *Hamilton College, Clinton, N.Y., USA.*

Michael Keren, *Hebrew University, Jerusalem, Israel.*

Krzysztof J. Ners, *Institute for East West Studies, Prague, Czech Republic.*

Plamen Puchev, *Technical University of Sofia, Bulgaria.*

Paul D. Reynolds, *Marquette University, Milwaukee, WI, USA.*

Richard Růžička, *Prague, Czech Republic.*

Michael Thomas, *Technical University of Dresden, Germany.*

Alexander V. Vilensky, *Institute of Economics, Russian Academy of Sciences, Moscow, Russia.*

Paul Westhead, *University of Warwick, UK.*

Rolf Ziegler, *Ludwig-Maximilians University Munich, Germany.*

Foreword

This book contains a collection of contributions to the 'Second Freiberg Symposium on Economics', which took place at the Technical University Bergakademie Freiberg, Germany, from September 9-11, 1993. The Technical University of Freiberg founded in 1765 which over two centuries had developed an outstanding reputation in mining, the natural sciences and engineering which it had been able to maintain even in Socialist Germany had to undergo severe changes during the process of transition. With a new faculty of Economics and Business Administration being installed in 1991, it was obvious for the organizers of the conference (and editors of this book) to choose the topic of the transformation which has been going on in East Germany and the other post-socialist countries of Eastern Europe as a subject for a scholarly meeting.

The papers presented here all deal with the question of how far the serious economic problems in the countries analyzed can be overcome by the creation of new and small business firms. Under the aspect of a long-term development, so-called 'top-down privatization', i.e. the privatization of state-owned enterprises, does not offer an adequate basis for a continous economic upswing. Bottom-up privatization, i.e. the founding of new enterprises, is seen as a prerequisite for a successful transformation. The contributors of the volume provide a host of empirical information and analyze on this transformation process from below in contrast to 'top-down privatization'. It is not at all surprising that the experiences in the attempts to employ the two strategies of transformation vary from country to country in the post-socialist area. It becomes clear from the various articles that bottom-up transformation may be seen as a major opportunity for economic recovery, but that, at the same time, such a process demands considerable time and that no quick relief for the ailing economic situation in Eastern Europe is in sight. The scholars who have contributed their expertise show much can be done to accelerate transformation and that bottom-up requires thorough and extensive support by government policy to yield satisfactory results.

The editors gratefully acknowledge the invaluable help provided by Herrmann Fink and Sandra Le Blanc in checking language and style of the articles, many of them written by non-native speakers. Special thanks go to Anja Helbig for providing the photo-technical version of this book.

We hope that 'The Economic Impact of New Firms in Post-Socialist Countries: Bottom-Up Transformation in Eastern Europe' will make a fruitful contribution to the discussion on the solution of economic problems in the transforming countries of Eastern Europe.

Freiberg

Horst Brezinski
Michael Fritsch

1 Introduction: the scope for bottom-up transformation in post-socialist countries

Horst Brezinski and *Michael Fritsch*

1. Two ways for the switch to a private market economy

The fall of the iron curtain and the drastic changes in the political system of former socialist countries in Eastern Europe has led also to a collapse of the economic planning system and to a dramatic downturn of economic performance. It has become a widely shared view that in order to cope with these economic problems a transformation of the Eastern systems to a Western-type market economy is necessary. Viewing an economy as a population of firms, there are two alternatives for such a transformation of post-socialist economies: 'top-down' and 'bottom-up'. Whereas top-down denotes the privatization of state-owned enterprises, bottom-up characterizes the change of economic structures that is due to the establishment of new enterprises or to the development of the private firms that already exist. The articles collected in this book deal with the prerequisites, the scope and the impediments of bottom-up transformation, analyze the respective experiences made in post-socialist countries of Eastern Europe and draw conclusions as to the most feasible and appropriate policies to implement this kind of transition from a command economy to a free market system.

The bottom-up strategy can be seen to rest on two foundations: the experiences with small and new firms in Western market economies and the severe problems of top-down privatization. Because the importance of the small firms sector in Western market economies is quite frequently misunderstood, we will begin our introduction in briefly summarizing main findings of the respective research (Section 2). Section 3 gives a description of the potential role small and new firms might play in post-socialist countries. Section 4 contains an overview on the collected papers.

2. The role of new and small firms in Western market economies

In the countries of the West, small and new firms have attracted the attention of major research and of economic policy only during the past 15 years. The initial impulse was the well-known and heavily criticized 1979 study by David Birch, the 'Job Generation Process' (Birch, 1979). In his analysis, based on US employment data, Birch concluded that during the 1970s small and particularly new firms were the major source of new jobs. This finding induced euphoric reactions and severe skepticism as well. Some saw small firms as a solution to the problems of unemployment and stagnation while others expressed considerable doubt concerning the empirical analysis. In fact, Birch's way of preparing his data proved to be questionable and further research showed, that the results presented by him do not hold true universally for all periods of time (Acs and Audretsch, 1993; Sengenberger, Loveman and Piore, 1990). Nevertheless, his work has been of a strong impact on further research and stimulated numerous analyses of the importance of small and new firms in economic development.

The results of the foregoing research on the role of small and new firms in Western market economies may be summarized in a few conclusions:

- Small and new firms *may* be of great importance for innovation (cf. Acs and Audretsch, 1990) and employment; still this is no reason for general enthusiasm about small firms.
- This impact may considerably vary from country to country, region to region, and period to period of time.[1]
- Although some of the small and new companies perform very well, many of them are merely marginal and do not make substantial contributions to economic development; they provide poorly paid jobs for employees with only basic qualifications.
- In most countries small firms are discriminated against by economic policy and are faced with much more serious drawbacks than large firms.

There is a consensus among many researchers in the field that economic policy should focus more on the small-firm sector than is commonly the case. Yet, it may be said that the role small and new firms play in job generation in Western market economies is often overestimated.

A central feature of small and new firms is that they may be seen as indicators of the dynamic properties of an economic system. Growing new and small firms play an important part in the process of economic development once illustrated by Alfred Marshall (1920, 263) in his comparison of the economy to a forest, in which 'the young trees ... struggle upwards through the benumbing shade of their older rivals' and where the old trees sooner or later have to give way to the young ones. Marshall's 'ecological' perspective is similar to Schumpeter's view of economic development as a process of 'creative destruction'. Schumpeter (1942) argued that destruction or the economic decline of firms is a necessary component of economic development in order to set free resources for a better use by other actors. According to Schumpeter this development is driven by dynamic entrepreneurs who introduce 'new combinations' to contest the established market positions of existing firms. Therefore, new-firm start-ups can be looked upon as an indicator of the contestability of established market positions and of the openness of the economic system to innovation and entrepreneurial initiative.

Marshall's 'ecological' view and Schumpeter's perspective of 'creative destruction' have at least two important implications (Audretsch and Fritsch, 1994). The first implication is that exits of firms from markets are inevitable and constitute an essential element of economic development. As a consequence, one should not care too much

1 Cf. the contributions in Acs and Audretsch, 1993; Sengenberger, Loveman and Piore, 1990. For the impact of new firms on regional development see Reynolds, 1994; Audretsch and Fritsch, 1994; and Fritsch, 1994, 1995.

about the decline or dying of firms. A second implication is that in such a process of 'destruction' new firms and growing small firms are of central importance. They do not only challenge the already existing firms, they are, moreover, particularly necessary to make the process creative because deaths and exits without corresponding growth is only destruction and nothing more.

3. The potential role of small and new firms in post-socialist countries

These views expressed in the analysis of small and medium-sized enterprises in the West had a considerable impact on the perception of small and new companies in the transforming economies of Eastern Europe. The governments of these states as well as international organizations and institutions assisting them regard the setting up of a new private-enterprise sector to be a major task in the process of transition (EBRD, 1994). This view is based on the hope that small and new firms may make a considerable contribution to the solution of economic, social and political problems. It is also based on the insight that the process of top-down privatization turns out to be much more difficult than initially expected (Rühle and Winkler, 1994) and that financial resources to subsidize state-owned enterprises are no longer available. If top-down transformation does not appear to be a promising way to cope with such problems as unemployment and insufficient economic growth all hope rests in the bottom-up strategy, particularly in the emergence and growth of new private businesses.

In the post-socialist countries of Eastern Europe, bottom-up development is expected to meet four functions in the process of transformation towards a market economy (Werner, 1994; Hauer, Kleinhenz and von Schuttenbach, 1993):

- *First:* Small and new enterprises perform an important political task in creating a pluralistic society. The existence of independent entrepreneurs reflects the personal freedom granted to individuals and the decentralization of economic power. Individuals may change from dependent into independent persons exercising power and shaping a democratic society and economy. The right to establish an enterprise when, in whatever field, and wherever wanted, constitutes a shift from formal rights to material ones. Thus, small enterprises contribute to and safeguard the very existence of a modern democratic society. They stabilize economic order and guarantee a certain quality of life.
- *Second:* Small and new enterprises contribute to competition and may help to prevent market failure caused by market power and the dominance of a few big companies.
- *Third:* In addition, the small-firm sector has a structural function. Small firms are regarded as institutions which improve the flexibility of the economy as a whole, particularly in terms of innovation and the necessary adaptation to the rapid changes of demand and supply. Moreover, an increase in flexibility may assist in removing regional disparities. The birth and death of enterprises may make a considerable

contribution to the structural change needed for the national economy to be competitive in the world market.

- *Fourth:* The small enterprise sector is seen to have an impact on the employment situation. It is regarded as a means to compensate for the job losses caused by the decline and the labor-shedding of the big state-owned enterprises. Consequently, small enterprises may serve as a social cushion in the labor market.

Thus, the role of small and new enterprises in the process of system transformation is regarded as very positive. However as pointed out (above), these expectations are only partly supported by the experiences made in the market economies of the West.

4. Overview on articles

While the majority of the articles collected in this volume deals with the current state and the problems of bottom-up transformation in certain post-socialist countries of Eastern Europe, there are also contributions that analyze the potentials of transformation 'from below' from a more general perspective. In the next chapter, Paul Reynolds gives an overview of recent research on the role of entrepreneurship in Western-type market economies. Michael Keren then contrasts the bottom-up strategy with the top-down approach to transformation within a theoretical model (Chapter 3); according to his results the bottom-up strategy can - under normal circumstances - be expected to be much more promising than the top-down approach. Sergio Arzeni gives a critical review of the state and development of entrepreneurship in Eastern Europe stressing the now visible shortcomings of private firms and government policy (Chapter 4); given the still unfavorable conditions for private entrepreneurship in most of the post-socialist countries he is rather pessimistic with regards to a speedy economic recovery.

The national studies begin with the contribution by Alexander Chepurenko and Alexander Vilensky on small businesses in Russia (Chapter 5) and an article by Stephen Batstone and Paul Westhead on the current state and the peculiarities of Russian science parks aiming at developing new technology based firms (Chapter 6). Karel Haav then reports on small businesses in Estonia (Chapter 7) and Gabor Hunya analyzes the conditions for private entrepreneurship in Romania (Chapter 8). The two following papers deal with Bulgaria: Tatiana Houbenova-Delissivkova and Plamen Puchev report on the scope of bottom-up and top-down transformation in Bulgaria (Chapter 9); Derek Jones gives information on characteristics of a sample of Bulgarian small businesses (Chapter 10). Will Bartlett and Paul Hoggett compare the development of the small business sector in Bulgaria, Hungary, Macedonia and Slovenia, working out the differences in performance and initial conditions (Chapter 11). Krzysztof Ners compares the mass privatization strategy followed in Poland to the much more reserved policy of privatization in the Czech Republic stressing the advantages of a cautious top-down privatization (Chapter 12). Richard Růžička deals with the problems of entrepreneurs in a former socialist economy under transition (Chapter 13); although the empirical background of his contribution is the Czech Republic, large parts of his analysis should also be valid for other post-socialist economies of Eastern Europe. Hans-Peter Brunner gives a detailed description of the dramatic changes in the stock of firms in the industrial sector of Poland and East Germany during the first years of the transformation process (Chapter 14). The article by Michael Thomas reports on the origions and further characteristics of new East German entrepreneurs (Chapter 15); Thomas Hinz and Rolf Ziegler analyze the economic activity and the capital investment of new businesses in the region of Leipzig, East Germany (Chapter 16).

In a final contribution (Chapter 17), Horst Brezinski and Michael Fritsch give a short synopsis of the results of bottom-up transformation in Eastern Europe, summarizing the impediments for the transformation from below and drawing a number of policy recommendations for a strategy that focusses on small firms and entrepreneurship. Their main conclusion is that a bottom-up strategy seems to be the most promising way of transformation in the post-socialist economies of Eastern Europe but that it needs profound and intense support by government policies in order to yield satisfactory results. The articles collected in this book very clearly show that much more could and should be done in this respect.

References

Acs, Z. and D.B. Audretsch (1990) *Innovation and Small Firms*, Cambridge: MIT-Press.

Acs, Z. and D.B. Audretsch (1993) (Eds.) *Small Firms and Entrepreneurship: An East-West Perspective*, Cambridge: Cambridge University Press.

Audretsch, D.B. and M. Fritsch (1994) *Creative Destruction: Turbulence and Economic Growth*, Working Paper 94/10, Technical University Bergakademie Freiberg, Faculty of Economics and Business Administration.

Birch, D. (1979) *The Job Generation Process*, Cambridge/Mass. (mimeo).

European Bank for Reconstruction and Development (EBRD) (1994) *Transition Report*, London.

Fritsch, M. (1994) *New Firms and Regional Employment Change*, Working Paper 94/12, Technical University Bergakademie Freiberg, Faculty of Economics and Business Administration.

Fritsch, M. (1995); Turbulence and Growth in West-Germany: A Comparison of Evidence by Regions and Industries; *Review of Industrial Organization*, 10 (forthcoming).

Hauer, A., Th. Kleinhenz and L. von Schuttenbach (1993) *Der Mittelstand im Transformationsprozeß Ostdeutschlands und Osteuropas*, Heidelberg: Physica.

Marshall, A. (1920) *Principles of Economics*, 8th edition, London: Macmillan.

Reynolds, P.D. (1994); Autonomous Firm Dynamics and Economic Growth in the United States: 1986-90; *Regional Studies*, 27, 429-42.

Rühle, I. and A. Winkler (1994); Die Finanzierungssituation kleiner und mittlerer Unternehmen und Maßnahmen der Finanzsektorreform in Transformationsökonomien, in: Institut für Wirtschaftsforschung Halle (ed.), *Mittel- und Osteuropa*, 2, 21-40.

Schumpeter, J.A. (1942) *Capitalism, Socialism and Democracy*, New York: Harper and Row.

Sengenberger, W., G. Loveman and M. Piore (1990) (eds.) *The Re-Emergence of Small Enterprise - Industrial Restructuring in Industrialized Countries*, Geneva: International Labor Organization.

Werner, K. (1994), Zur Entwicklung kleiner und mittlerer Unternehmen in Mittel- und Osteuropa - Ein Überblick, Institut für Wirtschaftsforschung Halle (ed.), *Mittel- und Osteuropa*, 3, 7-21.

2 The role of entrepreneurship in economic systems: developed market and post-socialist economies[1]

Paul D. Reynolds

1. Introduction

Every political system in the world is concerned with entrepreneurial activity and considers it a critical issue. In North America the competitive advantages associated with a healthy entrepreneurial sector lead to regional competition in promoting business climates. Western European countries, concerned with evidence of economic stagnation, are trying to encourage entrepreneurialism among their citizens. Latin American countries are trying to adjust the formal systems that have driven most entrepreneurial activity (as well as most economic growth) outside the registered economy (de Soto, 1989). In the People's Republic of China, an uneven distribution of entrepreneurial opportunity is a constant source of political disruption. The formerly socialist countries are attempting to construct the infrastructure that will facilitate new firm formation, hoping this will enhance economic growth.

The history of all societies is a history of economic, social and political change. Most models of societies produced by economists, sociologists and others, however, have emphasized the processes under conditions of stability - stable productive systems, stable institutional structures, stable political systems (Baumol, 1968; Barreto, 1989). While substantial progress has been made in understanding the processes and mechanisms that coordinate supply and demand in stable socio-economic systems, these theories do not emphasize a major role for entrepreneurial activity. Recent attention to socio-economic change has lead to greater attention to the role of entrepreneurial activity. It is now clear that economic growth and change occurs when an appropriate level of entrepreneurial activity is present.

Recognition that all socio-economic systems constantly undergo change has created two challenges for scholars:

I What is the role of entrepreneurial activity in promoting change and enhancing economic growth and well-being?

II What are the conditions that foster or encourage an optimal level of entrepreneurial activity?

---

1 This presentation combines analysis and interpretations from three collaborative documents: two reflect jointly organized research endeavors (Reynolds and Storey, 1993; Reynolds, Storey and Westhead, 1994; Reynolds and White, 1993) and the third a team developed research proposal (Curtin, Morgan and Reynolds, 1993). Many of the analyses and commentaries are joint products and substantial contributions came from various colleagues: Richard Curtin, James Morgan, David Storey and Sammis White. They are not, however, responsible for any errors introduced into this consolidated version.

While these issues are at the forefront of the study of both developed economies (as in North America, Western Europe and Pacific-Rim Asia) and developing economies (as in South America, Africa, South-East and central Asia) they have a special significance for post-socialist countries. Post-socialist countries are considered to be those where the governments are shifting from the centralized coordination of economic activity to supervision of market mechanisms. These market mechanisms, an open system of free exchange, are assumed to coordinate supply and demand providing, under the right conditions, optimal benefits for all participants.

Research on entrepreneurship in developed economies has progressed significantly in the past several decades. A greater role for the entrepreneurial process has recently been provided in the conceptual schemes of major social science disciplines. In economics, most change in economic activity has been assumed to reflect entrepreneurial activity, the result of 'creative destruction' (Schumpeter, 1934). There is a substantial literature on market entry (and exit) that is relevant to the entrepreneurial process. In sociology, there has been a sustained focus on the entrepreneurial behavior of immigrant groups and a major effort in organizational analysis (population ecology) focuses on emergence of new categories of organizations and the conditions that affect organizational birth rates in these new niches. In geography and the study of subnational regions, considerable effort has been devoted to understanding the factors that affect the spatial distribution of businesses. Changes in spatial distribution may reflect actual business moves or the outcome of differentials in firm birth and death rates; separating the two is a major problem. Those concerned with the study of business organizations have devoted substantial attention to the resources, strategies, personality profiles, training and experience associated with successful new - entrepreneurial - ventures. Psychologists have been exploring the unique personality and cognitive orientations of those disposed toward or involved in entrepreneurial activity for some time. The major findings may have relevance to the shifts occurring in post-socialist economies.

The following covers some current research on entrepreneurship, focusing on developed countries. Several topics are reviewed: problems associated with systematic research on entrepreneurship; the role of entrepreneurship in economic change and growth; an overview of research on sub-national regional (or contextual) factors affecting the rate of new firm births; and an introduction to current research on the entrepreneurial process (the mechanisms by which individuals decide to pursue an entrepreneurial career option and establish a new business entity). The final section provides some preliminary comments on the application of these findings to the current transitions in post-socialist countries.

2. Complications in the study of entrepreneurship

As important as the study of entrepreneurship may be, there are at least two problems that complicate careful study of this phenomena.

First are the multiple conceptions of entrepreneurship. The widest possible definition includes any individual economic activity, even part-time self-employment in traditional tasks, as entrepreneurship. In this light, a person that takes small carpentry jobs on the weekend, or does sewing at nights in the home, is considered an entrepreneur. This may be constrained to include only full-time self-employment. A further constraint would include only businesses that create jobs or employment for others. Some may or may not include family oriented productive units - such as farms or restaurants or construction firms. A more restrictive definition would include only major changes in productive or economic activity as 'entrepreneurial'. Again there is some variation, as there are different views on the degree of innovation required. Another criteria that is often introduced is the growth rate; there are some that consider only those firms with high levels of growth as entrepreneurial. A further complication involves the extent to which entrepreneurship can be produced by existing businesses, as when a team of employees - and not independent individuals - create a new product line, technological process, or distribution strategy.

Clearly, there is no easy resolution to this definitional problem. Those with different scholarly objectives have focused on a variety of firm attributes: size of the business, degree of innovation, growth rate, individual versus corporate efforts. The following discussions tend to emphasize the implementation of a new business by individuals, alone or in teams, without substantial support from established businesses. Much of the existing data can be utilized to study new firm births. Most of these new firms, however, are doing traditional things, only a very small proportion represent substantial innovations, and the majority do not have high growth rates.

The second major problem is the diversity of procedures used to identify new business in advanced economies. In terms of cross national comparisons of entrepreneurial activity, the most useful measures are annual counts of new firms. Remarkably, no two developed societies use the same procedure for identifying new (or small) firms (OECD, 1991; ENSR, 1993). Some use official registries, where those with new businesses are required to notify the government of their presence. Some use new filings of business or value added taxes; this can be extended to any filing that implies business activity (such as business expenses associated with an individual income tax return). Others use new filings of taxes for employees; if a new filing for withholding of income tax payments or social security payments is found, it is assumed that a new firm has been created. Some countries use new membership in local chambers of commerce, which vary among countries in terms of legal status or completeness of coverage. These procedures are further complicated by diversity in the information obtained on the new business. In some cases it is not possible to separate those started by individuals, unaided by others, from new branches or subsidiaries put in place by established businesses. In such situations the new business may either be an autonomous startup or a branch or subsidiary. None of the government records provide any information on whether or not the new business represents innovation or change in economic activity.

The result of these complications is that precise cross-national comparisons are very difficult. Analysis is generally restricted to (1) very general comparisons (ENSR, 1993) or (2) analysis of variations within the countries (Reynolds and Storey, 1993). If the same patterns are found within countries, despite variations in measures, then it increases confidence that the underlying processes are similar. For example, it is generally found that most firms are started by young adults (25-45 years old) in all countries; the very young and those past middle-age are seldom involved. This pattern is unrelated to the definition or measure of a new firm birth and, hence, can be considered a very robust phenomena.

3. Entrepreneurship and economic change and growth

The entrepreneurial process and the formation of new firms are central to many features of market economies.[2]

First, and perhaps most significant, new firms are a major source of new jobs (Birch, 1981; Kirchhoff and Phillips, 1988). Analyses for Sweden (Davidsson, Lindmark and Olofsson, 1992 and 1994) and the United States (Reynolds and Maki, 1991, 142; Reynolds, 1994) are shown in Table 2.1. In both countries, careful delineation of autonomous firms from branch establishments indicates that about half of all new jobs are provided by autonomous firms - virtually all qualify as small and medium enterprises.

Table 2.1 Sources of job creation (per cent)

	Sweden: 1985-89	US: 1976-88
Independent firm births	19	25
Independent firm expansions	32	29
Branch births	11	32
Branch expansions	38	14
Total	100	100

Second, within countries some geographic regions appear to have much higher rates of new firm formation than others. In many cases, these high rates of firm births are associated with substantial regional prosperity. Classic examples include the so-called 'third Italy' where firm formation rates are much higher than elsewhere in Italy, as in the south. Other illustrations include the Gnosjo area of Sweden, always used as a Swedish example of an area of exceptional enterprise[3] - and wealth. Since the third Italy

2 Much of this section is adapted from Reynolds and Storey (1993) and Curtin, Morgan and Reynolds (1993).

3 Although they are used frequently as examples of 'enterprising' regions, it should not be assumed that low levels of unemployment and high levels of wealth always coincide. For example, while the Gnosjo area has a low level of unemployment it is, by Swedish standards, a low wage economy. In addition, analysis of 382 US labor market areas indicate that correlations between annual growth in jobs and annual growth in labor income are about 0.67 over the 1976-86 period; many labor market areas have labor income growth without job growth and many job growth without labor income growth (Reynolds and

and the Gnosjo areas have low unemployment, it has encouraged many to believe that the new firm formation has led to prosperity, producing jobs and reducing unemployment.

Analysis of the relationship between firm births and subsequent regional economic growth in the United States has found that while not all regions with high firm birth rates prosper, it is rare for regions that prosper not to have high firm birth rates (Reynolds and Maki, 1990, 1991). High firm birth rates may be, then, necessary but not sufficient conditions for regional economic growth. If such a relationship exists more broadly across other countries, it justifies policies to raise new firm formation rates on the grounds that this will lead ultimately to greater regional prosperity. An example of the correlations found between firm birth rates and percentage job growth (growth in positions, not in employment) is presented in Table 2.2. This summarizes patterns for 382 United States labor market (travel-to-work) areas over a 12 year period (1976-88).

Table 2.2 Correlation of firm births with job growth in following period: US 1976-88

	Correlation[4]
Business services	0.50
Wholesale	0.41
Health, education and social services	0.32
Manufacturing, non-durable	0.32
Manufacturing, durable	0.30
Construction	0.30
Consumer services	0.12
Transportation, communication, utilities	0.11
Retail (includes bars and restaurants)	0.09
Mining	– 0.06
Agricultural services (excludes agricultural production)	– 0.10
All economic sectors combined	0.31

For most industries, there is a clear positive relationship. It may be, of course, that firm births are reflecting an underlying process of economic growth rather than

Maki, 1990, 24).

4 Each correlation is the average for six pairs of two-year periods. For example, firm birth rates (independent establishments per 10 000 human population) for 1976-78 is correlated with the percentage job (not employment) growth for 1978-80 (with 1978 used as the base year). Firms cover all economic sectors except agricultural production. Job counts cover all economic sectors except government, military and agricultural production. The unit of analysis are 382 United States labor market areas, consolidations of the 3 124 counties based on 1980 census information on travel-to-work patterns.

providing a direct contribution. An attempt to explore this issue found statistically significant evidence of an independent impact on economic growth from new firm births (Reynolds and Maki, 1990).

Third, new firms are involved in a substantial proportion of innovations in the economy (Acs and Audretsch, 1988). New firms implementing innovations in product or processes often lead to the creation of entire industries. Further, these new firms may provide a major challenge to established firms and encourage them to improve their products, quality or service, or reduce prices. The fact that innovation based new firms are a small proportion of all new firms does not diminish their significance. Innovation, change and vitality in an economic system are associated with vigorous new and small firm sectors.

Fourth, the opportunity to pursue an entrepreneurial venture is a major career option for a substantial, perhaps growing, proportion of the population. While entrepreneurial and small firm activity have always been important in economic affairs (Granovetter, 1984), there is evidence of a recent increase in its significance in all advanced economies (Loveman and Sengenberger, 1990). It has become clear that starting a new business is, for many people, an important career option. Societies committed to maximizing freedom of economic opportunity may take actions to ensure that those wishing to pursue entrepreneurship are not prevented from doing so.

Fifth, the increasing diversity and heterogeneity of organizational populations, or market niches, accompanied by an increasing interdependence among the niches, are a major source of system efficiency and adaptativeness.

Overall, these features of the entrepreneurial phenomena make a strong case for giving it careful attention. Two separate analyses will be reviewed below. First, a recent study of the contextual factors (societal, institutional, regional) affecting the presence of entrepreneurship will be considered. Second, a preliminary study of the entrepreneurial process will be described. These transitions mark the changes as individuals begin to develop new firms and eventually put a new firm in place.

4. Contextual factors affecting birth rates

There is substantial variation in the annual birth rates of new firms (firms per 10 000 human population; new firms per 100 business establishments) across regions within countries. This fact may be used to pursue analysis of those processes or mechanisms that affect new firm births. A recent cross-national endeavour selected seven such processes for attention (Reynolds and Storey, 1993). The choice of processes reflects both the availability of suitable data and an informed judgement regarding processes likely to have a major impact on new firm births.

4.1 Hypotheses

(a) *Demand*. No process is more fundamental than reactions to increased demand for goods and services. It is reasonable to expect that as demand increases, more new firms will be founded to satisfy this greater demand. Two indicators of such growth were utilized. One was a measure of net population growth or immigration. (This may also reflect, however, a growth in the supply of potential entrepreneurs.) The second was an indicator of increases in personal or household income or a growth in regional Gross Domestic Product.

(b) *Urbanization/agglomeration*. There has, for some time, been attention to the relative advantages of urban areas as a context - or incubator - for new firms. This is considered to reflect the relative ease of access to customers as well as the inputs required (capital, labor, suppliers) to produce the goods or services. Urbanized contexts are frequently a source of entrepreneurs, educated individuals with business experience in their early and middle adult years. On the other hand, the costs associated with most inputs (physical space, wages, transportation) are somewhat higher in urban areas. This may offset the benefits of ease of access for new firms in some industries. Indicators of urbanization/agglomeration included population density (transformed to a normal distribution), the percentage of the population 25-44 years old, the percentage of the workforce in managerial positions, the percentage of the population with formal occupational training or post-high school degrees and - as an indicator of non-urban settings - the presence of secondary or vacation housing.

(c) *Unemployment/desperation*. When people lose their jobs with existing organizations and become desperate for a role in the economy, they may well turn to self-employment or attempt to start a new firm. This is more likely to occur when they feel committed to a given community, where their family may have been established for generations, and reluctant to move to other regions with job opportunities. On the other hand, higher levels of unemployment may indicate a reduction in disposable income and a reduced demand, decreasing the rate of new firm formation. Two indicators were used to reflect this process, the absolute level of unemployment and changes in the unemployment rate in the previous two years.

(d) *Personal, household wealth*. One of the primary requirements for founding a new firm is start-up capital. This may be provided by the entrepreneurs on the start-up team or borrowed from friends or family. Greater wealth in an area may indicate the availability of start-up capital or a reduction in borrowing costs. For individuals, this wealth is often in the form of home ownership. Land prices would be one alternative to dwelling values. Four measures were used as indicators of wealth controlled by individuals: household income, the presence of owner-occupied housing, housing prices and land prices.

(e) *Small firms/specialization*. There are a number of examples of regions with a reputation for adaptability and growth that are characterized by a high proportion of small firms and sector concentration. 'Flexible specialization' refers to an organization of economic activity that is both adaptable and robust while specializing on a narrow range of goods or products. Two indicators were utilized in an attempt to capture the basic elements of this process. The percentage of all firms that would be considered small was a primary measure, although the definition of firm size varied somewhat among the different countries. For most firm size was measured by the number of employees, for others it was the annual sales (turnover). The second measure was an index of sector concentration, based on the percentage of workers in the major economic sectors (from 10 to 15 categories, depending upon the country) covering all areas of activity. If there was complete uniformity with the same proportion of the workforce in all sectors, the index would be zero. If all workers were in the one sector, the index would be one.

(f) *Socialist voters*. The political complexion of the government could also influence business formation rates. For example, it could be argued that left wing or socialist local/regional governments are more likely to spend money and hence create demand in the locality. On the other hand, these expenditures may require higher tax rates which could depress demand. Left-wing (or liberal) governments might also indicate the presence of relatively negative attitudes to self-employment and entrepreneurship, and the absence of a local 'enterprise culture'. It could also be argued that regions dominated by small businesses are more likely to have a conservative government. This liberal-conservative dimension was measured by the extent of socialist (liberal) voting patterns in a recent election.

(g) *Government spending/policies*. There are at least two ways governments may affect the presence of new firms in a locality. One is through local spending which may increase demand and, wisely used, improve the local infrastructure: schools, health care, roads, police and fire services, and the like. The other is through programs providing direct assistance to new and small firms. Indicators of both were used to reflect the impact of government actions.

It should be mentioned that the technical procedures used to measure the indicators varied among the countries. For example, virtually every country has a different education system, so the measure of educational attainment (associated with the urban/agglomerative processes) is slightly different for each country.

The major focus of the analysis, then, is to determine if there is evidence that these processes are having an impact on firm births in advanced market economies. If more than one process is found to have an impact, the relative magnitude of the impact is also of some interest.

4.2 Analysis strategy

The objectives of the overall project, and the analysis within each country, was to determine the relative impact of different processes on firm births (Reynolds, 1991). The strategy was, therefore, to take advantage of the variation across regions that are considered 'natural', at least not deliberately controlled by any human agents or organizations. In order to track the effects of these natural variations, it is necessary to have reliable data for the different regions within a country. If regions that have - for whatever reason - higher unemployment in one period appear, in a following period, to have higher firm births rates when compared to other regions, it is reasonable to infer that unemployment is somehow related to the processes that lead to firm births.

In order to complete such an analysis within a single country, data reflecting important processes must be gathered for each region at frequent intervals, say every one to five years. While most Western or developed countries have extensive annual data on economic activity and population characteristics at the national level, it is - surprisingly - relatively rare for the regions within the countries. This lack of periodic, regional level data placed major constraints on the countries that could be included in this analysis. In fact, the countries that are represented (France, Germany [Western], Italy, Ireland, Japan, Sweden, United Kingdom, United States)[5] are among the very few with appropriate data (Keeble, Potter and Storey, 1990). Suitable data may be available in some other countries (such as Australia, Canada, the Netherlands, New Zealand, Norway, Switzerland), but teams could not be located nor resources assembled for analyses in time for inclusion for this comparison.

4.3 Spatial variation in firm birth rates

This analysis would not be possible if there were no variations in firm birth rates across the different countries. Comparisons across countries provide some evidence regarding the extent of this variation. There was, however, substantial variation in the procedures used to determine new firm births across most advanced countries. In fact, no two countries have, strictly speaking, the same procedure. This variation is fully represented in this cross-national comparison in several ways. For example, for the United Kingdom, new registrations for the Value Added Tax (VAT) were used as counts of new businesses. For Sweden and France it was new entries in business registers. German firm births were inferred from social administration files and in Ireland based on comprehensive annual censuses of manufacturing firms. Births in the United States were based on new entries into the files of a commercial credit rating service. The nature of the business entities also varied. Data in Germany, Japan and the United Kingdom was based on all new businesses, including independent start-ups and branch units. In Ireland, Sweden and the United States, it was possible to exclude branch births and focus on autonomous start-ups. Another important source of difference was the definition of a 'region'. For Ireland and the United Kingdom, the regions were administrative counties. For France and Japan, they were administrative regions and for Germany, planning regions. For Sweden and the United States, they were labor market (or travel-to-work) areas.

Despite the differences, and with considerable coordination among the different country teams, it was possible to develop birth rate indicators that were conceptually similar, even if the technical details differed. The two measures used in the analysis are presented in Table 2.3. The four columns on the left in Table 2.3. are related to annual firm births per 100 firms existing at the beginning of the period. The four columns on

---

5 Guesnier, 1994; Audretsch and Fritsch, 1994b; Hart and Gudgin, 1994; Garofoli, 1994; Davidsson, Lindmark and Olofsson, 1994; Keeble and Walker, 1994.

the right refer to annual firm births per 10 000 human population.[6] For each firm birth rate measure, the average across regions, the maximum, the minimum and the ratio of maximum/minimum is given. The top half of the table reflects new firm births in all economic sectors, the bottom new firm births in manufacturing (industry). All birth rates are for the middle to late 1980s.

Table 2.3 Firm birth rates and variation by country

	Annual firms births per 100 firms				Annual firm births per 10 000 persons			
	Avg.	Min.	Max.	Max./ Min.	Avg.	Min.	Max.	Max./ Min.
All sectors								
France	104	70	148	21	118	67	264	3.9
Germany	6	65	101	16	55	41	90	2.2
Italy	93	61	118	19	144	74	202	2.7
Sweden*	157	109	222	20	88	56	149	2.7
United Kingdom	14.3	7	21.2	3	72	42	107	2.5
United States	6.9	3.9	11	2.8	33	18	74	4.1
Manufacturing only								
France	-	-	-	-	-	-	-	-
Germany	56	37	73	20	68	45	120	2.7
Ireland**	70	41	110	27	223	107	427	4
Italy	87	58	171	29	268	127	510	4
Japan	60	42	84	20	67	41	127	3.1
Sweden	-	-	-	-	103	44	287	6.5
United Kingdom**	16.5	10.1	23.1	2.3	27.5	10	59.5	6
United States**	6	2.1	14.2	6.8	16.8	2.4	114	47.5

Notes: * Population 16-64 used as denominator, rather than size of workforce.
** Manufacturing workers used as denominators.
- Missing.

6 Rather than review the spirited debate regarding which is the 'right' measure of birth rates (Audretsch and Fritsch, 1994a), both measures are included in this analysis. If one assumes that new firms are generated or created by the existing firms, then the focus is on a birth related to the presence of businesses. If one assumes that businesses are created by individuals, some of which may not have jobs, then the focus is on the pool of potential entrepreneurs, the human population. For the analysis that follows, the exact measure has little impact on the major conclusions.

There is some variation among the different countries in the average values. This reflects differences in the technical procedures used to measure firm births in the different countries. Because of these technical differences, *cross-national comparisons of the average values are not appropriate*.[7]

There are, however, two major sources of similarity. First, the average values have the same order of magnitude. Annual births per 100 firms ranges from 7 to 16 per year for all industries; 6 to 17 for manufacturing. Annual births per 10 000 persons ranges from 33 to 88 for all industries and 7 to 28 for manufacturing. This is strong evidence that the same phenomena underlies data collection in all countries.

Second, the ratios of the maximum to minimum values are quite consistent. For all industries these range from two to three for annual firm births per 100 firms or two to four for annual firm births per 10 000 persons. Setting aside the United States, the same pattern is found for manufacturing firms, with maximum/minimum ratios of two to three for births per 100 firms and three to six for births per 10 000 humans. The greater range in the United States regarding manufacturing birth rates reflects the diversity across 382 labor market areas. Some rural labor market areas have virtually no manufacturing activity, other labor market areas, again mostly in rural areas, are distinctive for the absence of non-manufacturing economic activity.

4.4 Entrepreneurial processes and new firm birth rates

It is clear there is variation in new firm birth rates across the regions of all countries included in the analysis. The basic purpose is to determine if the indicators, reflecting the various start-up processes, can be used to predict, or explain, variation in firm birth rates. If indicators of the same process are found to be useful in linear models of new firm birth rates across all the countries included in this analysis, there is high confidence it would be important in the same countries in other time periods, say the 1970s or the 1990s, or in countries not included in this analysis.

Informed judgements regarding the relative impact of the different processes, based on an inspection of patterns of statistically significant coefficients in the linear equations (Reynolds and Storey, 1993; Reynolds, Storey and Westhead, 1994) are presented in

7 There has been considerable discussion among the various country teams regarding the difference in birth rates, particularly the lower birth rates for the United States and the rather high birth rates for Sweden, both of which have been able to separate independent businesses from all establishments for their analysis, eliminating branch establishments. There are a number of possible reasons for the lower birth rates for the United States, related to the original source of data, new entries in the files of a commercial credit rating service. Such a service would underrepresent self-employment, included in the registries upon which the Swedish data was based. Further, the figures represent the simple averages for all 382 US labor market areas which was not weighted to represent the population in each labor market area. One half of the US population resides in 81 of the 382 labor market areas, which makes it possible for a large number of sparsely populated rural areas to have a substantial effect on the average. The high rates for the United Kingdom probably reflect the use of new Value Added Tax entrants to measure business births, which includes self-employment (if annual turnover or sales exceed a certain level), independent businesses and branch businesses. As long as there is no reason to suspect a systematic bias across the regions within a given country, the analysis justifies confidence.

Figure 2.1. This indicates the relative significance of the seven different processes, each represented by one or more variables. Indicators of the different processes are available for from three to seven different countries.

Table 2.4 Overview of major results

	All economic sectors	Manufacturing only
Processes included		
1) Demand growth	Strong positive (5)*	Positve (7)
2) Urbanization/agglomeration	Positive (5)	Weak positive (7)
3) Unemployment/desperation	Positive (5)	Mixed (7)
4) Personal, household wealth	Weak positive (5)	None (7)
5) Small firms/specialization	Positive (5)	Strong positive (7)
6) Socialist voters	Mixed (3)	Weak positive (3)
7) Government spending/policies	None (4)	Weak positive (6)
Predictive success (Average explained variance)		
Births/10 000 people	70%	52%
Births/100 firms	69%	36%

Note: * Indicates the number of countries where one or more indicators of the process could be included.

For linear models predicting firm births in all economic sectors, the most significant process is growth in demand. Three processes have a consistent positive effect: urbanization/agglomeration; unemployment/desperation; and the presence of small firms and economic specialization. There is a weak positive effect from measures of household wealth. The presence of a liberal political climate has a mixed effect and there is no statistically significant impact from government actions (local spending or programs of assistance).

The pattern is slightly different for predictions of manufacturing firm births. A strong positive effect is found from the presence of small firms (presumably reflecting some specialization) and there is consistent positive effect from growth in demand. Weak positive impacts are found from processes associated with urbanization/agglomeration, a liberal political climate and government actions. There is a mixed pattern associated with unemployment/ desperation and no impact from variation in household wealth.

There are, therefore, two differences between the models developed to predict firm births in all sectors and in manufacturing. First, the all sector models are more successful and explain a higher proportion of the variance in birth rates. Second, the processes considered important vary somewhat between the two models. Note, however, that no processes have the opposite impact for the two predictions - a positive impact for one and negative for the other.

Several things account for these differences. First, manufacturing (firms, jobs or firm births) represents less than a fifth of economic activity in most regions and countries. When all sectors are considered, over half of all firms, jobs and firm births are in sectors oriented toward the local market - retail (including catering), construction, consumer services, health care services - where an ordinary citizen is the customer. As a result, models of the processes affecting firm births in all industries are dominated by the processes associated with consumer oriented commerce - population growth, urban context, or availability of small amounts of capital.

In contrast, the major customer for manufacturing firms are other businesses, often other manufacturing firms and ease of access to large populations may be less significant than other factors, such as input costs. For example, the largest birth rates in manufacturing in the United States occur in rural regions adjacent to the major urban regions. Similar patterns seem to be found in Germany and the UK, as well. The lower costs of land and labor and efficient transportation to other regions (by rail or road), and the movement to these rural areas of potential entrepreneurs for environmental and quality of life reasons (Keeble, Tyler, Broom and Lewis, 1992), may all play a part in this pattern. These rural regions, then, where the economic structure is dominated by a range of smaller firms, have higher rates of manufacturing firm births. As a result, measures of personal wealth - related to housing and land values - or urbanization/ agglomeration have little value in predicting manufacturing firm births.

4.5 Analyses across time: Japan and the United States

The previous analysis has suggested substantial stability across a number of countries at the same time, the late 1980s. It is possible, of course, that there is something unique about this period and that different patterns may be found in the past or be expected in the future. While it is not possible to track the future until it arrives, some analyses are available that relate to the past.

Identical analyses for multiple time periods were conducted for both Japan and the United States. This was possible only because comparable data was available for more than one time period. The analysis for Japan (LaPlant, 1992) involved predictions of manufacturing birth rates across 47 prefectures for four periods covering ten years: 1976-79, 1980-82; 1983-84; and 1985-86. Indicators of various start-up processes were developed for prior periods. It was found that no significant difference was present across the time periods. A comparable analysis was completed for the United States for six two-year periods between 1976 and 1988 (Reynolds and Maki, 1991). Specific historical time, even periods with different stages of the business cycle, had no impact on the US models. In fact, rather successful models - explaining over 60 per cent of the variance in firm birth rates - could be developed using 1970 data to predict birth rates 12, 14, 16 years in the future.

The stability in both Japan and the United States analysis appears to reflect temporal stability in the relative status of regions within each country. For example, those regions within the United States with the greatest relative population growth, greatest relative economic diversity, greatest relative personal wealth and greatest relative proportion of volatile industries change very little over the 1970s and 1980s.

It is clear that across eight developed economies in the late 1980s and across the late 1970s and 1980s in two developed economies the same patterns are found. Several regional characteristics are found to have a significant relationship to new firm birth rates: population growth; urbanized/agglomerative economy; presence of small firms and economic specialization; and, to a lesser extent, higher levels of unemployment and personal or household wealth. The precise mechanisms by which these contextual factors lead to the formation of new firms have not been firmly established.

5. The entrepreneurial process

The cross national analysis completed above helps to identify the critical contextual factors that encourage new firm births in different regions of developed countries. They do not, however, provide much information related to the actual process - referred to here as the entrepreneurial process - whereby a new firm is created. The entrepreneurial process is considered to start with one or more persons, as economic participants seeking a useful role in the economy, and ends, at some later time, with a viable business. Such a 'business', or new economic entity, may be a self-employment (full or part time), a single location enterprise with a few employees, or a multi-establishment firm that becomes a substantial competitor in its chosen markets.

Figure 2.1 Entrepreneurial process transitions

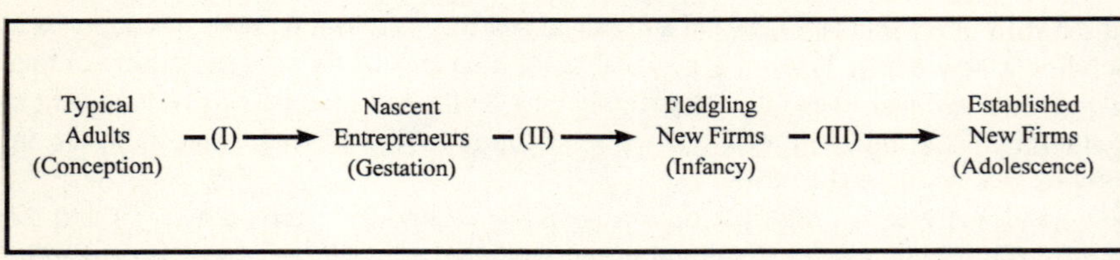

The process is marked by three transitions, outlined in Figure 2.1 (Curtin, Morgan and Reynolds, 1993).

I The decision by one or more persons to participate in the new firm gestation process and devote time and resources to founding a new firm thus becoming, in our language, nascent entrepreneurs.

II The successful fruition of these efforts - from gestation to firm birth - and the implementation of a fledgling new firm. (The majority of nascent entrepreneurs, however, appear to give up and withdraw before a new firm is established.)

III This transition marks the point where a fledgling new firm becomes an established new firm.

If a biological analogy is preferred, the conception of a new firm takes place when the first transition is initiated, a typical adult elects to become a nascent entrepreneur and implement the gestation of a new firm. Gestation would be that period when the nascent entrepreneur is trying to complete all the steps to found the fledgling new firm. That period when a fledgling new firm is becoming established and, most importantly, reaches a positive cash flow (monthly income exceeds monthly expenses) could be considered new firm infancy. Finally, the completion of the third transition, when the new firm has established itself and is more responsive to current economic conditions than to the gestation process and conditions of birth could be considered as 'new firm adolescence'. Some research has developed regarding each transition.

5.1 Transition I: typical adult to nascent entrepreneur

Estimating the prevalence of nascent entrepreneurs can best be done through surveys of representative samples of the adult population in a country or region. While some government data sets may provide information on the founding of new firms, there has not been - to our knowledge - any systematic effort to identify nascent entrepreneurs. A project just completed in Wisconsin (a state of five million with a diverse economic base in the north central region of the US) may be among the first efforts to systematically estimate the prevalence of nascent entrepreneurs (Reynolds and White, 1993). Part of an interview with a representative sample of adults asked the question: 'Are you, alone or with others, trying to start a new firm?' If the individual answered yes, they were asked a series of fifteen questions regarding the steps they had taken to put the firm in place. The first question asked if they had given 'substantial thought' to founding a new firm. The other fourteen questions were related to behaviors required to founding a new firm (preparing a business plan, saving money for start-up, assembling a start-up team, locating a site, hiring employees, etc.). About 95 per cent of those that say they are 'trying to start a new firm' report one or more behaviors, 85 per cent report five or more behaviors.

It was found that approximately 4.3 per cent of the respondents (typical Wisconsin residents over 18 years old) could be classified as nascent entrepreneurs. The percentage of adults from different categories that are considered to be nascent entrepreneurs are presented in Figure 2.2. The average value and the 80 per cent confidence intervals are provided. This is the interval that may include the true value 80 per cent of the time. (Multivariate analysis is not possible due to the small number of nascent entrepreneurs.)

Those most likely to initiate participation in the entrepreneurial process are: men; 30-39 years old; have completed high-school; have household incomes above the lowest level; are long term residences of the county (a local political jurisdiction); have a large network of work confidants and family members; and have a network with some members participating in the entrepreneurial process. While those not in the labor force are more likely to be nascent entrepreneurs, the majority of Wisconsin adults are in the labor force. About 80 per cent of all nascent entrepreneurs either have full time jobs or are running another business.

Figure 2.2 Prevalence of nascent entrepreneurs in Wisconsin: selected comparisons

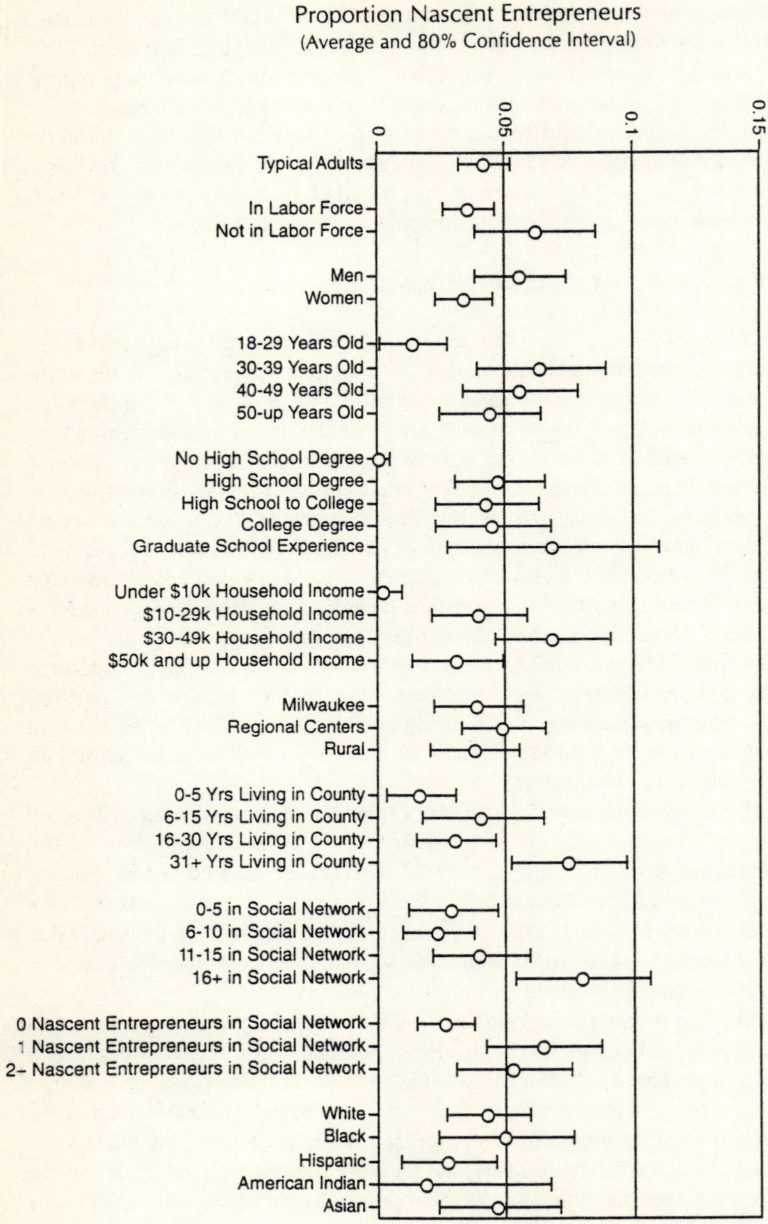

There is not much variation among those living in metropolitan, regional centers, or rural areas. In short, the typical nascent entrepreneur is well established in both their work career as well as the area in which they live.

There are some differences related to the ethnic background of the respondents. In general, these differences disappear when the context of the ethnic group is taken into account. Most of the differences among ethnic groups are related to differences in educational attainment, length of residence, household income and age distribution. There is little evidence of any 'cultural predisposition' to become involved with or avoid entrepreneurial activity.

5.2 Transition II: nascent entrepreneur to fledgling new firm

The best way to establish the prevalence of this transition is to identify a sample of nascent entrepreneurs and follow them (with periodic interviews) until they have (a) put a fledgling new firm in place or (b) given up. This has not, as yet, been possible for the sample identified in Wisconsin, simply because not enough time has elapsed to allow these outcomes to occur. (The survey was completed in the winter of 1993.)

However, another source of information is available to provide tentative estimates. At the same time nascent entrepreneurs were identified, discouraged entrepreneurs were also located. These were individuals that had tried to start a new firm and had given up. The month and year when each gestation behavior was initiated was obtained in the interview, along with the month and year when they gave up. This made it possible to determine the time between the initiation of the earliest gestation event and when the respondent gave up. About half gave up in less than six months and eighty per cent within 24 months. The average gestation period for those that gave up was 16 months. Comparable data on those that founded a fledgling new firm is not, as yet, available.

In addition, it is known that about 5 000 new firms with employees are started in Wisconsin each year. The typical firm is started by two individuals (two nascent entrepreneurs), indicating that each year about 10 000 nascent entrepreneurs successfully found a fledgling new firm. As there are about 150 000 nascent entrepreneurs at any one time, and we know that about 10 000 a year establish a fledgling new firm, it is possible to estimate the proportion of successful transitions for different estimates of the gestation period. For example, if the typical gestation period is 6 months, then three per cent of the nascent entrepreneurs are founding a fledgling new firm. If the typical gestation period is 36 months; then 20 per cent of the nascent entrepreneurs are founding a fledgling new firm. If we assume a typical gestation period of 16 months (the average before give-up for nascent entrepreneurs), then about five per cent are founding fledgling new firms.

Assuming it may take longer to start a firm than give up, and considering the tentative nature of these estimates, it seems reasonable to assume that no more than 10 per cent of nascent entrepreneurs are able to initiate a fledgling new firm.

5.3 Transition III: fledgling new firm to established new firm

There is a growing body of research on this third transition. Alternative analyses have developed two portrayals of the density probability function underlying the mortality of new firms. Some analysis supports the liability of newness argument that firm mortality is very high the very instant firms are founded (the precise definition of firm birth is vague) and then declines monotonically with age (Stinchcombe, 1965; Carroll, 1983; Freeman, Carroll and Hannan, 1983). Other evidence supports the inverted U shaped pattern, referred to as the 'liability of adolescence', where death rates are highest after a brief period where they are very low (Ben-Ner, 1988; Brüderl and Schüssler, 1990; Brüderl, Preisendörfer and Ziegler, 1992; Finchman and Levinthal, 1991; Preisendörfer and Voss, 1990; Reynolds and Miller, 1992). The controversy centers on the presence of high or low risk of death early in the life of the new firm. As much of the analysis has been done with a wide range of data sets with widely varying definitions of both 'new firms' and 'firm birth dates', it can only be resolved with the development of a panel that can track the development of a new firm prior to all definitions of a 'firm birth'. There is, however, agreement that a dramatic drop in the risk of discontinuance occurs after about four to five years. This point at which the 'drop in risk of firm death' occurs may be considered the transition from fledgling new firm to established new firm.

Preliminary evidence suggests, however, that about one-half of fledgling new firms that start with employees are still active five years after start up (Kirchhoff, 1992; Reynolds and Miller, 1992).

5.4 Transition sequence outcomes

Using data from various sources, then, we are able to provide an initial estimate of the probabilities that each stage of the transition is completed. These are presented in Table 2.5.

These indicate that for each 100 000 Wisconsin adults, we would expect about 4 000 to be nascent entrepreneurs at any give time. These would produce about 200 fledgling new firms each year and, in turn, half of these (100) may still be in business five years later.

It is clear that this analysis is representative only of the United States. There may be substantial differences in other developed societies and it is unlikely that the same transition probabilities are to be expected in developing or post-socialist countries. The benefit of the analysis is that it specifies the critical transition events for attention in future research. Variations across different countries - or countries in different stages of transition from centrally coordinated economies to market economies - may have substantially different success ratios at the different transitions in the entrepreneurial process.

Table 2.5 Entrepreneurial process transition proportion and new effects

	Proportion transition successes	Number of individuals	Number of firms
Typical adults		100 000	
Transition I	0.04		
Nascent entrepreneurs (Two per firm)		4 000	
Transition II	0.10		
Fledgling new firms			200
Transition III	0.50		
Established new firms (5 years old)			100

6. Potential for government influence on the entrepreneurial process

Can governments in developed countries actually affect new firm birth rates? There is no question they can discourage individuals from participating in the entrepreneurial process and depress the creation of new firms. If entrepreneurship is not actually prohibited, it may be discouraged by imposing onerous requirements, complex regulations or merely a slow reaction to requests for decisions required to implement the new business. A government that is unwilling or unable to control predators (criminal entrepreneurs) that may prey on new and small businesses should expect responsible entrepreneurial activity to be depressed.

Can, however, governments encourage entrepreneurship and firm births? Efforts to stimulate entrepreneurship may be divided into two categories, general efforts to enhance the capacity for all businesses to function effectively and specific efforts related to the entrepreneurial process.

The former efforts to facilitate the capacity of all business to operate, may be the most cost-effective strategy. Fundamental would be providing an efficient, effective infrastructure: transportation, banking and monetary system, health care, education, criminal and civil justice, and the like. For government requirements or programs that affect businesses directly, it may help to reduce the transaction costs for businesses as much as possible. This implies an effort to minimize bureaucratic complications, reduce delays in decisions that slow business adaptation, and generally treat the business community as an equal partner in providing a satisfactory work and economic life for all. Such general measures would do much to encourage firms - new and old, large and small - to expand business activity.

Perhaps critical in any government action to enhance entrepreneurship is an understanding of the scope of the phenomena associated with firm births. Two elements of this research reflect the massive nature of the entrepreneurial process. First is the substantial success of the linear models that use regional characteristics to predict new firm births. As presented in Table 2.4, a substantial amount of variation in firm birth rates was accounted for by relatively stable regional characteristics. Measures of government actions had very modest impacts in these models.[8] The most important processes - population growth, economic diversity and personal wealth - were not those easily affected by government action. It is, moreover, very unlikely that any government will deliberately increase unemployment as a mechanism to encourage entrepreneurial activity.

Second, entrepreneurial activity is a common feature of the life of the adult population in these countries, presumably absorbing time and personal resources. Table 2.6 presents the annual new firm births rates, taken from Table 2.3, in relation to other important life events: births and marriages. The analysis assumes that an average of two adults is associated with each new firm birth, a consistent finding in studies of new firm start-ups.[9] For the countries included in Table 2.6 from 1 in 103 to 1 in 192 residents are involved in marriages (each involving two people) and from 1 in 66 to 1 in 96 are involved in a live human birth (each involving two people) each year.[10] In a similar fashion, from 1 in 180 to 1 in 313 are involved in starting a new firm (each involving two people, on the average). Substantially more, perhaps ten times as many - 1 in 20, are involved in the earlier stages of the entrepreneurial process.

It seems clear that participating in the entrepreneurial process is as common as participating in important aspects of the family life course. It may be considered as a normal feature of many people's work career. It may be more prevalent - more widely expected - as the turbulence in established market economies increases.

A deliberate government policy to enhance entrepreneurial activity and new firm births should take into account the scope of the phenomena. It is clearly a major activity involving a significant proportion of the adult population. Perhaps as many as one in twenty are trying to start a new business at any one time. These people are willing to commitment substantial time and resources to pursuing this career option. Governments that wish to have a major impact on the prevalence and success of entrepreneurial initiatives should be prepared to invest substantial resources to the endeavour. Small-scale programs, such as the occasional twenty-firm incubator or token venture capital fund, may help a few firms, but compared to the overall scope of the phenomena the net impact will be small. This is probably why there was little

---

8 Though it should be noted that the UK study, which also analysed local variations in net changes in numbers of small businesses, found evidence of greater government policy impacts in reducing business death rates and, hence, increasing net growth of small businesses.

9 Surveys of new firms in the United States, with samples drawn from new firms with employees, consistently find that more than half are started by teams and that the average start-up team size is approximately 2.0 (Reynolds and Freeman, 1986; Reynolds and Miller, 1988). This assumption may not be appropriate in countries where new firm counts were based on new entries in registers unrelated to employment creation, such as new establishments in the value added tax listings in the United Kingdom.

10 Because of the differences in the way new firms are counted in the different countries, it is not appropriate to assume that firm birth rates can be precisely compared across countries and, in turn, that Table 2.6 indicates that higher levels of human births depress firm birth rates.

impact on firm birth rates associated with the presence of government assistance programs - they failed to reach most nascent entrepreneurs or new firms.

Just as determined governments have been able to affect human birth rates, determined governments may be able to affect firm birth rates. But it would be naive to suggest that it would be easy or could be accomplished quickly. One way to reduce the overall cost is to restrict assistance to certain regions - seen as being desperately poor and with low economic potential (Reynolds, Storey and Westhead, 1993);[11] to new firms in certain industries - those seen as having the highest potential; or to only those new firms seen as having a high potential for growth (Storey, 1991). Differential allocation of public resources, however, is always controversial and can only be resolved by the political process.

Table 2.6 New firms, start-up teams, birth rates and marriage rates

	Per 10 000 population			
	New firm birth rate	Start up teams**	Marriages*	Human births*
Germany (Western)	55	110	55	104
Sweden	88	172	52	112
United Kingdom	72	144	97	134
United States	33	66	97	151

Notes: * See The Economist (1991).
** Assumes two persons per new firm start-up.

7. Government intervention in developed market economies

Countries with a history of developed market economies have created a number of institutions, government agencies, professions and occupations, that are an integral part of a market economic system. Most market systems are designed under the assumption that there will be new business startups as well as business discontinuances. Efforts to encourage, enhance, or improve the entrepreneurial process are, in many ways, minor adjustments to this overall market context.

11 In both Western Europe and North America government's respond to poor, usually rural, regions in two ways: relocate people to more prosperous regions or relocate economic activity to the poor region. However, the emphasis seems to be quite different. In North America (at least in the United States) it is generally assumed that people should move to where there is economic growth and jobs are being created. Government programs are often created to facilitate this adaptation. In Western Europe, there seems to be much greater resistance to relocation (voluntary or otherwise) by individuals and families and a greater readiness by governments to encourage a shift of economic activities to 'poorer' regions.

Policies and programs of governments (international, national and regional) may influence the entrepreneurial process - provide these minor adjustments - in several ways.

(a) *Encourage conception*: Governments may modify the institutions and regulations that affect the capacity to initiate new firms, encouraging individuals to enter into the gestation process.

(b) *Facilitate gestation indirectly*: Governments may use public resources to improve or modify the overall economic infrastructure in such a way that it facilitates the gestation process. This would, indirectly, encourage conception.

(c) *Facility gestation directly*: Special programs may be developed to identify, inform and train nascent entrepreneurs interested in establishing new firms - acting as midwives in the gestation-firm birth stage of the process. These may focus on the three major activities involved in planning a new firm: a marketing strategy and program, organizing the delivery of the goods or services, and assembling and managing the financial resources.

(d) *Facility growth/survival*: Specialized efforts may be made to assist fledgling new firms following birth, providing post-natal care, as it were. This may take the form of counsel and advice, provision of resources, or sympathy and encouragement.

Almost all of the current efforts focus on facilitating or subsidizing the inputs associated with business start-ups. That is, providing training or planning assistance to any new firm, engineering or scientific assistance to high technology new firms, or financial support (or help in obtaining financial support) to entrepreneurs and new firms. The range and diversity of such problems is astonishing. In Wisconsin alone, only one of 50 states of the United States, about 400 such programs providing over 700 types of assistance were identified (Reynolds and White, 1993). This uncoordinated conglomerate of assistance is sponsored by variety of local, state and federal government units as well as business associations and voluntary groups. Most people starting new firms were unaware of the programs that would be of most help to them.

The efficiency and effectiveness of these programs in established market economies is, as yet, not known. They often are not able to locate or identify, and hence have trouble serving, their major clients - nascent entrepreneurs and new firm owner/managers. Application to post-socialist countries may have some value for some specific individuals or new firms, but an impact on overall, country-wide economic growth may be difficult to identify.

8. Special situation of post-socialist countries[12]

It would appear that at least four features of socialist countries, where there was centralized coordination of economic activity, are quite different from that of contemporary market economies: (a) ambiguity regarding ownership of property; (b) underdeveloped mechanisms for resolving civil disputes; (c) absence of a banking system and capacity for auditing financial flows; and (d) intolerance of diversity in personal economic success. A few brief comments on each.

(a) *Clear title to property*. The importance of property ownership varies dramatically among different businesses. In some, such as construction, consumer services and some types of health care, the property requirements are modest - the tools and equipment required by the craftsman or professional and, perhaps, a small amount of space in which to work. In retail the major property may be a small inventory and a location to operate. If the location is on the street, then ownership of the space is irrelevant. Others types of economic activity require a substantial physical investment and clear rights of ownership. Most manufacturing, transportation and wholesale distribution require fixed facilities, substantial equipment and often considerable inventory.

There are substantial reports that establishing private ownership of property, a right to property that will be respected by private citizens and government agencies, is both difficult and expensive in the post-socialist countries. In countries where a recognized title to property is expensive to obtain, one would not expect individuals to found new firms in industries where property rights are critical. Only existing large, well-financed organizations could afford the time and costs to establish clear title. Individual entrepreneurs would be more prominent in industries where property rights are less critical, such as traders and street corner entrepreneurs.

(b) *Market supervision and resolving disputes*. In a system where all economic activity is coordinated through government administrators, there is no need to have mechanisms to regulate economic exchanges between independent businesses. Administrative mechanisms can be used to resolve disputes between government agencies. When economic activity is conducted by a large number of autonomous firms, it is desirable that they focus on providing quality produces at low prices. Dishonesty, fraud, and misunderstandings occur in all societies, and those with established market economies have substantial mechanisms for resolving disputes associated with these problems; administrative mechanisms to regulate the markets and judicial mechanisms for resolving disagreements. These mechanisms attempt to be as objective and explicit as possible, leading to a massive amount of written

12 I am grateful for discussions on these issues with two people. First, Dr. Andrev V. Korneyv, Institute of the USA and Canada, Academy of Sciences of the USSR during his visits to the United States and my visit to Moscow and St. Petersburg. Second, with Dr. Peter Taumanoff of Marquette University, an economist with substantial personal experience with the Former Soviet Union.

procedures and rules, specialists in the procedure itself (lawyers), but a considerable reduction in uncertainty about the constraints or expectations in business exchanges.

Post-socialists societies do not seem to have created such procedures. It is clear that the large scale presence of organized criminal groups - which are supervising many of the retail and street markets in post-socialist countries - reflect the inability of the current governments to provide this supervision.

(c) *Capacity to trace and audit economic transactions*. One of the central features of developed economies is a pervasive, sophisticated banking system. All transactions of any significance are completed through bank account transfers. These transfers can, and often are, audited by outside individuals. This substantially reduces the potential for ordinary theft and misappropriation of funds. It makes it feasible for any organization (government agencies, financial institutions, or private business) to have a large number of people involved in financial matters, as it is possible to verify the economic actions of all individuals.

Most financial transactions in post-socialist countries appear to use cash. Cash transactions are very difficult to trace and any independent assessment of financial flows is difficult to check. This substantially reduces the number of people that may be trusted to handle the finances of a business. Restricting financial management to a small group of individuals that trust each other because of other social relationships (marriage or family related) places a considerable constraint upon the size and complexity of business organizations. It may be interpreted as an extremely high administrative cost that, in turn, places a major constraint on the capacity of a business to grow.

(d) *Tolerance of economic inequality*. A major feature of market economic systems is the diversity in individual economic well-being. It would appear that such diversity is an integral and necessary feature of market systems; its presence provides an improved standard of living for all participants, even those that have relatively low incomes. Not every self-made millionaire in market economies is loved and respected, but their presence is usually tolerated with little acrimony.

There is little question that one of the objectives for the system of centrally coordinated economic activity and collective ownership of all capital, as proposed by Marx, was to reduce the extent of economic inequality present in Britain and Europe in the late 1800s. It may have been greatest in Britain, where Marx lived as he developed his ideas; poor himself, he found this inequality quite distasteful. He suggested that if all in a socialist society would provide the same hours of work, it would be appropriate for all to receive the same economic rewards. In his view, it was morally inappropriate for some to have more economic wealth than others.

A widespread judgement that it is morally wrong for some to have greater wealth than others can be a substantial disincentive to entrepreneurial activity. Those that wish to pursue new ventures to improve their personal economic wellbeing may be discouraged from such actions if success leads to criticism or abuse by their social contacts - their friends, family and neighbors. The energy required to avoid criticism or abuse for being successful will certainly distract entrepreneurs from making further contributions to the economy.

Institutions, agencies and professional groups have emerged in established market economies to resolve or manage the first three problems; there has been a willingness in developed market economies to pay the costs to develop unambiguous property ownership, non-violent resolutions of disputes and measures for supervision of financial flows. This allows some measure of predictability in the conduct of an established business or creating a new business. Those whose contributions result in greater personal wealth generally do not spend much effort hiding from society. In this context, there is a focus on economic outcomes, either increasing productivity, reducing costs or providing a new good or service.

These four features would seem to have a major impact on the potential for entrepreneurial activity in current post-socialist countries. Ameliorating these constraints may do much to improve the functioning of the market system, including an enhancement of the entrepreneurial process.

9. Conclusions

This discussion has reviewed research related to the following question:

I What is the role of entrepreneurial activity in promoting change and enhancing economic growth and wellbeing?

A substantial amount of research is now underway to increase understanding of the entrepreneurial process in market economies. However, market economies have been established with the assumption that some level of new firm creation and existing firm discontinuances are to be expected. There is, without question, a substantial amount of time and resources devoted by ordinary citizens to the entrepreneurial process. Current research may be considered as efforts to explore the details of the entrepreneurial process such that the current government and economic institutions may be adjusted to increase the efficiency and effectiveness of the system. Some headway has been made regarding part of the second question:

II What are the conditions that foster or encourage an optimal level of entrepreneurial activity?

Much is known about the conditions that foster entrepreneurship. The optimal level of entrepreneurial activity for a society is not known. Some scholars are concerned that misdirected entrepreneurial energies may produce a net social loss (Baumol, 1990), but this is related to specific 'entrepreneurial' initiatives, not the overall level of activity. As yet, no society has been identified that appears to have an 'excessive' level of entrepreneurship. Countries with post-socialist economies are confronted with the task of putting a number of features in place to facilitate market mechanisms. As they create the infrastructure that will facilitate market economies, they may - at the same time - create a context that encourages entrepreneurial activity. Special programs - providing direct assistance to entrepreneurs and new firms - may have less impact in the near future than improving the overall context for market economies. After all, most of those that start new firms in developed economies receive no special assistance or funding from any public or government sources.

References

Acs, Zoltan and David Audretsch (1988); Innovation in Large and Small Firms: An Empirical Analysis; *American Economic Review*, 78, 678-90.

Audretsch, David B. and Michael Fritsch (1994a); On the Measurement of Entry Rates; *Empirica*, 21, 105-13.

Audretsch, David B. and Michael Fritsch (1994b); The Geography of Firm Births in Germany; *Regional Studies*, 28, 4, 359-66.

Barreto, Humberto (1989) *The Entrepreneur in Microeconomic Theory: Disappearance and Explanation*, New York: Routledge.

Baumol, William J. (1968); Entrepreneurship in Economic Theory; *American Economic Review*, 58, 63-9.

Baumol, William J. (1990); Entrepreneurship: Productive, Unproductive and Destructive; *Journal of Political Economy*, 98, 893-921.

Ben-Ner, Avner (1988); Comparative Empirical Observations on Worker-Owned and Capitalist Firms; *International Journal of Industrial Organization*, 6, 7-31.

Birch, David A. (1981); Who Creates Jobs?; *The Public Interest*, 65, 3-14.

Brüderl, Josef and R. Schüssler (1990); Organizational Mortality: The Liabilities of Newness and Adolescence; *Administrative Science Quarterly*, 35, 530-47.

Brüderl, Josef, Peter Preisendörfer and Rolf Ziegler (1992); Survival Chances of Newly Founded Business Organizations; *American Sociological Review*, 57, 227-42.

Carroll, Glenn R. (1983); A Stochastic Model of Organizational Mortality: A Review and Reanalysis; *Social Science Research*, 12, 203-329.

Curtin, Richard, James Morgan and Paul Reynolds (1993) *Panel Study of Entrepreneurial Dynamics Pilot Study*, Ann Arbor, Michigan: University of Michigan Institute for Social Research, Proposal Submitted to the National Science Foundation, August 1993.

Davidsson, Per, Leif Lindmark and Christer Olofsson (1992) *Business Volatility and New Firm Formation in Sweden*, Umea, Sweden: Umea Business School, Working paper.

Davidsson, Per, Leif Lindmark and Christer Olofsson (1994); New Firm Formation and Regional Development in Sweden; *Regional Studies*, 28, 4, 395-410.

de Soto, Herman (1989) *The Other Path: The Invisible Revolution in the Third World*, New York: Harper and Row.

The Economist (1991) *Pocket World in Figures*, London, UK: Economist Books Ltd.

European Network for SME Research [ENSR] (1993) *The European Observatory for SMEs: First Annual Report*, Zoetermeer, The Netherlands: EIM Small Business Research and Consultancy.

Finchman, M. and D.A. Levinthal (1991); Honeymoons and the liability of adolescence: A new perspective on duration dependence in social and organizational relationships; *Academy of Management Review*, 16, 442-68.

Freeman, John, Glen R. Carroll and Michael T. Hannan (1983); The Liability of Newness: Age Dependence in Organizational Death Rates; *American Sociological Review*, 48, 692-710.

Garofoli, Gioacchino (1994); New Firm Formation and Regional Development: The Italian Case; *Regional Studies*, 28, 4, 381-93.

Granovetter, Mark (1984); Labour Markets and Establishment Size; *American Sociological Review*, 49, 323-34.

Guesnier, Bernard (1994); Regional Variations in New Firm Formation in France; *Regional Studies*, 28, 4, 347-58.

Hart, Mark and Graham Gudgin (1994); Spatial Varations in New Firm Formation in the Republic of Ireland; *Regional Studies*, 28, 4, 367-80.

Keeble, David, Jonathan Potter and David J. Storey (1990) *Cross National Comparisons of the Role of SMEs in Regional Economic Growth in the European Community*, Coventry, UK: University of Warwick, SME Centre. Report to the ECC.

Keeble, David, Peter Tyler, Geoff Broom and Jonathan Lewis (1992) *Business Success in the Countryside: The Performance of Rural Enterprise*, London, UK: Her Majesty's Stationary Office for the Department of the Environment.

Keeble, David and Sheila Walker (1994); New Firms, Small Firms and Dead Firms: Spatial Patterns and Determinants in the United Kingdom; *Regional Studies*, 28, 4, 411-27.

Kirchhoff, Bruce A. (1992) *Firm Failure Fantasies and Entrepreneurial Survival: The US Experience*, presented at Small Business in the Global Economy: New Structures for Development, 24-27 May 1992, Montreal, Canada.

Kirchhoff, Bruce A. and Bruce Phillips (1988); The Effect of Firm Formation and Growth on Job Creation in the United States; *Journal of Business Venturing*, 3, 261-72.

LaPlant, David J. (1992) *The Effects of Regional Economic Characteristics on New Manufacturing Establishment Formation in Japan*, Milwaukee, Wisconsin, USA: Department of Economics, Marquette University, MA essay.

Loveman, Gary and Werner Sengenberger (1990); The Re-emergence of Small Scale Production: An International Comparison; *Small Business Economics*, 3, 1-17.

OECD (Organization for Economic Cooperation and Development) (1991) *Statistical Data on Small and Medium Enterprises*, Directorate for Science Technology and Industry: Industry Committee, Report Prepared for Working Party No. 9 of the Industry Committee on Industrial Statistics (6 June 1991), Paris, France: OECD.

Preisendörfer, P. and T. Voss (1990); Organizational Mortality of small firms: The effects of entrepreneurial age and human capital; *Organizational Studies*, 11, 107-29.

Reynolds, Paul D. (1991); Strategies for Cross-National Comparisons: Matching Research Issues and Analysis Objectives; *Small Business Economics*, 3, 245-260.

Reynolds, Paul D. (1994); Autonomous Firm Dynamics and Economic Growth in the United States, 1986-1990; *Regional Studies*; 28, 4, 429-42.

Reynolds, Paul D. and Steve Freeman (1986) *New Firm Contributions to Pennsylvania*, Vol. 2 of 1986 Pennsylvania New Firm Survey, Washington, DC: Appalachian Regional Commission.

Reynolds, Paul D. and Wilbur Maki (1990) *Business Volatility and Economic Growth*, Final Project Report Submitted to the Office of Advocacy, US Small Business Administration, Contract SBA 3067-0A-88.

Reynolds, Paul D. and Wilbur Maki (1991) *Regional Characteristics Affecting Business Growth: Assessing Strategies for Promoting Regional Economic Well-Being*, Project Report submitted to Rural Poverty and Resource Program, The Ford Foundation, Grant 900-1013.

Reynolds, Paul D. and Brenda Miller (1988) *1987 Minnesota New Firms Study*, Minneapolis, MN: University of Minnesota, Center for Urban and Regional Affairs.

Reynolds, Paul D. and Brenda Miller (1992); New Firm Gestation: Conception, Birth and Implications for Research; *Journal of Business Venturing*, 7, 1-14.

Reynolds, Paul D. and David J. Storey, (1993) *Local and Regional Characteristics Affecting Small Business Formation: A Cross-National Comparison*, Paris, France: Organization for Economic Cooperation and Development.

Reynolds, Paul D., David J. Storey and Paul Westhead (1993) *Cross-National Comparisons of the Variation in New Firm Formation Rates' Coventry*, United Kingdom: University of Warwick, Centre for Small and Medium Enterprises (Report Submitted to the European Commission).

Reynolds, Paul, David J. Storey and Paul Westhead (1994); Cross-national Comparisons of the Variation in New Firm Formation Rates; *Regional Studies*, 28, 4, 443-56.

Reynolds, Paul D. and Sammis B. White (1993) *Wisconsin's Entrepreneurial Climate Study. 1993*, Madison, WI: Wisconsin Housing and Economic Development Authority. Final Report.

Schumpeter, J.A. (1934) *The Theory of Economic Development*, Cambridge, MA: Harvard U. Press.

Stinchcombe, A.L. (1965) Social Structure and Organizations, in March, J. G. (ed) *Handbook of Organizations*, Chicago, IL: Rand McNally, 142-93.

Storey, David J. (1991) *Should we Abandon Support to Start-up Businesses?*, Coventry, United Kingdom: University of Warwick, Centre for Small and Medium Enterprises, Discussion Paper No. 10.

3 A dynamic evolutionary perspective on transformation

Michael Keren

1. The problem

It is now clear that the privatization process in Eastern Europe, i.e. the process by which existing SOEs (state-owned enterprises) are becoming private firms,[1] is proceeding at a much slower pace than even the greatest pessimists have expected. There are several reasons, but the one I would like to stress is quite simple: the existing SOEs have very little value, if by the value of an SOE or a firm we denote the present value of its expected stream of profits (Keren, 1992a). The reason is that these firms cannot be thought of as maximizers or even satisfiers of any simple index, but rather as fairly stable coalitions of actors, workers, managers, suppliers and buyers, tied together by a network of implicit agreements. Considerable political skill is required to change these hidden contracts, and it is, therefore, very hard to modify the firms' mode of operation unless strong entrepreneurial leadership guides these reforms along. In other words, without turning them over to private entrepreneurial management there is little chance for any change in their mode of operation. Privatization is an all but necessary condition, though by no means a sufficient one, for transforming an SOE. Privatization from above has, however, been shown to be a drawn out affair: the difficulties of turning state assets over to private ownership have been outlined by many authors (Berliner, 1992). Consequently, the only hope of the transforming countries lies in the bottom-up growth of a new private sector, and the crumbling of SOEs through spontaneous privatizations initiated from below.

But bottom-up regeneration is fraught with great difficulties. New firms have to strike roots on the ruins of the crumbling monofirm, an environment which preserves much of the heritage of the old socialist system. The latter was in general a highly conservative regime which aimed at freezing the existing organizational state in order to secure each member of the coalition his present position, and was, therefore, - in spite of lip service - quite hostile to the intrusion of anything new, to any innovation. And it was destructive of the institutions of private property and free economic activity which it saw as the germ of capitalism, the dreaded alternative. Now all of these institutions have to be rebuilt, i.e. many new organizations have to be formed and the mode of operation of existing ones has to be seriously modified. Many of these organizations produce public goods and must, therefore, be governmental; others can and should be private, but depend on a public framework which has to pre-exist. Thus, the transformation of the state organizations and the growth of the private sector are interdependent.

1 A much wider definition of the term is used in Kornai (1991).

In other words, the transformation process is an extended process of transition of the economy from one state, the centralized monofirm consisting of large and inefficient SOEs and coordinated by its top-heavy planning and management apparatus, to a market populated mainly by competing private firms. The path between the two is long and arduous, but the final length and cost of transition may depend on the policies adopted by the government. A simple quasi-dynamic model is introduced in Section 2, to underscore the time-dependent nature of the process and to make the analysis of the process and the policies which affect it possible. The model is simulated in Section 3, to check its consistency and see whether the claims of the text do indeed follow.

The obstacles on the way to the establishment of a new private sector are manifold, and of these it is only a small selection that is discussed:

(i) The environment: the institutional environment which has evolved was designed to favor the state sector. In particular, the institutions of private property have been suppressed for many decades, with the result that the protection the state can offer the entrepreneur in his transactions with other economic units is quite feeble. The police are inexperienced in the protection of the individual and in the fight against organized crime, the sector that seems to be in the van of private economic activity, and the courts were designed to protect the institutions of the state, not (the previously banned) private economic activity.

(ii) Resources: the old state sector has control of many of the resources needed for the establishment of new firms-land, old capital equipment, and preferential access to others, particularly to credit. This may be a serious obstacle on the way of the bottom-up transformation.

(iii) The nature of the entrepreneurs: the origins of the nascent entrepreneurial class determine its character and the type of contributions it can provide. In Eastern European economies this class is composed mainly of ex-cadres, renegades of Djilas' 'new class', and of ex-black marketeers. Both have learnt their entrepreneurial trade as an underground activity and are unlikely to be trustworthy, and both are not members of the new elite. New historical research is turning up evidence on the importance of credence and reputation in early commercial developments in the middle ages (Greif, 1993). Honor among thieves is not sufficient here: it is ordinary businessmen and citizens who may require the services of firms founded by this class, who have to be able to take the word of these entrepreneurs. Life in the shadow of the law does not breed the credibility that is needed for this class to be a catalyst in the healthy growth of its customers.

Two of the points listed, (i) and (ii), provide the state sector with advantages, and disadvantage the small new private sector. They thus place a hurdle on the way of bottom-up transformation. But at least in the short run small firms in the private sector also have advantages: they are free from any interference by the state, in particular from prying by the tax collector. Though these advantages may not persist, they many be helpful in the formative stages. It may be thought that the advantages and disadvantages balance each other, and that the net position of the new sector does not require any additional improvement. There is a problem with this supposition: both advantages and disadvantages do not affect all parts of the small firm sector alike. They may, therefore, lead to an adverse selection of untrustworthy entrepreneurs. These selection biases are discussed in Section 4, using the notation introduced in Section 2. Section 5 takes into account point (iii) above, which has been disregarded in Section 4. The concluding Section 6 assembles the policy recommendations which are embedded in the previous sections.

2. The model

Assume that at $t=0$, before the start of the process of transformation, Eastern European economies consisted of large SOEs, all parts of a single monofirm. These enterprises were, as a rule, inefficient. The end of the transformation process, as is widely agreed, is to restructure the economy and to turn it into a largely privately run efficient and competitive economy. To achieve this, some of the SOEs have to be transformed into efficient firms, competitive in the world market. Most of these should be private, but some, as in all capitalist countries, are likely to remain publicly owned.[2] The vision of the future includes a large sector of new private firms that will take the place of the existing SOEs, those that do not manage to transform themselves into successful efficient firms. The first question concerning this vision relates to existence: does a feasible path to the target economy exist? Other questions concern the choice between existing paths, i.e. which of them is the shortest, which is the best? The full agenda of this research should answer all three questions. The present paper tries a stab at just one: suppose there exists a possible trajectory, what are the policy steps that may help the transition along?

At $t=0$ industry consists of old SOEs, the set X, all large and inefficient. The same symbol, here and elsewhere in the paper, is used to refer to the set and to its power, i.e. to the number of firms in the set: it is not expected that this will create any confusion. This $X_0=X$ is the number of SOEs at $t=0$. At each point in time these X firms belong to one of the following sets:

B, the set of bad, inefficient firms. At the start $B_0=X$.
G, the set of good, successfully transformed firms. $G_0=0$.
D, the set of dead firms, also empty at $t=0$.

D will be formed by SOEs that fail in their attempt at conversion, and by firms which die without even trying to transform themselves. At any stage of the transition $B_t+G_t+D_t=X$.

In addition, at each point in time there is a pool of M new entrepreneurial firms, which produce either tradable or non-tradable goods, the sets R and N respectively. Thus $M_t=R_t+N_t$. I consider the distinction between the two types of firms to be

2 But compare 'Halle-luja Chorus' (The Economist, 1993a, 31), which discusses the shift of traditionally municipally produced services to the private sector in Halle, a town in the ex-GDR.

important. The R-sector provides the economy with consumers and producers services of which it was starved by the previous regime. It is a necessary condition for the growth of the entrepreneurial sector, because it allows each firm to specialize in a given line. It is useful for the G-sector, too: although the very size of the SOEs makes it easier for them to produce their own inputs, one of the essential steps in turning the old SOEs into efficient and more flexible firms is to reduce their vertical integration. R-firms belong to that part of the small-firm sector that may grow large if successful or be wound up if it fails. This is the most promising part of the entrepreneurial sector, its potential growth node. This paper focuses on the rate at which these two flows of private firms enter the economy and on the ratio between them. For simplicity all firms are assumed to use a single unit each of L and K: the distinction between the two types of input is introduced below. It is initially assumed that a unit of L together with a unit of K produces one unit of output and provides one unit of income. All firms are thus of equal size and scale effects, which is the main *raisons d'être* of the G-sector, are disregarded: an alternative would be to add a size symbol to distinguish between the members of X and of M, but notational simplicity takes priority.

The first step of transition is the dissolution of the top of the monofirm, the coordinating organs of the *ancien régime*. Henceforth, it is assumed, all firms of all sets compete in the market. Consumers are constrained by their income, $I_t=B_t+G_t+N_t+R_t$. Their utility function is

$$Ut = \beta B_t + G_t^{\gamma} R_t^{(1-\gamma-\nu)} N_t^{\nu}\ ; \quad \beta,\gamma,\nu > 0; \quad \beta < 1; \quad \gamma+\nu < 1.$$

The output of the B-SOEs provides little utility to the consumers; this is why each unit of output provides a utility of $\beta<1$. Each firm in the new sector $G \cup R \cup N$, provides on the average a unit-utility, except that the proportions between the three types matter. This is because, unlike under the *ancien régime*, here firms are specialized, and the substitution between the tradables and non-tradables counts. The latter supply the services neglected under socialism, and the former the importables, either directly through substitution or indirectly via exports. The G- and the R-sectors are, nevertheless, kept distinct: this is to account for the fact that the transformed G-firms are the suppliers of scale-requiring products, goods whose production is very inefficient at the low scale of the R-firms. On the other hand, R-firms supply high-tech products, which require flexible production, not the forte of the ex-B firms, even those that have been successfully transformed. However, the G+R sector is the mainstay of future development, since both sectors produce the modern goods whose markets are growing, and successful units in both may be the nuclei of future multinationals. Furthermore, the G+N sector creates externalities that are essential for the entry of R-firms:

$$\pi_r = \pi_r(e, G_t + N_t); \quad \delta\pi_r/\delta\,(G + N) > 0; \quad \delta\pi/\delta e > 0,$$

where e is the real exchange rate. The simple assumptions on the utiliy function lead to simple price functions: $p_r=p_g=e$; $p_b=\beta<1$, and p_n depends on the size of the N-sector relatively to the others:

$$p_n \lesseqgtr 1 \qquad \text{if} \qquad N_t / I_t \lesseqgtr \nu.$$

There is a further implication here: since the resource cost of each B-firm is 1 and its income only β, the B-sector makes losses of $(1-\beta)B_t$ per annum, and these have to be covered by a tax on the remainder of industry: the symbol τ denotes the tax. This aspect will be discussed in detail later.

Consider the decisions of the SOEs on the one hand and those of the entrepreneurs on the other. The SOE, considered as a decision maker here, i.e. a team, has to decide at each point of time whether to attempt transformation. It is driven by a desire for self-preservation. If it does nothing it is in danger of being bankrupted and driven out of existence: δB_t are transformed into D-firms at each point of time, where δ is a government decision variable. Bankruptcy may also be the outcome of an unsuccessful attempt at transformation, and a share of those who try transformation fail and exit: this share is denoted by ε. The proportion ε declines with the profitability of the G-sector, π_g, on which more below: $\varepsilon = e\ (\pi^g)$, and $\varepsilon' < 0$. If ϕ is the proportion trying to reconstruct, then $\phi = \phi\,[\,\varepsilon\ (\pi_g),\ \delta,\ \tau_g\,]$; and $\phi_\varepsilon < 0$, $\phi_\gamma > 0$, $\phi_\tau < 0$.

As for the entry decisions of the entrepreneurs, here profitability is the objective. Let us separate the entry decision into two steps: the entrepreneurial decision to start up a new firm, and the location in the N- or R-sector. This separation is easier under the assumption, maintained for the present, that N-entrepreneurs and T-entrepreneurs are identical *ex ante*. Entries, m_t, depend on the general conditions in the private sector, i.e. on positive externalities created by the G- and N-sectors, and on the costs of other inputs, denoted here p_k, which are discussed below. Thus, $m_t = m\ (p_k,\ N_{t-1} + G_{t-1})$, $m_1 < 0$, $m_2 > 0$. The choice whether to enter the R- or the N-sector depends on p_n/e and on τ_n/τ_r. Thus $m_t = n_t + r_t$, where $n_t/r_t = f\ (p_n/e,\ \tau_n/\tau_r)$, and $f\ (1, 1) = \nu/(1 - \gamma - \nu)$. Section 4 contains a brief discussion of the simulations.

3. The simulations

The consistency of the model of the previous section was tested in a series of simulations. In particular, an attempt was made to establish whether the predicted outcomes do indeed occur. Not all possible variations of the model have been tried out, and some of the variables were kept constant. The main aim has been to check whether δ, the variable that represents the hardness of the budget constraint, i.e. the hardness of the resolve to weed out loss-making enterprises, could lead to faster growth in the middle and long run at the price of a deeper immediate decline of output.

Figures 3.1 and 3.2 (see appendix B) illustrate the role of some of the variables introduced in Section 2. In both figures δ progresses from 0.05 in panel a, via 0.1 in panel b, to 0.2 in panel c. In Figure 3.1 the effect of the size of the G- and N-sectors on the rate of entry of new firms is strong, and the depression at the beginning of the transition period is shallow, though deeper when δ is large. This depression is followed by a fast rate of output growth, with the new sectors, R and N, growing faster the greater δ is. Figure 3.2 reports the case of a lower effect of the G- and N-sectors on entry, and here the superiority of the high δ policy is not at all obvious.

Various values for the interaction variables have been tried. Another coefficient which, not surprisingly, has been shown to have an effect on the rate of growth of the new sectors is ϕ_δ, i.e. the effect of δ on the rate of exit from the old sector into the G-sector. Appendix A contains the exact numerical specification of the simulated model.

4. The effects of policy variables

The policy variables introduced in the previous section are discussed under the headings of the relevant policy fields.

4.1 The basic institutions of the market

As mentioned in the introduction, some basic institutions of the capitalist economy were destroyed by decades of communist rule, and these institutions have to be revived before a healthy growth of private economic activity can commence. Since much has been said on this subject, my own comments will be brief.

The very institution of property ownership, basic to any market economy, has been undermined by the socialist regime, by the very fact that all property in the economy was ostensibly owned by the nation at large. The exact subdivisions of this final holding body did not matter enough (as they would, e.g., in a network of fully owned subsidiaries and their mother corporation in a capitalist economy). Private ownership of most assets was strictly forbidden, and this prohibition has now to be reversed. What are the steps required to revive the institution of private property? The first step is a change in the law, undertaken in each country by its legislative organization (and this term, rather than the term 'organ' which is usually used, has been picked on purpose). This has surely been effected at least partially[3] in all countries of the area. Next comes the delineation of the assets, the decision on which state body, which SOE, is the rightful owner of each of the assets owned by the state. This operation is usually supervised by the privatization organization which has been put up in each and every country, and is a major organizational undertaking. This is an essentual step in the so-called commercialization or 'corporatization' of SOEs. Another part of this operation is the decision on Who Owns What in the private sphere: ownership claims rooted in the pre-socialist era become important in the time when the restitution of ownership, or the distribution of some state assets to past owners is on the public agenda. For these tasks legal institutions have to be in existence and to be in working order. And legal institutions here means legal organizations, the courts, law firms or private law offices,

3 For example, Russia has just started to prepare the framework of private property in agriculture.

and the executive organizations such as the police, to enforce the decisions of the courts and see to it that ownership rights can be consummated.

The stress on organizational tasks is intentional. It serves to underscore the fact that new functions and newly determined procedures require new, or at least changed, organizations. New organizations are networks consisting of labor with the proper skills. The members of these new organizations have to learn to carry out their act together, and it may take some time before they have been run in and can start working effectively in unison. In many cases old organizations which carried out similar tasks or carry a name tag that is reminiscent of the new function, may be retooled, their workers reeducated, taught new 'tricks', and the unlearning of old tricks may be a condition for learning the new ones. It may seem that time may be saved when organizations are merely retooled, but restructured organizations may continue to carry out some of the old procedures, inherited from their past.[4] Either process takes both time and resources, and is, therefore, expensive but singularly indispensable. Much of it is in the nature of the production or public goods, and can be undertaken only by the state. Even if the state is overloaded by pressing tasks, this is a task of prime importance.

Some of the services mentioned above should be supplied by private bodies, e.g. private lawyers. Are the existing lawyers competent to serve as advisors and representatives of private interests? Even this is questionable. Who is to accredit them? It should be remembered that the time element here consists of two steps, first organization-building, then 'production' of the required services by the new or reconstructed organization. In view of the large backlog, the latter task is bound to take considerable time.

I have used a considerable amount of space to amplify on a single aspect of the institution-building task of the state, simply to emphasize how difficult, time-consuming, and costly this is to be. Since this is a self-understood precondition for the growth of a healthy private economic sector, this is not included among the variables mentioned in the model.

4.2 Privatization policies

It is generally agreed that the great bulk of SOEs has to be privatized. The meaning of the term privatization is less widely agreed upon. One has to reexamine the aims of the process to decide which of the various strategies under review in the region do indeed merit the designation.

The aims of privatization, as far as economists are concerned, is to turn the SOEs into efficient and innovative producers. Keren (1993) has an extensive discussion of the reasons why privatization is necessary. The principal upshot is that the soft budget constraint, the guarantee which state firms possess that their existence is not in danger, is the main cause of their traditional 'don't rock the boat' mode of behavior. To change

---

4 See, for instance, 'How to start an Airline with 5 000 US$' (The Economist, 1993b, 67), where the entrepreneur '...refused to hire former Aeroflot cabin crew...' for the new airline he founded.

this mode of behavior means to destroy habits which have grown over time, to disrupt links with other members of the network which makes up the enterprise, with workers, management, suppliers, or clients. All this is bound to meet resistance. Only strong outside pressure can break down this resistance to change. The most effective pressure is the threat to the very existence of the organization. As long as continued survival is not in doubt, SOEs continue to operate in a conservative manner. But survival cannot be credibly threatened under socialism. As a part of a large organization, whose own existence is not in doubt, the supervising hierarchy finds it next to impossible to devise ways of terminating the life of an SOE, even if it is clear that its performance is not acceptable, and SOEs know that their umbilical cord can never be severed. This is why privatization is necessary, and why only organizational changes that ensure the end of the automatic support line, the soft budget constraint, deserve the designation 'privatization'.

An alternative with which many countries toy, is to hand SOEs over to holding companies. If these holding companies were to be private foreign investment funds or unit trusts or the like, each of which had control of a very small number of these SOEs, the threat of closing them down or reorganizing them if their performance were unsatisfactory would be credible. Not so, however, if all industrial SOEs are divided among a small number of nationally owned companies that specialize in holding nationally owned firms. These holding companies themselves are likely to threaten their SOEs with closure when their performance is unsuccessful only if they themselves are likewise threatened. It is true that the ostensible objective of the holding company would be to produce profits, but however that was also the aim of SOEs under reform regimes (Keren, 1992b). Holding companies may tend to form coalitions with their flock of SOEs, and this tendency would be strengthened if the holding companies themselves were manned by previous employees of the state apparatus.

Another alternative is to hand the SOEs over to their workers. Here the danger is similar: a worker-managed enterprise is a legitimized coalition-led firm, and such a firm will find it very hard to change its mode of operation. As a result the enterprise is unlikely to reorganize itself. Politically, on the other hand, such a firm has a much greater power to fight against its own demise. Hence, this too is no real alternative, and the worker-managed enterprise does not deserve the designation of being privatized.

All that remains is sale to private units, a lengthy affair, which raises the need to weigh up equity against efficiency, the fair price against the speed of disposal. Existing management, previous members of the *nomenklatura*, have the best means of obtaining control over SOEs or their parts, and the fastest way of disposing of the SOEs may be to let them nibble those parts of the enterprises which they deem to be capable of functioning profitably. Efficiency should permit such disposal. However, the voices that claim that brakes should be applied will be strengthened, and, thus telling, slow speed and equity should take precedence over efficiency. Incentive problems also arise, when the privatizers know that they are putting themselves out of a job when they have accomplished their task and sold off profitably all ex-SOEs in their portfolio.

There is another perspective on the treatment of SOEs: the weight of industry in Eastern European economies is far too large, its structure is biased toward heavy industry, and it is often too specialized to be able to change its line of business. A significant share of the SOEs can therefore never be sold. These SOEs are characterized by a negative value, that is, by a negative expected flow of profits. They have to be wound up sooner or later, and for plain economic reasons this should be sooner rather than later. Some of these SOEs belong to the proudest collections of the communist state and many of them took opposition to the *ancien régime*; it may therefore seem ungrateful and unjust to punish them in this manner. But if they are kept alive for too long, i.e., to use the symbols of Section 2 if δ is kept very low, then they endanger the whole transition process, or, in the least, slow it down considerably.

The conclusion of the previous paragraph is that the government cannot remain uninvolved in the affairs of the state sector, because it was to play the role of the executioner and at the same time of the judge that decides which SOE should cease operations. A related reason is that some help has to be given to the entrepreneurial sector in the acquisition of resources. This has a stock and a flow dimension. The stock refers to the fact that the SOEs have frozen in them considerable assets that are not directly related to the production process. They possess real estate, land and buildings in urban centers, used machinery and transport equipment, all of which are required by the private sector. Some of these assets are transferred to the non-state sector through the spontaneous or decentralized privatization that hives off parts of the large SOE. This is, however, a very incomplete process, that may leave too many of these assets locked away, unused, in SOEs that are, in effect, awaiting liquidation. A high rate of liquidation of B-firms is therefore beneficial, also because it frees these assets. Another means may be the reorganization of SOEs, an attempt to save those parts in them that may have a chance of surviving through vertical and horizontal disintegration - unless, of course, this is already being accomplished by spontaneous privatizers. A low δ is therefore harmful since it tends to lock these assets into their unused state, raising their price to the entrepreneurial sector.

The flow dimension relates mainly to the availability of credits. This has two dimensions: the macroeconomic dimension of the pressure on resources, and the distributive aspect. The former is related to δ through the pressure on national resources by the need to bail out loss-making SOEs; the latter because banks tend to give precedence to large SOEs in the allocation of scarce funds.

To summarize: a reduction in δ has the following detrimental effects:

(i) It reduces ϕ, the rate at which B-firms try to transform themselves.
(ii) It increases the government deficit, and thus the rate of taxation, τ. Since a high τ hinders the entrance of M-firms and reduces ϕ, this too reduces the rate ϕ.
(iii) If τ_n is harder to collect than τ_r, an increase in τ also raises the gap $\tau_r - \tau_n$, which raises the n_t/r_t ratio, i.e. hinders the growth of the R-sector.
(iv) It reduces the amount by which K-resources which are locked in SOEs, which would be freed upon dissolution. A similar effect would be obtained by the very hardening of the budget constraints which would have been signalled by a higher δ: it leads B-firms to try to increase their cash flow, i.e. to sell off the K-resources which they command at a faster rate. This too is conducive to an increase in m_t.

An increase in δ imposes an obvious cost, i.e. the costs of higher unemployment in the immediate future. This is a highly visible cost, very painful and unpopular, and the authorities are naturally disinclined to enforce it. The argument that indirect steps to maintain employment in the old SOEs may lead to greater harms is not easy to sell. This does not reduce the significant invisible and indirect costs of a low δ.

4.3 Macro policy

Macroeconomic policy is a separate area, which can and should be discussed independently of the micro-problems which are the focus of this book and this paper. I therefore take it for granted that inflation in the Eastern European economies has to be brought under control, and that the only question of interest is whether there may be certain weapons in the arsenal of the inflation-fighter that may harm the transformation process and should, therefore, be avoided.

There is just one instrument on which I would like to focus: the exchange rate (e in Section 2). The exchange rate is often chosen to be one of the 'nominal anchors' used to assure the public that the authorities are in earnest and will not allow prices to rise. The freezing of the rate is also used to stop the cost push, to uncouple cost rises from price rises. This is, however, a very dangerous weapon, one that can fault the whole transition process. When the nominal exchange rate is used as an anchor, it is all but inevitable that the real exchange rate becomes overvalued. The anchor is needed as long as prices are rising, and at the time when the exchange rate is fixed rising prices assure us of a true appreciation of the domestic currency.

The direct effect of an appreciation, of a reduction in e in the model, is to slow down the development of the R-sector, the sector that may promise the future development of growth nodes in the economy. The same cause may also slow down the rate of conversion of B-firms into G-firms: the fate of the ex-GDR, whose industry was killed by an overvalued exchange rate, is a case in point, even though an extreme one. There are also positive examples: it is widely agreed that the undervaluation of the DM after the currency reform of the late 1940s was an important stimulus to the German Miracle of the 1950s and 1960s: the case of Japan and other East Asian tigers may be similar. This is not all: the over-valued rate also leads to balance of payment problems, and if a devaluation is not acceptable, this leads to administrative means of reducing imports and increasing exports. These administrative methods - import licensing, direct export promotion and tampering with the price system - are more dangerous in an ex-communist economy than elsewhere: through the back-door they bring back the previous means of coordination. Subsidies to enterprises that are deemed to be temporarily harmed bring back the soft budget constraint.

If the exchange rate has not to be used to fight inflation, then all other instruments become more indispensable. Monetary poliy has to be very strict, and all possible steps have to be taken to balance the budget. In other words, any talk of a Keynesian policy, in the sense of a less contractionary macro-policy, is out of place (Kornai, 1993). In particular, the efficient collection of taxes becomes very important. The new private sector in many East European countries apparently manages to avoid paying taxes altogether. Any lightening of the net, and such lightening is unavoidable, will affect R-firms before it does N-firms, because the former are more likely to be unable to avoid contacts with the government, e.g. when permits of various kinds have to be obtained. The N-sector is likely to be a supplier of the private sector, while the R-sector's clients are likely to include government agencies as well as the private and the foreign sectors. Hence in the short run it seems that τ_r is likely to increase, and this advantage of the new sector will be lost for R-firms. It may seem too costly for the tax collector to widen the net and try to catch the N-firms. It may also meet internal resistance because it may deprive the staff of bribes and lead to conflicts with organized crime. It is, therefore, essential, on microeconomic as well as on macroeconomic grounds, to improve the net even further, so that the advantage that the N-sector has and which may divert investments into production exclusively for the local market, away from exportables, will be removed.

5. Mafia = Robber Barons?

Does it matter which type of entrepreneurs are bred, what is their character, their credibility? If it is mainly the Mafia and members of the old nomenklatura who control industry, will it not be a replay of the 19th Century US History with its robber barons who pioneered modern industry in the US and the world at large? It is not easy to answer this question: one view could be that it does not really matter who obtains initial control of the industry, because if the first private owner is unsuccessful, a better one will replace him. This need not be the case[5] if a substantial chunk of industry were controlled by a Mafia that becomes successful commercially because it succeeds in rent seeking activities, i.e. in obtaining favorable conditions by coercing business associates into deals they would not have entered freely, or by taxing competitors by imposing high transaction costs on them (e.g. by running a protection racket). Furthermore, there is a great difference between the types of industrial empires which the robber barons put up at the turn of the century, and those that are most promising today. The efficiency condition for the industries which thrived at the turn of the century was large- scale, and the very ability to create large organizations was an essential gift of the robber barons. This is not the case at present, when flexibility and an advanced scientific basis provide advantage. The Mafia and the nomenklatura networks might have been competent at building the large empires required for the old, heavy, scale-dependent industries. However they have no comparative advantage in high technology, in knowledge dependent industries. The R-sector represents the knowledge-based industries in which the evil networks have no advantage.

If this distinction is valid, then the question arises whether the government has, in its armory, any instruments that may favor the entrance of one type of entrepreneur rather

5 This need not be the case in general: see Nelson (1991), who argues convincingly that one should not impose too much determinism on the actions of economic actors, that these have some discretion in selecting their policies.

than the other. The most obvious priority is the fight against crime, against extortions, and against Mafia-type murders.[6] This is hard because the police were trained and organized to defend state and not private property by means which differ from those of Western police forces. This comes on top of the fact that the police, a mainstay of the previous regime, are in general dispirited. The tight controls of the previous regime have left a system where hardly anything is allowed without a special official permit. Many of these were of no consequence in the highly centralized administration, where orders from above were sufficient to smooth the way for any project that received the consent of higher ups. With the loss of this vertical control in the post-socialist regime, these stamps of approval become a license for *blat*, for bribes. These controls are much easier to disregard for those that deal with the private local market, much harder to avoid for those whose economic activity transcends these bounds. Once you are selling to the authorities, importing or exporting, you are put at a disadvantage. And the actors in the R-sector are, therefore, much more open to these pressures of the rent-seekers than those of the N-sector. Consequently, it is best to dismantle all those licensing requirements that were of little hindrance before transition started.

The adverse side is characterized by those impositions of the center that are unavoidable: these should be imposed on all sectors alike. Otherwise they provide the N-sector with an advantage and militate against the R-sector (see discussion of taxation in subsection C of Section 4).

6. Bottom up transformation: policy implications

The title of this book implies that bottom-up transformation is just one among several possible alternative transformation policies. The implication of much of the reasoning of this paper is that bottom-up is the only feasible transformation policy. The apparent alternative of transition from above, of building the market economy from within the existing state sector is plainly not feasible, because the old SOEs are in the wrong branches of the industry, are much too big, and have built into themselves inefficient operation procedures that make them unviable in a competitive market environment, and that are very hard to root out. The best hope remaining for SOEs is privatization from below, the so-called 'spontaneous' privatization. Though lacking in equity, the efficiency gains of relieving the state of the burden of ownership gain precedence (Berliner, 1993).

It may, therefore, seem that the government's role in the transition is secondary. But this is plainly not the case: the government's involvement in the process is essential. It is questionable whether the transformation can take root without it, and the path the political body may take in its absence may lead it into a *cul de sac*. But the government has few tasks in the field that used to be called industrial policy: all it has to do here is to control the old government sector that cannot be steered by indirect means, and, more

---

6 'Banking in Russia: No Foreigners Need Apply' (The Economist, 1993c, 76) reports that Mafia attempts to elbow into the lucrative banking industry. Ten bankers were shot in the first seven months of 1993.

specifically, try to phase it out as fast as possible. Its main positive role is to construct a public sector that can provide the type of services which are taken for granted in the Western market economies: protection of property, law and order, and the efficient collection of taxes.

The government should be constrained in the type of instruments it is using: there is a single caveat - avoid an overvalued exchange rate, one of the greatest obstacles on the path of a smooth and desirable development; an overvalued exchange rate is an invitation to a stop-go policy which which will discourage the growth of an efficient export sector.

This menu of policies is not easily implemented, in particular because it constitutes such a break with the past. The human resources needed to carry it out are in short supply. And there is no past example one can point to and say: 'Here is your model'.

References

Berliner, Joseph S. (1992) Strategies for Privatization in the USSR, in Keren, M. and G. Ofer (eds.) *Trials of Transition: Economic Reform in the former Communist Bloc*, New York: Westview Press, 215-37.

Berliner, Joseph S. (1993) The Gains from Privatization, in *The Former Soviet Union in Transition, Vol. 1*, Study Papers submitted to the Joint Economic Committee, Congress of the United States, Washington, DC: US Government Printing Office, 240-54.

Greif, Avner (1993); Contract Enforceability and Economic Institutions in Early Trade: The Maghribi Traders Coalition; *American Economic Review*, 83, 529-48.

Keren, Michael (1992a) The Socialist Firm, the Value of Capital, and Transition to Capitalism, in Keren, M. and G. Ofer (eds.) *Trials of Transition: Economic Reform in the former Communist Bloc*, New York: Westview Press, 239-53.

Keren, Michael (1992b); The New Economic System, the New Economic Mechanism, and the Yugoslav LMF: Bureaucratic Limits to Reform; *Economic Systems*, 16, 89-111.

Keren, Michael (1993); On the (Im) Possibility of Market Socialism; *Eastern Economic Journal*, (1993, forthcoming).

Kornai, János (1991); The Principles of Privatization in Eastern Europe; *The Economist* (forthcoming).

Kornai, János (1993) *Transformational Recession: A General Phenomenon Examined through the Example of Hungary*, Francois Peroux Lecture, mimeo, Budapest (forthcoming, Economie Appliquée).

Nelson, Richard R. (1991); Why Do Firms Differ, and How Does it Matter?; *Strategic Management Journal*, 12, 61-74.

The Economist (1993a) *Halle-luja Chorus*, 14 Aug.

The Economist (1993b) *How to start an Airline with 5 000 US$*, 14 Aug.

The Economist (1993c) *Banking in Russia: No Foreigners Need Apply*, 7 Aug.

Appendix A: the simulations

1. Constants

$\delta \in \{0.05, 0.1, 0.2\}$a
$\nu = 0.3$
$\beta = 0.7$
$\phi = +\phi_0 + (\phi_\delta * \delta) - (\phi_\varepsilon * \varepsilon)$
$\phi_0 = 0.03$
$\phi_\delta = 1.0$
$\phi_\varepsilon = 0.2$
$\phi_{\tau g} = 0.4$
$\varepsilon = +\varepsilon_0 - \varepsilon_{\pi(G)} * \pi_G$
$\varepsilon_0 = 0.2$
$\varepsilon_{\pi(g)} = 0.4$
$\tau_n = 0$
$\pi_g = 0.2$
$m = m_0 + m_{p(k)} * p(k) + m_{G+N} * (G_{-1} + N_{-1})$
$m_0 = 0.05$
$m_{p(k)} = 0.01$
$m_{G+N} \in \{0.05, 0.1\}$[a]
$p(k) = 0.005$
$e = 1$

2. Variables

$D_t = D_{t-1} + \Delta D_t$
$G_t = G_{t-1} + \phi * (1 - \varepsilon) * B_{t-1}$
$B_t = 1 - G_t - D_t = (1 - \phi - \delta) * B_{t-1}$
$N_t = N_{t-1} + \Delta N_t$
$R_t = R_{t-1} + \Delta R_t$
$I_t = G_t + B_t + N_t + R_t$
$\Delta D_t = (\delta + \phi * \varepsilon) * B_{t-1}$
$\Delta M_t = M_0 - M_{P(K)} * P(K) + M_{(G+N)} * (N_{t-1} + G_{t-1})$
$M_0 = 0.01$
$M_{p(k)} = 0.4$
$M_{(G+N)} = 0.05$
$f_t = f_{PRAT} * (P_n/E - 1) - f_{\tau\Delta} * (\tau N - \tau_R)$
$f_{prat} = 0.6$
$f_{\Delta\tau} = 0.3$
$P_n = \nu * I_t/(N_t + 1/\infty)$
$\Delta R_t = \Delta M_t/(1 + F_{t-1})$
$\Delta N_t = \Delta M_t - \Delta R_t$
$\tau_t = (1 - \beta) * B_t$
$\tau_r = (\tau - \tau_N * N_t)/(R_t + G_t + 1/\infty)$

[a] Sets contain the values used in simulations.

Appendix B:

Figure 3.A1 Panel a; delta = 0.05, high (G+N) sensitivity

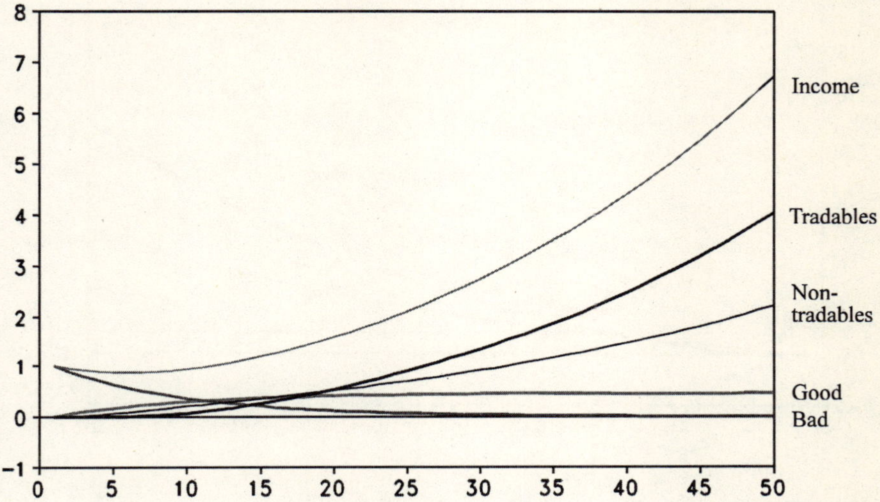

Figure 3.A2 Panel b; delta = 0.1, high (G+N) sensitivity

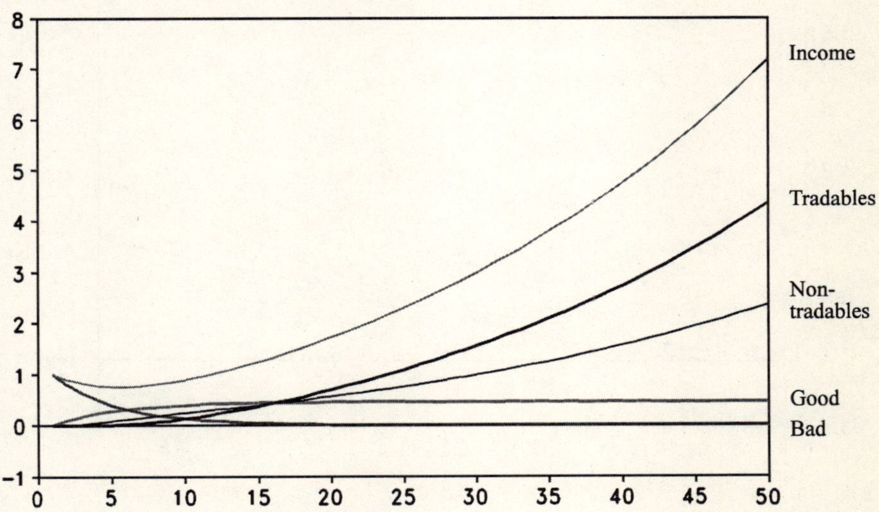

Figure 3.A3 Panel c; delta = 0.2, high (G+N) sensitivity

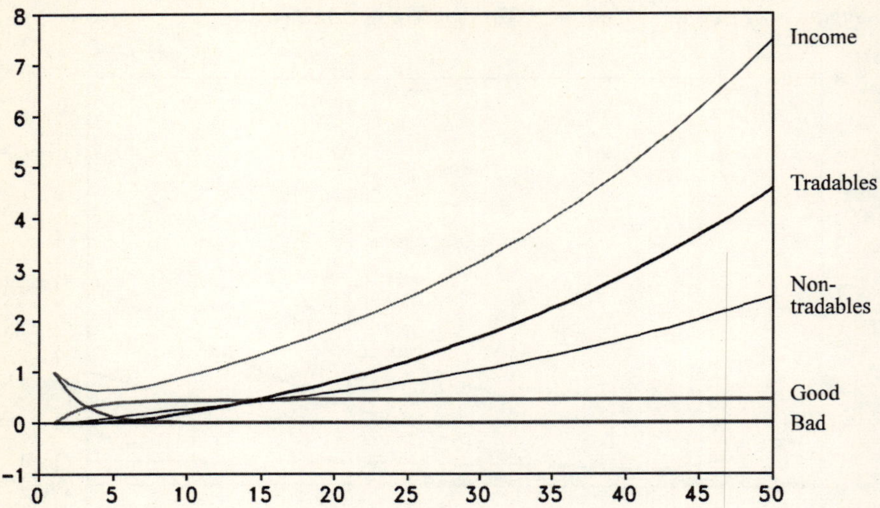

Figure 3.A4 Panel a; delta = 0.05, low (G+N) sensitivity

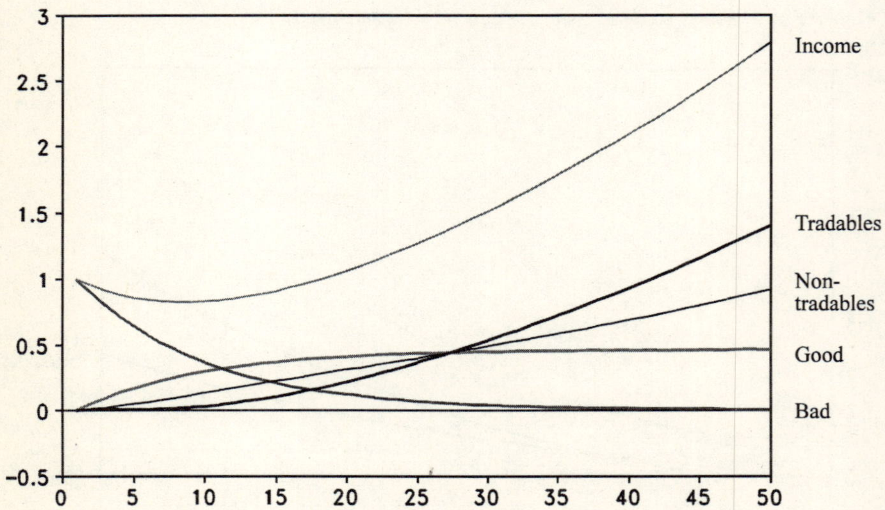

Figure 3.A5 Panel b; delta = 0.1, low (G+N) sensitivity

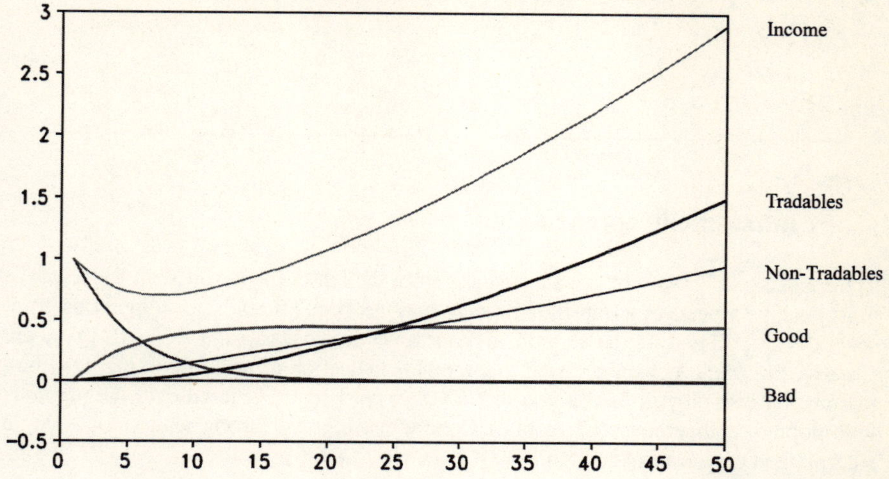

Figure 3.A6 Panel c; delta =0 .2, low (G+N) sensitivity

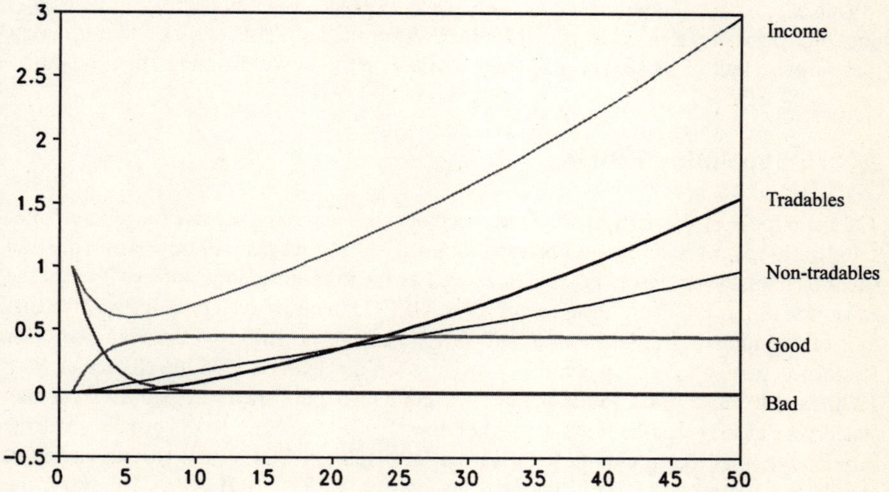

4 Entrepreneurship in Eastern Europe: a critical view

Sergio Arzeni

1. A burst of entrepreneurship

The spontaneous growth of private business since the fall of the Berlin Wall is one of the most positive aspects of a transition process that has been otherwise disappointing from several viewpoints. At the summit in Vancouver in early April 1993 with President Clinton, President Yeltsin declared that the best indication of progress in the transition to a market economy in Russia was that 60 000 new firms registered over the previous few months, compared to 70 years of Communist regime, during which not a single enterprise had been incorporated.

By the end of 1993 Poland leads the league of former Communist countries moving towards entrepreneurship with two million unincorporated businesses and roughly 60 per cent of Gross National Product (GNP) generated by the private sector. Taking only the urban labour force, at the end of 1991, Hungary had eight incorporated businesses per 1 000 people and Czechoslovakia had 160 unincorporated businesses per 1 000 people (The Economist, 1992).

This explosion of entrepreneurship took place spontaneously and the result was largely unexpected for Western advisors and for local governments. This was a bottom-up event that surprised all of those who still think and act on top-down planning and schemes.

2. Disappointing EBRD

The main focus of Western advice to new democracies was basically macroeconomic, i.e. stabilization, convertibility and privatization - three key words. Entrepreneurship and small business were largely neglected, as well as the microeconomic approach, with the exception of the EC Phare Programme. The OECD countries even established a special tool to 'promote entrepreneurship and SMEs', called the EBRD (European Bank for Reconstruction and Development). However, when they passed from the charter of May 1990 used to raise funds to the operational guidelines published in April 1991, it was stated very clearly that the Bank would not directly lend to SMEs on the grounds of 'cost efficiency', that the minimum loan was set at 5 million ECUs, and that this amount should not exceed one third of the total investment (EBRD, 1991, 17). This way, the main agency set up by the OECD-G24 countries to foster entrepreneurship in Central and Eastern Europe neglected entrepreneurship and small firms while focusing on size: infrastructure investments and privatization. The initial structure of the EBRD, which hinged on two departments (development bank and merchant bank), reflected this fundamental choice. Now, following the departure of Mr. Attali, things may change but the fundamental focus will not be the small firm.

3. Part-time entrepreneurship

For the most part, spontaneous, bottom-up, entrepreneurial development took place without Western assistance and without government aid. In fact, all Central and Eastern European governments experiencing a drastic fall in fiscal revenues are trying to raise money by heavily taxing new entrepreneurs who, for survival, are pushed into tax evasion.

A main feature of East European business creation is that many new businessmen are partially self-employed, so that they often still keep on a paid job in the public sector or in a state-owned company. What we have been observing is a mass phenomenon of part-time entrepreneurship, probably unique in history. The problem is that the practice of a double job (one in the public and one in the private sector) makes sense in terms of microeconomic pragmatism but is problematic in terms of public ethics and social morality. The key policy issue here is, therefore, to choose what matters most: to encourage people to try out a business idea with a social safety-net (the public sector salary) or to discourage some people - the most 'entrepreneurial' - to take advantages that others are not willing or capable to take, thus risking social tensions between the winners and the losers in the game for the transformation of the economy.

4. Social barriers to entrepreneurship

The fate of entrepreneurship development in Central and Eastern Europe, largely depends on this issue, where the biggest obstacle to capitalist development is the psychological barrier, the entrenched and lingering logic of egalitarianism, still ingrained in the minds of people. The results of the Polish elections in 1993, which returned former Communists back to power, are a consequence of these social implications related to entrepreneurial development. Forthcoming elections in other countries in transition to the market economy may prove the effects of this untackled policy issue to be even more worrying.

In Poland, the ex-Communists have become strong advocates of capitalism and socialism at the same time. Former Communist party spokesman Jiri Urban now possesses one of the largest Polish fortunes and, in several countries former Nomenklatura bosses have turned themselves into entrepreneurs, causing a great deal of resentment among the population that sees the same people - whatever the regime - always reaping the benefits. Nevertheless, the enthusiasm with which ex-Communists embraced capitalism is mitigated by their continued nostalgia for the past. This is a negative development because, in the difficult and uncertain march towards the free market and a competitive economy, political leaders must reject the past completely and must be adamant in not wanting to go back to a dreadful regime of horror. As in the

Bible, when Moses was leading the people of Israel away from Egypt, through the desert, towards the Promised Land, he had only one negative certainty to convince his suffering brothers to continue the march: there was nothing good under the Pharoahs' regime, although everyone had shelter and food, because it was slavery. Anyone who now discovers something positive in the Communist ideology and experience undermines the refusal of the past, aggravates the pains of the transition and draws out the duration of the same pains. This is why it is so important to understand and support grass-roots entrepreneurial growth in Central and Eastern Europe.

5. Good and bad entrepreneurship

In this respect, the work of William Baumol is extremely useful. He argues that 'while the total supply of entrepreneurs varies among societies, the productive contribution of the society's entrepreneurial activities varies much more because of their allocation between productive activities such as innovation and largely unproductive activities such as rent seeking or organized crime. This allocation is heavily influenced by the relative pay-offs society offers to such activities. This implies that policy can influence the allocation of entrepreneurship more effectively than it can influence its supply' (Baumol, 1990).

Translated into the reality of Central and Eastern Europe, this means that the relative rewards for different types of entrepreneurial activity (the innovative and productive, the rent-seeking and unproductive, the criminal and negative) have profound effects both on patterns of entrepreneurial behaviour and on the rate of economic growth, which depends on entrepreneurial development.

Under Communism, any form of entrepreneurship was illegal and criminal. In fact, this prohibition did not stop the flourishing of a black market economy largely using a foreign currency, the dollar. Like many prohibitions in history (e.g. alcohol) as well as in the present (drugs), entrepreneurship previously banned is now legal. This simple act *per se* is not enough, and government neglect is not commendable. In fact, black market entrepreneurship was largely associated with extensive corruption in the system. In a sense, the vast and informal exchange of large and small favors that characterized the corruption in some societies may even have played a positive role at a point in history when it provided the oil in the wheels of a crippled system. However, it is now time to clarify things. Crime must be stamped out, not only because it is intrinsically bad, but also because it provokes entrepreneurial misallocations, encouraging ambitious and creative people to embark on illegal activities if they are not effectively prosecuted. However, a clear distinction should be made between criminal activity (i.e. drug pusher or 'racketeer') and informal activity (i.e. selling apples without any authorization). The informal or underground economy should be allowed to expand and government should avoid any measure, such as taxation or heavy red tape that discourages entrepreneurs to move naturally from the informal to the regular economy.

6. Service sector entrepreneurs versus manufacturing entrepreneurs

A clear weakness in Eastern European entrepreneurship is that it is heavily concentrated in the service sector, with little activity in farming or manufacturing. By the end of 1991, already up to 80 per cent of Polish shops and restaurants were privately owned, representing about 10 per cent of private business. Almost 80 per cent of Polish agricultural production comes from farming enterprises. The challenge of entrepreneurship in Eastern Europe is to promote entrepreneurship in manufacturing. It is the ability to predict how consumer demand will change and to find cost-efficient ways of supplying new products that govern business success in manufacturing. And in this field, I contend that entrepreneurial culture needs to be rediscovered and reinvented - with Western partnership - in Eastern Europe. I, therefore, disagree with Professor Johnson when he argues that 'the idea that East Europeans need to be taught the basic facts of economic life was always absurd. Forty years of rationing, shortages and thriving black markets were an excellent course in elementary economics - better, perhaps, than a century or two of capitalism, whose beneficiaries take the miracle of supply and demand for granted' (The Economist, 1992, 73).

All this ignores the fact that a successful firm is not only one that is capable of rapid responses but is competent in innovation, management discipline and the capacity to muster accumulation towards progress in production and productivity. The barriers to entry in small commerce or trade, in self-employment or survival entrepreneurship are very low. But, if we want a Schumpeterian entrepreneur, there is a great deal of work to do.

The Harvard Business School's working definition of entrepreneurship is 'the pursuit of opportunity beyond the resources you currently control' (Stevenson, 1992) . However, Joseph Schumpeter, who added the notion of innovation to the definition of entrepreneurship, regarded the entrepreneur as a man who transforms events into opportunities, performing functions which are always innovative, leading to the creation of new goods or services by combining the different factors of production in an original way. Therefore, for Schumpeter, a cobbler who sets up a shop in a village or a chain of footwear shops is not an entrepreneur. For Schumpeter, to become an entrepreneur, the cobbler must either produce new models of shoes or modify (possibly improve) the process of shoemaking or invent or develop a new distribution system, such as franchising - to sell shoes world-wide, as McDonalds did for hamburgers and Benetton for sweaters. He allowed for many kinds of innovation, e.g., in the areas of process, market, product, factor and even organization (Schumpeter, 1942).

Anyone can see that these sorts of innovation and these types of entrepreneurs are lacking in Central and Eastern Europe and that there is a need to teach the basics of what constitutes a business and how it works. Confusions and misunderstanding about what is meant by 'entrepreneur' are quite common, even in the West - not to speak of the East. For instance when people qualify an entrepreneur as a risk taker, they focus upon only one aspect of *some* entrepreneurs and probably a small percentage of them. In fact, while risk taking is an important element of entrepreneurial behavior, it is clear that many entrepreneurs bear risks grudgingly and only after they have tried to get others to absorb risk for them. Furthermore, once established, the life of any entrepreneur is concentrated on trying to avoid the greatest of all risks that hangs over his head like a sword of Damocles: bankruptcy.

This sort of concept and fact ought to be taught even in OECD countries. Who could credibly deny the Eastern Europeans' need to be educated about these basic business principles?

As pointed out by Professor Stevenson, Sarofim-Rock Professor of Entrepreneurship at Harvard University, 'one issue that is frequently raised in discussions on entrepreneurs in Central and Eastern Europe is the notion of equating entrepreneurs with scoundrels, thieves and other people who break the law. Surveys of successful entrepreneurs in the United States repeatedly revealed ethics as the most important thing to teach. Trust, and getting other people to trust you, is an overall important issue in entrepreneurship, because without trust you can never get resources from other people' (Stevenson, 1992). This leads to understanding the real meaning of entrepreneurship that goes beyond small business or start-ups, because people who have developed some fairly large businesses in OECD countries are still very entrepreneurial. They are certainly also not just the high-flying, fast-living, unscrupulous promoters. They will never create anything with sustaining value. It is an approach to management and it starts with opportunity. We should always bear in mind Stevenson's lesson: 'Everything you will ever make as an entrepreneur comes from three activities: something coming in the door, something being transformed and something going out of the door. All the rest of your company is overhead' (Stevenson, 1992).

7. A ministry for entrepreneurship?

Having said this, we have to acknowledge that more effective action and more resources should be devoted to fostering the growth of entrepreneurship in Central and Eastern Europe. The Polish government has been the first in history, to my knowledge, to create a Ministry for Entrepreneurship. (We do not know, at the time of writing, whether the new Polish Government will keep this Ministry.) That is not enough, because the Ministry was without portfolio, but it has been beneficial in providing a coherent framework for donor-led initiatives - enabling everybody to know who is doing what - and a set of useful measures and institutions.

Governments and international donor or assistance organizations must understand that smaller manufacturing firms play a vital role in translating new scientific and technological knowledge into economic wealth. They also provide the pool of companies from which larger international businesses can emerge. The trouble is that their managers frequently lack the strategic management skills needed to allow their businesses to grow. There is not enough encouragement from the government for these firms to expand and there is not enough affordable credit for them.

Successful lending to small business requires local knowledge in the form of a dense network of experienced branch managers. Locally-based business support organizations are needed to upgrade the quality of services that may enable agglomerations of SMEs or creation of industrial districts made up of clusters of small firms. Forms of partnership between industrial districts in the West and in the East should be tried out.

Recent literature suggests that - due to the structural change that occurred in OECD countries over the last 10-15 years - while small firms may generally be less profitable than larger firms, their ability to identify and occupy niches can lead to an elimination of profitability differentials (Porter, 1990).

8. Firm-to-firm tutoring

The future of local, bottom-up entrepreneurship in Central and Eastern Europe, and the overall success of the transition process will depend on the local entrepreneurs' capacity to accumulate and generate internal cashflow and on whether local governments create a climate conducive to small business development. As for Western bilateral and multilateral assistance programs, they should provide less consulting (often discredited or resented) and encourage Western SMEs - not so much the large firms - to go into Eastern Europe and to act as *role models* and embark on tutoring programmes. According to Mr Carlo Borgomeo, the Chairman of the Committee for the Development of Young Entrepreneurs in Italy, 'You become an entrepreneur by doing it, not by going to school', and he has proved his theory by nurturing more than 5 000 aspiring young business people under an innovative system of business tutoring. The concept of providing external consultants as midwives to nascent companies is also being pursued in France, Britain and Germany.

However, what makes tutoring different is that it is designed to sow and then fertilize the seeds of an entrepreneurial culture in areas where it is so manifestly lacking, such as Southern Italy. Furthermore, the tutor is not an individual but a company, and a scheme can be seen as a form of enterprise creation by means of enterprise. Italian Law 44/86 on Youth Entrepreneurship has led to the creation of 20 000 jobs and 600 manufacturing firms in its first six years. This is an example of 'forced' entrepreneurship associated with a strategy of local development. It works in Southern Italy and may also work in Central and Eastern Europe. Company tutoring is potentially a much more effective means of launching small businesses than more formal management training schemes, which may only partially equip the entrepreneur for the daily problems which he or she will undoubtedly confront.

Industrial districts and company tutoring are two innovations that should be introduced into programs to promote small business in Central and Eastern Europe. However, it is high time to question technical assistance as well. Writing reports, as do so many Western consultants, is meaningless without operational follow-up and implementation of projects that commit all parties to result-oriented objectives. 'Career' consultants proved inappropriate for the practical needs of the local economies in Central and Eastern Europe. Furthermore, they only know how to operate in more advanced market settings and too often make recommendations that cannot be translated into practical implementation because of the lack of Western-style company structures there.

Bottom-up pressure from disappointed would-be entrepreneurs will be an important spur to an improvement in support schemes to small firms. However, to achieve results, stronger local business associations, capable of lobbying effectively for private sector interests, must be created and nurtured (CENSIS, 1993).

References

Baumol, William J. (1990); Entrepreneurship: Productive, Unproductive and Destructive; *Journal of Political Economy*, 98, 893-921.

CENSIS (1993) *Entrepreneurship in Central Europe*, Milan: Franco Angeli.

European Bank for Reconstruction and Development (1991) *Operational challenges and priorities: initial orientations*, London, April, 17.

The Economist (1992) *Pioneers of Capitalism*, 4 April, 78.

Porter, Michael (1990) *The Competitive Advantage of Nations*, London: Macmillan Press.

Schumpeter, Joseph A. (1942) *Capitalism, Socialism and Democracy*, New York: Harper & Row.

Stevenson, Howard (1992) The Nature of Entrepreneurship, in Abell, Derek and Thomas Kollermeier (eds), *Dynamic Entrepreneurship in Central and Eastern Europe*, Amsterdam: EFER-Elsevier.

5 Small businesses in Russia

Alexander J. Chepurenko and *Alexander V. Vilensky*

1. 'Small Entrepreneurship' - the issue of the concept

Economic reforms in Russia started with the passing of the Cooperation Law which formed the legal basis for economic activities in the non-state sector of the economy. (In the 'shadow' economy small construction companies, consumer and transport services operated and prospered under the full dominance of planned economy.) But several years went by before a broad basis for private entrepreneurship and small business was created.

Despite the market economy policy proclaimed by the political leaders and supported by the majority of the population, small business in Russia is now developing at a slow pace. In addition, this process is painful and extremely contradictory.

First of all, it is necessary to determine what such terms as 'small enterprise' and 'small entrepreneurship' mean in the specific conditions of a transforming economy. Otherwise it remains unclear what the statistical and empirical information entails in the context of small entrepreneurship in Russia.

These terms have not been defined yet in Russian legislation neither in their economic nor juridical meaning. However, it is evident that such indicators as annual turnover, profit and profitability cannot be considered as criteria for defining small enterprises at times of huge inflation and an approximate assessment of economic activity. The only valid and available indicator is the number of employees in an enterprise. Moreover, even this indicator largely depends on the various sectors of the economy, the amount of monopolization and other circumstances.

Russian legislation defines small enterprises by the number of employees working in the enterprise including those working on contracts. This indicator differs from branch to branch. There have been proposals to define this differentiation more precisely.

Table 5.1 Definitions of small businesses by sector

Sector	Upper limit of employment for a business to be classified as 'small'
Industry	up to 200
Construction	100
Wholesale trade	50
Agriculture	50
Science and non-productive sectors	25
Retail trade	15

Thus, the bill 'On State Support for Small Entrepreneurship in the Russian Federation', to be discussed below, recommends classifying small enterprises by means of the following employment criteria listed in Table 5.1.

The Russian Department of Statistics distinguishes six groups of small enterprises:

- individual private small enterprises,
- business companies and societies (closed companies),
- small state and municipal enterprises,
- joint-stock companies (open companies),
- cooperative enterprises,
- other enterprises.

'Small entrepreneurship' is seen as economic activity by persons engaged in management and control of their businesses. Classifying an enterprise as small it appears reasonable to take into account the role of its owner(s) in production and management processes. In our opinion, an enterprise is to be considered small if its owner(s), in addition to controlling the company, participate in everyday business activities by their personal effort. In other words, we suggest combining the economic-juridical concept of 'small entrepreneurship' with the social phenomenon which the Germans call 'Mittelstand'.

2. Number, role and place of 'small entrepreneurships' in the Russian economy

All quantitative estimates of small and medium-sized business in Russia are approximate ones only. There are practically no reliable statistics and experts' estimates vary greatly. The results of the industrial activities of small enterprises are demonstrated in Table 5.2. During 1992, in spite of deteriorating general economic conditions for the creation of small enterprises, the number of small businesses with individual or collective ownership increased by almost 100 000 (Table 5.3).

According to information by the Russian Chamber of Commerce, the number of small enterprises was one million by the end of February 1993. Their share in the GNP was 15.0 per cent in 1992. About two-third of the 800 000 private enterprises created in 1992 were small ones. 85 per cent of non-state commercial banks also were small and medium-sized enterprises. Compared to the figures given by the Russian Chamber of Commerce, experts of 'Business World' usually make lower estimates. According to these sources the number of small enterprises was 250 000-270 000 in mid-1993, more than half of which were engaged in media and food business, 10 per cent were active in industry, 10 per cent in science and scientific services, 20 per cent in construction. However, official information, published in 'Delo', a supplement to 'Russian News', reads differently; it estimates the number of small enterprises in 1993 at 460 000. Obviously, the truth should be somewhere between 300 000 and one million.

Table 5.2 Industrial small enterprises in the Russian industry (end 1991)

Branches	Number of enterprises	Per cent of the total number of enterprises in respective industry	Per cent of total output (current wholesale prices) in respective industry	Number of employees (in thousands)	Per cent of employees in respective industry
Russian Federation	10 778	48	5.2	874	5.1
including:					
Energy	51	20	0.5	5.4	0.6
Fuels	121	27	0.4	8.5	1.0
Ferrous metals	52	23.6	0.5	5.7	0.7
Non-ferrous metals	30	12.6	0.8	2.8	0.3
Chemicals and petro-chemicals	136	22.3	1.2	14.2	1.6
Mechanical engineering and metal industries	1 256	25.5	1.4	123	14.0
Timber, wood-working & paper	2 066	54	6.4	153	17.5
Construc-tion materials	933	44.8	9.5	97.1	11.1
Glass, china	32	21	1.9	3.7	0.4
Textiles	809	36.9	2.1	71.1	8.1
Food	3 181	64.8	21.5	297	33.9
Micro-biology	7	15.6	1.7	1.0	0.1
Pharma-ceuticals	11	4.8	0.5	1.3	0.2
Printing and publishing	1 352	86	19.7	43.8	5.0

Source: RSPP (1992).

Since 1991, the number of employees working in registered small enterprises has increased by 1.4 per cent and reached 2.8 million. This constitutes 86 per cent of the total number of employees in non-state enterprises. In addition, more than two million persons (4.6 per cent of all employees) worked under varying contractual assignments. In 1992, limited companies were rapidly created. Since the beginning of the year, the percentage of small enterprises has increased by 4.6 per cent and reached 24 per cent of all enterprises.

Table 5.3 Small enterprises created in 1992

	Number of enterprises		Number of employees		
	Total	Per cent	(in thousands)	Per cent total	01.01.1992
Total number of enterprises	189 834	100	2 824.6	100	1.4
including:					
Private individual	52 030	27.4	536.6	19.0	1.7
Companies & societies	45 221	23.8	631.8	22.4	2.7
Cooperative enterprises	43 813	23.1	749.5	26.5	82.3
State and municipal	15 804	8.3	390.4	13.8	1.3
Joint-stock companies	9 844	5.2	167.6	5.9	2.3
Other enterprises	23 122	12.2	348.6	12.4	1.7

Source: Goskomstat (1993).

3. The development of small entrepreneurship in Russia

There are two major ways of creating small firms:

- breaking up large enterprises into smaller ones,
- creating new small enterprises.

After the adoption of the Law on Cooperation in 1986 the first small enterprises appeared as cooperatives. In the beginning it was assumed that mostly students and retired persons would make use of the possibility of creating small private enterprises in the service sector (food, etc.). However, the opportunity of small-enterprise creation was mainly seized by employees engaged in the state sector or in the 'shadow' economy.

In the beginning Komsomol organizations actively participated in this process of 'small' entrepreneurship development. Dwellings, cooperative enterprises, science centres, farms and leasing enterprises were established by young people. Entrepreneurship by young people was facilitated by former Komsomol leaders using their formers contacts in the economy. The economic structures which developed at that time quickly generated capital and, nowadays, many of them have been transformed into large commercial enterprises with economic activities which are far from being 'small'.

The Law on Enterprises and Entrepreneurship Activity passed by the Russian Federation in 1991 made no provision for cooperative forms of businesses. It regulated the creation of limited companies and open joint-stock companies. Since the adoption of the law, small enterprises have begun to develop into limited companies. Enterprises, formerly consisting of physical persons only became shareholders in new limited companies. Since the law provided privileges and favorable conditions to small enterprises, a process of establishing small state enterprises began, especially in the construction industry and in the sciences.

The next stage was characterized by the *buying-up* of small enterprises, the transformation of cooperative enterprises to joint-stock companies, and by the leasing of enterprises with the option of buying them in the future. This situation presents a rather mixed picture of what could be called 'Russian small entrepreneurship'. The situation might be illustrated by four basic small-enterprise processes of creation:

Figure 5.1 Legal forms of private enterprises according to the Law on Privatization (1986-1988)

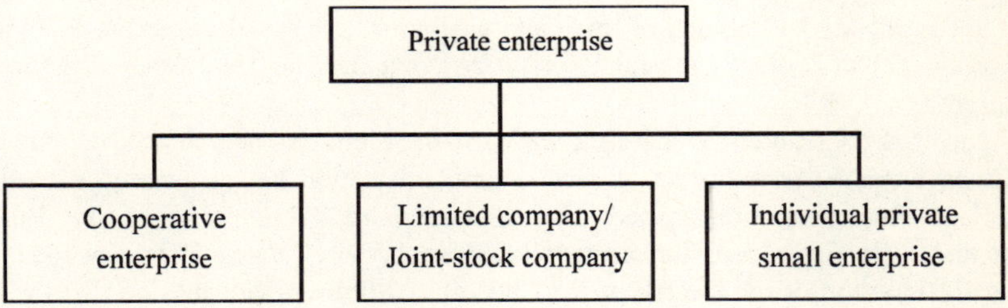

Figure 5.2 Legal forms of private enterprises in industry (1989-1991)

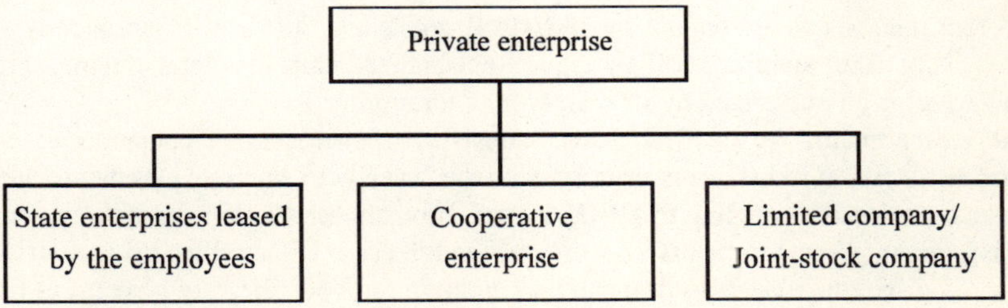

Figure 5.3 Legal forms of private enterprises in trade and services in 1992

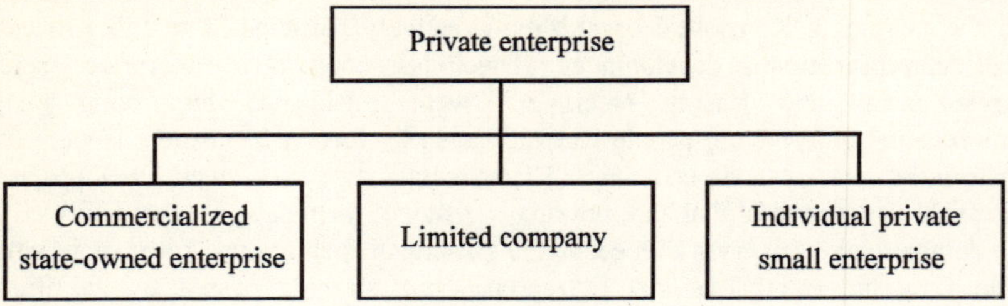

Figure 5.4 Legal forms of start-ups (since 1991)

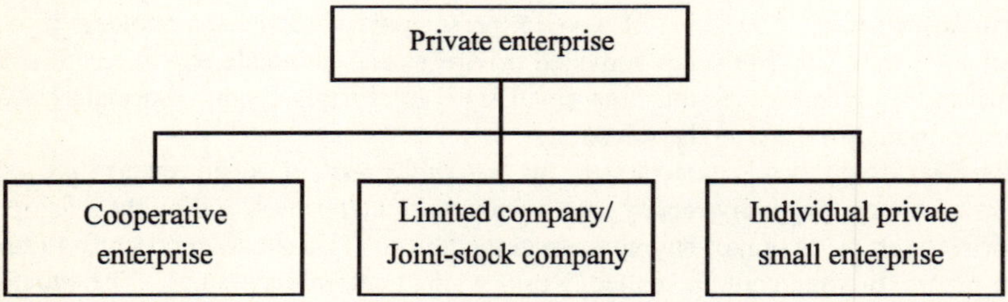

Figure 5.1 was operated between 1986-1988 after the adoption of the Law on Privatization. After the formal obstacles to private entrepreneurship have been removed, we now see the logical completion of this scheme. Figure 5.2 was operated between 1989-1991, the period characterized by 'nomenklatura' privatization. It applies also to the ongoing privatizing of small and medium-size industrial enterprises. Figure 5.3 is typical of large-scale 'small' privatization under the 1992 State Privatization Program.

Figure 5.4 constitutes the classical way of 'small' entrepreneurship development in Western terms. As a matter of fact its implementation began somewhat earlier. Officially implementation started after the adoption of the Law of the Russian Federation 'On Enterprises and Entrepreneurship Activity', dated 1 January 1991, and after the adoption of the Decree of the Council of Ministers No. 406 of 18 July 1991 'On Measures of Support and Development of Small Enterprises in the Russian Federation'. The first document legalized 'small' entrepreneurship, but did not give any definition of it; the definition was determined by the Decree of the Council of Ministers.

All four methods were used during 1987-1991 with some time lag. Consequently, we can speak of four main 'waves' of 'small'-entrepreneurship development in Russia. Each 'wave' is characterized by its own type of entrepreneurs.

The entrepreneurs of the first 'wave' consisted of members of cooperatives who derived their capital mostly from criminal activities usually in small wholesale and retail trade and services. According to a 1991 investigation almost 40 per cent of respondents working in 'small' entrepreneurship were engaged in criminal activities prior to private business legislation being passed, mostly speculating in goods illegally brought in from the West. 22.5 per cent had criminal records, every fourth respondent had friends engaged in crime. As a matter of fact, managers of small enterprises frequently prefer former criminals among their personnel, because they are very experienced and cautious employees.

The second 'wave' of entrepreneurs is represented by managers of state industries who, using their experience, contacts and knowledge of the market, put ineffective industrial capital to efficient work in their business. Almost one half of these respondents (46 per cent) came from industrial enterprises and scientific-industrial institutes, 15 per cent from ministries and various state administrations, and 2.4 per cent from the CPSU and Komsomol elite.

The third 'wave' was constituted by businessmen who, in the past, had worked as managers in private retail trade, services, transport and construction companies. They used the capital created in the shadow economy to purchase equipment and to legalize organizational schemes of resources.

The fourth 'wave' consisted of a variety of persons: farmers, craftsmen, scientists, artists, consultants in production and/or marketing, employees in tourist services, banks, insurance companies and engineering. 72 per cent of the respondents from the Moscow area had a higher education, 2.4 per cent held doctoral degrees. The usual main resource which they invest in their businesses, often original and quite competitive, is know-how. Having practically no major contacts or other resources, this fourth wave is practically unprotected from the political and economic risks which accompany private entrepreneurship. Consequently, such entrepreneurs have to be systematically supported by the state.

Priority state support for 'people' entrepreneurship could create a great social basis for the reforms within one to two years. This would promote the institutional and structural reforms by a social consensus. Voucher privatization is no solution to this problem.

4. Social value attached to entrepreneurship

It is common knowledge, not only in the West, but also in Russia, that the main difficulty in entrepreneurship development is the people's hostile attitude towards privatization. Collective traditions make for tendencies to have equal incomes and standards of living. However, our research and evidence from various opinion polls provide a different picture. Opinion polls by the Russian Independent Institute in December 1992 indicate that about 80 per cent of all people dream of private entrepreneurship. Moreover, 28 per cent seriously think of starting their own businesses. According to other data, in 1993, 3.3 per cent of all Russian people already had their own business, 28.7 per cent would like to and 49.1 per cent were in the process of setting up their businesses.

However, the answer to the question 'Are you making any practical steps to start your own business?' presents a more realistic picture: five per cent of the respondents have already tried to register their enterprises, they have attempted to get loans and other resources; 29 per cent have not undertaken any steps so far, but were going to do so soon; 66 per cent (as in 1992) have not taken any action and are not going to take any such action in the near future (Nedzvetsky, 1993, 14-5).

Apparently, there is no more moral, social and/or psychological barrier to small business development in Russia.

5. Difficulties of small entrepreneurship in Russia

A large number of economic, political, legal, social, moral, and organizational problems cast serious doubts on small businesses' ability to survive and grow without powerful and purposeful state assistance. What are the most severe problems?

First of all the difficulties are connected with the macroeconomic situation of the country. In 1992, the Yeltsin/Gaidar goverment concentrated market reforms in Russia on a rapid financial stabilization. As a result a strict taxation system with relatively high tariffs was introduced, both for small and large enterprises. For the same reason, the government refused to compensate the population for the devaluated deposits in state savings banks. This devaluation had been caused by the liberalization of consumer goods prices which resulted into an acute shortage of funds available for the establishment of new and the expansion of existing small enterprises.

The measures taken by Yeltsin/Gaidar and later by the Chernomyrdin administrations failed to achieve financial stabilization and the lack of loan funds continues to be an aspect of the lasting financial crisis. Commercial banks have raised the interest on credits to almost 200 per cent. Moreover, banks refuse long-term credits even to important clients, to say nothing of the small enterprises. The absence of loan funds has turned into the most serious restraint in the creation of new and the expansion of existing small enterprises which are unable to introduce urgently needed technical innovations and to replace obsolete production technology (see Appendix 5.1A).

Small business suffers mainly from the 25-40 per cent month inflation rate, production decline, monopolism and the disintegration of the traditional system of internal and international division of labour. Under such conditions it becomes impossible for small business - which usually does not dispose of an adequate market information and/or broad and established connections - to invest, cover overheads, and find suppliers as well as customers. To this will have to be added organizational problems: a weak self-organization of small enterprises; slight beginnings only of commercial/industrial and craft chambers, exhibitions, branch business associations; underdeveloped consulting and information services; absence of reliable statistics.

Furthermore, there are moral problems, because the population who predominantly support small business, and the business people themselves become convinced (based on their experience) that in today's Russia prospering business is done mainly by representatives of the mafia and 'nomenclature'. As a rule energetic persons who do not carry the burden of a criminal or party-political past and are ready to invest their talent into commercial activities and production, have to withdraw from business shortly after the start. This produces a negative impact on public psychology and the reforms in general.

Yet, the essential organizational problems for small enterprises, especially in production and intellectual services, have to do with the shortage in competent enterprising and the lack of honest and honorable people who might be entrusted with the projects in the private sector. The absence of business ethics is seriously impeding the development of a civilized non-criminal entrepreneurship and intensive business contacts particularly with the countries of the West.

Finally, there are political problems of 'small' business. It is an official axiom that stability in a society depends on the existence of a middle class and that the creation of adequate conditions for middle-class reproduction may save the Russian economy from a shock which, first of all, concerns 'small' business owners. Yet, instead of a real policy to avoid such a shock there were proclamations which, as the 2nd International Congress on 'Small Business in Russia' of July, 1993 in Moscow showed, are perfectly understood by the Russian businessmen. During times of acute political crisis and conflicts between parliament and the President, both sides try to make advances to 'small' entrepreneurship, in their own interests. At the same time, a corrupt bureaucracy, the main obstacle to 'small' entrepreneurship in Russia, manages to strengthen its position in the local and federal state structures.

6. 'Small' entrepreneurship and the policy of the state

In 1992, the Yeltsin and Gaidar government assumed that state stimulation and guidance of the process of small-business formation were tasks for the second stage of reforms, i.e. the stage following the introduction of market mechanisms, market relations, after overcoming the financial and economic crisis in Russia. But by the end of that year, it became evident that in order to continue the reforms the state had to take urgent measures to support small business. It also became clear that it would be necessary to combine state support for small business with the anti-crisis policy of the government. From the spring of 1993 on, the Chernomyrdin government has considerably accelerated the organizational preparation for the establishment of a united federal system of state support for small business.

During 1991-92, several state bodies of the Russian Federation were established to support small enterprises. But the creation of such bodies focused at the leaders of the competing political teams within the government and the Supreme Soviet. Moreover, due to the acute budget crisis neither the government nor the Supreme Soviet were able to allocate the necessary funds for the support of entrepreneurship and for the due maintenance of the apparatus of officials of the state bodies for that support. Therefore, the issues of the support of entrepreneurship were relegated to the background. Only by the spring of 1993 the organizational structure of state support acquired some system, though a rather unsteady one. By presidential decree the Department of Entrepreneurship Support of the Ministry of Economic Affairs was nominated as the main coordinator of the supporting small-enterprise policy. Now, this policy has to be worked out and put into practice by

- the Council for Support of Entrepreneurship of the Russian government;
- the Board of Entrepreneurship Support of the Russian Federation State Committee on Anti-Monopoly Policy and Support of New Economic Structures (Anti-Monopoly Committee);
- the subdivision of the State Committee on Industrial Policy;
- the Department of Organization, Property Management and Entrepreneurship of the Russian Federation's Council of Ministers;
- the Fund for Support of Entrepreneurship and Competition Development of the Anti-Monopoly Committee;

also by the subdivisions for small-business support of various committees, departments, state industries and joint-stock companies established on the basis of the former ministries of the USSR and the Russian Federation. However, despite the variety of state bodies, in practice, small business still cannot count on any serious support of any of them. None of the state bodies has the means for a due support of entrepreneurship.

Nevertheless, the Russian state budget for 1993 provides 25 billion roubles for the support of small entrepreneurship. But until October 1993 not a single rouble had been allocated and only the organizational schemes for the distribution of the funds have been worked out.

Meanwhile work was begun on a newly integrated federal program of state support for entrepreneurship mainly created by the Ministry of Economic Affairs of the Russian Federation. It forms part of the third integrated program of support of entrepreneurship development and includes the one created in the USSR. It can only be hoped that this new program will not remain unclaimed as happened to previous and similar programs. In addition, this program will have to reflect the whole condition of small businesses in the Russian economy. It will consist of the following parts:

- financial and tax support;
- technological support;
- organizational support;
- support of instruction and consultancy;
- support of the foreign economic activities;
- stimulation of small business cooperation;
- assistance in the marketing of small-enterprise production through channels of state orders and their provision with deficit raw materials.

Some provisions of the future integrated Federal program have already been or will be reflected in the Russian economic law. So far, the only privilege of small business has been some deferent of tax liabilities for enterprises in priority sectors of industry. A 1993 decree stipulates that privileges be granted to small enterprises whose activities promote the structural reorganization of the Russian economy, the achieving of conversion programs, and the development of socially significant industries. The

Ministry of Finance has prepared and forwarded to the Council of Ministers and the Supreme Soviet proposals on differential preferential taxation and accelerated amortization for small businesses, on the creation of state guarantees for credits and on preferential credits to small enterprises. The government and the Supreme Soviet have also received similar proposals on the amount and procedure of state support for small business from other state departments and Russian non-state free unions and associations of small business. Motions to alter the law on enterprises and enterprising activities have been prepared and several new laws have been worked out. They take into account the characteristics of small business and the specific character of state measures for its support.

Specialist participation in all this legislative work makes us hope that the opinion of 'small' entrepreneurs on the priorities of economic reform will be taken into account to warrant their interests (see Appendix 5.2A). But there is a long way from a draft to a law, and many Russian laws, as practice has shown, remain only on paper.

As to the drafts of the 'Law on State Support of Small Entrepreneurship', its first version was worked out by a team of experts convened by the Anti-Monopoly Committee of the Russian Federation. After the draft had been submitted to various government agencies, the major textual criticism of the draft was that it should reinforce positions of the public administration. Moreover, some state agencies quickly began to prepare their own drafts in which they claim the supremacy of their respective departments in the general structure of state bodies which are to support entrepreneurship. Some associations and unions of the Russian 'small' entrepreneurship act alike and try to consolidate their own exclusive monopoly rights in the future law, so as to warrant the interests of the Russian entrepreneurship. The result has been a dozen draft laws on the state support of entrepreneurship collected by the Supreme Soviet of the Russian Federation. Therefore, it is unlikely that this law will be adopted by the Supreme Soviet and put into economic practice before 1994. So far, no agreement has been reached, not even whether the law will be directly in force or will serve as the basis for further legislation by the Russian Federation or by its subjects. The latter has a reasonable motivation to do so because under present Russian conditions supporting entrepreneurship mainly is the task of the local and regional state agencies. The federal government obviously lacks the resources for the implementation of any effective policy of entrepreneurship development.

In the course of 1992-1993, the local and regional authorities have taken independent measures to support 'small' entrepreneurship irrespective and at times even regardless of the federal government policy. In many regions local semi-state funds for entrepreneurship support were created by state property privatization, local taxes, etc. It is well-known that such funds were set up in Buryatia and the Novgorod region. In various regions small entrepreneurship support programs are now spelled out and put into practice.

Taking into account the real situation of the Russian economy and policy, the specific feature of the Federal program of 'small' entrepreneurship support and development is that it generalizes the available regional programs. Drawing up the federal program provisions means going through regular consultations with the regions (subjects of the Federation). It is hoped that the implementation of the organizational state measures on the Federal and regional levels which began in 1992-93 will permit small business to assume an adequate role in the market reforms and become a vital part of the new market economy in Russia.

References

Expert Institute RSPP (1992) *Russian Small Business: Business Conditions, Perspectives of the Development*, Moscow.

Goskomstat (1993) *Main Characteristics of Cooperative and Small Enterprises Activity in Russia in 1992*, Moscow.

Nedzvetsky, S. (1993); Who will start private business?; *Reforma*, 5, 14-5.

Appendix

Figure 5.A1 Sources of initial capital of Russian small business owners

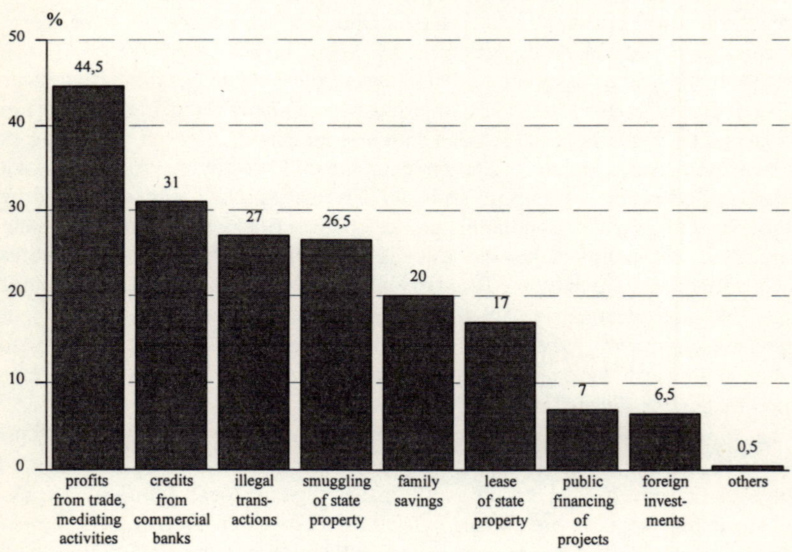

Figure 5.A2 Priorities of economic reform in the opinion of Russian small business owners

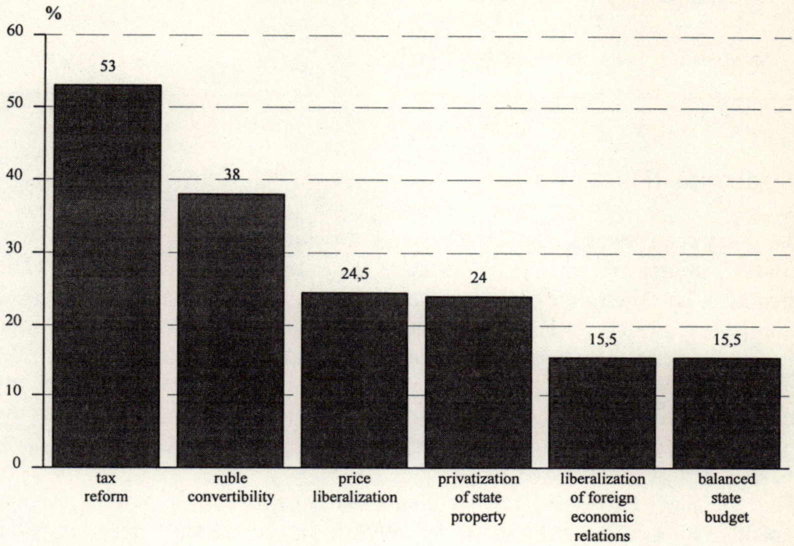

6 The development of science parks and new technology-based firms in Russia

Stephen Batstone and *Paul Westhead*

1. Introduction

It has long been argued that low economic growth in socialist economies could be attributed, at least in part, to deficiencies in technology and innovation. Lack of competition has been viewed as a prime cause of technological stagnation (see for example Nove, 1983). The lack of competition in the former Soviet Union is clearly related to the monopolistic structure of industry which has prevailed despite successive attempts at reform. As a result, the average size of manufacturing enterprises in 1990 comprised more than 800 employees (IMF et al., 1991). This compares with an average employment size of manufacturing enterprises in the European Community of sixteen employees (EIM, 1993).

The role played by small and medium-sized enterprises in providing a source of competition for established firms has recently been attracting much attention within the Russian Federation (Tsiganov, 1992). A burgeoning science park movement is now evolving which may play a role in this process of demonopolization. Small new technology based firms (NTBFs) are being created by entrepreneurs taking advantage of recent changes legalizing private business ownership, many of whom are seeking the assistance of science parks. This paper examines the present stage of development of the science park movement and the manner in which it is evolving. It should be borne in mind that evaluation of Russian science parks is at a very early stage.

The CIS Business Incubator Science Park Association (BISPA) is the coordinating institution which has been attempting to develop appropriate developmental role models for assisting NTBFs and promoting the Russian science park movement. Formerly known as the Higher Education Science Park Association, it has hosted several international conferences on the role of science parks (see Armit, 1992), as well as initiating training for science park managers. In April 1993 there were eighty-six members of BISPA across the former Soviet Union, although only thirty-four science parks conformed to the BISPA approved concept of a science park. Moreover, only ten of these are presently operational (according to Dr Shukshonov, the chairman of BISPA). The description of Russian science park activities in this paper is based upon collected materials and interviews with science park managers, government officials and entrepreneurs located at eight science parks which are members of BISPA. This information was collected during the latter half of 1992 and 1993.

Whilst there is now a substantial body of literature examining the science park concept in developed Western capitalist economies, this is not so for economies in transition. A number of questions and issues arise in evaluating the contribution of the science park movement within the current Russian transition process: What are Russian science parks? What roles do they seek to play? Do they differ both in terms of objectives and operationally from those found in developed Western capitalist economies such as the UK? How do they assist NTBFs? Answering these questions should provide insight into whether promotion of science parks may help to drive the Russian economy towards competition and entrepreneurship, seen by many as the prime movers of human action and initiative (Kirzner, 1973). This paper is an attempt to start the process of finding answers to these questions, although it should be stressed that these are still early days in the evolution of the Russian science park movement for a proper evaluation.

Our task, in seeking to understand the Russian science park movements, is not an easy one. Cultural obstacles litter our path, obscuring our comprehension of the rapidly changing realities of Russian economic life. Our approach is thus exploratory and should be read as the attempts of Western observers to understand how Russians are attempting to mould Western institutions to fit the peculiarities of their economy. The present study is a pilot study to the development of a longitudinal tracking exercise monitoring the development of Russian science parks. Our analysis is based largely around secondary analysis of materials collected as part of the development of a large management training program for Russian science parks, coordinated by the University of Warwick Science Park, into which the SME Centre at the University of Warwick has a significant training input.

The paper is organized as follows. First, in the following section, we relate the development of a science park movement to the notion of the new competition (Best, 1990) emerging in global markets, in which characteristics such as entrepreneurship play a key role. Elements of the new competition are to be used as a framework for evaluating key features of the development of the Russian science park movement to date. The section includes detail on the stated objectives of the Russian science parks surveyed. In section three the link between science parks and innovation is examined and it is noted that there is evidence that Russian science parks appear to implicitly accept a version of the linear model of innovation. Section four contains the main empirical data on the parks arranged under four main headings which comprise elements of a collectivist entrepreneurial approach. These are: (i) firms, (ii) the production chain, (iii) sectoral competition and cooperation and (iv) strategic industrial policy.

We conclude by arguing that Russian science parks are developing in a somewhat different fashion than their Western counterparts, as might be expected. This different pattern of evolution, however, influenced as it is by history, culture and the active political process, makes it difficult to predict how effective Russian science parks will be both in assisting in demonopolizing Russian industry and in encouraging productive entrepreneurship.

2. Science parks and the new competition

The promotion in Eastern Europe and the Former Soviet Union of science parks and the related notion of technopolis has been endorsed in a recent United Nations report on entrepreneurship (United Nations, 1992) as a possible element in promoting what Baumol (1990) has termed 'productive' entrepreneurship. Productive entrepreneurship contrasts with two other types of entrepreneurial behavior, unproductive and destructive, and unlike these other types it is desirable within a society because it is linked to the process of both individual and social wealth generation which it is believed leads to economic development. Baumol draws on Schumpeter's (1987, 132) characterization of the function of entrepreneurship, which was to 'revolutionize the pattern of production by exploiting an invention or more generally, an untried technological possibility for producing an old one in a new way'.

In a less often remarked upon but potentially equally significant comment, Schumpeter noted in the paragraph following his well known characterization of entrepreneurship that as society becomes increasingly technologically sophisticated much innovation becomes routinized, with teams of training specialists increasingly influencing further technological progress. The consequences of this is that possibilities for profitable individual action are frequently replaced by bureau and committee work. We would argue that this requires entrepreneurial action through teamwork in firms and by governmental bodies (see Best, 1990; Eisinger, 1988), and that in comprehending the role of science parks in furthering technological progress we must examine such features. This requirement is reinforced in the Russian case where the state still plays such a significant role in almost all realms of society.

We consider two facets of such collectivist entrepreneurial action. These are firstly the elements of what Best (1990) has termed 'the new competition'. This approach considers four main features of a collectivist entrepreneurial approach: firms, the production chain, the sector and government. It provides a useful framework for empirical analysis of Russian science park activity. The second facet is what Eisinger (1988) terms 'the rise of the entrepreneurial state'. This examines the final element of Best's new competition, the role of government in greater detail. The entrepreneurial state is seen by Eisinger as being active in creating markets through promotion of high technology venture finance provision and international promotion of regional economic activity. It also stresses the important role played by smaller firms.

Central to Best's approach is the role of small firms. Russian small business has a chequered history. Traditionally small business was regarded as a subsidiary sector within Soviet society. Little capital investment meant that small enterprises were equipped with obsolete plant and equipment, whilst employees tended to come from the less skilled members of society (Antosenkov, 1991). With the advent of legislation to support small business already passed and still being drafted (see IMF et al. 1991; Economic Commission for Europe, 1992; State Committee on Antimonopoly Policy of the RSFSR, 1991), there seems to be an increasing recognition of the important role which small business can play in the development of economies. Certainly it is true that this legislation has meant a rapid rate of formation of new businesses (see Tsiganov,

1992; Zavrakhanov, 1992). The regulatory environment towards small business is, however, still extremely hostile (Gibb and Gibb, 1992) and the relationship between state and small business is in many ways still an uneasy one. One area where this is perhaps less so is in the area of small NTBFs, where the active relationship between the state as sponsor of science parks and the firms, many of which were spawned by state institutions, perhaps makes a reconciliation between state interests and private property easier to achieve.

Promotion of entrepreneurship in Russia should not be understood as a simple process of drafting legislation. As Ardishvili and Cardozo (1993) point out, Russian society is still basically mercantilist with an emphasis upon redistribution rather than creation of wealth. Different groups in society are treated favorably in a situation where independent entrepreneurial activity may be discouraged. Nevertheless, Russian entrepreneurs still exhibit a strong sense of dissatisfaction with Government officials who are perceived to fail to meet entrepreneurs' requirements (Sterlin and Kozlov, 1993).

The appreciation of the role of technological innovation in revitalizing economically deprived localities has increasingly led policy makers to a concern with the creation of NTBFs as one potentially productive form of entrepreneurship. This has been evident not least in the promotion of start-up NTBFs in a variety of property led 'incubator' environment clusters. Typical of these are science parks where 'the local university would act as a growth pole, being a locus of high technology information to established industrial firms and, at the same time, being a source of new technology based firms' (van Dierdonck et al. 1991, 111). The role of science parks in promoting technological innovation via NTBFs has not been without trenchant criticism. Oakey (1985, 64), for example, warned that:

> 'without the generation of production to create the critical mass of technical production skills, the new science parks are unlikely to reach … self-sustained growth of the development. A degree of 'ivory towerism' is inherent in … the setting up of science parks'.

He argues further that much science park promotion is an attempt by universities to adapt to political circumstances. Whilst his arguments were developed in the UK experience, this latter argument, as we shall see, also appears to carry some weight in the Russian context.

This is not to say that science parks are without utility, simply that the empirical evidence does not support the contention that the science park performs a growth pole function. The utility of science parks appears to derive from the location of firms on the park, the agglomeration of high technology businesses serving to confer local reputational benefits. Thus, it may argued that science parks should be viewed as agents of local economic development. This view sits neatly alongside the assertion of the United Kingdom Science Park Association (UKSPA) that 'no two science parks are alike … [and] … It is not possible to judge the success or otherwise of a single science park without taking account of its age, location and characteristics' (Grayson, 1993, 119).

In order to understand the relevance of these arguments to the Russian case it is necessary to look more carefully at why age, location and characteristics of science parks matter so much. This analysis is presented in the next section. Before this we consider related empirical evidence on the objectives stated by those groups which have set up science parks in Russia.

The eight parks on which we have detailed information are at different stages of development. All of them are integrated into a higher education institute with strong research traditions. The main differences arise in virtue of experience of operation of a science park, integration with local industry, the importance of the property component and the nature of the management team. Of those parks reviewed Ufa and Tomsk must be considered the most developed.

The Ufa Technopark was established in 1991 by twenty founders which included amongst others two banks, local government bodies, various large enterprises and a higher education institute. The objectives of the park were to assist in the R&D process in order to progress towards commercialization of various technologies; to assist in the conversion process from military to civil production; and to improve innovation within larger enterprises. Perhaps the most mature park is to be found at Tomsk. Much of the development of Tomsk has been initiated by the entrepreneurial Director of the park who raised funds through commercial ventures in raw materials, consumer goods and timber processing worth more than two million US dollars. He has personal investments in more than fifty per cent of the companies involved in the science park and has even set up an exclusive nightclub in Tomsk as part of his personal vision of the overall science park service package. The park presently offers help and support to firms with exhibitions, markets, support services and investments. It works closely with the local regional administration.

Two experienced parks are Zelenograd and Moscow State University. What sets these aside from Ufa and Tomsk is that local industry seems to have relatively less involvement with the parks. The objectives of these two parks are slightly different to those found at Ufa. For example, in the case of Zelenograd there is no apparent strategy for conversion related work, helping defense industries in developing technology or businesses. The weakness of links with local industry seem to have meant that firms that are generated as a result of the science park have a far greater orientation towards foreign markets than was found at Ufa. Given the previous high dependence of Zelenograd industry on the defense industry, it seems initially somewhat strange, in the absence of more detailed research into the matter, that linkages with the conversion process are so weak. Moscow State University Science Park was formed approximately four years ago. A similarity with Zelenograd is the lack of direct evidence of relationships with local industry. The objectives stated by the park are to support the creation and growth of NTBFs, particularly as spin-offs; to create employment for technically qualified graduates; to lend assistance to regional redevelopment through stimulating a shift in the structure of local industry; to support exports of innovative businesses; to assist in technology transfer and to generate an entrepreneurial spirit amongst those involved with the Moscow State University.

Three younger science parks are those at Saratov, St Petersburg (LETI) and MEPHI (Moscow). At present they lack a resource base and experience, although in the opinion of one science park expert, David Rowe, who is the Director of the University of Warwick Science Park, they appear to have the potential to emulate the two best developed science parks, Ufa and Tomsk. Saratov Technopark was founded by seventeen organizations which were mainly engaged in defense work. Technopark LETI in St Petersburg was formed as a result of a project called Ekko park which was oriented towards ecological technologies. This was revised due to a lack of available projects for commercialization and the current strategy is to grow organically using the skills base provided by the University. Because the park is still at an early stage of development it has not yet been incorporated as a legal entity. The basic goals of the park are to promote the scientific potential of the higher education institute; to attract highly qualified personnel; to provide equipment for use in developing innovative products and processes; to attract investment; to control the innovation process; to create a structure which influences the innovation process from fundamental research to commercialization; and to train and retrain scientific and technical personnel. The MEPHI science park is based around a ten member association and at present is still in formation. It is a belief of the park, in contrast to some of the others, that it needs to clearly differentiate itself from the Moscow Engineering Physics Institute (MEPHI) which is the most prominent partner. The key objective of the institute is to provide employment for graduates and to generate research income. In common with all of the other parks, there was a goal of commercializing technologies arising from the research of staff from the institute.

The final science park considered is one which is driven by property investment considerations. The Baltic International Technopark has been described by the rector of the Baltic State University as 'an area for cooperation between European companies and the defence industries of Leningrad'. The objectives of the technopark are to make local technology-based products competitive within world markets through encouraging foreign know-how and new technologies; to assist enterprises in privatizing; to provide international sources of information through technology-based databases; and to engender a local spirit of enterprise through transferral of Western management practices.

It should be stressed that the physical infrastructure of the parks is in most instances rather underdeveloped. Certainly, on many of the parks there will in time be reason to believe that they may be partially driven by property investment considerations. Founding organizations have in many cases pledged land or buildings, the value of which frequently comprised much of the stated founding capital of the parks. This land or the buildings may often be inappropriate to the needs of a well planned science park either in virtue of poor location, shoddy state of repair or mismatched facilities. Many of the parks have grandiose plans to develop substantial property complexes ranging from start-up incubator units to hotel accommodation. At present, however, much of these proposed developments should probably be regarded as no more than speculation. In their current stage of development the science parks, on the whole, should not be seen as property based, but rather as service organizations providing a range of business support facilities to new technology based firms.

As we can see, although there are many similarities in the objectives states by the science parks, there are also several differences. It would appear that some of these may be related to the age of the park. Others, however, appear to relate more to the location of the park and the relation with the local industrial base. The exact nature of these differences is, however, a matter for further research and is outside the scope of this paper. To understand, in more general terms the importance of the local industrial base to the innovation process means examining the relationship between science parks and innovation.

3. Science parks and innovation

Science parks are a form of collaboration between institutes of higher education and industry. They are a potential mechanism for technology transfer and technological progress leading to local economic developments. Piore and Sabel (1984, 287) describe the potential relationship between a university and its local community in terms of innovation in rather romantic terms:

> 'Thus, the university campus is like the corner cafe where Italian artisans solve one another's problems and share - or steal - one another's ideas; a place where Proudhon might have taken Marx to show him where cooperation and competition meet'.

Whether this either is, or ever can be, an appropriate description of the industry-higher education relationship in Russia remains to be seen. Certainly, it would appear that the objectives of those setting up science parks do appear to be to encourage cooperation between industry and education in order to promote NTBFs. The key question, however, is whether science parks are the appropriate means of achieving the objectives stated.

Under central planning innovation tends to come from above, with little incentive being provided for independent entrepreneurial activity, which may even be resisted because of its destabilizing effects on the status quo. Where enterprises are restricted in their ability to make independent decisions the incentive to innovate may be severely weakened, and the likelihood of a process of creative destruction driving economic development is severely diminished, if not impossible. Features likely to lead to a lack of desire to raise product quality or introduce new products include fixed prices and employment levels regardless of technological change; responding to planning targets rather than customer demands; lack of competitive pressures and of horizontal links which may encourage learning-by-doing (Sayer and Walker, 1992). Obviously much of the legislation introduced as a result of the reform process initiated by Perestroika has changed the rules of the game by which enterprises must operate (see IMF et al., 1991), yet it is an empirical matter whether the features mentioned above, which are almost polar opposites of the requirements for the new competition, are still having an effect on NTBFs in Russia. The role of the political process under central planning, which Sayer and Walker note centralizes *a priori* the allocation process, may have given those who stood to be negatively affected by innovation the power to resist change. The extent to which political pressures still hold sway will thus affect the possibilities for legislative change leading to real technological change through innovative activity which may be commercialized to form the basis of an emergent new competition in Russia. The barriers faced by small firms which were mentioned previously, many of which are erected by government officials, do not on the surface lend optimism. Nevertheless, in assessing the prospects for economic development through technological promotion two features should be considered.

The first of these is Schumpeter's (1987) argument that the social position of the entrepreneur is related to the importance of the entrepreneurial function in the social process. Schumpeter argues that in capitalism the bourgeoisie depends economically and sociologically upon the entrepreneur and that in cases of success the bourgeoisie class absorbs entrepreneurs together with their families and connections as a source of revitalization. This would also appear to be a useful argument in economies in transition, such as Russia, with the exception only that we replace bourgeoisie with 'nomenklatura'. With the change in allocation mechanisms demanded by new legislation it makes sense for those who were actively involved in the political process prior to reform, holding economic power as a result of the political process, to seek to retain some elements of power by aligning themselves with the newly legitimatized entrepreneurial class. We might conjecture, on this basis, that technological innovation will not be resisted where it is linked to older power structures such as government bodies and government sponsored research institutes. If this hypothesis were shown to be true it would provide a rationale for willingness to support the concept of science parks in general terms, though it would also help to explain the need for different policy emphasis in different locations according to the varied nature of the local nomenklatura structures.

The second point is that when examining economic development it is important to consider the dynamism of production and that this will exhibit considerable sectoral variation. As Rostow (1990, 15) notes:

> 'Leading sectors are determined not merely by the changing flow of technology and the changing willingness of entrepreneurs to accept available innovations: they are also partially determined by those types of demand which have exhibited high elasticity with respect to price, income or both'.

The importance of demand in understanding the possibilities for Russian science parks is fundamental. To concentrate solely on the supply side conditions of prevailing practice would be to commit a grave error. The stage of growth of any sector is a complex interplay of 'the dynamics of market demand, risk-taking, technology and entrepreneurship' with a whole range of non-market considerations which are 'deep in history, culture and the active political process' (ibid. 15).

For Russian enterprises the possible types of markets and distribution channels available within the domestic market are quite different than those found within more widespread global markets. The effective strategies for exploiting new technologies will therefore tend to vary according to the nature of the market being targeted. Since many parks have stated objectives of developing technologies for world markets, the nature of, and changes in, global demand in various sectors is likely in the longer term to be a key determinant of the pattern of development of Russian science parks.

One particularly pertinent reason for a focus on demand side issues is the underdeveloped law and enforcement concerning the protection of property rights to be found currently in Russia. This enables new technologies to be easily copied and distributed in the domestic market. Use of domestic distribution channels such as the *Birzhy* auction markets may contribute to the problem facing an innovator seeking to exploit initial high price and income elasticity of demand by treating technological innovations as simple commodities, distinguishable by price rather than quality. Working to establish international reputations for quality may be one feasible shorter term strategy for individual firms seeking to maintain high price elasticity for their products in the face of price competitive and largely unregulated domestic markets. The ability of firms to effectively pursue such a strategy, however, will depend on the ability of firms to market themselves to the needs of international customers. As we shall argue presently though, many firms may have an incentive to market themselves vigorously towards domestic influences, thus providing a countervailing tendency.

Whilst the relationship between technology diffusion and economic development must be analyzed in terms of both supply side and demand side forces, the question of *how* science parks can assist in equilibrating the changing flow of technology with a changing composition of demand still needs to be resolved. In the context of development of science parks in the UK, Massey et al. (1992) argue that the reality of science and technology on these parks fails to connect with a rhetorical promotion of the concept, justified in terms of the so-called linear model of innovation. Relatively few scientists actually become entrepreneurs, and the role claimed for small firms is exaggerated. The linear model of innovation tends to ignore the interplay between the forces of supply and demand and views innovation as largely a supply side phenomenon where the nature and composition of demand is assumed fixed.

Much evidence casts doubt on the notion of a simple linear process connecting research, production and commercialization, so Massey et al. claim. Since this appears to be a fundamental starting point in any underlying rationale for the existence of science parks, it is important to understand both the structure and implications of this model and its implications. The likely consequences of this model in terms of industrial development can be appreciated through highlighting the particular forms of division of labor which the linear model of innovation presupposes (for detailed discussion see Massey et al., 1992).

Three types of division of labor would appear relevant to the present discussion. These are the technical division of labor which splits tasks vertically by nature of specialization within an organization; social division of labor which allocates economic activity between organizations; and the spatial division of labor which divides labor by geographical location. The influence of each of these potential divisions of labor will depend upon the maturity of the park and the associated level of demand for its activities, together with the location of the park and the regional specialization in particular types of technologies which was a characteristic feature of the development of Soviet industry. Hence, stressing the importance of the division of labor highlights why we should choose to focus upon the age, location and characteristics of the parks. It also serves to highlight the importance of demand side factors.

Viewing innovation as a linear process involves conceiving a set of interrelated activities as a series of stages. Starting with basic research, through applied and development stages, the process leads in a seemingly inexorably fashion to new product and process possibilities. These typically require a further prototype stage before commercial realization, production and diffusion. The metaphor of a chain captures the essence of this stage approach nicely. The strength of a chain comes both from the individual elements and the linkages between each part. This is equally true with the linear model of innovation, where both the role of organizational forms, such as research teams promulgating new ideas, through to small enterprises profiting from commercial opportunity, together with linkages between these different organizational units contribute to the overall process of innovation. It is the combination of both specialized organizational forms, performing well-defined roles within a larger process, and the co-ordination of linkages between different organizations, which are presumed to be the key features leading to the overall strength of this process.

In the absence of detailed consideration of demand side factors the extent to which the innovation process is split into discrete stages, divided across different industrial enterprises and in different locations will be determined by supply side factors, assuming the existing pattern of industrial demand to be fixed. Were this to be an accurate assumption then the linear model of innovation would seem to be a reasonable approximation to the role of science parks. As we have already noted, however, in analyzing Russian science parks the changing composition of demand, together with the differences between domestic and international markets for science park production, do mean that it is unrealistic to treat demand parametrically.

Discounting for a moment complications borne out of consideration of demand side factors, there is still merit in addressing the linear model of innovation, since the presumed role of science parks in the linear process of innovation fits nicely with the second of two policy questions which emerge from the model. Whilst the first of these addresses the question of appropriate mechanisms for generating new ideas through government support for basic research, the second considers the speed of the transmission mechanism connecting basic research with development and commercialization. Massey et al. (1992) consider the science park model to be one clear solution to this latter problem though not, perhaps, a unique one. In the context of developing science parks in the former Soviet Union we shall see presently that the first of these policy questions also assumes considerable significance.

The empirical appropriateness of addressing this linear model of innovation in order to understand the development of science parks in the former Soviet Union is well highlighted in Figure 6.1. This is taken from publicity material produced by Moscow State University Technopark. It clearly shows the basic structure of the linear model of innovation. This model is used as the basis for a justification of the activities pursued by the management of this science park. Whilst other parks do not set out this model quite so explicitly, descriptions of the nature of activities pursued together with the manner of support offered lead to the conclusion that this model is widely used as a starting point for the development of science parks in the former Soviet Union.

Figure 6.1 MSU science park model of the innovation process

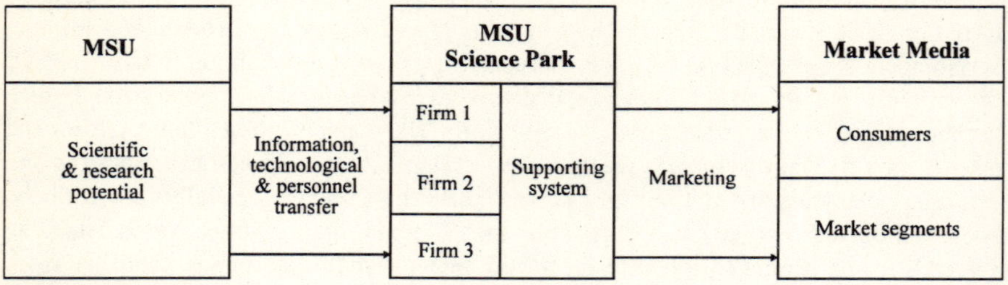

4. Russian science parks - how do they compare?

4.1 The role of science parks in Russia

The development of science parks in Russia must be viewed in the context of the military conversion process, and understood in relation to the historical development and destruction of alternative attempts at promoting technological innovation such as the science production associations (see Cooper, 1991a, b). These associations were an attempt to vertically integrate production activities in the sphere of technology by linking enterprises right through from fundamental research through to serial production.

A typical process might start with a higher education research institute being asked by a ministry to develop a solution to a particular technological problem. This would lead to the development of a prototype and this would be produced by a separate plant using jobbing facilities. Testing would occur, followed by product revision before an acceptable model was produced. Much of the activity to this point, when connected with defense work, typically took place in closed scientific cities with a strong specialism in particular technologies. Once an acceptable technology was developed this was usually passed onto serial production plants which were often located elsewhere for mass production. In some ways this pattern of production has appealing features. First, it allows for external economies of scale through regional agglomeration of similar types of technologies. Second, it considers the need to integrate various stages of the production process. The quasi integration of activities within the association rather than just between separate enterprises should in principle have helped to overcome production bottle-necks. Finally, the model should have permitted rational resource planning and monitoring of investment in technological projects at various stages.

The science production associations were broken up in the late 1980s and many enterprises which were formerly part of such an association were left to fend for themselves in the market place. Clearly it was perceived that the supposed benefits of the science production associations had not been realised.

Science park developments may be a possible means of overcoming the partial vacuum in policy to assist technological development and innovation, which arose as a result of the dissolution of the science production associations. Science parks in Russia are an attempt at creating new institutional forms which preserve some elements of the previous industrial system, together with the expertise of the scientific elite, whilst trying to realise comparative advantage from research and development activity within an economic and social infrastructure in which the rules of the game have been radically altered. However, by trying to retain some of the more successful elements of the old system there is implicit recognition that simply changing legislation does not necessarily alter institutional behavior and norms of behavior (see Yamin and Batstone, forthcoming). The changing legislation opens up new opportunities for new ways of organizing economic activity but it does not necessarily guarantee that the behavior of economic agents faced by new institutions and organizations will respond in entirely predictable ways.

The rest of this paper tries to assess how science parks have contributed to reorganization of technology-based economic activity in Russia. We must question whether the new organizations and institutions observed in developing science parks in Russia have led to patterns of behavior similar to those found on Western science parks, such as those in the UK which are often similar in aim and basic legislative and organizational form to Russian science parks, or whether a totally new model of economic development is being created. Best's (1990) framework of the new competition can help to give us some insight into this. Best argues that a new competition is evolving in international markets based on a need to economize on time. Whereas mass production is concerned with economies of time in throughput the new competition must also consider economies of time in implementing new technologies. This is obviously a very relevant concern for science parks, if they are going to aid NTBFs in forming part of the new competition in Russia, such that Russian technologies can compete in world markets, since as we have seen in the previous section, one of the rationale for science parks was to provide a speedy transmission mechanism for technology diffusion.

There are four main elements to Best's approach. The first of these is the entrepreneurial firm. This is seen as a firm which stresses teamwork and strategy in order to establish competitive advantage. Continual innovation in product, process or organization is seen as the source of strategic advantage. Such innovation will tend to be incremental and not restricted to specialist engineers. Instead it will be viewed as a social process of problem solving. In order to achieve such innovation a major requirement is for organizational flexibility, with the entrepreneurial firm pursuing a strategy of continuous learning and improvement.

The second element of the new competition comprises the production chain. Here the requirement is for each phase of production to be co-ordinated. A number of forms of co-ordination may be possible, but Best notes that the particular arrangements that sustain co-ordination of economic activity between firms will depend upon social arrangements. One such arrangement is the scientific industrial district (Piore and Sabel, 1984), similar in concept to science parks. The co-ordination may come from a shared set of values of firms all engaged in similar types of technological applications.

Piore and Sabel see problems, however, with this mode of market organization. There are two specific problems which may arise out of the scientific industrial district which may damage the basis upon which firms cooperate with one another as well as compete. The first of these is that when firms relocate due to expansion, community ties binding firms together are broken. Second, when firms expand to new locations whilst keeping their home bases, the existence of subsidiaries means that management attachment to the original location is weakened. This may lead to a lack of commitment to the workforce. Further problems may arise out of the conditions causing the possibilities for expansion.

Much expansion of scientific industrial districts has occurred because of military sponsorship. In Russia this is now seriously declining and whereas in a growing market there is less need for firms to cooperate, Piore and Sabel argue that the failure of firms to cooperate in the past can seriously weaken the ability of firms to cooperate in the future. To the extent that the science production associations were built on growing military demands, albeit with unsatisfactory levels of integration and communication between enterprises, therefore, there is reason to believe that the decline in these markets will mean that cooperation between firms may become more problematic. It may be hypothesized that this effect is likely to be greatest in localities and sectors where there were previously science production associations One surprising corollary of this line of thought is that those science parks which have relatively little attachment to the local industrial base may actually be better placed to develop aspects of the new competition than those which are linked to the conversion process and based around older, larger enterprises. Additionally, the use of serial production plants by the science production associations may have already done much to weaken regional allegiance by local management to the local workforce. The objective of some of those science parks seeking to provide technical employment locally may be an important counter to this.

The third element which needs consideration within Best's theory is the nature of the sector. Best argues that sectoral strategies can evolve from the actions of private firms within a sector developing a capacity to jointly overcome new challenges and grasp new opportunities. An important element in encouraging this may be the restriction of price competition in order that the sector can compete on the basis of product quality or innovation. Finally, this sectoral cooperation may typically be joined to a strategic industrial policy on the part of government. Eisinger (1988) argues that it requires a reorientation of the goals of public policy so that government concentrates on creating new markets through demand side measures such as promoting science parks and innovation, assisting fast growth small firms with the capacity for job generation and providing venture capital where private investors would otherwise perceive risks as being too great.

One interesting question which such an approach raises concerns the nature of the relationship between the state and science parks. If government actively attempts to generate new technologies through promoting organizations such as science parks an apparent paradox arises. On the one hand it may be in the interests of many state officials to maintain the status quo, whilst on the other hand active promotion of innovation via the science park concept may speed up a process of change, which weakens positions of power derived largely from the monopolistic structures of Soviet times. One possible effect which our earlier discussion suggests is that state promotion of science parks may create an incentive on the part of entrepreneurs within Russian society to align themselves with the science park movement in order to gain access to state credits and industrial support which may offer a degree of protection from the ravages of the marketplace. This would dictate that economic effort is likely to be directed towards effective marketing to receive state subsidy and retain a soft budget constraint (Kornai, 1986) which may enable norms of behavior to be largely maintained within a new organizational form. So long as the soft budget constraint is retained, either by the science park as a whole or the individual firms attached to it, there may be little incentive to properly market new technologies either to the domestic market or internationally. If this is an accurate representation of current practice on the part of science park entrepreneurs, management teams and state officials, then it would offer a way out of the above paradox. It would suggest that the process of change within Russian society, brought about through channelling innovation diffusion through science parks, should largely preserve existing structures of social relationships and help to protect the position of privilege of state officials to whom entrepreneurs and science park management must still retain allegiance for effective preservation of the soft budget constraint.

4.2 A first assessment

Although we are interested in the extent to which the elements of the new competition can be found on Russian science parks, we cannot at this stage give a completely satisfactory overview in this pilot study. Nevertheless, we do attempt to provide some insight by looking at elements of Russian science park practice. We use the four modes of the new competition as an organizing frame for this purpose. As mentioned earlier, a number of sources of information on the eight Russian science parks analyzed here are used. These include: (i) interviews by the Director of Warwick Science Park with science park managers (30 science park managers and six representatives from founding organizations), sixteen entrepreneurs, and four local authority officials, as well as briefing reports compiled on each of the science parks (ii) publicity material produced by the science parks, (iii) materials collected by a Warwick MBA student studying Moscow State University science park, and (iv) information collected by one of the authors from science park teams as part of a management training program for Russian science parks.

4.2.1 Firms as collective entrepreneurs?

The first empirical issue in assessing the development of aspects of the new competition is the nature of firms to be found on Russian science parks. To provide a context for comparison with practices found elsewhere, some stylized features of firms to be found on Western science parks are also presented.

Drawing upon the North American literature on young high technology companies it has been asserted by Bullock (1983) that the typical firm will record substantial change with age. A process of 'hardening' is suggested, whereby companies initially sell highly analytical technical solutions for specific problems before moving on to standardized and simplified products for a more general market. The evidence on this transition from 'soft' to 'hard' activities is inconclusive. In the UK it appears that 'there is little evidence of any shift from "soft" to "hard" activities' (Monck et al., 1988, 139). Due to the early stage of development of science parks in Russia it is not possible to test this hardening hypothesis. Of more importance in the present context are the consequences of entrepreneurs starting up in 'soft' activities. Thus we are interested, firstly, in whether the typical market is indeed for 'soft' specific problem oriented solutions as described above, and secondly, what the consequences of the firms' strategies are.

There are two main advantages during the early development of a firm proposed by Bullock, for the formation of 'soft' companies by academic entrepreneurs, these are firstly the low risk arising from minimal capital investment, and second the opportunity to assess the existence of a market. The evidence from a sample of firms on Russian science parks makes it hard to judge at this stage whether there is development from soft to hard activities. This is an issue that we should be able to judge more fully through tracking the development of Russian science parks as they mature. Nevertheless, the evidence does suggests that the majority of firms formed by academics at present are in soft activities and that low initial capital entry requirements coupled with relatively high rates of return have made such activity more attractive than harder manufacturing activity.

In terms of entering a market it should be noted that the firms on Russian science parks are in many respects quite different from their UK counterparts. On most parks many of the firms were spawned from the activities of the local higher education institutes. In many cases there was not an obvious market opportunity which led to the formation of a firm, but rather the opportunity to apply for more funding for research from state sources. This is probably not surprising in many ways since it is consistent with individuals who have become used to reliance upon state maintained soft budget constraints (see Kornai, 1986).

Many of the companies found on Russian science parks were trading profitably, usually in domestic markets. There were relatively few examples of successful foreign currency earnings. A typical way in which firms acquired capital for start up was to engage in arbitrage in general commodities prior to starting an NTBF in order to generate capital reserves. Several months of trading in this way could provide required capital in many cases without resort to banks which tended to be seen as charging exorbitant rates of interest.

Obtaining property is one of the most serious obstacles facing Russian entrepreneurs with bribery and connections frequently required (Gibb and Gibb, 1992). This is obviously an important consideration in analyzing the role of science parks, which are generally property based initiatives. Several of the parks held competitions based on the submission of a business plan to decide which firms should have access to science park facilities and property. In many cases property was offered at subsidized rates, or even free.

Many of the firms on which we have information did not undertake any production and so it is difficult to know whether there was much innovation based upon learning. Where firms are engaging in production, most of the manufacturing process is subcontracted. The supply-led development of technology often seems to lead us to infer that much of the technology does not appear to have been designed with particular customer groups in mind and it is difficult to see how much of it will ever reach commercialization.

4.2.2 The production chain

One of the interesting features about Russian science parks is their belief in many instances that they will play a role throughout the innovation process. As we have seen, this process will likely as not fail to follow the neat linear pattern upon which many of their activities are premised. The relationships between science parks, the NTBFs to be found on them and the local community is not always clear. Certainly there is much variation by park. One issue which needs addressing in future work is how the science park can assure quality. As we have noted much of the technological innovation which has derived from science parks serves the domestic market. On the supply side there is much effort by many of the parks to provide management training activity and assistance with overcoming bureaucratic obstacles. The nature of Russian distribution channels, however, may serve to thwart many of these efforts. Much activity at present is being channelled through auction houses known as Birzhy. These trade in general in unbranded commodities. For example, in Zelenograd an auction house deals in electronic components. Because there is no possibility of controlling quality from the end destination much of the traded produce is not of top quality. More to the point, the production strategy is one of produce first, find a buyer later. This strategy also seems to extend to the technology process, where an attitude amongst many NTBFs appear to be innovate first, think of the purpose of the innovation later. Such a strategy sits rather uneasily alongside the requirements of the new competition.

4.2.3 Sectoral competition and cooperation

The third element to consider is the extent of sectoral competition and cooperation. Here it should first be noted that at the design stage there is often relatively little competition faced by Russian NTBFs. In many cases, though, it is the production stage which generates value added. Unfortunately, due to various problems with property rights many designs are quickly copied and manufacture often takes place with more than one subcontractor. This might be thought of as some kind of downstream joint sourcing by design teams, but unfortunately in many instances it leads to an inability to control quality. This occurs frequently because many subcontract deals are negotiated on a one-off basis. This provides no incentive to engage in long term cooperative practices.

One point which should be mentioned where the science park may play a very positive role is that most of the science parks appear to have spezialised in particular types of technology. This may give hope that the sorts of shared values leading to cooperation described by Piore and Sabel may yet evolve. Also the science park may play a valuable role in co-ordinating different stages in the production process. Given the poor experience, however, of the science production associations and the relatively underdeveloped stage at which most Russian science parks currently find themselves it is difficult to see at this stage exactly how this will occur. Certainly current practice does not seem to fit neatly with Best's theory. We should be wary before rejecting it out of hand as irrelevant though, since there does not as yet appear to be sufficient evidence to properly judge the prospects for both competition and cooperation springing out of science park activities.

4.2.4 Strategic industrial policy

In terms of strategic industrial policy this is probably the area where present Russian science park activity fits most neatly with Best's theory. Both central government assistance through the Ministry of Higher Education, Science and Technology policy and local government assistance at a number of levels, have frequently been pro-active in seeking to develop new markets based around innovations arising out of NTBFs. The coordinating role of BISPA serves to give worldwide exposure to the Russian science park movement whilst local initiatives on many of the parks have helped to secure some foreign capital. Mainly, though, this has come from foreign Government assistance programs such as the UK Know How Fund, which has for example funded development work on Zelenograd science park, rather than from foreign direct investment. A crucial question which must be examined as these parks develop, however, is how the role of Government is expected to change as the firms on the parks develop and become more successful, thus generating increasing competition in Russian society which may tend to break up existing institutions. The relationship between state and science parks and NTBFs may well be an interesting feature to monitor as these parks develop.

5. Conclusions

We have seen that promotion of NTBFs on Russian science parks fits in with a general strategy of promotion of small business by government in Russia. Much of the technological innovation which is currently emerging from NTBFs has only limited commercial application, and is often derived from academic spin-offs where the goal is just as likely to be to gain access to research grants as to genuinely enter markets. In any case, at present much of the activity on Russian science parks is only being sold on the Russian market. There appears to be relatively little meaningful internationalization. Whether this is an inevitable consequence of the early stage of development of science parks, which means that as yet many are ill-equipped to assist NTBFs in attracting foreign capital and selling overseas, or whether it represents more fundamental weaknesses due to structural difficulties which make it problematic for Russian industry to adapt to changing market conditions is something we cannot gauge yet.

We have asked several questions in the course of this paper. The answers to these may now be briefly summarized and drawn together to enable us to conclude with an evaluation of the current state of development of Russian science parks, based upon the evidence currently available. We asked first of all whether promotion of new technology based firms would assist in the process of demonopolization of Russian society through promoting competition. The answer to this question is that it is difficult to know whether this is happening because the nature of competition is so different within the present Russian economy from what is presumed to exist theoretically within existing market structures. Examining the strategies of competing new technology based firms mainly illustrates that there is more utility to be gained in terms of understanding how markets actually develop through standing back to observe the unfolding process of competition than by imposing pre-existing theoretical frameworks which presume a rational evolution of market structure between monopoly and competition. Quite simply, what we learn is that it is inappropriate at the present stage to ask whether in order to learn more about how markets function, it is not yet clear whether science parks are being used to assimilate entrepreneurs into a nomenklatura class.

In discussing various issues related to the theory of entrepreneurship, and the practice of science parks in Western economies, we have raised several questions. We addressed the nature of competition now emerging in Russia and concluded that it is dissimilar in many respects to that found elsewhere. We considered the question of what science parks mean in a Russian context. In particular, we focussed on what roles they play; how they differ from Western parks and amongst themselves; and the typical services offered. Age, location and characteristics of the parks were found to be crucial in explaining differences. We also asked whether science parks were the appropriate organizational form for meeting the objectives that parks set themselves. This proves to be a particularly difficult question to answer since it presumes a particular path down which the Russian economy might evolve. Our comments concerning the nature of competition lead us to believe that we cannot predict the nature of the turbulent Russian economy accurately enough to answer this question. Nevertheless, we should note that at a micro-micro level some parks do appear to be achieving partial success in meeting the objectives set for themselves.

In addition to various questions raised, the paper also formulated certain hypotheses. Given the nature of this paper, as an early stage report on the science park movement in Russia, it is inappropriate to give categorical responses to such hypotheses. It is perhaps more worthwhile giving a progress report based on evidence collected to date.

The first hypothesis conjectured that innovation would be accepted best where linked to old state structures. This in turn would provide a rationale for different approaches being found in markedly different geographical locations characterized by the socio-economic infrastructure found in the regions. The evidence to date certainly suggests differing levels of state support for the various parks in different regions as well as parks seeming to direct their attentions to alternative market distribution channels in different locations. This suggests some evidence for the latter part of our hypothesis. On the direct relationship between innovation as practised through science parks and state structures there appears to be no clear evidence. These are sensitive issues, and given the absence of more detailed evidence, it would be inappropriate to surmise which parks are apparently more tied to old structures and old ways of thinking than others. This certainly seems an issue worthy of greater exploration. A second hypothesis suggested that parks not attached or related to localities dominated by the old science production associations may have the best chances of success. Unfortunately, we have not yet been able to collect sufficient data to properly address this. Examination of the issues, however, strongly suggests that it merits further attention.

What this paper has attempted to show is that Russian science parks are different than many found in the West. Some of these differences are undoubtedly attributable to the early development of the science park concept, but other differences are likely to be the result of cultural, historical and political influences on Russian society. It is not sufficient to note simply that Russian science parks are different, however, for as we have seen, there are marked differences between the science parks in Russia. Many of these differences appear to be attributable to age, characteristics and objectives of the science parks and their development. The extent to which these differences (both between Western and Russian science parks and comparatively between Russian science parks) can be successfully disentangled, however, is something which lies beyond the scope of this paper. To attempt a full evaluation of the role, function and performance at this early stage of development is not a realistic objective. The task carried out in this paper was to set out the appropriate parameters for evaluation. This is a more manageable objective which may in time yield insight into which strategies adopted by Russian science parks lead to successful patterns of economic development.

This pilot study shows us that there are many issues which a longitudinal tracking study of the Russian science park movement can address. The framework provided by Best appears to be a useful conceptual starting point for understanding how science parks may be expected to assist in Russian economic development, as well as in assessing specific successes and failures. Over time we hope to be able to compare the development of the Russian science park movement with that found in the UK. We shall draw on a major longitudinal study of science park firms and matched off-science park firms conducted in 1986 and 1992 for the UK component. This has attempted to evaluate the contribution of science parks in the UK (Monck et al., 1988; Westhead and Storey, 1993). These studies provide a basis for some comparative analysis on science parks in Russia compared with the UK. Due to different methods of data collection, inevitable given problems of analyzing Russian institutions, comparison will only be possible at an aggregate level. Nevertheless, such analysis should serve to highlight key features in the development of Russian science parks.

Acknowledgements

We are very grateful to David Rowe for permission to use materials compiled by him for the purposes of the European Bank for Reconstruction and Development sponsored project 'CIS: Training for Science Park Management and Training Teams'. The opinions stated here represent the views of the authors alone. Any errors or misinterpretation of information remains the sole responsibility of the authors.

Appendix

Selected Source Materials on Russian Science Parks:

Cieszynski, B. (1993) *Russian Science Parks Operations and the Changing Russian Economy: a case study of Moscow State University Science Park*, Unpublished MBA dissertation, University of Warwick.

Moscow State University (undated) *Moscow State University Science Park: Concept in Brief*, Publicity material.

______ (undated) *Moscow State University: Business incubator and communication centre*, Publicity material.

Rowe, D. (1993a) *CIS Training Program - Moscow,* Unpublished training program consortium briefing note.

______ (1993b) *Summary Report on the Visit to Russian Science Parks*, Unpublished briefing report.

______ (1993c) *Moscow State University Science Park*, Unpublished briefing report.

______ (1993d) *Zelenograd Technology Park*, Unpublished briefing report.

______ (1993e) *Technopark in Moskvorechje*, Unpublished briefing report.

______ (1993f) *Technopark LETI*, Unpublished briefing report.

______ (1993g) *Baltic International Technopark*, Unpublished briefing report.

______ (1993h) *Saratov Technopark*, Unpublished briefing report.

______ (1993i) *Technopark Bashkortostan - Ufa*, Unpublished briefing report.

University of Warwick Science Park Ltd. (1993) *CIS: Training for Science Park Management and Training Teams*, unpublished project proposal.

Zelenograd Science Park (1993) *Zelenograd Scientific and Technological Park*, Publicity material.

References

Antosenkov, E. (1991); Small Enterprises and Employment Problems in the USSR During the Transition to a Market Economy; *Labor and Society*, 16, 25-36.

Ardishvili, A. and R. Cardozo (1993) *Socio-Political Structure of a Society as a Determinant of Entrepreneurial Behaviour: The Case of Post-Communist Russia*, paper presented at the Third Annual Global Conference on Entrepreneurship Research, Lyon, March 8-10th.

Armit, R. (1992) *Internationalizing Technology Transfer*, Proceedings of the Technology Transfer Society Annual Meeting and Conference, Atlanta.

Baumol, William J. (1990); Entrepreneurship: Productive, Unproductive and Destructive; *Journal of Political Economy*, 98, 893-921.

Best, M. (1990) *The New Competition: Institutions of industrial restructuring*, Cambridge: Polity.

Bullock, M. (1983) *Academic Enterprise, Industrial Innovation and the Development of High Technology Financing in the United States*, London: Brand Bros. and Co.

Cooper, J. (1991a) *The Soviet Defence Industry: Conversion and Reform,* London: Pinter.

Cooper, J. (1991b); Military Cuts and Conversion in the Defense Industry; *Soviet Economy*, 7, 121-42.

Economic Commission for Europe (1992) *Economic Survey of Europe in 1991-2,* New York: United Nations.

EIM (1993) *The European Observatory for SMEs*, 1st annual report for EC DG XXIII.

Eisinger, P. (1988) *The Rise of the Entrepreneurial State*, London: University of Wisconsin Press.

Gibb, A. and Y. Gibb (1992) *A Study of the Regulatory Environment for Small Business in Russia*, 1, Durham University Business School.

Grayson, L. (1993) *Science Parks: an experiment in high technology transfer*, London: The British Library.

IMF, World Bank, OECD and EBRD (1991) *A Study of the Soviet Economy* (3 vols).

Kirzner, I. (1973) *Competition and Entrepreneurship*, Chicago: University of Chicago Press.

Kornai, J. (1986); The Soft Budget Constraint; *Kyklos*, 39, 3-30.

Massey, D., P. Quintas and D. Wield (1992) *High Tech Fantasies: Science Parks in Society, Science and Space*, London: Routledge.

Monck, C., R. Porter, P. Quintas, D. Storey and P. Wynarczyk (1988) *Science Parks and the Growth of High Technology Firms*, London: Croom Helm.

Nove, A. (1983) *The Economics of Feasible Socialism,* London: Allen and Unwin.

Oakey, R. (1985); British University Science Parks and High Technology Small Firms: A comment on the potential for sustained economic growth; *International Small Business Journal*, 4, 58-67.

OECD (1989) *Industrial Policy in OECD Countries*, annual review, Paris: OECD.

Piore, M. and C. Sabel (1984) *The Second Industrial Divide: Possibilities for prosperity*, New York: Basic Books.

Rostow, W. (1990) *The stages of Economic Growth* (3rd ed.), Cambridge: Cambridge University Press.

Sayer, A. and R. Walker (1992) *The New Social Economy: Reworking the division of labor*, Oxford: Blackwell.

Schumpeter, J. (1987 [first published 1943]) *Capitalism, Socialism and Democracy*, London: Unwin paperbacks.

State Committee on Antimonopoly Policy of the RSFSR (1991) *PROGRAM: To Support Business Activity in Russia,* Mimeograph, Moscow.

Sterlin, A. and V. Kozlov (1993) *Emerging Entrepreneurship in Russia: Entrepreneurs' perceptions of their social and economic function*, paper presented at the Third Annual Global Conference on Entrepreneurship Research, Lyon, March 8-10.

Tsiganov, A. (1992) *Small Business in Russia*, Conference on Small Business in the Global Economy, May, Montreal, Canada.

United Nations (1992) *World Economic Survey*, 1992, New York: UN.

van Dierdonck, R., K. Debackere and M. Rappa (1991); An Assessment of Science Parks: Towards a better understanding of their role in diffusion of technological knowledge; *R&D Management*, 21, 109-23.

Westhead, P. and D. Storey (1993) *An Assessment of Firms Located On and Off Science Parks in the United Kingdom*, Unpublished Mimeograph, SME Centre Warwick Business School.

Yamin, M. and S. Batstone (forthcoming) Institutional Obstacles to Marketization, in Cook, P. and F. Nixson (eds.) *The Move to the Market: Trade, Industries and Policy Reform in Transitional Economies*, London: Macmillan.

Zavrakhanov, I. (1992) *The Development of the Small Business Sector in Russia,* Paper presented at the International Conference on Small Business, Montreal, May 24-27.

7 Big problems of small businesses in Estonia*

Karel Haav

1. Introduction

The problems of all post-socialist or, more precisely, post-totalitarian states are similar. They have all been the victims of Soviet imperialism, which violently introduced its type of totalitarian regime and centrally planned economy. Due to the degree of dependency on the developments in Russia the situation in the Baltic states and in the other former Soviet republics differs from that in the Central European post-socialist nations. The difficulties of Central European states, e.g. Poland and Hungary, have been subject to research for many years and pertinent literature abounds (e.g. Blanchard et. al., 1992; Clague and Rausser, 1992; Kornai, 1992; OECD, 1992; Rosati, 1992). Only now, such literature is available on Estonia and the other Baltic states.[1] With Haav (1988, 1991a, 1991b, 1992) and Ruutsoo (Haav and Ruutsoo, 1990) having analyzed mainly the social problems of Estonia's economic, political and national development.

The present article aims at providing additional information on the most recent economic and social developments in Estonia, and at enabling an understanding of the problems of post-totalitarian states and of the consequences of the Soviet regime. The paper focuses on the following issues:

- macro-economic situation;
- reorientation of foreign trade;
- free enterprise development;
- problems of small businesses in Estonia.

2. Macro-economic situation in Estonia

During the short period of independence between the two World Wars, Estonia's economy developed rapidly. The standard of living in the Republic of Estonia was comparable to that of Finland. It is remarkable that by the end of 1930s the total value of Estonia's exports was greater than that of Finland. Now, Finland belongs to the most

* The author is thankful to Mrs. Sirje Rogova (Statistical Office of Estonia) and Mrs. Kaja Kell (Bank of Estonia) for statistical information, and to Mr. Jüri Estam (Estonian Television) for revising a first draft in English.

1 For example, Arkadie and Karlsson, 1992; Dellenbrant et al., 1992; Hansen and Rocha, 1993; Joeste and Kaevats, 1991; Kahk, 1992; Knobl, 1992; Liuhto, 1991 and 1992; Norgaard, 1992; Sepp, 1992.

developed Western welfare states while Estonia ranks lower than less developed European countries like Greece and Portugal, and can be compared to Central European countries like Poland. This is one result of the fifty years of Soviet occupation. In all countries that have moved from command economies to market economies, the economic situation has continued to deteriorate. In Estonia, the GDP declined by 12 per cent in 1991, and by 30 per cent in 1992 in comparison to the previous year. The consumer price index rose by 210 per cent in 1991 and by 1 176 per cent in 1992 (Pollisinski, 1993). Compared to the 1991 level, industrial output diminished by 40 per cent. Agricultural output has roughly dropped by one half during the past two years. Trade turnover declined more than five times during 1991 and 1992 (Rajasalu, 1992a) and average wages increased from 98.3 EEK in 1991 (in comparable currency) to 528.7 in 1992, i.e. more than five times. Yet, real income declined more than twice. The unemployment rate remained surprisingly low (one per cent in 1991 and 10 per cent in 1992 and 1993).

According to data published by the Vice-Director of the Institute of Economics of the Estonian Academy of Sciences, Estonia's economic output was cut in half from 1990 to 1992. The agency estimated Estonia's GDP to be equal to approximately 1 500-2 000 US$ in 1990, to 1 120 US$ in 1991 and to 800 US$ per capita in 1992 (see Rajasalu, 1992a and 1992b). The average figures (3 700 US$ for Estonia and 2 600 US$ for the Soviet Union) for 1991, published in the World Bank study on Estonia (Hansen and Rocha, 1993) seem to be too high.

Actually, the economic indices of Western and Eastern European countries should not be compared directly. Corrected data should be used which take into account the differences in real purchasing power in the various countries. Thus, the corrected GDP per capita for the first half of the 1980s would be (Dyker, 1992, 16-17):

- 9 000 US$ in the North and West of Europe;
- 6 000 US$ in the South of Europe;
- 5 000 in Central and Eastern Europe.

The last figure could also apply to the Estonia of the 1980s. But, in the meantime, this figure has decreased by at least one half. Consequently, the economic output in Estonia is more than four times lower than that in developed European states. The standard of living is probably five to six times lower in Estonia than in the EG. The same conclusion could be drawn on the basis of the Big Mac Index. In 1990 this index was four to five in more developed and two to three in the less developed European countries (Järve, 1993). In Estonia, average pay per hour was about five EEK and the average price for a McDonalds' hamburger was six EEK in the beginning of 1993. Thus, the Big Mac Index is less than one in Estonia.

In August 1991 Estonia restored its independece. The mass movement for political and economic sovereignty started earlier, in 1987, soon after the beginning of the crisis of the Soviet Bloc. The decentralization of large state enterprises began in 1987. Various forms of private property and enterprises were allowed in 1990. The introduction of the Estonian currency - the Estonian crown - on June 20, 1992, ended Estonia's financial dependency on Moscow. The privatization of state property and the restructuring of industry continues. The most outstanding achievement of Estonia's economy was the reorientation of foreign trade from East to West in 1992 (Table 7.3). Traditionally, almost one-half of its economic output was exported with about 94-95 per cent going to other parts of the Soviet Union.

At the beginning of 1993 the economic decline in Estonia came to a halt. Economic output increased slightly (three per cent) during the first three months of 1993 and monthly inflation amounted to two to three per cent. The prediction of the annual inflation rate (25-30 per cent) is likely to occur.

The progress of Estonia's financial and economic reforms is appreciated by the World Bank. John Hansen, senior World Bank economist, believes that Estonia might experience economic growth in 1993, Latvia at the end of 1994 and Lithuania not before 1995 (Hansen, 1993). He considers Estonia to be a great model of adequate policy-making for the Baltics and other countries.

3. Foreign trade

A highly important factor in Estonia's economic development is the expansion of her foreign trade. One of the main purposes of the Estonian monetary reform of 1992 was to stimulate this process, and Estonian businessmen managed to reorientate their foreign trade from the East to the West (Tables 7.1-7.3).

Approximately 45 per cent of the home market's gross product was provided by export of 1993. Export of Estonian goods increased more than ten times in monetary terms (but much less in real terms) in 1992 and is likely to double by 1993 (Table 7.1).

Table 7.1 Foreign trade of the Republic of Estonia (million Estonian kroon)

Year	Exports	Imports	Balance
1990	262	342	-80
1991	510	445	65
1992	5 548	5 128	430
1993 (first half)	4 185	4 421	-236

Source: Estonian National Customs Board and Bank of Estonia, 1993.

Estonia's primary export items are agricultural produce (meat, milk and related products), timber and timber products, textiles and metals (see Table 7.2). Unfortunately, the export of agricultural goods from Eastern to Western Europe is restricted by the European Community. Estonia's export structure is very similar to that of less developed countries. Estonian businessmen serve as mediators in trade with metals (from the East to the West) and second hand cars (from the West to the East).

Table 7.2 The structure of Estonian foreign trade (in per cent)

Items	Exports				Imports			
	1990	1991	1992	1993 (first half)	1990	1991	1992	1993 (first half)
Food-stuffs	20.9	18.3	16.5	21.3	14.9	17.8	8.7	13.8
Minerals	3.2	5.2	11.2	8.0	7.5	12.0	28.0	19.0
Chemicals	14.0	15.7	7.0	4.8	16.8	11.5	7.6	5.7
Timber	4.7	5.9	7.9	9.2	2.2	2.4	3.9	2.7
Textile	24.5	26.4	14.0	12.2	23.1	19.0	8.3	12.4
Metals	3.8	3.6	13.5	14.1	10.0	9.4	4.7	4.9
Machines	10.1	11.6	5.5	8.5	12.7	14.0	18.3	18.9
Vehicles	1.3	1.0	6.5	10.6	3.4	3.8	12.7	13.6
Other	17.5	12.3	11.6	11.3	9.4	10.1	6.8	8.8
Total	100.0	100.0	100.0	100.0	100.0	100.0	100.0	100.0

Source: Estonian National Customs Board and Bank of Estonia, 1993.

Table 7.3 Estonia's foreign trade partners (in per cent)

States	Exports				Imports			
	1990	1991	1992	1993 (first half)	1990	1991	1992	1993 (first half)
Russia	55.1	56.5	20.8	19.0	51.8	45.9	28.4	21.0
Other CIS	30.1	26.8	12.5	8.2	22.3	27.4	5.3	5.7
Latvia	5.7	7.7	10.6	7.1	4.7	5.1	1.4	2.5
Lithuania	3.1	3.8	1.3	2.4	3.2	6.3	1.7	3.0
Finland	1.1	2.3	21.0	23.0	1.6	2.0	22.6	25.3
Germany	0.3	0.2	4.3	7.9	2.3	0.8	8.3	9.8
Sweden	0.4	0.5	7.7	11.0	0.1	0.8	5.8	9.2
Other Western Europe	0.5	1.0	11.5	12.0	2.9	2.4	8.5	5.9
USA	0.6	0.1	2.1	2.2	3.2	3.7	3.5	2.4
Canada								
Other	3.1	1.1	7.0	7.2	7.9	5.6	3.5	15.1
Total	100.0	100.0	100.0	100.0	100.0	100.0	100.0	100.0

Source: Estonian National Customs Board and and Bank of Estonia, 1993.

4. Development of free enterprise

The number of new firms is rapidly increasing in Estonia. Under command economy and state monopoly there was a trend toward a concentration of firms in order to facilitate control by the state ministeries. At the end of the Soviet occupation there were only about seven hundred industrial enterprises and three hundred state and collective farms in Estonia. In 1987 the decentralization of large state enterprises began.

Table 7.4 Number of firms in Estonia

Indices	1988	1989	1990	1991	1992	1993
No. of firms	1 795	4 007	6 084	10 346	21 051	34 677
Start-ups	1 212	2 142	4 790	11 369	12 369	
Closures			65	593	1 257	
% of Start-ups	67.3	53.5	78.7	109.9	58.8	
Firms per 1 000 inhabitants	1.1	2.5	3.8	6.5	13.2	21.7
Starts-ups per 1 000 inhabitants	0.8	1.3	3.0	7.1	7.7	

The indices in Table 7.4 were computed by the author on the basis of data from the Statistical Office of Estonia. The number of firms rose from 1 795 at the beginning of 1988 to 34 677 at the beginning of 1993, i.e. an increase of 19.3 times (see Table 7.4). Each year the number grew by more than fifty per cent, the legalization of private firms (1990) even by more than one hundred per cent. The number of new establishments rose from 1 212 in 1988 to 12 369 in 1992, i.e. 10.2 times (see Table 7.4). However, new start-ups per 1 000 inhabitants prove to be a better indicator of economic acitivities. In 1992 the start-ups figure in Estonia (7.7) was many times higher than in Western countries. In 1987, the analogous figures were 1.0 in the Netherlands, 1.5-1.8 in the United Kingdom, 2.2 in Sweden, 2.9 in Denmark, 2.5-3.2 in Norway, 3.9 in France and 4.8 in Germany. The number of self-employed people in Estonia (about 5 per cent) is still two to three times lower than in Western countries. In 1990, according to Basic Statistics of the European Community (1992), the percentage of employers, self-employed and family members was 7.9 in the USA, 8.9 in Sweden, 11.3 in Norway, 14.6 in Finland, 18.2 in the EC, 24.7 in Japan and 48.6 in Greece.

In 1987 the Soviet Union granted permission to set up small state enterprises, producers' cooperatives and joint ventures. During the period from 1987 to 1990 most new firms were cooperatives. Since 1990, all other forms of enterprises have been allowed in Estonia, and the joint-stock company became the most common legal form of business organizations. The first two joint ventures the Soviet Union had were established in Estonia in 1987.

Table 7.5 Ownership of Estonian enterprises (as of January 1993)

Property	Number	Per cent
State	1 677	4.8
Municipal	260	0.7
Private	24 412	69.4
Cooperative	4 686	13.3
Foreign	3 645	10.4
Other	514	1.4

Source: Luup and Ehrlich (1993).

Now there are two main forms of foreign capital participation in Estonia: joint ventures (limited liability type) and joint-stock companies with foreign shareholding. In April 1993 there were more than 4 000 enterprises with foreign capital participation in Estonia. The total amount of foreign capital of these firms amounted to more than 2.2 billion EEK (it made about 1 500 EEK or 110 US$ per inhabitant). The most important foreign investors came from Sweden (37.7 per cent of total foreign capital), Finland (30.0 per cent), CIS (10.6 per cent), USA (4.5 per cent) and from the Netherlands (3.5 per cent). Most new firms are very small. According to the Statistical Office of Estonia (Rogova, 1992) fewer than three per cent of employees are on the payrolls of two thirds of Estonia's companies. Only five per cent of the country's firms have more than one hundred employees and employ more than 70 per cent of Estonia's labor force.

There have been great changes in the activities of the firms. The most important phenomenon is the rise of services. Services consisted of about one third of Estonia's economic output and labor force, by the end of the Soviet occupation. Now, most new firms are engaged in trade and services. The more important fields of activity of Estonian firms at the beginning of 1993 were (number of firms as percentage of total) trade and services (33.3 per cent), manufacturing (17.0 per cent), finance and business (16.4 per cent), agriculture and forestry (14.9 per cent), construction (8.8 per cent), transport and communications (3.8 per cent) and other activities (5.8 per cent).

Taking into account that market services averaged 48.2 and non-market services averaged 14.3 per cent of the total economic output of the European Community in 1990 (Eurostat, 1992, 26), it can be concluded that the structure of Estonia's economy is developing similar to that of other European countries.

A special group of small family businesses are private farms. There were about 600 estates in Estonia in the nineteenth century, 135 000 farmsteads in the Republic of Estonia, and 300 state and collective farms at the end of the Russian occupation. Now, the large Soviet-type farms are broken up, over 8 000 private farms and many cooperatives and joint-stock companies have been established. While the Estonian agriculture served as a huge milk and meat factory for Moscow and Leningrad and almost 50 per cent of Estonia's milk and meat production was sold to Russia at very low prices during Soviet occupation, Estonian agricultural production declined roughly by a factor of two from 1990 to 1993. On the other hand the export of agricultural products to Russia is diminishing, as the export of milk and meat products to Western European countries has been limited by the European Community. Imports of foodstuffs from other countries into Estonia are unrestricted. There is no state support policy for agriculture. At the same time prices for fuel, agricultural engineering and construction materials have risen many hundred times during the last few years. As a result, Estonian farmers have to sell their products at prices below the cost of production, e.g. farmers are paid only one Estonian crown for one liter of milk while the cost price is about two to three crowns.

It is difficult to assess the role of private firms and farms in the Estonian economy. Privatizing small state firms in trade and services began in 1990, and by 1992 a majority of them were in private hands. According to the Statistical Office of Estonia, during the first half of 1993, the trade turnover generated by state and municipal wholesalers was 33 and by retailers 14.2 per cent of the total. Mass privatization of large state enterprises began in 1993. It is expected that the majority of such companies will be sold within two to three years. The share of private firms in Estonia's industrial output has been estimated at around 20 per cent in 1991 and 30 per cent in 1992. The share is likely to be 40 per cent in 1993.

The entrepreneurial spirit of Estonians is relatively high. According to various sociological surveys, about 15-20 per cent of the economically active persons wish to set up their own firm or farm; many others (20-30 per cent) would like to become shareholders. All things considered, almost one half of the economically active population is interested in the active use of their financial and material resources. That data may easily be compared with the results of a 1989 British Social Attitude Survey, in which 47 per cent of a random sample of 780 British adults stated they would like to be self-employed (Jowell et al., 1990). The proportion of British self-employed people is slightly over 10 per cent. At the beginning of 1993 the equivalent number of Estonians was about 5 per cent. The possibilities for Estonians to become self-employed are very limited. According to a study of the saving behavior of Estonians, only 11 per cent of the population have relatively high savings (more than 4 200 Estonian crowns or slightly more than 300 US$) (Loogma and Pettai, 1993). The Estonian privatization program aims at enabling people to acquire real assets. Over 200 000 Estonians have claimed the property or compensation for property nationalized under the Soviet rule. Nearly all economically active citizens will get vouchers enabling them to purchase their dwellings or participate in the privatization of state firms.

5. Problems of small firms

Private ownership of the means of production and free enterprise were prohibited in totalitarian Marxist societies. After the collapse of socialism in Eastern Europe, the freedom to engage in economic acitivities was guaranteed. Unfortunately, the monopoly of the state in the economy has not yet been removed from all post-socialist countries.

The old socialist monopolist structures and patterns, e.g. the policies, economies and the educational system of the post-totalitarian societies are still present. It is not likely that democracy will automatically replace communist dictatorship. According to Zbigniew Brzezinski, the most probable stages in the retreat from Communism are communist totalitarianism, communist authoritarianism, post-communist authoritarianism and post-communist pluralism (Brzezinski, 1989). But this is a rather optimistic view. We all know that Western societies are not totally democratic either. Representative democracy does not exclude the influence of the golden rule of oligarchy. Important political decisions are made by the leaders of ruling political parties in democratic Western states, despite the fact that the segment represented by members of political parties usually does not exceed one per cent of the entire population. Thus, it is no wonder that oligarchical tendencies are even stronger in post-totalitarian societies. In Estonia, the desire to obtain monopolistic power and enjoy privileges is characteristic not only of the old political and economic organizations, but also of the new organizations and their leaders. The struggle is for the redistribution of power and privileges and not so much for their abolition (Haav, 1992). It is symptomatic that the early post-communist governments of Estonia did not have any explicit economic policies and that various steps towards a market economy did not correspond to each other (Reiljan, 1993). In July 1993, the Minister of Economics started to organize a council to work out a new concept of economic policy. Unfortunately, the creative problem was approached as an administrative one and established a new corporatist structure from a limited number of Estonian prominents. This has been realized by Estonian entrepreneurs, too, and the Estonian Chamber of Trade and Commerce has initiated an alternative institution.

As there was no free enterprise in Estonia, there could not be any research either. But it was possible to study the problems of management in state enterprises. A lot of economic and some sociological empirical investigations were conducted in Estonia during Soviet occupation since the mid sixties. Estonian economists started to approach Estonia's economy on the basis of neoclassic theories of macro-economics many years ago. But neoclassical economics ignores the role of the enterpreneur. Traditionally, the microeconomists and management specialists are not able to consider the problems of firms in a wider economic and social context. As many researchers were not satisfied with the traditional narrow and one-sided approach to entrepreneurship, new concepts of social networks and social entrepreneurs are being developed in many Western countries. The network approach would be fruitful for transitional countries, too (see e.g. Albach, 1994). The new theories and concepts of entrepreneurship and economic transition are not well known in Estonia.

The respective empirical investigations are suffering from their weak theoretical basis in Estonia. It is hard or even impossible to interpret, compare and generalize about the results of various investigators if the theoretical and methodological bases of their research is not clear. The Estonian Market Research Institute regularly evaluates the problems of Estonia's economic development. Eighteen prominent Estonian experts ranked the significance of ten factors of economic development in July 1993. According to their opinion, the main retarding factors are (in percentages of importance as assessed by the experts): lack of capital (89 per cent of the experts), low demand on the domestic market (89 per cent), weak economic policy (89 per cent), unemployment (56 per cent), lack of qualified labour force (45 per cent), inflation (39 per cent), exports barriers (33 per cent), weak international competition (33 per cent), imbalance in the state budget (28 per cent), and the foreign debt (22 per cent). Most experts consider a lack of capital to be the most important factor hurting the economic situation in Estonia.

In view of these experts' opinions, it is not difficult to realize that the three most important factors are connected with the financial policy of the Government and the Bank of Estonia. The repeated devaluation of the Estonian currency (Rajasalu, 1992b) resulted in a supply shock and the decline of demand and production. According to John Hansen (World Bank), the real exchange rate of the Estonian currency on the basis of its purchasing power was not 1 DM = 8 EEK, but 1 DM = 2.7 EEK in June 1992, and 1 DM = 5.4 EEK at the beginning of 1993 (Hansen and Rocha, 1993): this exchange rate stimulated export (see Tables 7.1-7.3) and strengthened the Estonian crown. The currency reserves of the Bank of Estonia have increased by more than three times between June 1992 and July 1993. The Estonian commercial banks have enough money to grant credits to Estonian businessmen. But due to high risk and inflation (two to three per cent per month in 1993) they are not interested in lending money. When granting loans, they charge high interest rates (over 50 per cent per year at the beginning of 1993, and 30-40 per cent in the middle of 1993). Another problem is that most new entrepreneurs are unable to employ a good business planning.

The Estonian Small Business Association (ESBA), representing more than 300 small and medium-sized firms, has submitted proposals to the Government on how to support small start-ups. It suggests to:

- create a special fund of to provide credits to small and medium size enterprises (SME);
- work out and implement an export credit system;
- change the tax system, increasing the role of indirect and diminishing the role of direct taxes;
- complete the introduction of market legislation;
- stop the preferential treatment of state enterprises and to guarantee the equality of different forms of property;
- provide opportunities for the participation of SMEs in the privatization of state firms.

ESBA conducted a public opinion poll among Estonian entrepreneurs in 1993 (see Klaamann, 1993). 138 entrepreneurs assessed the relevance of 61 factors determining the development of free enterprise. The most important factors negatively affecting Estonian businessmen were high interest rates, low demand in the domestic market, and difficulties in obtaining long-term credits. The majority of respondents considered taxes of firms to be too high, especially the income-tax and value-added-tax burden. The businessmen wanted taxes to be lowered. They suggested that

- income tax should not exceed 18 per cent (the actual average income tax was raised from 27 to 35 per cent during the monetary reform of June 1992);
- VAT not be more than 10 per cent (it was raised from 10 to 18 per cent in June 1992);
- social tax be lowered to 13 per cent (at this time 20 per cent of a workers income);

- health-insurance tax be lowered to 9 per cent (at this time 13 per cent of a workers income).

According to Estonian economists, taxes are not high in Estonia. In comparison to Eastern and Central European countries they are on an average level. The nominal share of the total tax burden is estimated to be 37.9 per cent of GDP, but tax receipts (taking into account tax avoidance) are estimated at 33.3 per cent in 1993 (Eero, 1993). The main debtors are some large state-owned firms. In July 1993, 35 large enterprises owed more than one billion EEK to the state (among them 'Eesti Polevkivi', the Estonian Oil-Shale Company, 82.6 million and the textile company 'Balti Manufaktuur' - 56.9 million EEK). On August 1, 1993 the total amount of unpaid taxes was almost 360 million EEK. It is difficult to obtain statistical data from new small firms; and thus, small firms can easily avoid paying taxes.

Table 7.6 gives a brief systematic review of main problems in different aspects of free enterprise development in Estonia.

Table 7.6 Overview on main problems facing entrepreneurs in Estonia

Entrepreneurs	Real estate	Investments
• weak business ideas and plans • low business ethics • many consultancies • little research into entrepreneurship	• hard to obtain land and buildings, no market in immovables and securities • slow and corrupted privatization.	• hard to obtain credits, high interest rates • small foreign investments.
Business society and culture	**State**	**Foreign policy**
• low demand in domestic market • easy to disregard laws, avoid taxes, cheat clients	• incomplete and contradictory legal system • weak economic and foreign policy, weak control of state firms, no support to small firms and farms • weakness of police and courts of justice • corruption	• economic pressure and military threat from the expansionism of Russia • difficulties in getting rid of Russian occupation and annexion and their results (colonization, assimilation, stagnation)

6. Some conclusions

There are some signs giving hope that Estonia will overcome the total crisis caused by Soviet occupation and Russian colonial policy. The Estonian monetary reform in 1992 put an end to the exploitation of Estonian national recources by Moscow. It stimulated the reorientation of Estonia's foreign trade from the East to the West and Russia lost its privileged role in trade in 1992. And yet, Estonia's economy still depends on the import of fuel and raw materials from Russia. Estonia's independence and recovery always remain vulnerable to the expansionism of Russia.

Despite macro-economic stabilization, Estonia's economy is still in a deep depression. A rapid political restructuring is taking place before a radical restructuring of the economy. There is strong competition between various groups of the old and new political and economic elite. But these groups are struggling more for the monopoly of power than for democratic - right, left or centrist - policy. This is the reason, why most important political organizations and institutions still have oligarchical and corporatist structures as the partocracy in the Soviet Union had. And those who have obtained power do not hurry to change the policy of their predecessors or to express their own priorities.

Under these circumstances, the role of radical social reform and of higher education could be decisive. It could facilitate the concentration of Estonia's intellectual potential aiming at working out concepts for democratic political and economic development, and in doing so, East-West cooperation could prove to be vital.

References

Albach, Horst (1994) *The Transformation of Firms and Markets - A Network Approach to Economic Transformation Processes in East Germany,* Stockholm: Alquis & Wiksell.

Arkadie, Brian van and Mats Karlsson (1992) *Economic Survey of the Baltic States. The Reform Process in Estonia, Latvia and Lithuania*, London: Pinter Publishers.

Blanchard, O., R. Dornbusch, P. Krugman, R. Layard and L. Summers (1992) *Reform in Eastern Europe*, London, Cambridge: The MIT Press.

Brzezinski, Zbigniew (1989) *The Grand Failure*, New York: Charles Scribners's Sons.

Clague, Chr. and G.C. Rausser (eds.) (1992) *The Emergence of Market Economies in Eastern Europe*, Oxford, Cambridge: Blackwell.

Dellenbrant, Jan Ake, Ole Norgaard and Helle Willumsen (eds.) (1992) *The Politics of Transition in the Baltic States*, Collection of papers from the Parnu Seminar, 16-19 January 1992, Aarhus: University of Aarhus.

Dyker, David (ed.) (1992) *The European Economy*, London and New York: Longman.

Eero, Endel (1993) *Riigieelarve Tasakaalust ja Kova Krooni Tugevusvarust* [On the Balance of Estonia's State Budget], Postimees, July 26.

Eurostat (1992) *Panorama of EC Industry*, Statistical Supplement, Brussels, Luxembourg: Eurostat.

Haav, Kaarel (1988) *Kui Hästi Tasub Töötada?* [Does It Pay to Work Hard?], Tallinn: Eesti Raamat.

Haav, Kaarel (1991a) *Estonian Managers in State and Non-State Enterprises Getting Rid of the Command Economy*, Paper presented at the East-West Management Symposion in Konstanz, February 11-13, 1991.

Haav, Kaarel (1991b) *On the Projects of Property Reform and Expectations of People in Estonia*, Proceedings of the International Conference 'Privatization versus Democratization', Tallinn: Ministry of Economics, Vol. II, 63-66.

Haav, Kaarel (1992) *Getting Rid of the Totalitarian Regime: The Case of Estonia*, Proceedings of the International Conference 'Assets and Liabilities of Independence', Trento.

Haav, Kaarel and Rein Ruutsoo (1990) *Eesti Rahvas ja Stalinlus* [The Estonian People and Stalinism], Tallinn: Olion.

Hansen, John (1993) *World Bank Predicts Gradual Economic Recovery for Baltics*, An Interview given to The Baltic Oberserver, April 30 - May 6.

Hansen, John and Robert Rocha (eds.) (1993) *Estonia. The Transition to a Market Economy*, Washington D.C.: The World Bank.

Järve, Tonu (1993) *Elukallidust ja Palku Vorreldakse Hamburgeri Abil* [Comparison of the Standards of Living on the Basis of McDonalds], Ohthleht, February 26.

Joeste, Marje and Ülo Kaevats (eds.) (1991) *The Baltic States. A Reference Book*, Tallinn, Riga, Vilnius: Encyclopedia Publishers.

Jowell, R. et al. (1990) *British Social Attitudes: The 7th Report*, Aldershot: Gower.

Kahk, Juhan (ed.) (1992) *Estonia and World War II - a Damages Report*, Tallinn. Estonian Academy of Sciences.

Klaamann, Vaho (1993); Eesti Ettevolust Häirivad Probleemid, [On Problems of Estonian Entrepreneuship]; *Äripaevg*, 73, 20.

Knobl, Adalbert (ed.) (1992) *Economic Review Estonia*, Washington D.C.: IMF.

Kornai, Janos (1992) *The Socialist System. The Political Economy of Communism*, Oxford: Clarendon Press.

Liuhto, Kari (1991) *The Interaction of Managerial Cultures in Soviet-Finnish Joint Ventures*, Turku: Turku School of Economics and Business Administration.

Liuhto, Kari (1992) *Developing Estonian Entrepreneurship in Economic Transition*, Turku: Turku School of Economics and Business Adminstration, Business Research Center and Institute for East-West Trade.

Loogma, Krista and Iris Pettai (1993); Eestlane Soovib Säästa 55,000 Krooni [An Estonian Is Willing to Save 55,000 EEk]; *Äripaev*, 54, May 15.

Luup, Laine and Rutt Ehrlich (eds.) (1993) *Invest in the Future: the Future is Estonia*, Tallinn: Informare Ltd.

Norgaard, Ole (ed.) (1992) *Transition in the Baltic States: Politics, Economy, National Minorities and Foreign Policy*, Research, Aarhus: University of Aarhus.

OECD (1992) Economic Outlook No. 52, December 1992, Paris: Organisation for Economic Cooperation and Development.

Pollisinski, Kaupo (ed.) (1993) *Eesti Panga Bulletään. 1993 I kvartal*, Tallinn: Eesti Pank.

Rajasalu, Teet (1992a) *Estonian Economy at the Dawn on Independence*,Tallinn: Institute of Economics, Preprint.

Rajasalu, Teet (1992b) *Eesti Majanduse Prognoos 1992. ja 1993. Aastak* [The Prognosis of Estonias Economic Development for 1992 and 1993], Tallinn: Institute of Economics, Working Paper.

Reiljan, Janno (1993) *Reformimine Toimub Ilma Ühtse Majanduspoliitikata* [There is No Coordination in the Economic Policy of Estonia], Kaubaleht, March 26 - April 23.

Rogova, Sirje (ed.) (1992) *Eesti Ettevotlus 1991*, Aastal Tallinn: Eesti Vabariigi Statistikaameti Peaarvutuskeskus.

Rosati, D.K. (1992) *The Politics of Economic Reform in Central and Eastern Europe*, CEPR Occasional paper No. 6.

Sepp, Urmas (1992) *Current Problems and Perspectives of the Estonian Economy*, Tallinn: Institute of Economics, Estonian Academy of Sciences.

8 Private economy in an etatist environment: the case of Romania

Gábor Hunya

1. The legacy of the past

The development of private economic activity started after the fall of the Ceausescu regime from nothing. Only some private farming was allowed earlier which operated under strict government control (compulsory deliveries, state-controlled prices on the peasant markets). No private craftsmen, no small-scale retail trade had been in private hands. State property was in the course of expansion even during the 1980s when many socialist countries experimented with some private initiative and state enterprise autonomy. Individual thinking was suppressed, the population intimidated, so that it took several months after the fall of the Communist regime before private initiative started to develop. Even later, the social basis for a market economy has remained rather small. Social behavior is not in line with the necessities of market exchange: sincerity and trust are downgraded as social values (Daniel, 1992). Corruption is widespread, private economy and state bureaucracy have developed a kind of symbiosis.

State control over the economy was eased but remained more substantial than acceptable in a market economy. The incompleteness of macroeconomic liberalization and stabilization, the delay of the privatization and the bankruptcy of state-owned enterprises and the widespread state interference in the economy can be regarded as the main current obstacles to the development of the private sector.

2. Legal framework of the private economy

After December 1989 the transitory government initiated hesitant changes; market economy based on private property was not declared as the aim of transformation. Decree 54/1990 of February 1990 gave the first legal possibility to establish private businesses in the forms of personal or family ventures, as well as of private small enterprises, but only with up to 20 employees (see Hunya, 1990). This limitation of size, representing a relict of socialist thinking did not prove to be a tremendous obstacle at this initial stage. The state wanted to check the way private initiative was to develop. The National Agency for Private Initiative was called into being with the task to authorize each private application for start-up after having checked its 'viability' and 'social importance'. Despite its bureaucratic role, this authority, which later became the National Agency for Privatization and Small Enterprise, proved to be an initiator of market-oriented reforms and defendant of the interest of private economy in government disputes.

After the general elections, a new government was founded in June 1990 for a legislative period of two years. The government's programme[1] initiated the introduction of the legal framework of a market economy during this time. The corporate act and the transformation law, which abandoned the size-limit on private firms, were passed in August that year.[2] Small private enterprises had to be converted into partnerships; most of them took the form of limited liability company. Private entrepreneurs and family associations could continue their activities. At the same time, the corporatization of state-owned enterprises (SOEs) took place. SOEs in infrastructure and basic industries were converted into autonomous enterprises ('regie autonome'), most of the others into commercial partnerships with the state being the single owner. The privatization of the latter group was foreseen, while in the first no private participation was envisaged. The management of the majority of state-owned enterprises found it easier to remain under close state control a fact which guaranteed survival and provided for an adequate supply of energy and imports. Some state owned joint stock companies succeeded to become 'regie autonome' during 1992. Being saved from privatization, they continued their rent-seeking behavior.

The foreign investment law of April 1991 opened the country to foreign investors, gave guarantees against nationalization, and provided tax-holidays for investors. Restrictions on the purchase of land by foreigners and on the repatriation of profits earned in domestic currency remained. The amendment to this law in June 1993 (Tribuna Economica, 1993) allowed the full transfer of profits, but the restriction on land-ownership was not eliminated. As the political and operational risks of investment projects is considered high, most of the foreign investments have strengthened the small-scale private sector.[3]

The law on privatization passed in August 1991 provided the main institutional framework; it took over a year to set up these institutions, so that the sale of assets started in 1993 only. The law put 30 per cent of SOEs' shares into Private Ownership Funds to be privatized by vouchers and the rest into the State Ownership Fund to be privatized by sale. Local authorities began in 1990 with the renting out of shop-space mostly on a non-competitive basis to private entrepreneurs. This activity became later more organized, retail outlets and small restaurants were rented out in increasing numbers. The sale of such premises started only in late 1992 in the framework of the assets-privatization program.

After three years of transformation, the basic legal framework for market economy is now in place in Romania, but much of the operation rules are still unclear. Rules of the game are too often directed by ministerial decrees, the application of which is negotiable.

---

1 See Government of Romania (1991); for an assessment of the program see Demekas and Khan (1991).

2 For an English translation of relevant laws see Romanian Development Agency (1992).

3 For factors of investment and credit risk see Hunya (1993).

3. Macroeconomic environment

Both the current depression of the Romanian economy and the rudimentary market-economic framework increase the risks of private investments and put limits on its development. GDP in 1992 was 32 per cent lower than in 1989, in real terms, and a further decline of 5-10 per cent can be expected for 1993.[4] The unofficial sector may have tempered the decline of production. Official data on consumption (private consumption, retail trade turnover, real wages, income of the population), however, indicate a substantial shrinking of private demand as well Although the recession has, first of all, affected the state sector - while the private one has been growing - the decline in purchasing power of most of the population has put a demand-side limit on the expansion of the private sector. Nevertheless, private companies can be extremely profitable and expand in an economy with still surviving shortages and segmented markets.

Economic transformation has been slow in Romania compared to Central European reforming countries. Until very recently, price-liberalization was incomplete. Stabilization attempts have been half-hearted, so that inflation is at 200 per cent p.a. for the third consecutive year now. Inflation makes economic calculations unreliable and increases the risk associated with private investment (see Daianu, 1992).

The foreign exchange situation is precarious, convertibility does not function. This is one of the deterring factors for foreign investments. The inter-bank foreign exchange market develops an exchange rate under the supervision of the National Bank of Romania at which demand exceeds supply. The private sector has to rely on its own foreign exchange earnings and has practically no access to the inter-bank market. State-owned commercial banks discriminate against the foreign exchange claims of small private businesses. The recently established Eximbank of Romania plans to introduce a more favorable practice.

Interest rates are kept artificially low, the central bank refinancing rate being 70 per cent p.a. and commercial bank lending rate even lower than that. Commercial banks prefer lending to large state-owned companies, access to bank-loans for the private sector is limited. Exceptions are better-established foreign trade companies and those able to offer real estate as collateral. They can also rely on the services of three private commercial banks. The financial sector is severely underdeveloped, the payment morale is low, especially regarding public sector organizations. In this respect the Romanian economy is 'unimaginably primitive' (Dumitriu, 1993).

---

4 The macroeconomic development is constantly monitored by The Vienna Institute for Comparative Economic Studies (WIIW). See: WIIW Members' Information Bulletin, various issues.

4. Scope of the legal private activity

Private ventures absorbed a remarkable proportion of unemployed persons, some of them relying on unemployment benefits while active in the private sector.[5] There is also a wide illegal private economy, the size of which may only be estimated with surveys. Employment in the private sector outside agriculture is estimated to 1.5 million by the Romanian Development Agency, but the Ministry of Labour registered only 0.45 million, less than the number of private firms and entrepreneurs in the statistics.

Table 8.1 Share of the private sector in the economy (per cent)

	1991	1992	Jan-June 1993
GDP	21.5	25.5	...
agricultural GDP	81.2	82.0	...
non-agricultural GDP	4.0	4.6	...
exports (in convertible currency*)	19.1	26.1	25.8
imports (in convertible currency*)	17.5	32.3	28.9
retail trade	21.9	44.9	45.9
services for the population	16.4	26.0	43.9

Note: * = US$ based

Source: Monthly Bulletin of Statistics, different issues.

The share of the private sector in the GDP produced outside agriculture was only 4.6 per cent in 1992, up from 4 per cent in the previous year (Table 8.1). This reveals a substantial backwardness of Romania if compared to Poland and Hungary, where the private share in non-agricultural GDP exceeds one third. Almost half of the retail trade and of services to the population in Romania is carried out by the private sector. The private share in foreign trade was almost 30 per cent in 1992 but declined to 26 per cent in the first half of 1993, because the issue of licences to fill central quotas was restricted, and duties increased.

There has been a fast and uninterrupted increase in the number of private ventures for the last two and a half years (Table 8.2). The relatively small (depreciating with inflation) statutory capital necessary for a start-up encouraged entrepreneurs to set up businesses in the form of legal partnerships.

5 According to a survey, 46 per cent of unemployed persons had secondary incomes in 1992. See Lazarsfeld (1993).

Table 8.2 Number of firms in the Romanian economy

	Regie Autonome	State	Private	Person	Small	Foreign
17/12/90	-	-	-	70 477	23 023	
30/06/91	299		19 491*	122 849	21 399	
31/12/91	693	7 577	76 255	154 472	-	8 022
30/06/92	758	8 423	146 466	180 861	-	
31/12/92	859	7 885	199 902	196 306	-	21 056
30/06/93	912	8 251	266 061	207 846	-	22 887

Notes: * For 30/06/91 state-owned and private companies together, because the corporatization of state-owned enterprises and of private small companies was under way.

'Regie Autonome' = autonomous state-owned enterprise
State = State-owned company in corporate form
Private = Private company in corporate form (including mixed)
Person = Natural person and family association
Small = Small private company before corporatization
Foreign = Private companies with foreign participation

Source: Monthly Bulletin of Statistics, different issues.

The number of family ventures has, therefore, been growing rather slowly for the last year, while the number of private companies increased by 82 per cent. Private agricultural units, not registered as firms, are not included in these figures and, thus, not a subject of the present paper.[6]

All data in this paper refer to registered firms leaving unknown how many of them are operational. The National Trade Register Office reports a negligible number of firms going out of business. We also have no data on unregistered private business activity. There are, however, certain incentives (besides the disincentive of taxation) to legalize private ventures. Only registered companies can operate in foreign trade and lease or buy shop-space. The minimum statutory capital for a limited liability company, lei 100 000 equals two months average salary, which can be no major obstacle to set up legal ventures.

There is no information on the distribution of private firms by activities, as most of them registered production, domestic trade and foreign trade simultaneously as their field of activity. Nevertheless, their contribution to retail sales and foreign trade turnover reveals the main fields of interest.

6 The land of the former agricultural cooperatives was distributed among the original owners, so that four-fifths of the agricultural production comes from the private sector.

Almost one tenth of the private companies have foreign participation, including those 100 per cent foreign-owned. The foreign part of the statutory capital of foreign direct investment projects registered until mid-1993 reached US$ 600 million, which is much less than in the more advanced Central European reforming countries, but more than in insolvent Bulgaria. The inflow of foreign capital through the banking system is even smaller, some US$ 120 million are recorded in the capital account between 1991 and the first quarter of 1993. The rest of the statutory capital has either never been paid, or represents foreign contribution in kind.[7] The average capital per project is very small which is not surprising if we consider that foreign capital participated in only three privatization cases.

As a Romanian speciality, small private ventures operate to a large number in the form of joint ventures with foreigners. Turkish, Syrian, Jordanian, Lebanese and Iraqi capital participates in small-scale retail and foreign trade ventures. These countries contribute with 24 per cent to the number of projects, but only with 3 per cent to the registered foreign capital. Near-Eastern trading skills seem to make up for missing local experience. Small joint ventures with Hungarian (3.5 per cent of projects, 0.5 per cent of capital) and German participation operate in regions of national minorities. The most important foreign investment projects, however, are those of British, American, Italian and German large companies.

5. Regional distribution of private companies

The private sector is concentrated in the capital, major ports and border regions as well as in the most developed areas[8]. Bucharest with 10 per cent of the population has more than 20 per cent of the total number of private companies and also of companies with foreign capital registered in the country. The size of companies in Bucharest is larger than elsewhere; almost half of the foreign capital is registered there (end of May 1993: 48.7 per cent, US$ 230.8 million). Central location, proximity to government offices, a large and diversified local market are among the factors of attraction.

The density of the private sector (measured by the number of companies per 1 000 inhabitants in the counties 'judet') next to Bucharest is second highest in Constanta (major port), third in Cluj (centre of Transylvania). Both places are regional or country-wide distribution centres. They are followed by the Western border regions of Timis and Oradea. As half of the foreign trade is done with Western Europe and Hungary is the most important transit country for Romanian imports and exports, these regions are attractive for trade activities. There is a very low presence of the private sector in Moldavia which is rather off the track of international transport. Open borders (in view

7 On methodological problems of measuring foreign direct investment flows and the major characteristics of such flows see Hunya (1992).

8 The source of regional data is the Monthly Statistical Synthesis No. 18, May 1993 of the National Trade Register Office. Data on the total number of firms published here is slightly different of those by the National Commission for Statistics included in Table 8.1.

of the envisaged economic and political integration with the neighbouring Republic of Moldavia) promoted unregistered trade but not legal private activity.

Companies with foreign participation show a similar regional distribution to private companies. The Eastern and the Western 'ports', i.e. the counties of Constanta and Bihor have the highest share in the invested foreign capital. In addition, the counties of Cluj, Timis and Hargita are also important sites concerning the number of projects, less so, however, regarding the amount of invested capital.

6. Results of small-scale privatization

The genuine private sector partly relies on the premises leased or bought from state-owned companies. This process goes on in an organized way under the provisions of the privatization law of August 1991.[9] Bottom-up development of the private sector is thus linked to privatization proper.

The National Agency for Privatization manages a small-scale privatization program, the selling of assets (shops, hotels, restaurants, workshops, individual machines etc.) at auctions. One third of the selected assets have been sold by now: 1 534 assets in 1992, with total value of lei 15.9 billion and another 764 assets in the first half of 1993, in the value of lei 14.4 billion.[10] The total number of employees working with these assets was 11 088. More than 80 per cent of the selected assets originally belonged to companies in trade and tourism. The new owners are mostly domestic private firms.

In spite of these results, the genuine private sector has benefited very little from the privatization-proper. State-owned companies sit on hardly utilized assets without making them available for the private sector. Asset stripping and privatization through bankruptcy, the two most common ways of transfer of public property to private owners in Poland and Hungary, hardly exists.

7. Private initiative in the grip of state authority

The government office in charge of small and medium-sized enterprises, organized recently as the Romanian Development Agency, has partly concentrated its activities on the legal supervision of start-ups and partly on representing the interests of the private economy at government level. Its success has been rather limited in the latter field, as economic policy-making is a constant battlefield between conservatives and reformers, where the conservative forces based in the ministries of industry and agriculture, and partially in the ministry of finance, successfully block more courageous steps.

The private sector has to face non-transparent bureaucratic procedures with widespread corruption. Financial, health and other authorities harass the private sector,

9 For the legal and institutional framework of privatization see the chapter 'Romania' in Frydman, Rapaczynsky and Earle (1993). Recent results are presented in Hunya and Virág (1993).

10 Data-base of the National Agency for Privatization.

and, thus, keep it under close control. As a side-effect, tax collection may be more efficient in Romania than in other Eastern countries. Private enterprises report higher profit rates than state-owned ones - an unusual phenomenon in Poland or Hungary. Programmes for SME promotion are at the conceptual stage only, without domestic financial background. The Guarantee Fund For Private Entrepreneurs, which could have the aim to support investors to obtain credit, was authorized in August 1992 but was not yet operational a year later.

It is usually left to foreign experts and foreign aid to promote private entrepreneurship in Romania. There was a program developed in the framework of PHARE to set up information centers and incubators for the private business (Costariol, 1993). A related decree was issued in August 1993, which envisages the coordinated spending of foreign funds targeting small and medium-sized enterprises[11].

Incomplete liberalization and stabilization have left quite extensive state control in the spheres of price-formation, availability of foreign exchange, credits, import and export licences. Vaguely formulated laws and contradictory regulations governing private business leave wide discretionary rights to the bureaucracy. Corruption and favoritism govern the interaction of state bureaucracy and the private sector. The completion of liberalization and a successful stabilization could put limits on state interference. The state would have more important tasks to fulfil, like the guarantee of the safety of private property and the enforcement of laws and contracts.

The slow space of privatization of state-owned assets is a further obstacle to private sector development. While selling state property as 'enterprises' is usually complicated and slow everywhere, offering workshops, hotels, shops, machines and industrial real estates to private firms can be rather successful. State-owned companies should, therefore, be disintegrated and sold as assets without the inherited financial and organizational burden. The genuine private sector would need this cheap way of expansion. The lack of a fast process of top-down privatization hinders bottom-up development.

References

Costariol, M. et al. (1993) *The Small and Medium-sized Enterprise in the Transition Process: the Case of Romania*, Venice Mestre: CNA Veneto and Euro-in-library.

Daianu, D. (1992) *The Changing Mix of Economic Disequilibria during Transition - a Romanian Background*, Paper presented at the 2nd EACES Conference, Groningen, 24-27 September 1992.

Daniel, D. (1992) *Transformation and Legacy of Backwardness - Thoughts from a Romanian Perspective*, Paper presented at Georgetown University on January 29, 1992.

11 Romania got ECU 10 million for SME promotion form the European Communities in the framework of the PHARE programme.

Demekas, D. and M. Khan (1991) *The Romanian Economic Reform Program*, IMF Occasional Paper No. 89, November 1991.

Dumitriu, I. (1993) *Company Management and Capital-Markets Development in the Transition of Romania. Russian and East European Finance and Trade*, Summer 1993.

Frydman, R., A. Rapaczynsky and J. Earle (1993) *The Privatization Process in Central Europe*, Budapest: Central European University Press.

Government of Romania (1991) *The White Book of the Romanian Reform*, Bucharest, May.

Hunya, G. (1990); Privatwirtschaft und Privatisierung in Rumänien; *Südosteuropa*, 10.

Hunya, G. (1992); Foreign Direct Investment and Privatization in Central and Eastern Europe; *Communist Economies and Economic Transformation*, 4.

Hunya, G. (1993) *Romania 1993: Country Report and Risk Assessment*, in WIIW Country Report and Country Profiles, No. 6, The Vienna Institute for Comparative Economic Studies, September.

Hunya, G. and Z. Virág (1993); Hesitant Privatization in Romania; *Members' Information of The Vienna Institute for Comparative Economic Studies*, 8.

Lazarsfeld, Paul (1993) *New Democracy Barometer*, Vienna: Society for Social Research.

Romanian Development Agency (1992) *Law Digest for Foreign Investors*, Bucharest, February 1992.

The Vienna Institute for Comparative Economic Studies (WIIW), *WIIW Members' Information Bulletin*, various issues.

Tribuna Economica (1993), No. 31, July, 23.

9 The small private firms in Bulgaria and the impact of the economic reform on their growth and future

Tatiana Houbenova-Delissivkova and *Plamen Puchev*

1. Prerequisites

Until the beginning of the political and economic reforms in Bulgaria in November 1989 the development of the entrepreneurial small and medium-sized firms was deliberately suppressed by the system of central planning. Unlike countries like Poland with its considerably big private agrarian and craftsmanship sector, and unlike the former GDR and Hungary with their traditions and efforts of providing for the co-existence of state enterprises and small private firms, there were not even partial efforts towards creating private entrepreneurship prior to the Bulgarian reforms. In addition, the rights of the agrarian and craftsmanship cooperatives were considerably limited.

Between 1983 and 1987 Bulgaria undertook an experiment to create small and medium-sized production facilities within the structure of the state enterprises which, however, did not lead to any substantial changes in the framework of socioeconomic conditions (Puchev, 1990).

Since the liquidation of the monopoly of the Communist party in 1989, there has been a marked tendency among intellectuals as well as in the programs of the newly created Bulgarian parties to emphasize the importance of the small business sector for the economic reform itself as well as the significance of the so-called 'middle class' for the success of democratization. Based upon the historical experience and the contemporary conditions for the small business sector in the developed Western economies, it was assumed that this sector represents an important factor in the national economy of these countries and that it provides new jobs. The small firms also play a significant role in the training and qualification of workers. Their flexibility and innovative potential and their ability to adapt to the fluctuations of the business cycle were also taken into consideration.

Due to the lack of entrepreneurial tradition during the relatively long period of a centrally planned economy, the Bulgarian society has become used to wait for economic changes to be imposed 'from above'. It appears interesting to observe to what extent the development of a vital sector of small and medium-sized firms has become a priority of the state policy of reforms and what forms this development has taken. On the other hand, the key element in the transition process from a command economy to a market system is the transformation of the role of the government in macroeconomic policy and in the promotion of economic development. Thus, the proper choice of a set of policies favorable to private-sector growth is a vital issue of the economic reform. Of course, the deep economic crisis in Bulgaria reduces the range of flexibility of such a policy. The process of macroeconomic stabilization with its anti-inflationory restrictions contradicts the concepts of a state policy of subsidizing small businesses. In this context it is also interesting to show how - in spite of the restrictive effects of the stabilization policy and without proper institutional support - the small private sector develops under the impact of the market forces. The economic liberalization has stimulated the growth of the private firms but their further development needs to be supported by adequate economic and legal measures.

2. 1989-1993 macroeconomic framework for the private sector development in Bulgaria

It is almost accepted that in the former Eastern countries, according to the level of achievement in economic reform and democratization, there are three types of states. The economic crisis in each of the three state categories differs in its dimension as well as in its course. During the four years since the end of 1989 the economic crisis in Bulgaria has proven to be much deeper than in other countries, and economic recovery has not yet taken place. Compared to Central European countries, Bulgaria lags behind in economic transition. While positive changes occurred as a result of economic liberalization and democratization, the reform in Bulgaria could not reach the macroeconomic stabilization targets initially set for 1991 and postponed to 1992-1993. Since the end of 1993 the Bulgarian economy has entered another cycle of financial destabilization without having achieved macroeconomic stabilization.

There are substantial deviations between the targets of the government policy set for the state budget and the balance of payments and the results represented by such important quantitative parameters as growth and structure of GDP, inflation, unemployment, budget deficit and national debt, balance of payments and foreign debt, real income and consumption. The economy is still in a deep crisis and the economic environment remains uncertain. The pendulum of disequilibrium has moved from one extreme to the other; and while some disequilibria have been overcome new ones have appeared.

According to the IMF data for 1993 the rate of inflation in Bulgaria was 70 per cent, compared to 13 per cent in the Czech Republic, 40 per cent in Poland and 20 per cent in Hungary. In Eastern Europe, only Romania and Albania have a higher inflation than Bulgaria. Unemployment in Bulgaria in 1990-1993 was also much higher than in the Czech Republic, Hungary and Poland. The dynamics of the economic indicators show that while in Hungary, Poland and the Czech Republic and Slovakia the slump has bottomed out, Bulgaria, Romania and Albania have not reached the lowest point yet.

Though under conditions of restrictive monetary, fiscal, and budgetary policies, the creation and survival of private firms was a risky and uncertain process, the results as a whole may be encouraging. To a certain extent the private sector - represented mainly by the small and medium-sized firms - may be considered to be the major stabilizing factor in the transitional economies. While in the countries which are advanced in their economic reforms, e.g. Hungary and Poland, the share of the private sector in the GDP in 1992 was 34.0 and 47.5 per cent, the Bulgarian share was the lowest among all

Central European countries. As a result, the Bulgarian private sector does not yet sufficiently respond to supply in terms of job creation, self-employment, supply and the marketing of goods, etc. The economic environment for the private sector still lacks the prerequisites to grow. Neither the much delayed privatization process, nor the external economic relations are changing the prospects for lowering inflation, for increasing demand and the opening up of new business opportunities and for improving the access of private firms to the credit markets.

Given this situation it appears important to analyze the problems of the stabilization policy and their impact on the creation of a dynamic and vital private sector which may become a future structural element of the reforms and serve as an alternative to non-efficient state enterprises. It is difficult to say how long it will take for private firms to replace the inefficient state firms. There are some vested economic interests of private firms that demonstrate why the privatization process may be delayed. So far, the state enterprises have played an important role in the start-up of some private firms, especially in the trade and services sectors. The symbiosis of some state and private firms during the period of transition has been a way of mutual survival, though allegations of spontaneous privatization have become quite common. The losses sustained by state firms have burdened them only in so far as the private firms attached to them have been able to avoid inefficient investment. As a rule this type of relation will have to be terminated either by the ongoing process of privatization or by changes envisaged in the management of state enterprises and state property.

At the end of 1992, the economic stabilization in Bulgaria has entered a critical phase. According to the Annual Report of the Bulgarian Agency for Economic Co-ordination and Development (AECD) 'the complexity of the situation is a result of the interrelation of problems which have to be solved under the condition of political uncertainty, limited choice of alternatives and unfavorable external environment' (Agency for Economic Co-ordination and Development, 1993, 1). By the end of 1993, the economic situation had not changed much and a new cycle of financial destabilization started with a sharp depreciation of the national currency (the lev), more price shocks, the introduction of a VAT system, and a sharp rise in the basic rate of interest to fight inflation.

The macroeconomic analysis of Bulgaria's transition to a market economy by an independent group of experts of the Institute of Economics (IE) of the Bulgarian Academy of Sciences and by the AECD arrived at the conclusion that, in spite of the institutionalization of private property during the past four years, the targets of the stabilization program have not been reached and that there is progress only in implementing the economic reform as a package and follow-up policies. This critique is not meant to deny the positive results. The positive achievements of the Bulgarian transition to a market economy made possible the establishment of a new economic environment and the motivation of private-sector creation. The results may be characterized by the recent economic development of:

- A diminished role of state interventionism and implementation of economic policy instruments instead of purely dirigist directives.

- Nearly all prices having been liberalized and the avoidance of hyperinflation (at least for the time being).
- The gradual emergence of a consumer market is to replace the producer market.
- The fact that enterprises and institutions are now forced to operate under stricter budget constraints.
- More opportunities for entrepreneurs in the decentralized management of the national economy.
- A growth in the creation of private firms which involves more people in the process of economic decision-making.
- Entrepreneurs in the private sector acting at market conditions without any protection whatsoever.
- Rising unemployment with hidden unemployment being transformed into an open one. This has created an environment of social and economic uncertainty and has resulted in greater motivation of labor and private initiative to start new businesses.
- The stopping of the dollarization of the economy and confidence in the national currency have become a main concern of the monetary and exchange rate policies.
- An openness of the economy which has increased on account of significant steps towards liberalization of internal and external economic relations.
- Important economic legislation (on privatization, restitution of land and other property, foreign investment, banking, tax laws, settlement of bad loans of state enterprises etc.) having been adopted (Angelov et al., 1992, 2).

The substantial discrepancies between the targets and the results of the stabilization of the Bulgarian economy have a negative impact on the creation and the functioning of the private sector. There was a continuous drop in the GDP between 1990-1993, the rate of growth at 1990 prices decreased from –9.1 per cent in 1990 to –16.7 per cent in 1992 and to –12.4 per cent in 1992. For 1993 the estimate decline is –6.2 per cent. At the present time the economy is operating at half of its capacity. The industrial and agrarian production has been reduced to the level of the mid-1970s. The public and personal consumption has been reduced considerably and by the end of 1992, 69.7 per cent of the households earned incomes at or below the social minimum level. The GDP decline at constant 1990 prices is expected to continue in 1994, although at a slackening pace: three per cent in 1994 and zero growth in 1995 (Angelov et al., 1994). Unemployment, having reached an estimated 17 per cent in 1993 in some regions and branches, is now nearly 50 per cent and keeps growing mainly due to the ongoing restructuring of the state enterprises. Still, the private sector has been on the rise, though on a moderate one. Its share in GDP will continue to grow. From 15.6 per cent in 1992, it is expected to reach 27.0 per cent in 1994, 34.0 per cent in 1995 and some 40.0 per cent in 1996. Its share will rise fastest in services and agriculture and slowest in industry. It is to be noted that these data also take into consideration the production of the cooperatives (Angelov et al., 1994, 43).

The drastic contraction in the domestic demand under the stabilization policies has caused a sharp decline in the GDP and employment. In 1992 the state budget deficit reached 11 per cent of the GDP and in 1993 it is expected to be no less than eight per cent. Interest payments for servicing the domestic debt have exceeded 28 per cent of the aggregate budget expenditures. If the expenditures for servicing the external debt of the country is added to this, the foreseeable future may see a sharp rise of such expenditures to more than 40 per cent. By the end of 1992 the external debt had reached 12.95 billion US$ and the ongoing negotiations with private creditors leave the expected expenditures for the servicing of the external debt open.

In general, further difficult adjustments in the structure of the GDP of Bulgaria are to be expected. For 1993 the only sources of foreign credit will be the international and economic institutions, although the amount of such foreign finance will hardly be large. If an agreement on the Bulgarian foreign debt up to 1995 is reached with the commercial banks, a gradual recovery in the supply of foreign credits and investments appears possible.

At this time the inflow of foreign direct investments is extremely modest, a future increase could add to the GDP used in Bulgaria and thus contribute to economic recovery. According to the official data of the Association of the Foreign Investors in Bulgaria (BIBA), the 1990-1993 foreign capital inflow in Bulgaria was 26 times less than the capital inflow for Hungary and 6 times less than that for Romania. Although the exactness of the data on foreign capital investment in Bulgaria may be disputable, it is believed that by the middle of 1993 the volume will be between 300 and 650 million US$. Adding the official credits granted to the Bulgarian government by the IMF, the EC and the World Bank, foreign financing amounts to nearly 1.1 billion US$ for the entire period since the start of the economic reform. Expectations for a foreign capital inflow have proven to be too high, and given the unfavorable external environment on the Balkans and the uncertainty of the domestic political and economic climate in Bulgaria, only a moderate rise may be foreseen for the near future.

Foreign capital investment may be important to the development of an entrepreneurial culture and a managerial experience of the small and medium-sized firms. A recent study by the Center for Democracy in Bulgaria points to a high degree of satisfaction of foreign companies working in Bulgaria in their ventures with Bulgarian private firms. This may also be indicative of the fact that, due to the lack of proper state regulation and surveillance of the economic activities, such joint ventures enjoy some advantages. Still there is a need of further improving the process of learning by doing in Bulgarian small firms by joint ventures with foreign capital.

The restrictive macroeconomic policy and the slow speed of the economic reform combined with inconsistent measures in Bulgaria have caused much criticism in the society during the past three years. Tight monetary, budgetary and income policies have created strong disequilibria and provoked social discontent. The burden of the anti-inflationary restriction was unevenly distributed among the macroeconomic instruments with the main burden being the lowering of real incomes, the raise of the interest rates and credit ceilings. This monetary policy was evaded with short-term anti-inflationary functions at the expense of function as an instrument of serving the real economy through financial intermediation and functional savings-investment support.

The restricted monetary and budgetary policies have been harmful to the bank-financing of the small and medium-sized firms and have proven be to major difficulties in the functioning of the private firms as a whole. The financial condition of still prevailing state and private firms is difficult and there is large-scale insolvency. For the state firms a government-approved package for the depreciation of bad loans was approved in September 1993. The financial instability of the private sector is still to undergo unpredictable difficulties.

This process of decapitalization in the economy and accumulation (net, in particular) was reduced to a symbolic minimum by the beginning of 1993. Due to the contraction of gross accumulation (for capital investment and, to a larger extent, for working capital growth) the ratio between final consumption and gross accumulation has changed rather unfavorably. Although, in real terms, consumption will not increase, its share may reach a maximum of about 90 per cent in 1994. It will then slowly turn downwards at the expense of accumulation, mainly for investment. An optimistic forecast might be that there could be a sharp rise in the volume and share of fixed capital formation during the next years and especially by the end of the decade.

It is no exaggeration to emphasize that during the next few years, and up to the end of the decade, both quantitative and qualitative parameters of the economy will be determined mainly by the performance of the state sector. This appears inevitable, even if privatization (not yet successfully designed) will accelerate. Large-scale privatization, however, is a complex and continuous process. More direct effects for the private sector are connected with 'small privatization' which has been under way, although to some extent delayed, in its implementation, particulary at the municipal level.

The full impact of the privatization process will presumably be experienced by the end of the decade, while the important issue still remains the marketization of state enterprises and the creation of a competitive environment in which private firms will operate. Thus, the installation of the economic, legislative and institutional prerequisites for a competitive market environment will have to face and cope with a number of problems. One of the most controversial problems during the transition is the need to adopt a new tax legislation and to completely reform the tax system. During the transition period the delay in the adoption of the tax reform is inevitably connected to a spontaneous process of accumulation and redistribution of wealth. Dubious consequences are to be expected for the private sector development.

The lack of capital, labor and goods markets in Bulgaria is another characteristic aspect of the economy. The following institutional reforms have been delayed: the restructuring and reorganization of the banking system, comprehensive reforms of the tax system and the establishment of an efficient tax administration, institutionalization of a budget auditing agency, adoption of a bankruptcy legislation, stock and commodities exchanges, etc. Delays in the systematic and institutional reforms reduce the efficiency of the monetary and fiscal policies, while the state is forced to redirect the resources saved by the elimination of subsidies, price increases and restrictive income policies to loss-making or low-profit state enterprises in order to avoid the loss of jobs and the rise of social unrest. Thus, there is a trend to continue the uneconomical reallocation of resources in favour of a number of inefficient state enterprises.

Such conditions are detrimental to the interests of the nascent private sector which is left without any support. Furthermore, it has to perform under conditions lacking fair competition because of the delay of the proper demonopolization of the domestic market.

The policies of the state still lack the proper mechanisms to promote private entrepreneurship and to secure the maintainance of competition in the market. There has been pressure and attempts to adopt special legislation for the small and medium-sized firms in Bulgaria but there is still a lot of uncertainty in terms of outcome.

Some Bulgarian experts have characterized the contemporary situation as one of uncertainty, surmising that 'the Bulgarian economic policy is wavering from one extreme to the other, from the absurd attempts at centralized planning in the greatest details to leaving the reform at the mercy of spontaneous factors, while at the same time completely ignoring the role of the state' (Ikonomika, 1993a, 15). Though drastic to some extent, such judgement is illustrated by the following opinion: 'The state does not create the appropriate conditions for the development of private business. The private initiative based on crime and speculations as well as on a spontaneous privatization is encouraged on the sly and there is a regeneration of the wild primary accumulation of capital known to have existed in Bulgaria at the end of the 19th and at the beginning of the 20th centuries' (Duma, 1993a).

The problems discussed seriously complicate the designing and implementation of a consistent state policy in favour of private entrepreneurship. The main purpose of the state policy is the implementation of the macroeconomic stabilization, but the delay in the reform and the need of a better sequencing of proper measures has diminished the chances of achieving the targets. A number of elements, mechanisms and instruments still lack the success of the reform. Under these conditions the private sector development may be considered a logical consequence of the abolishment of the monopoly of state property in the Bulgarian economy and a spontaneous reaction of the population to the processes of social-economic democratization. This is the reason why the contribution of the private sector to the economy is spontaneous.

3. Tendencies and problems in the development of the small business sector in Bulgaria from 1989-1992

The regulative framework for the creation of small private firms was passed in the beginning of 1989. This may explain why soon after the political changes in November 1989 the number of small firms increased to 13 000. Towards the end of 1990 and in 1991 this number was further increased to 54 000 and 213 000. By the end of 1992 small private firms numbered nearly 339 000 (see Figure 9.1). Nearly one half of these firms are one-man businesses. This figure is typical of the fact that nearly 10 per cent of the Bulgarian working population have registered their own private firms.

Evaluations of the share of the private sector (which in Bulgaria has been represented by small and medium-sized private firms) in the creation of the GDP differ considerably. According to the President of the Union of Private Economic Enterprises (UPEE), the share of the private sector is not higher than 4-5 per cent, whereas the experts of the AECD believe it to be nearly 50 per cent (Bulletin of the Agency for Economic Co-ordination and Development, 1993, 3). It is quite possible that this indicator is exaggerated as it contradicts the results of a number of other authoritative studies.

Figure 9.1 Number of registered small private firms in Bulgaria in 1989-92

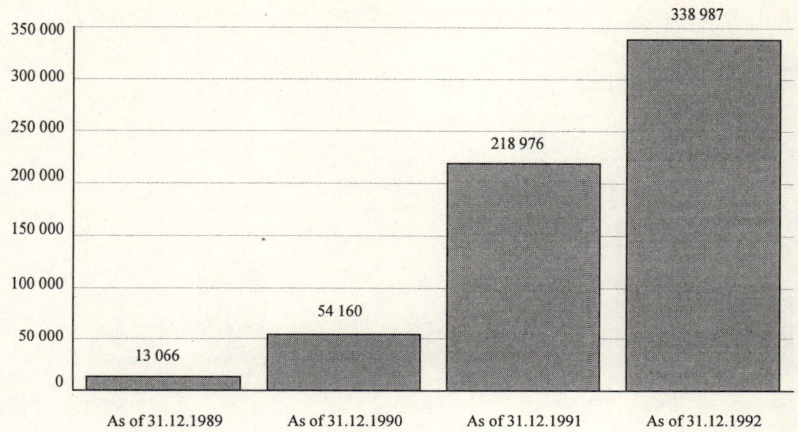

Source: Ikonomika Journal, February 1993, p. 29, National Statistics Institute.

The spheres of activities of the newly created Bulgarian small firms are similar to those in other Eastern European countries. Thus, most of the firms start their activities with trade and services since start-up capital in this sector is not so much needed (see Figure 9.2). 97 per cent of the newly created firms start with a capital of three to 15 thousand leva.[1] A comparison with the Eastern provinces of Germany shows that start-up capital here exceeds 12 000 DM. Due to the high interest rates during the past three years of reform, nearly 60 per cent of the entrepreneurs begin their activity with their own capital, 20 per cent resort to financial support from their families, and about 10 per cent rely on some form of financial support from other private firms. Only 10 per cent of the firms rely on credits drawn during their start-up period. Besides the high nominal rates of interest - which in the first half of 1993 were within the range of 50-60 per cent on an annual basis - another unfavorable impact has been exercised by the lack of programs dealing with financial support for private entrepreneurship.

Although the growth of the private sector and the appearance of new small and medium-sized firms has been a positive trend between 1990-1993, the private sector is experiencing serious credit difficulties, inadequate banking services provided to the small firms, and inflationary pressures of the economy. There has been a coincidence of the creation of risk-based new small firms, deep recession, and a crisis of state

1 The exchange rate of the lev to the DM in July-August 1993 is 16 leva for 1 DM.

enterprises. All this has caused the banks to plunge into loan activities without observing the proper criteria of lenders, which usually lower the risk of doing business with small firms by refusing credits without adequate guarantees (Houbenova-Delissivkova, 1993).

Figure 9.2 Spheres of activity of Bulgarian small private firms (in per cent)

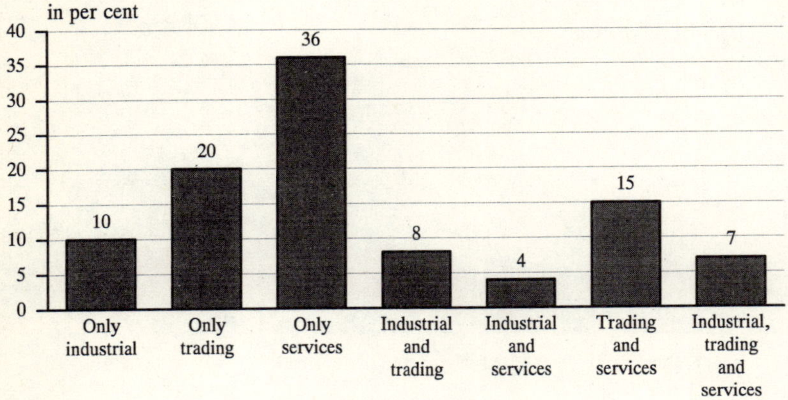

Source: Ikonomika Journal, February 1993, p. 30.

Moreover, the technological condition of the private firms is unsatisfactory. According to a recent study, hardly seven per cent of the private entrepreneurs evaluate the technologies used as 'corresponding to the average level of a given branch'. Over 50 per cent of the respondants recognized that the fixed assets in their firms are 'technologically obsolete, though still physically intact'. It becomes understandable why in recognition of the limited capital potential in newly created private firms, there is a large number of fixed assets that were bought from state enterprises or from other sources as 'second hand' acquisitions. This fact deserves special attention because the low standard of fixed assets and technology used in private firms may have negative consequences for the development of the private sector as a whole.

In most of the newly created private firms personnel does not exceed 30 persons and the great majority (93 per cent) belongs to the so-called 'microfirms', i.e. enterprises with fewer than 10 employees. Only 2.2 per cent of the private firms interviewed employ more than 30 persons (see Table 9.1).

In spite of some optimistic evaluations asserting that at present nearly 20 per cent of the population capable of working are employed in the private sector this figure is no higher than eight per cent in Bulgaria.

Some observations on and conclusions from the present state and development of the small private business sector are given in a study of a Dutch-Bulgarian team under the auspices and funding of the PHARE programme during the first half of 1992.

Table 9.1 Distribution of Bulgarian private firms according to the number of employees

Number of employees	Per cent
Sole entrepreneurs	37.2
Up to 5	44.8
6-10	11.0
Up to 10	93.0
11-15	3.1
16-25	1.3
26-30	0.4
11-30	4.8
31-50	0.9
51-75	0.5
Over 75	0.8
Over 30	2.2
Total	100.0

Source: Ikonomika Journal, February 1993, p. 30.

According to this survey, only 17 per cent of the private firms in Bulgaria are at the stage of a 'relatively high degree of development', another 19 per cent are at 'an average level', and the remaining 64 per cent are considered to be at a 'low level of development'.[2]

The troublesome conclusions on the characteristics of firms by class of development in this survey (Dutch Research Institute for Small and Medium-sized Business, 1992, Vol. A, 28-30) have been confirmed by the most recent data on the course of the economic reform in Bulgaria. There is a trend of deepening discrepancy between those firms registered and those companies truly functioning. According to the data of the National Statistical Office for July 1993, current bookkeeping comprises only 70 000 firms.

This coincides with the official opinion of the UPEE that only one fifth of all officially registered private firms in Bulgaria engages in some kind of economic activities (Ikonomika, 1993b, 30).[3] The rest of the firms have either not started doing business due to unfavorable economic conditions or have meanwhile stopped their

2 Dutch Research Institute for Small and Medium-sized Business (1992) under the PHARE programme; the authors of this paper have participated in the study on behalf of the Bulgarian part of the team.

3 According to the legislation in Bulgaria the registration of the new firms is done by the Court and the observation of the firms' activities is done by the National Statistical Office. There is a considerable disparity between the number of the registered and the really acting firms observed by the national statistics.

activities in some cases, even because of bankruptcy. For the time being the real situation in the second group of firms cannot be analyzed more accurately because in Bulgaria there is no system to monitor and controll this process.

According to another survey done by the National Statistical Office among 5 000 private entrepreneurs during the first half of 1993, almost 80 per cent of the firms interviewed are engaged in trade with every third firm intending to change the object of its activity because of difficulties due to the economic crisis. These data are indicative of the rising general instability in the national economy. This rise has been greater in 1993 compared to 1992 when the PHARE study forecasts the danger of a worsening situation for the small private firms because of the delay in institutional support. As a main reason the latest survey underlined the unfavorable economic environment. Only 16 per cent of the firms in the survey intended to increase their staff significantly. Most of the firms do not plan to make any new investments.

During the first half of 1993 a considerable rise by 60 per cent in the turnover of private commercial firms was observed, followed by the transport firms (9 per cent) and the food trading firms (7 per cent). These figures appear in comparison to the same period of 1992. The private sector producing food such as bread, milk, meat products, and beverages has been growing due to the high domestic demand and the more favorable conditions after the demonopolization of this sector of the economy.

Another feature of the development of the small private firms is this low degree of involvement in foreign capital participation. Of the current 3 600 joint ventures with foreign partners most are small and commercially specialized. The foreign capital is usually an insignificant amount. The main foreign partners in these small joint ventures are Greek, Turkish, Arabian or former USSR citizens.

The evaluation of the impact of the economic environment and of government policy on small private firms during the past three years tends to be rather negative at the microlevel. The negative assessment by the entrepreneurs of their environment is related not only to the general economic crisis but to the lack of proper government policies for small and medium-sized firms. In most cases the pessimism of the entrepreneurs leads to the prevailing opinion that not much support can be expected from any Government schemes or facilities, and that improvement of the economic environment in general lies in the future.

Such results were provided by the 1992 PHARE programme survey. They have been confirmed by a number of sociological inquiries in Bulgaria in 1993. According to a study by the Bulgarian team of Eurobarometer of Gallup International in the spring of 1993, 53 per cent of the Bulgarians are dissatisfied with the democratic development of the country, mainly because of the economic decline (BBSS Gallup International Study Eurobarometer, 1993). In another inquiry among 1 402 Bulgarians in April 1993, 78 per cent find the most serious problem of the country to be the rising crime, followed by the poor state of the national economy (73 per cent). The social fatigue becomes even more pronounced when taking into consideration that a rising number of the Bulgarians interviewed see the negative changes in the country to prevail (46 per cent of the interviewed in 1993 compared to 31 per cent in 1992) (National Sociological Survey, 1993).

An important problem for the future development of the small private sector will be the further course of the legislative and institutional reform in Bulgaria. As has been shown in the PHARE program survey, the Bulgarian entrepreneurs encounter numerous difficulties in their business environment. With regard to the general framework of economic activities the greatest problem for small private firms is the high taxation (87 per cent of the respondants) followed by unfavorable economic conditions (81 per cent), inadequate legislation and policies (78 per cent), poor infrastructure (62 per cent), bureaucratic procedures (62 per cent), lack of credits (61 per cent), high cost of social security (60 per cent), undeveloped banking system (42 per cent), and corruption in official institutions (42 per cent) (Dutch Research Institute for Small and Medium-sized Business, 1992, 46).

Corruption in the official institutions has become a rather disputed problem in 1993. As the Member of Parliament Mr. V. Vulckanov declared: 'What successes could the police, the tax administration, the customs office, etc. have against the various forms of crime if they themselves have become its conductors' (Duma, 1993b). The Vice-President of the Economic Commission of the Parliament St. Stoilov in an interview underlined the uncontrolled pressure of some economic groups and private banks on the real economy: 'This has been one of the paradoxes of our development during the past three years. The real economy declines and is in a deep depression but the banking sphere increases its profits... There is information about the degree of the secret or open privatization of a number of banks. Parliament has not dealt with this problem yet und we deserve sharp criticism from society' (Continent, 1993). According to the Governor of the Bulgarian National Bank Prof. T. Vulchev: 'A priority of our reform is the stabilization of the government and official institutions, the infrastructure and the domestic order, because businessmen as well as ordinary citizens are suffering from their weaknesses and sometimes even complete collapse' (168 Hours, 16.08.1993).

Serious constraints for business development as seen by the small private firms are connected with the maintainance of their offices and other facilities, the provision of equipment and machinery, qualified personnel and workers, raw materials, technical services, consultancy services, and distribution channels as well as the compliance with the law. The problems within the firms are ranked as follows: marketing problems (42 per cent), accounting and statistics (30 per cent), business plan (28 per cent), exporting (18 per cent), management and organization (17 per cent), production technology (16 per cent) (Dutch Research Institute for Small and Medium-sized Business, 1992, 84).

An important aspect of the small private business development is its interrelation with governmental and non-governmental institutions. Among government institutions, entrepreneurs recognize the importance of the Ministry of Finance (41 per cent), Municipality Authorities (36 per cent), the Ministry of Industry and Trade (35 per cent), Ministry of Labor (33 per cent), District Authorities (26 per cent), the National Small and Medium-sized Entreprises' Council (20 per cent), the Small and Medium-sized Enterprises' Fund of the Ministry of Industry and Trade (20 per cent) (Dutch Research Institute for Small and Medium-sized Business, 1992, 36-38).

According to the PHARE survey, the ranking of the non-governmental institutions by the private entrepreneurs is as follows, mainly depending on these institutions: Bulgarian National Bank (71 per cent), commercial banks (67 per cent), First Private

Bank (67 per cent), Bulgarian Foreign Trade Bank (59 per cent). As to the other institutions they are of a lesser significance for the small private firms with a clear trend of a diminishing role of the Bulgarian Economic Chamber, the Union of Labor Co-operatives and other former organizations which are slow to adapt to the needs of the developing private businesses. The entrepreneurs of private firms have difficulties in obtaining the necessary information and consulting services, particularly during the start-up periods. Thus the PHARE survey showed a lack of trust in such organizations as the Bulgarian Economic Chamber as well as the Union of Labor Cooperatives, the Central Cooperative Union, and a number of newly created private business associations (Dutch Research Institute for Small and Medium-sized Business, 1992, 37-38).

The private firms emphasize the need for business-support schemes and the need for subsidized or preferential credits, tax reductions and tax holidays, a need to improve banking services and to make access to risk capital possible (see Figure 9.3).

Figure 9.3 Critical private firms' attitude against institutions and infrastructure

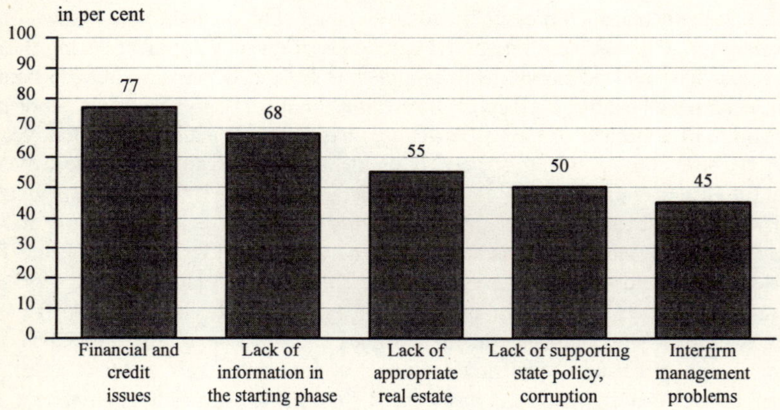

Source: Dutch Research Institute for Small and Medium-sized Business (1992), Vol. 5A, pp. 32-41.

These problems lead to the conclusion that the relations between the small business and the macroeconomic environment of the institutional infrastructure and the government policies are burdened with difficulties which constitute bottlenecks to the small private-sector development. It is obvious that so far the general economic crisis in Bulgaria at governmental level has not allowed to carry out special programs for the support of small private firm as it has been experienced in EC and West-European countries. The reasons for this are complex, they may be summarized as follows:

- The effects of the macroeconomic stabilization and its restrictive monetary policies have reduced the start-up business opportunities for small firms because of high interest rates and a lack of access to credits.

- The spontaneous privatization has stimulated the creation of small firms as a way out of the economic stagnation. Some of the new firms have made successful attempts of making use of second-hand equipment and of fixed assets of former state enterprises but this legacy of the past is the reason for a comparatively low-level technological equipment of the small private firms.
- The development of the small private firms has been dynamic in the trade and services sectors. Foreign investment and joint ventures are most active in this sphere while there still is reluctancy to take the risk of new investments in the production cooperation.

4. Conclusions

As a result of the three years of economic reform in Bulgaria two groups of economic problems in the development of the small private firms become distinguishable:

(1) Socio-economic problems typical of the East European countries in the transitional period. For the future development of the small private sector, a state of the macroeconomic environment will be decisive, the proper choice of priorities in structural adjustment policies with regard to the enterprises' adjustment in the transition period will be essential, the demonopolization, deconcentration and restructuring of the state sector and its future transformation into private sector with its close interdependence with flexible small private firms will be necessary.

To a great extent the future development of the private sector will be closely connected with the promotion of the modern entrepreneurial tradition, the development of the system for labor reorientation and qualification, promotion of communication business systems as well as the creation of business support systems for the private sector etc.

The summing up of the evaluations of the present impact of all these factors, on the small private sector development in Bulgaria, is mostly unfavorable. Concluding our analysis it can be said that the situation of the small private sector in Bulgaria is very similar to that of the private sector in East European countries other than the Central European countries. In general, the small private sector in Bulgaria is not contributing much to the economic reform.

(2) The lack of a specially designed government policy for the small private sector at the present stage is rather controversial. It is difficult to determine whether the lack of a properly designed government policy to stimulate the development of the small private firms is a real consequence of the impossibility of such a policy or whether it is merely a chance missed in providing support for a macroeconomic stabilization. In our opinion the Bulgarian case relates much more to the second option. In the future much will remain desirable for the promotion of business support systems for the private sector.

References

Agency for Economic Coordination and Development (1993) *Annual Report for 1992*, Sofia, Bulgaria.

Angelov, I., St. Dulev, Al. Dimitrov, T. Houbenova-Delissivkova and N. Gulubov (1992) *The Bulgarian Economy up to 1995*, Sofia.

Angelov, I., St. Dulev, T. Houbenova-Delissivkova, V. Yotzov and V. Konsoulov (1994); Economic Outlook of Bulgaria (1994-1996); *Bulgarian Economic Review*, April.

_______ (1993) *BBSS Gallup International Study Eurobarometer*, Spring.

_______ (1993) *Bulletin of the Agency for Economic Co-ordination and Development*; July, 3.

_______ (1993) *Continent*, 31.07.-1.08.1993.

_______ (1993a) *Duma*, 25.05.1993

_______ (1993b) *Duma*, 28.08.1993.

Dutch Research Institute for Small and Medium-sized Business (1992) *Survey of the Nascent Private Sector in Bulgaria*, 6 volumes.

Houbenova-Delissivkova, T. (1993) *Small Business and the Banks:what has gone wrong in the learning by doing process and how to improve relations*, Paper presented at the International Conference IntEnt '93, Wien, July.

_______ (1993a) *Ikonomika*, 1.

_______ (1993b) *Ikonomika*, 2.

_______ (1993) *Ikonomika Journal*, National Statistics Institute, February.

_______ (1993) *National Sociological Survey*, April.

Puchev, P. (1990); A note on the government policy and the new entrepreneurship in Bulgaria; *Small Business Economics*, 2, 73-7.

_______ (1993) *168 Hours*, 16.08.1993.

10 The nature and performance of small firms in Bulgaria

Derek C. Jones

1. Introduction

As some have noted (e.g. Acs and Audretsch, 1993) much of the debate on small firms in former socialist countries uses limited empirical data. To improve on the available data, 'stylized facts' on the nature of the three main organizational types of small Bulgarian manufacturing firms - private, state and cooperative - were assembled during the period 1989-1992. In addition some comparisons with small firms in other former socialist economies are made in this paper.

Another objective is to present *preliminary* evidence on the comparative 'performance' of small versus large firms and also on different legal forms of small enterprise. Such data are relevant to debates on the role of small firms in post-socialist economies (e.g. Clague and Rausser, 1992), including the matter of economically preferred forms of ownership.

To address these issues we will draw on new sample survey data for manufacturing firms - private, state and independent. This simultaneous gathering of enterprise data that are representative of the underlying populations of manufacturing firms, and which vary by both size and ownership, constitutes an unusual resource. In the main sections of the paper we will first describe the nature and scope of Bulgarian small firms, then make comparisons with small firms in other former socialist economies and finally consider their performance. We will continue, however, in the next section by briefly reviewing Bulgarian industrial policy on small firms.

2. Economic context and industrial policy[1]

Before discussing key legislation on small firms, we will briefly note some important features of the Bulgarian economy since the late 1980s, i.e. since discussion of the need for small firms (often as part of a strategy of 'privatization') first seems to have begun.[2] First, unlike Poland and even the former GDR and Hungary, there was no private sector to speak of in Bulgaria during the communist era. The starting point on the road to restructuring was one where almost all of the economy was state-owned and where even in 1988, the year prior to the political revolution, there were probably no private firms

1 This section draws heavily on Jones and Rock (1994).

2 However, we do not systematically examine the slew of other micro and macro policies designed at least in part to encourage market-type behavior. For discussion of 'marketization' including attempts to restructure management (and stabilization) see World Bank (1991) and Wyzan (1993).

at all in Bulgarian manufacturing. Also, the cooperative sector (which was part of the socialized sector) was quite small compared to countries such as Poland; this was especially the case in the industrial sector. In turn this predominant type of industrial organization led to fantastic economic concentration; giantism without small firms was the order of the day (Jones and Meurs, 1991; Jones and Parvulov, 1992).

Second, the beginnings of the transitional process in general were marked by an economic context that was extraordinarily unfavorable, even when compared to many other Eastern and Central European economies. This is the case on matters such as: the level of external debt; the enormous dependence on CMEA markets; and severity of the disruption to trade and loss of markets because of the recent conflicts in the Balkan and Middle East region.[3]

Until the replacement of the dictator, Zhivkov, after a bloodless coup in November 1989, there were some modest innovations in industrial policy towards small firms. Under the communists, several initiatives (mainly Decree 12 and 33) were introduced and supportive institutions were established (notably the Bulgarian Industrial Association) to foster the development of new firms within the state-owned sector (Puchev, 1990). However, in practice only a minority of these small firms were autonomous and in the aggregate these firms barely affected the existing size distribution of firms and the prevailing mode of giantism (Jones and Meurs, 1991, 320-3).

Potentially a more important change was the introduction of Decree 56 in January 1989. This new commercial code led to the entry of new private enterprises and by the end of February 1990 more than 14 000 (of a total of 15 500) registered firms were private firms. However, few of these enterprises actually operated, and those that did typically were quite tiny.

The political revolution of November 1989 was followed by the rapid emergence of political pluralism, much of which coalesced into the United Democratic Front (UDF). However, it was the Bulgarian Socialist Party (the BSP, formerly the communists) that received a mandate in the first free elections in June 1990. For much of this period small firms emerged in an uncoordinated way - as *ad hoc* privatizations. This 'wild', 'quiet' or 'spontaneous privatization' involved the sale of portions of state-owned assets at their listed book value. Due to accounting practices under the previous system, in many cases these values had little relationship to any probable market valuation. This period of privatization has been condemned by some as one of self-serving and scandalous grand theft on the part of managers and communist party members. However, the scale of these privatizations is not clear since no data appear to exist.

After the fall of the Socialist government subsequently a coalition caretaker government headed by the UDF under Dimiter Popov emerged. As a result this period was also characterized by political deadlock and no such legislative activity in fact took

3 Representatives of all parties acknowledged the need for 'restructuring', of which 'privatization' was a part, because of a rapidly deteriorating economy since the mid 1980s. For elaboration of the economic conditions when privatization began see World Bank (1991).

place.[4] In particular, the Popov government failed to enact a comprehensive privatization law.

One hallmark of this period was the so-called small privatization of mostly service and retail units. This began at the end of 1990 after the new more liberal ministers took office in December. Several small auctions (both open bid and solicited tenders) occurred on an irregular schedule. However, the small privatization program in fact led to very little transfer of ownership and little raising of revenue, with property sales including a few gas stations (Jones and Rock, 1994).[5]

Following new elections in November 1991 for the first time a non-socialist party alone formed the government. For most of 1992 it was the UDF, led by Prime Minister Filip Dimitrov, that was in the driving seat. However, since the balance of power was held by the party that represents the ethnic Turks, the position was often tenuous, and it proved difficult to introduce or even effectively implement new laws. Unsurprisingly the situation proved to be unstable and in November 1992 the UDF government fell. This latest political stalemate was resolved with the emergence of a new coalition government (in January 1993) under the leadership of Lyuben Berov.

During this period the focus clearly shifted to the privatization of large-scale firms. However, there was also evidence of renewed interest in government support for small firms. Perhaps the best example, following the passage of Decree 108 of June 1991, was the introduction of a fund to help to provide diverse forms of assistance to small firms (Bartlett, 1993, 17) in September 1991. The growth of various institutional support agencies, such as the Union of Private Economic Enterprises (UPEE), was also evident during this period.

But the major change was the introduction of the new policy on competition in late 1990. Major structural changes began as some horizontally organized firms in the food industry were split and their regional subsidiaries given economic and legal independence. In March 1991 a large scale de-monopolization process was initiated. This break-up of many state monopolies would naturally be expected to lead to major changes in the size distribution of Bulgarian firms (Jones and Parvulov, 1992).

3. The scope and nature of the Bulgarian small firm sector

3.1 Changing scope of the small firm sector: 1985-1992

The upshot of all of the foregoing is that, in all probability, the small firm sector has continued to grow during this period, though the rate of increase has varied, especially for different legal forms of enterprise. For private firms there have been continuing

---

4 However, a major stabilization program was introduced. Policies included: price liberalization; deciding to let the leva float; wage controls; and a tightening of macro fiscal and monetary policy. For more discussion and evaluation of the success of these policies see Wyzan (1993).

5 Also during this period the slow process of restitution of land to former owners was begun. For accounts see Jones and Rock (1994) and Bogetic and Wilton (1992).

large increases in the number of new firm registrations: by the end of 1990 there were 69 000 firms and this number had grown (according to differing estimates) to between 130 000 and 180 000 by the end of 1991. By February 1992 there were about 200 000 new firms registered; by mid 1993 about another 10 000 had been added. Hence, it appears that the growth rate in the number of new private firms has been falling. As far as industrial distribution is concerned, data obtained from the Union of Private Economic Enterprises (reported in Bartlett, 1993) indicates that 25 per cent of the new private businesses are in manufacturing, 24 per cent in services, 17 per cent in construction and 15 per cent in trade.

At the same time, the absence of any reliable and comprehensive system of gathering information means that it is impossible to obtain reliable data on even basic indicators for small Bulgarian firms such as mean/median sales or employment.[6] It seems, however, that the size distribution of new private Bulgarian firms is heavily skewed towards the very small. Thus, data provided by the Central Statistical Institute indicate that throughout Bulgaria in the middle of 1992 there were only 130 private sector *manufacturing* firms with 10 or more permanent employees. Data such as these strongly suggest that the impression of small firm economic activity revealed by crude registration data is probably exaggerated. Equally, the official data do not catch informal/ underground economic activity. In these circumstances it is not surprising that estimates of the size of the *overall* private sector and its economic significance range widely. While the official estimates vary from 5-7 per cent of GDP, claims have been made that the private sector accounts for up to 37 per cent of the overall economic activity, with more than 50 per cent in some sectors such as retailing.[7]

For firms that originate in the state-owned sector, official data indicate the general trends in the distribution both of legal forms of enterprise and their size. Thus, the most recent population data (e.g. Jones and Parvulov, 1992; Parvulov, 1991) show an abrupt reversal in the growth of giantism. However, these data are limited since they give no clear indications of whether firms are independent (particularly important for some cooperatives) or whether firms have attained a joint stock status. Also, reflecting problems with the central gathering of data during times of transition and of fiscal crisis, they tend to be rather outdated.

Consequently, during such turbulent times, survey data may be more current and also enable one to more reliably and finely determine the main trends in ownership and size. The results of such a panel survey[8] for manufacturing firms beginning as SOEs, that was representative of employment in such enterprises in the principal urban areas from 1988-1992, are shown in Table 10.1.

6 Estimates by the Union of Private Economic Enterprises suggest that the average firm employs fewer than four people with the highest average (of 7.6) in construction. However, these estimates do not appear to be based on reliable sampling methods. By using a sample that is nationally representative, Anachkova et al. (1992) estimate that in 1990 the average size of a new firm was about 3.

7 For example see AECD (1993).

8 See the Appendix for details of the sampling method.

In 1988, 92.1 per cent of manufacturing firms were state-owned. By 1990 this number had slightly fallen to 89.7 per cent with further declines in 1991 to 80 per cent and in 1992 to 76 per cent. The same table indicates that during the same period the percentage of joint stock companies in which the state had a significant (often a 100 per cent) ownership position increased steadily from 1.4 per cent in 1988 to 12.7 per cent in 1992.

Table 10.1 Property forms in large manufacturing sample (per cent)

Property Form	1988	1989	1990	1991	1992
State	92.1	90.5	89.0	80.0	76.0
State-joint stock	1.4	1.6	1.6	10.3	12.7
(Independent) Cooperative	5.7	6.9	7.3	7.9	8.5
Private		0.2	0.4	0.8	1.8
Other	0.8	0.8	1.0	1.0	1.0

Notes: 'State' refers to organizations that are controlled by central bodies. In some cases ownership is municipal, in other cases cooperative. Private includes limited and unlimited liability legal forms.

Source: The sample of 495 firms is drawn from the Bulgarian Management Survey. (For a description, see the Appendix and Jones, 1993.)

Even as early as 1988, there were enterprises in which respondents reported that they were independent cooperatives. These enterprises accounted for 5.7 per cent of the sample in 1988 and registered a significant growth to 8.5 per cent of the sample by 1992. But fully fledged private firms were always a rarity in those manufacturing firms that were once state-owned; even by 1992 they represented only 1.8 per cent of the sample.

In terms of the size distribution of small firms the sample data show that in 1991 36.4 per cent of manufacturing state firms employed fewer than 250 workers. Fewer than 16 per cent had 1 000 or more workers. This represents an extraordinary turnaround from the situation prevailing as recently as 1989 when: only 15.9 per cent of state manufacturing enterprises had 500 or fewer employees; only 4.9 per cent of firms employed 200 or fewer workers (Jones and Parvulov, 1992, table 2); and 66.6 per cent of all state manufacturing firms had 1 000 or more workers (with 21.8 per cent having 5 000 or more). Similar processes were apparently underway amongst firms designated as cooperatives. Thus, in 1991 60 per cent of sample firms employed fewer than 250 workers and only 13 per cent had 1 000 or more employees. In other words, the growth of the small firms sector *in general* has been remarkably rapid.

3.2 The nature of small manufacturing firms

In this chapter we will report preliminary results from our attempt to develop an improved portrait of small Bulgarian manufacturing firms. Since at least outside of the private sector there have been so few tiny manufacturing firms and also because firms of all sizes typically have been contracting employment since late 1990, we consider all firms with, on average, fewer than 250 employees during 1991 as 'small'. Our sample survey data (described in the Appendix) has been compiled for 105 private manufacturing firms, 123 small state firms and 23 small independent cooperatives.

3.2.1 Private firms

Reflecting the novelty of Bulgarian private enterprise in 1992, unsurprisingly a large number of firms (83 per cent) had been in existence for fewer than two years; in fact, in the middle of 1992 the average private firm was 16 months old. Essentially all firms had been independent organizations since December 1991 and typically there was no state participation in ownership. Nearly all private firms (97.1 per cent) began from scratch (rather than as spin-offs from large state-owned firms.) Of the various possible legal forms of private ownership,[9] about 47 per cent of the sample were headed by a single owner with a similar proportion (48 per cent) representing partnerships. Relatively few (five per cent) firms had adopted the legal form of limited liability.

Different measures are used to present information on the average size of private sector manufacturing firms in 1991 and also in the first half of 1992. For the entire year 1991 the average private manufacturing firm sold goods worth 1 245 million leva (roughly 50 000 US$) and produced goods worth about the same amount (in fact, 1 278 million leva).[10] At the end of 1991 average employment was a roughly over 20 workers. Unsurprisingly the bulk of the sample, in fact 94.3 per cent of firms, employed 50 or fewer workers at the end of 1991. Large private manufacturing firms were extraordinary - only one firm employed more than 250 workers. Average profits amounted to about 125 000 leva. In 1992, by annualizing data for the first half of 1992, sales were now 871 000 leva, output 844 000 leva and profits 128 000 leva. In mid 1992, average fixed assets stood at 368 000 leva (about 15 000 US$). Almost four in ten small firm entrepreneurs expected to increase employment during the period June 1992-June 1993; only 14 per cent anticipated the need to make job cuts.

In 1992 on average 87 per cent of a firm's fixed assets were owned by the firm, with 10 per cent leased and only one per cent rented. By far the biggest source of capital were owners' savings, which typically accounted for 60 per cent of the total. On average bank credit amounted to 25 per cent of capital supply. The average level of capacity utilization in the middle of 1991 was reported to be 73 per cent. A year later this was

9 According to the commercial code of May 1991 'private' firms may assume diverse legal forms. These include various forms of partnership (differing according to the number of partners and authorized capital) as well as companies with either unlimited or limited liability.

10 Substantial differences exist in these figures according to legal form. Typically, values for firms that have 'limited liability' are much higher.

essentially unchanged. Also in June 1992, a surprising number of firms - almost one third - reported that they could produce current levels of output with fewer workers. Furthermore, these firms reported that overmanning was quite extensive and averaged almost 23 per cent of the workforce. Since there do not seem to be any legal or institutional constraints preventing private employers from releasing workers the explanation for this behavior must lie elsewhere.

Turning to sources of inputs, the situation for private firms was very different from that for capital supplies. There was an overwhelming dependence on state-owned firms for supplies of raw materials for use in the manufacturing of product. As far as the destination of products was concerned the bulk of output was sold in domestic markets; on average exports accounted for only three per cent of sales although this value did increase a little in 1992 compared to 1991. While bartering of a final product was not unknown it was typically unimportant. Information on the importance of the principal customers of private sector small firm manufacturers was also gathered. This shows that there was considerable dispersion in the dependence on the top three customers. In more than one in four cases the top three buyers accounted for more than 75 per cent of sales, suggesting a continuation of the strong vertical links that characterized the old command economy arrangements. But in more than a third of the cases, the top three customers bought less than one quarter of sales.

Turning to the extent of product market concentration, 14 per cent of respondents believed that they had a complete monopoly in the product market. However, the norm was one where producers perceived the existence of strong competition. Indeed almost 44 per cent of firms believed that they faced competition from at least 50 other producers. As far as the range of products is concerned, 45 per cent of respondents indicated that they had increased the range during the previous year. Only 10 per cent had decreased the product range while the balance had not changed matters. While 40 per cent of respondents said that they set prices as a mark up on production costs, 20 per cent indicated that their prices were set in the marketplace; the balance reported that they used a combination of these methods.

During the year preceding the survey, while 39 per cent of respondents had increased their labor force, only 16 per cent employed fewer workers. As such the typical employment dynamic was very different than in large state sector manufacturing firms which typically reduced employment by an average of 31 per cent in the preceding year (Standing et al., 1993).

On average, at the end of 1991, the labor force was structured as follows: 44 per cent of a private sector manufacturing firm's employment was female, less than a fifth were under 25 years old and almost a quarter were over 54 years of age.

As far as payment systems are concerned, the most preferred form of compensation in private manufacturing was the usage of piece rates (53 per cent) while time rates were used by 38 per cent of respondents, and other systems of payment in remaining firms. About one in ten firms reported using a profit sharing system. Typically the payment of non-monetary benefits (e.g. food, consumer goods) was unimportant in small Bulgarian private firms, and amounted to an average of 3.85 per cent of production worker earnings. The average worker received earnings of more than 2100 leva - about 89 US$ a month.

More than 77 per cent of respondents reported hiring workers on civil contracts during the preceding year.[11] Skilled workers were most apt (in 54 per cent of cases) to be hired using such contracts; non-managerial specialists were the second group most likely to be hired under such an arrangement. However, respondents reported that while in four of ten cases workers on civil contracts were unlikely to receive different pay than were employees on labor contracts, in more than three in ten cases, civil contract workers were likely to receive better pay, and in only 16 per cent of all cases was the pay apt to be less.

Representation of employees by trade unions was essentially absent in the private sector. The existence of unions was reported in only five per cent of cases. In all cases the trade union was CITUB, the union that succeeded the old 'official' unions (Jones, 1992). In firms where unions existed, on average, about seven per cent of the workforce were members of CITUB.

Nearly all respondents replied that they operated only one shift and that this has not changed recently. More than half of the respondents (58 per cent) indicated that their current operations required a greater degree of technical knowledge than had been the case a year ago. Fewer than two per cent believed that there had been a decrease in technical complexity; in the bulk of the remaining cases matters had not changed. Consistent with these responses, 31 per cent of respondents reported that they had introduced new technology during the last two years.

3.2.2 Small state firms

Despite the novelty of smallness in the state sector, only a small number of small firms (3.3 per cent) had been in existence for fewer than two years in 1992. In fact the average small state firm was 27 months old. What basically seems to be happening is that, while all firms had begun as (parts of) state firms being part of the centrally administered system, in 1992 all sample firms viewed themselves as operating autonomously - they were all spin-offs from large state-owned firms.

In 1991 the average small state firm had annual sales of 13 274 million leva (about 530 000 US$), fixed assets of 4 794 million leva (about 190 000 US$), and a labor force that averaged 182 workers during the year though had fallen to 153 by the end of the year. Among all state firms, only 4.9 per cent employed fewer than 50 workers. Reflecting their sense of being independent entities, 72 per cent of small state manufacturers responded that their main source of capital was internal. Only 8.2 per cent of firms listed allocations from the government as the main source of capital, with 16 per cent replying that the local bank played the key role. Assets were leased by fewer than two per cent of the small state firms.

In the middle of 1991 the average level of capacity utilization was reported to be 66.5 per cent; a year later the level had fallen to 63.3 per cent. Also in June 1992, almost two thirds of firms reported that they could produce current levels of output with fewer

11 Reflecting the uneven nature of the available data, not all measures are available for all enterprise types/size classes.

workers. Furthermore, these firms reported that the average level of overmanning was almost 21 per cent.

Turning to sources of inputs, the bulk (70 per cent) of small state firms obtained their main raw materials by paying cash locally (rather, for example, than from allocations by the government [6.4 per cent]). As far as final products are concerned, the bulk of output was destined for sale in domestic markets; on average, exports accounted for only three per cent of sales though this number did increase a little in 1992. Considering information on product markets for several size classes of state firms (large and small), it is apparent that the smallest firms are least export-oriented. Thus, whereas the exports of firms with fewer than 50 employees accounted for about 2.75 per cent of output, for firms with 251-500 employees the corresponding figure is 18.8 per cent and for firms with more than 1 000 employees it is 35.8 per cent. That small state-owned manufacturing firms principally play the role of filling domestic niches for their larger state fellows is also indicated by the typical tendency of smaller firms to engage in the bartering of output. About ten per cent of small state firms believed that they had no serious competitor for their principal product. At the same time almost 16 per cent of firms believed that they faced competition from 50 or more firms and another 42 per cent of the sample perceived that they faced from 11-50 competitors.

As far as price setting is concerned, however, in 63 per cent of all cases small firms still see the government as playing the key role. Only about a third of the time did small state firms see that they set prices alone. Interestingly, the sample was more or less equally divided on the question of changes in the range of products during the preceding two years. Whereas 32 per cent responded that they had increased their product range, 29 per cent said that their number of products had fallen and 37 per cent reported 'no change'.

Almost 93 per cent of small state firms reported that they had decreased their labor forces during the period from January 1990 to December 1991; only 4.1 per cent reported that they were employing more workers during this period. For the average small firm, the labor force fell by more than 16 per cent. As to the structure of the labor force, at the end of 1991, on average 45 per cent of a small state-sector manufacturing firm's employment was female, about 11 per cent was under 25 years old and almost eight per cent was over 54 years of age. Workers in the smallest state firms (with fewer than 50 workers) were the best paid of all state sector workers. On average they received 2 030 leva per month and there does not seem to be an obvious sectoral explanation for this phenomenon. This compared with 1 260 leva for workers in firms with 51-100 employees, and 1 440 leva in firms with 101-250 employees. The most preferred form of compensation in state manufacturing firms was the implementation of piece rates (57 per cent) while time rates of various kinds were used by about 39 per cent of respondents and other systems of payment in remaining firms. Approximately one in five small state firms reported using a profit sharing system.

More than 68 per cent of respondents reported hiring workers on civil contracts during the preceding year. Skilled workers were most apt to be hired using such contracts. Representation of employees by trade unions was very strong in small state firms -averaging 83 per cent in firms with fewer than 50 workers and 73 per cent in other firms with fewer than 2 509 employees. While in most cases the preferred trade union was CITUB, the union that succeeded the old 'official' unions, the new union Podkrepa, was also present. Nearly all respondents replied that they operated only one shift and that this has not changed recently. A little over half of respondents (50.4 per cent) reported that they had introduced new technology during the last two years.

As for the immediate outlook for small state firms (at the end of 1991), most firms (46 per cent) expected no change in employment during 1992. While 22 per cent anticipated the need to make further job cuts, 29 per cent expected to increase their labor forces.

3.2.3 Small cooperatives

As in the state sector, until recently smallness has been quite scarce in the cooperative sector (Jones and Meurs, 1991). However, despite the novelty of smallness in the cooperative sector, surprisingly in 1992 only 4.3 per cent of firms reported that they had been in existence for fewer than two years. The average small cooperative in manufacturing was 32 months old. As in the state sector what seems to have been happening is that small cooperatives were beginning to appear as spin-offs from the previous large and state-controlled cooperatives.

In 1991 the average small cooperative firm had annual sales of 7 676 million leva (about 300 000 US$), fixed assets of 1 954 million leva (about 75 000 US$) and a labor force that averaged 169 workers during the year, though had fallen to 147 by the end of the year. Among all cooperatives in the sample, only 8.7 per cent had a labor force with 50 or fewer workers.

Reflecting their sense of being independent entities, 87 per cent of small cooperative manufacturers responded that their main source of capital was internal. No firms listed allocations from the government as the main source of capital, with 9 per cent replying that the local bank played the key role. Assets were leased by no small cooperatives.

In the middle of 1991 the average level of capacity utilization was reported to be 75 per cent; a year later the level had fallen to 72 per cent. Also in June 1992, almost 70 per cent of small cooperatives reported that they could produce current levels of output with fewer workers. Furthermore, these firms reported that the average level of overmanning was almost 22 per cent.

Turning to sources of inputs, the bulk (81 per cent) of small cooperatives obtained their main raw materials by paying cash locally. Not a single small cooperative stated that its principal sources of raw materials were allocations by the government.

As far as the destination of products was concerned the bulk of small cooperatives' output ended up being sold in domestic markets; on average exports accounted for only 4.2 per cent of sales though this did increase a little in 1992 compared to 1991. When it comes to price setting, in 56 per cent of all cases small cooperatives still see the government as playing a key negotiating role; by comparison, almost 40 per cent of respondents reported that they set prices alone. On the question of changes in the range of products during the preceding two years, only 24 per cent responded that they had increased their product range. This contrasts with 48 per cent who said that their number of products had fallen, while 29 per cent reported that there had been no changes.

While 78 per cent of small cooperatives reported that they had decreased their labor forces during the period from January 1990 to December 1991, 13 per cent reported that they were employing more workers (with the balance indicating that matters were unchanged). For the average small firm, the labor force fell by about 13 per cent. As far as the structure of the labor force is concerned, at the end of 1991, on average 44 per cent of a small state sector manufacturing firm's employment was female, about 11 per cent was under 25 years old and almost 9 per cent was over 54 years of age.

Workers in smaller cooperatives were paid much better on average than were workers in larger cooperatives. On average workers in firms with fewer than 50 employees received 1 160 leva per month while those in the 101-250 size class earned 1 320 leva on average. These sums were compared to the average of 840 leva per month for workers in firms with 250-1 000 employees and 960 for employees in firms with more than 1 000 workers. In terms of preferred forms of compensation in small cooperatives, sample firms were evenly divided between piece and time rates. About four in ten firms reported using a profit sharing system. Almost 61 per cent of respondents hired workers on civil contracts during the preceding year. Skilled workers were most likely to be engaged under such contracts. Representation of employees by trade unions was quite strong in small cooperatives - averaging 55 per cent in firms with fewer than 100 workers and 70 per cent in other firms with fewer than 250 employees. While in most cases the preferred trade union was CITUB the new union Podkrepa, was also present.

Nearly all respondents replied that they operated only one shift and that this has not changed recently. Only 27 per cent of small cooperatives reported that they had introduced new technology during the last two years.

At the end of 1991, consistent with their reports concerning overmanning, many small cooperatives expected that the process of shedding labor still had ways to go. In fact 40 per cent of firms anticipated that more jobs would be lost. But, surprisingly, even more firms (44 per cent) expected no change in employment during 1992. The remainder (17 per cent) expected an increase in labor forces.

3.3 Comparisons by size and ownership

By drawing on the foregoing we will summarize some of the similarities and differences between small Bulgarian firms with different forms of ownership (see Table 10.2). We will also make use of the available data to draw comparisons between the average small firm and its large counterpart. When such comparisons are made, the principal observations are as follows.

Major differences exist concerning employment dynamics by both size and ownership. Nearly all large (state and cooperative) firms cut their workforce during 1991 - on average by 31 per cent (Standing et al., 1993). By comparison, fewer small cooperatives cut jobs - only about three in four - and small state and cooperative firms shed workers at about half the rate in large firms. Even more striking is the fact that only 16 per cent of private firms cut employment and that the average small private sector firm *added* workers during 1991. Also, a greater fraction of private firms expected to have to add workers when compared with small state and cooperative firms. The average small private firm is considerably smaller than its cooperative or state counterpart. Relative to a state firm, a small private firm sells one tenth as much, has a capital stock that is 1/13 as large and a labor force that is 1/10 as big.

Table 10.2 Descriptive statistics: Bulgarian small firms: 1991

	Private	State	Cooperative
Average sales (thousand US$)	50	530	300
Average employment (mid 91)	16	182	169
Average employment (end 91)	20	153	147
per cent firms fewer 50 employees	94	5	9
per cent firms raising employment	39	4	13
per cent firms reducing employment	16	93	78
Women in workforce (per cent)	44	45	44
Workforce < 25 years old (per cent)	< 20	11	11
Overmanning (per cent firms)	23	21	23
Average wage (leva per month)	2 100	1 600	1 250
Profit sharing (per cent firms)	10	20	40
Degree of unionization	5	75	65
Average age small firm (months)	16	27	32
No competitors (per cent sample)	14	10	n.a.
> 50 competitors (per cent sample)	44	16	n.a.
Average capacity utilization (per cent)	73	67	72
Exports (per cent sales)	4	3	4

Source: Surveys of private, state and cooperative manufacturing firms (see Appendix).

Small private firms are overwhelmingly internally financed by owners' savings. But both small state and small cooperatives as well as large state and large cooperatives rely on internally generated funds. In only 11 per cent of the large state firms were allocations by the government the main source of capital. At the same time private sector firms are much more likely to use bank loans than other small and large firms. Neither leasing nor foreign private capital was of any significance on average for any small or large Bulgarian firm.

In a number of respects all small and large firms were surprisingly similar. Thus, all forms of small and large firms claimed similar levels of capacity utilization (63-72 per cent) and similar levels of overmanning (about 20 per cent). The proportion of women in the labor force was basically similar in all forms of small and large firm as was the use of piece rates and civil contracts. Levels of perceived competition were surprisingly similar in all forms of enterprise. However, sometimes there were differences with some large firms. Thus, while no type of small firm was primarily export oriented, the average large state firm exported more than 17 per cent of its output, i.e., more than twice the amount for small state firms.

Private sector firms had labor forces that contained greater proportions of both younger and older workers than did state or cooperative firms, both large and small. Profit sharing was a form of compensation that was four times as likely to be preferred by cooperatives (large and small) as private sector firms and twice as likely as in small and large state firms.

Since the average wage in large firms with above 1 000 employees was 1 740 leva per month, workers in very small state firms were better paid (2 030 leva per month) though employees in large firms did earn more than workers in small firms with 50-250 workers. In large cooperatives the average worker earned 960 leva, significantly less than employees in smaller ones. However, on average, best paid workers were in the private sector, although there is some evidence that they did not receive benefits comparable to those earned by workers in the state and cooperative sectors.

It was no surprise to find that trade union density was much higher in both small state firms and in small cooperatives compared to small private firms where very few workers were union members. However, trade union membership was much more prevalent in both small state and small cooperative firms than in large state firms and in large cooperatives. Unlike patterns observed in Western countries, member commitment to the new trade unions in Bulgaria is clearly strongest in smaller firms.

Probably these differences may be explained by in the varying origins of the firms, in particular by the fact that private manufacturing almost always began *de novo* and that private firms are much newer - for example typically 50 per cent younger than a small cooperative.

4. Comparisons with other former socialist economies

When drawing comparisons of the size and composition of Bulgarian small firms and small firms in other former socialist economies, we note that the available data for other countries are particularly rich for features of small *private* firms (e.g. Webster, 1992a and b; Swanson and Webster, 1992; Charup and Webster, 1993). However, in such comparisons it must be remembered that such an exercise is fraught with unusual difficulties - there are, for example, enormous problems in the precise definitions and measures of key variables. Also, differences in the nature of the private sector across countries reflects variation in the pace of privatization policies. At the same time, if a comparative exercise reveals major differences, conceivably these may persist across countries even after the extent of privatization becomes more uniform.

Table 10.3 summarizes some of the principal features of the average small private firm in several former socialist countries for which 1991 data are available. Compared to small firms in Hungary, former Czechoslovakia, Poland and St. Petersburg, from the standpoint of the size of the average workforce, the average Bulgarian private firm is always considerably smaller - by at least a third.[12]

12 The very high rates of union membership in small state firms and in small cooperative firms also suggest that, as such firms privatize, membership levels in small private firms in the future may increase.

Table 10.3 Comparisons of small firms in different post-socialist economies

	Bulgaria	Czechoslovakia	Poland	Hungary	St. Petersburg
Average monthly sales (thousands US$)	4.2	26	47	109.4	4.8
Average labor force	20	42	32	44	74
Firms <50 employee (per cent)	94	80	90	78	n.a.
Main source start-up capital = own/family savings (per cent)	60			52	67
Value of equipment (US$ thousands)		244.5	132.3	320.5	
Women in labor force (per cent)	44	57	53		42
Average wage (monthly, US$)	89	151	155	207	13 (unskilled) 30 (skilled)
Average cost of labor (monthly, US$)			297	303	31.3
Union density (per cent)	5	0	0	<5	n.a.
State firms as primary source of inputs (per cent)	>90	80	71	74	77
0 competitors (per cent)	14				33
>50 competitors	44	20	42	n.a.	<20
Value of exports (per cent)	4	33	17	36	3
Average age of firm (months)	16			75 per cent>36	22

Source: For Czechoslovakia: Swanson and Webster (1992); Poland: Webster (1992a); Hungary: Webster (1992b); St. Petersburg: Charup and Webster (1993); for Bulgaria: the author's survey.

Also the size dispersion of the population is different. Whereas very few Bulgarian manufacturing private firms employ more than 50 people, in Hungary and former Czechoslovakia, one in five private firms has more than 50 workers. An even larger difference exists in average sales, except when compared with private firms in St. Petersburg.

There are important differences between Bulgarian private firms and other private firms in terms of origins, product and capital markets. Compared to small firms elsewhere (including St. Petersburg) an unusually large proportion of Bulgarian small private firms began as independent start-ups. Bulgarian private firms are typically much newer than private sector firms elsewhere. From the standpoint of input supplies, Bulgarian small private manufacturing firms are unusually dependent on state firms. While many of the private Bulgarian firms regard themselves as pure monopolists, the bulk perceive that they face an environment that is unusually competitive compared to firms in nascent private sectors elsewhere. Finally, and importantly, as Bulgarian private firms export a tiny fraction of their production (four per cent) they differ greatly from firms in Hungary, Poland and the former Czechoslovakia.

There are also interesting differences concerning the nature of labor markets and associated institutions. Relative to other small firms in former socialist economies (except St. Petersburg), Bulgarian small firms pay poorly - at least 40 per cent less (though the pay differential with bigger firms is not necessarily very big). While trade union membership is quite low (about five per cent) this is qualitatively different than the typical situation elsewhere.[13] Also, it appears that the structure of the labor forces differ. (Note the smaller fraction of the female labor force in Bulgaria.) Finally there is the suggestion that the nature of the typical compensation system may vary, with profit sharing being more prevalent in Bulgaria than in other small private firms.

5. The performance of small firms

For diverse reasons, including weak or perverse incentives for managers and absence of competitive pressures, the conventional wisdom is that large firms in the former centrally administered economies are technically inefficient. The corollary is that small firms would be expected to be relatively more efficient than large firms and that, therefore, diverse measures should be taken to foster the spread of small firms. Another important issue concerns the appropriate forms of ownership for these new small firms. While some seem to argue that only small *private* firms will have the desired efficiency advantages, others argue that small firms that are not private may also be potentially efficient and hence argue for a policy that encourages a broader range of forms of ownership (e.g. Estrin, 1991; Murrell, 1991).

For the most part, empirical evidence for Bulgarian firms on these issues is lacking. An exception is Parvulov (1991) who, by using several partial productivity indicators, finds that small and medium firms outperformed larger firms in 1988-89. However these exercises could only be undertaken for state firms and since then there have been significant changes in the economic context. Hence, to provide additional evidence that

13 This is especially striking when it is noted that, whereas the Bulgarian sample is for the largest private firms, in the studies by Webster and her colleagues, the samples are representative of all size classes and do not even exclude tiny firms. Equally, however, whereas the Bulgarian private sector did not contain any firms that formerly had different forms of ownership (e.g. cooperatives) this is not the case elsewhere, especially in the Northern tier trio.

bears on these issues, we extended the approach adopted by Parvulov. We used partial productivity indicators to see whether or not there were differences in performance, on average, for small firms compared to large firms and, within a given size class, for different legal forms. In Table 10.4 we present such information where performance is measured by: sales per worker; value added per worker; sales per unit of fixed assets; value added per unit of fixed assets and costs per unit of sales. In addition we computed the capital-labor ratio. The means are presented for the three main types of ownership and for different size categories.[14]

Table 10.4 Performance indicators by size and ownership

	Private	State					Cooperative		
		<50	51-100	101-250	251-1 000	> 1 000	50-250	251-1 000	> 1 000
Sales per worker	54.5	111.8	65.3	76.9	142.1	141.0	46.9	22.4	28.9
Sales per unit fixed assets	38.8	11.8	7.3	4.0	4.6	3.8	19.6	4.6	4.7
Value added per worker		57.9	20.5	–49.8	46.1	25.0	20.8	20.4	18.9
Value added per unit of fixed assets		8.3	6.1	–3.3	1.7	1.1	14.7	3.4	2.6
Capital labor ratio	15.3	82.9	27.9	25.4	69.9	50.5	12.7	5.8	41.2
N	66	6	21	96	162	53	23	12	5

Notes: All values are in thousands of leva. In 1991 the exchange rate was about 25 to 27 leva per US$.

For state firms, these data show that capital productivity (sales per unit of fixed assets; value added per unit of fixed assets) was higher for the smallest firms (below 100 workers) compared to larger firms (250 or more workers). While sales per worker were typically much higher in bigger state firms, this was not the case with value added. Hence, there was no consistent pattern by size in state firms for labor productivity. While the capital-labor ratio was lower in most small firms (compared to large firms), surprisingly state firms had the biggest capital-labor ratio with fewer than 50 workers.

Broadly speaking, the picture of cooperatives points to a better comparative performance of small cooperatives. Thus, capital productivity (sales per unit of fixed assets; value added per unit of fixed assets) is always higher for the smallest size firms

14 Thus, despite our best efforts, the fluidity of the federal statistical gathering efforts means that there may be omissions from our sample of the largest private sector manufacturing firms. The novelty of the new accounting frameworks means that inevitably there also may be measurement errors for key variables such as fixed assets.

(below 100 workers) when compared to larger firms (250 or more workers). In addition, sales per worker are considerably higher and value added per worker slightly higher in the smaller cooperatives.

Unfortunately, because of the different data gathered in the different samples, comparisons across the different legal kinds of enterprise, do not enable us to draw many comparisons. The available data do not point to a clearly and consistently better record for any particular legal form of enterprise. However the data do suggest that private sector firms are clearly the strongest in terms of capital productivity - an unsurprising finding given the relatively low capital-labor ratios of private firms. In conjunction with our earlier findings on the significantly smaller average capital stock of private firms, this points to the embryonic nature of Bulgarian capital markets, especially to their inability to allocate sufficient capital to private firms.

6. Conclusions

We reported findings drawn from new survey data of small manufacturing firms in the private sector as well as in the state sector and independent cooperatives. We also compared some of our findings with those for large state and cooperative firms and with small private firms elsewhere. In addition we undertook a preliminary analysis of the performance of these different forms of enterprise.

Before reviewing our findings we must stress again that the nature of the available data means that we must be cautious in interpreting these findings.[14] These caveats notwithstanding, we find that:

(a) While the *private manufacturing* sector is not very extensive, because many small cooperative and state-owned manufacturing firms exist, in terms of its *overall* importance in the economy, the Bulgarian small firm manufacturing sector probably is quite well developed compared to other former socialist economies. (Equally, the available data do not permit very precise statements to be confidently made about the size of the Bulgarian small firm sector.)

(b) The characteristics and behavior of Bulgarian small firms often differ considerably depending on the forms of ownership and when compared to large Bulgarian firms. There are important differences by legal type in employment levels and employment dynamics, average age, sources of capital, the prevalence of profit sharing, average levels of worker earnings and degree of unionization.

(c) Small Bulgarian firms often differ from those in former socialist economies. Compared to small private manufacturing firms in other restructuring economies, Bulgarian small private manufacturing firms are, indeed, smaller, more dependent on the state, exposed to extraordinary levels of competition, not export-oriented and employing a relatively small proportion of women in their labor forces.

(d) Productivity indicators of performance show that small Bulgarian manufacturing companies typically are less capital intensive and reflect a higher capital productivity than larger Bulgarian firms. There is no evidence of a clearly and consistently better performance by any particular legal form of business organization.

A number of implications of our findings concern the size of the small private-firm *manufacturing* sector. While much has been done to promote a private sector - e.g. new legislation - the small-firm sector,, remains tiny. In part this testifies to the fact that much of the energy has been focussed elsewhere, e.g. on the problem of trying to rapidly privatize large state-owned manufacturing firms. The conditions conducive to the entry of new small firms have remained less than ideal. Agreeing with North (1990, 76ff.), established sectors such as manufacturing (unlike relatively underdeveloped activities such as services), do not seem to have sufficiently appreciated the informal and formal rules that confront individual entrepreneurs and inhibit the emergence of prospering private manufacturing firms. While it is clear that more work is needed to determine precisely what the impediments to the expansion of the private sector are, the following considerations may be pertinent.

The fact that the private sector, in general, is characterized by many tiny and new firms means that collective action by supporters of that sector (e.g. employer associations) probably will be difficult. In part this reflects the deficiency of the information available to business owners and the difficult logistics of preference formation. On the other hand, fast changing situations mean that some of these advocates of an emerging private sector probably have had to allocate scarce resources to more pressing issues and thus are less effective in coalition building. The newness of policies to promote private firms, past policies which prevented an export-orientation toward the West, an inconsistent small-firm policy focusing on restitution and spontaneous privatization, seem to have inhibited the development of ties between different private-sector firms. Hence, there appears to be a need to increase the scope and nature of the institutions designed to assist the private sector.

At the same time, such ideas as path dependency, first-mover advantages, market power and corporate life-cycle (Müller, 1992) suggest that the choices to be made within the years to come will have long-lasting consequences. Our preliminary findings suggest that industrial policy should not focus on encouraging one single form of ownership and exclude the others. Yet, for these and similar matters there is a clear need for on-going and preferably longitudinal research.

References

Acs, Zoltan J. and David B. Audretsch (eds.) (1993) *Small Firms and Entrepreneurship: an East-West Perspective*, Cambridge University Press.

Agency for Economic Coordination and Development (AECD) (1993) *Annual Report*, Sofia.

Anachkova, Bistra, Derek C. Jones and Ivailo Parchev (1992) *Who are the New Entrepreneurs?*, mimeo, Dept. of Economics, Hamilton College.

Bartlett, Will (1993); Small Firms in Bulgaria and Hungary: The Importance of Initial Conditions; *MOCT-MOST*, Spring.

Bogetic, Z. and John Wilton (1992); Bulgarian Market Reform: Beating the Odds, Transition; *World Bank*, Vol. 3, No. 6.

Charup, Joshua and Leila Webster (1993) *A Survey of Private Manufacturers In St. Petersburg*, Private Sector Development Department Working Paper, The World Bank, Washington, DC.

Clague, C. and G.C. Rausser (eds.) (1992) *The Emergence of Market Economies in Eastern Europe*, Blackwell.

Estrin, Saul (1991); Some reflections on Self-Management, Social Choice and Reform in Eastern Europe; *Journal of Comparative Economics*, 15.

Jones, Derek C. (1993); The Effects of Employee Ownership on Productivity in Command Economies: Evidence from Poland; *Managerial and Decision Economics*, 14.

Jones, Derek C. and Mike Meurs (1991); On Entry in Socialist Economies: Evidence from Bulgaria; *Soviet Studies*, 43, 311-28.

Jones, Derek C. and Svilen Parvulov (1992) *Industrial Organization in a Restructuring Socialist Economy: Evidence from Bulgaria*, Hamilton College, Department of Economics, Working paper No. 91/10, New York.

Jones, Derek C. and Charles Rock (1994) Privatization in Bulgaria, in Estrin, S. (ed.), *Privatization in Central and Eastern Europe*, Longmans.

Müller, Dennis (1992); The Corporation and the Economist; *International Journal of Industrial Organization*, 10, 147-70.

Murrell, P. (1991); Can Neoclassical Economics Underpin the Reform of the Centrally Planned Economies?; *Journal of Economic Perspectives*, 5.

North, D. (1990) *Institutions, Institutional Change and Economic Performance*, Cambridge University Press.

Parvulov, Svilen (1991) *Economic Features of Bulgarian Small and Medium-Sized Establishments During 1988-89*, mimeo, Institute of Economics, Sofia.

Puchev, Plamen (1990); A Note on Government Policy and the New Entrepreneurship in Bulgaria; *Small Business Economics*, 2, 73-6.

Standing, Guy, Gyorgy Sziraczki and James Windell (1993) *The Bulgarian Labor Flexibility Survey*, papers presented at ILO conference, Sofia, May.

Swanson, D. and Leila Webster (1992) *Private Sector Manufacturing in Czech and Federal Republic: A Survey of Firms*, The World Bank Industry and Energy Department Working Paper, Industry Series Paper No. 68 (December 1992).

Webster, Leila (1992a) *Private Sector Manufacturing in Poland: A Survey of Firms*, The World Bank Industry and Energy Department Working Paper, Industry Series Paper No. 66 (December 1992).

Webster, Leila (1992b) *Private Sector Manufacturing in Hungary: A Survey of Firms*, The World Bank Industry and Energy Department Working Paper, Industry Series Paper No. 67 (December 1992).

World Bank (1991) *Bulgaria: Crisis and Transition to a Market Economy 2 vols.*, The World Bank, Washington D.C.

Wyzan, Michael (1993) Stabilization Policy in Post Communist Bulgaria, in Somoqyi, Laszlo (ed.), *The Political Economy of the Transition Process in Eastern Europe*, Elgar.

Appendix: the samples

The three samples are for different forms of ownership and were gathered during the summer of 1992. The data were gathered by enumerators who administered instruments devised by the author sometimes in collaboration with teams including colleagues from the ILO and Charles Rock.

This list of the largest *privately* owned manufacturing firms was derived from the records of the Bulgarian Central Statistical Institute. All 130 such firms were contacted; 105 provided information.

The state and cooperatively owned firms are a subset of a sample for which the design proceeded at two levels. First, five groupings of the 320 municipal districts in Bulgaria were selected on the basis of their geographic and urban variability, reproducing in the aggregate the country-wide industry distributions, and minimizing data collection costs (Sofia, Pernik, Pleven, Burgas and Plovdiv). Second, within each of the five regions, population enumeration lists of enterprises that were state and cooperatively owned in 1988 were compiled by the Central Statistical Bureau. The number of sampled establishments per region was set to reproduce the population proportions of establishments per region. The five regions contained a population of 727 state and cooperatively owned enterprises. Within each region, within major industry categories, establishments were ordered by size and the largest were selected - approximately two-thirds - up to the desired sample size of 500. Thus, the sample contains 69 per cent of the population of establishments but it was selected to reproduce population establishments distribution by industry and region. In terms of employment, the sample firms contain about 95 per cent of all employees in state and cooperative manufacturing in the five regions. In order to facilitate more meaningful comparisons with private firms, in this paper the sub-sample of firms comprises all (338, large and small) *state* (including 123 small and medium firms) and all 38 *cooperative* firms that regarded themselves as *independent* entities, including 23 with fewer than 250 workers.

Acknowledgements

This paper has benefitted from comments from Jeffrey Pliskin, Charles Rock, Svilen Parvulov and participants at the International Conference on 'Bottom-Up Transformation in Eastern Europe: The Role of Small and New Firms in Post-Socialist Countries' Technical University Bergakademie, Freiberg, Germany 9-11 September 1993. Help from IRIS (and earlier, for partial support of data collection, from NSF SES 9010591) is acknowledged. I am also grateful for the valuable research assistance of Kosali Ilayperuma and Murat Ozvardar.

11 Small firms in South East Europe: the importance of initial conditions*

Will Bartlett and *Paul Hoggett*

1. Introduction

Much of the recent analysis of economic transition and transformation in Eastern Europe has focused upon the role of macroeconomic stabilization policy, the privatization of large state-owned enterprises and the 'sequencing' of these reforms (Clague and Rausser, 1992; Richter, 1992; Siebert, 1992). Only a few contributions have touched on the equally important aspect of 'transformation from below' (Acs and Audretsch, 1993), involving the creation of new small firms on the basis of a resurgence of entrepreneurial activity. Moreover, much of the discussion of this aspect of economic transformation has concentrated on the northern and central parts of Eastern Europe to the neglect of the southern part. Since the northern economies were at the outset rather more developed than the southern economies this focus has tended to obscure some of the key differences between the emergence of entrepreneurship and new small firms in different Eastern European economies (as well as in other aspects of economic performance; see Smith, 1991).

In this paper we present a preliminary comparative study of the development of the small firm sector in Bulgaria, Hungary, Macedonia and Slovenia. Even within this set of central and South East European economies there are some important diversities in initial conditions, circa 1989, which we regard as having important consequences for the subsequent path of the economic (and social and political) transformation. The most obvious divergencies relate to the degree of decentralization and marketization of the economies prior to 1989, with Bulgaria at one extreme having a virtually completely centrally planned economy, Hungary having experimented with devolved management within a reformed centrally planned economy for a number of years and both Macedonia and Slovenia, within the former Yugoslavia, having the most extreme form of economic decentralization within the system of 'enterprise self-management', with some similarities to Western European cooperatives but with a poorly defined property rights structure which opened the door to destabilizing political interference at the microeconomic level (Uvalic, 1992).

* One of the major problems confronting researchers investigating the small business sector in Eastern Europe concerns the lack of reliable and comparable forms of data. On the principle that inadequate data is better than no data at all we have endeavoured to construct a number of tables in this paper which would enable us to make tentative comparisons between Hungary, Bulgaria, Slovenia and Macedonia. Nevertheless we admit that the kind of questions that we are asking here are ones which cannot be fully answered on the basis of existing data. At the moment we are beginning an analysis of a small scale survey of our own on the small business sector in Hungary, Bulgaria and Slovenia.

In this paper we argue that these differences in initial conditions and experience of market and quasi-market forms of economic relations, combined with associated differences in the political and social attitudes towards the growth of entrepreneurial activity, have influenced the way in which the small firm sector has begun to develop in these economies. Consequently public policies in the field of small business development and training for entrepreneurs will be likely to differ in each. Eastern Europe, and still less South Eastern Europe, should not be treated as a consistent regional bloc.

2. The issues

2.1 Smooth transition or chaotic transformation?

Initially most observers expected that the process of change in Eastern Europe would follow a pattern of a smooth transition to a capitalist market economy. This view was based upon a focus upon an imagined end state. The market economy was considered as a natural phenomenon, towards which the economies of Eastern Europe would gravitate, led by Adam Smith's invisible hand, once the restrictions on individual entrepreneurial effort were lifted. Subsequent events have shown this optimism to be misplaced. The process is more one of a chaotic transformation. No end state can be predetermined to this transition. It is becoming clear that the process of transition is highly unpredictable, and will be determined by an interaction of both political and economic (and social) forces. In order to understand the transformation process it will be important to focus upon differing initial conditions, rather than final end states. This does not mean that initial conditions will determine the path of the transformation, either, since the path taken will be continuously adjusted and affected by a whole series of system states as the process evolves.

2.2 The concept of transition in economic dynamics

In the study of economic dynamics and structural change a commonly used model is one of systems which adjust to random shocks by shifting smoothly from one equilibrium position to another. The concept of transition describes the path taken between equilibria. In the Eastern European context such an adjustment process would involve a shift from a predominantly large scale state-owned sector to a predominantly small scale privately owned sector. The length of time taken to traverse this path might differ, according to various factors (e.g. the sequencing of reforms), but all East European economies would be expected to arrive at a common finishing post, or end state. This would be the 'natural' structure of a market economy. This perspective tends to confuse both analytical and normative stances. As Chavance (1991) notes what is required is an 'open' concept of transition, one open to the possibility of a whole variety of end-states, including ones which have no precedent. Such an approach does not preclude the possibility of a normative view of a desired end-state so long as this view is explicit rather than hidden.

Recent developments in the study of economic dynamics however, have introduced a quite different image of the process of structural change. Dynamics can be chaotic, and can involve unpredictability, and non-smooth transformations of systems. Such chaotic dynamics have been discovered in quite simple models of system evolution over time. A feature of these models (called the 'butterfly effect') is that the path of the actual dynamics typically depends sensitively on initial conditions. Even quite small differences in starting positions can generate wild differences in the path followed by a system, and lead to quite different end states or regions within which turbulence continues to exist (Gleick, 1988).

This general discussion of the theory of economic dynamics suggests that a careful study of the process of transformation in each individual East European country will be required in order to arrive at policy conclusions which will differ from case to case.

2.3 *The political economy of transformation*

One of the most important considerations in studying the processes of transformation and the development of the small scale sector in Eastern Europe is an understanding of the essentially political as well as the economic nature of the changes which are taking place. The principle reason for this is that markets do not simply evolve of their own accord, but are created by policy makers and interest groups (Weiss, 1989). Indeed it is one of the paradoxes of the demise of communism that the potential role of the state may actually be enhanced in the dimension of system guidance and regulation. The appropriate methodology to use to understand the transformation is thus one of political economy, rather than pure economics.

2.4 *The causes of entry of new firms*

Economic theory contrasts two models of new firm entry (Storey and Atkinson, 1993). One is based upon the industrial economics model of barriers to entry. This model emphasizes the 'pull' forces of new profit opportunities to explain the entry of new firms in particular sectors. The pull forces will be offset by a series of barriers to entry such as the degree of concentration in an industry, the size of set-up costs and the more or less conscious barriers created by the strategic actions of incumbent firms (advertising, product differentiation, strategic investment in spare capacity and so on). Edith Penrose, in her book 'The Growth of the Firm' emphasizes how the number of new small firms can expand at the peak of a boom period as large firms face internal barriers to growth due to managerial diseconomies of scale, and new small firms enter the 'interstices' of the economy to fill the gaps left by the major players.

The other main model emphasizes the importance of labor market conditions in guiding individuals' choices between wage employment, remaining in unemployment (perhaps to wait for or search for a better job offer), or various forms of self-employment which might include establishing a new firm. This model emphasizes that the number of new small firms in an economy can grow even during a period of recession as a defensive reaction to unemployment or low wages in traditional employment. The model also encourages a more differentiated concept of the entrepreneur. For example research in the UK indicates that the strong emphasis upon self-employment within many ethnic minority communities is a consequence of their experience of discrimination within the paid employment sector (Ward, 1991); Curran and Blackburn (1991) suggest a similar effect may account for the rapid growth of female self-employment in the UK in the 1980s.

There is no reason to believe that these two accounts of new small firm entry are mutually exclusive. Furthermore in the context of Eastern Europe, where market type arrangements are often starting from a zero base, it may not just be desirable but imperative to combine both models. It may also be necessary to retain a flexible stance towards the possibility that the influence of political and institutional factors may be so strong that purely economic models of small firm entry are inadequate.

2.5 Conditions for small firm entry within the labor market model

In stressing the choice to be made between wage employment, remaining in unemployment and self-employment, the labor market model relies upon some assumptions which do not necessarily hold in the Eastern European context. For example Eastern European economies prior to the beginning of the transition varied considerably in terms of the scale of self-employment which was possible. In Hungary, Slovenia and to a lesser extent Macedonia, quite widespread forms of artisan/craft based small scale private production were tolerated throughout much of the post-war period. In Hungary the limit to the number of employees permitted in such enterprises was gradually raised throughout the 1980's. Similarly the ability to 'choose' unemployment is only a recent right bestowed upon the population of Eastern Europe. Political factors play a crucial role here. For example whereas Slovenia has opted for tight controls on money supply, a fair degree of economic restructuring and what it hopes will be high but temporary levels of unemployment, in Macedonia, as in neighbouring Serbia, the absence of any kind of control over money supply led to hyper-inflation in conditions in which unemployment was already high. Only the unilateral declaration of independence in 1991, and the successful implementation of a macroeconomic stabilization policy, has enabled Macedonia to avoid the economic catastrophe which Serbia has experienced. But real wages in Macedonia have continued to decline, and the boundary between wage employment and unemployment becomes increasingly tenuous, indeed wage employment increasingly resembles a form of disguised unemployment.

Eastern European countries not only vary according to when unemployment first appears as an officially recognized category but also in terms of the social provision for unemployment once it is recognized. Indeed, with unemployment benefit covering only 60 per cent of the unemployed in Bulgaria and 78 per cent in Hungary it is not surprising to find 'a ready supply of new entrepreneurs' (Bartlett, 1993). One is reminded here of some recent research in the UK on the impact of enterprise schemes for the young unemployed in the North East of England which suggested that the willingness of young people to try out self-employment had more to do with a culture of survival than a culture of enterprise (MacDonald, 1991).

So a labor market approach would stress the importance of conditions such as the availability of wage employment, the costs and benefits of remaining either unemployed or in disguised unemployment, and both the possibility and relative advantage of choosing self-employment. As we have seen, the prevalence of such conditions varies considerably in Eastern European countries both before and after 1989. Since 1989 political choices, particularly relating to the degree of real economic restructuring undertaken, and monetary and pricing policies, have contributed substantially to this variation.

In addition to the above factors it is possible to identify some other conditions which will contribute to the ability and willingness of individuals to set up new forms of small enterprise. In the context of Eastern Europe, cultural attitudes towards entrepreneurialism can play an important role in either encouraging or deterring individuals regarding this choice. Little research has so far been done on this subject in the Eastern European context, with the exception of Hungary where a strong body of research has recently focused upon the question 'who are the entrepreneurs?' (Kuczi and Vajda, 1990; Lengyel, 1989). The evidence suggests that in Hungary ideological factors no longer inhibit entrepreneurial inclinations but rather that it is the fear of uncertainty and failure which is the real barrier. Moreover it is the existence of 'social capital', particularly the 'capital of connections', which leads actors to expect success rather than failure. Inter-generational traditions of enterprise are known to be an important determinant of choice of self-employment in the West (Curran and Blackburn, 1991). Clearly this factor is going to be of lesser importance in the East given that few previous generations will have had direct experience of self-employment themselves. Nevertheless within all of the former communist regimes a second economy existed, one rooted in household survival strategies which were necessary to cope with the shortage economy. In some countries, such as Hungary, this second economy was semi-tolerated by the official regime (Sik, 1993) and the inter-household and community networks upon which it was based now provide a crucial means of acquiring the skills, information and capital necessary to start up new enterprises in either the formal or informal sectors.

Membership of the nomenklatura, however, is likely to contribute to the social capital an individual may bring to his or her choice about self-employment. However, the relationship between the 'nomenklatura effect' and small firm development is unclear. In Hungary the scale of spontaneous privatization (which as Mizsei (1992) notes is given the more pejorative title 'nomenklatura privatization' in Poland) has been such that much of the existing economic elite has been able to find a place within the newly privatized organizations. Our initial research in Slovenia and Macedonia reveals that in these countries, too, previous elites have been flexible enough to manage the process of change even though here little spontaneous privatization has occurred. In Bulgaria, however, official attitudes towards what is known as 'wild privatization' are extremely hostile, but given that little in the way of real privatization has so far occurred it is still too early to tell what role existing economic elites will play in any processes of change which occur. Where the nomenklatura has survived intact it is, therefore, unlikely that in these countries choice of self-employment will be driven primarily by experience of unemployment; rather it is more likely to be seen as an opportunity to jump directly from waged employment in the state sector into small firm ownership.

2.6 *Conditions for small firm entry within the industrial economic model*

It is probable that the 'nomenklatura effect' may be more important in terms of barriers to entry than it is as a push factor. Where traditional economic elites have been able to ride the transition to become elites within the newly privatized or corporatized sectors it is quite possible that they may provide a formidable economic and social barrier to the entry of new firms. However, this is likely to vary considerably according to sector; it is most unlikely to occur in those sectors such as trade and industrial services which were quite undeveloped under the command economy system. It is most probable to occur in sectors such as manufacturing which in some senses had become 'over-developed' under previous regimes.

The degree of industrial concentration within sectors is also likely to be a major potential barrier. Industrial concentration was high in all Eastern European countries prior to the transition even in those countries such as Hungary which had experimented with forms of decentralization. The main exception here relates to former Yugoslavia where the self-management model combined elements of economic decentralization with forms of internal market. Thus, comparing our four case study states, industrial concentration is highest in Bulgaria and lowest in Slovenia. One of the paradoxes of the privatization process in Hungary (spontaneous privatization on the one hand but limited success with planned privatization on the other) is that while parts of the economy have now been radically restructured other parts remain almost completely unchanged. Even with these provisos industrial concentration generally remains at much higher levels than one would now expect in Western-type economies, and as a consequence patterns of sub-contracting are still largely undeveloped.

Another major barrier to entry relates to the capital intensity of production. In Eastern Europe this is a particularly salient factor given the difficulty potential entrepreneurs have in raising any kind of investment capital. On the one hand the historical accumulated indebtedness of major state firms has led banks to charge very high interest rates. Thus, for example, in Hungary interest rates have barely dipped below 30 per cent since 1989 and this in itself acts as a major deterrent to entrepreneurs even if they were able to offer security which the banks would be willing to accept. On the other hand few potential entrepreneurs have much capital of their own and where it does exist it often assumes the form of property which banks in some countries (i.e. Hungary) refuse to accept as security. In both Slovenia and Macedonia, however, banks do accept property as security. Moreover, there is a substantial amount of private wealth held by Slovenians in the form of foreign currency savings-deposits in Austrian banks. Clearly the state could play an important role in enabling entrepreneurs to overcome this barrier to entry through the development of loan guarantee schemes, cheap credit and so on, but for this to occur governments would have to overcome their reaction to any forms of state involvement. Thus, for example, we find that at the moment an enabling strategy for the state in small business development is entirely absent in Bulgaria and pretty rudimentary in Hungary, despite the work of the PHARE program (Hoggett and Kallay, 1993). Only in Slovenia, where a Ministry for Small and Medium-Sized Enterprises has been established, does it seem that a policy response may be emerging equivalent to the scale of the problem (and opportunity) presented.

In concluding this discussion it is worth reflecting that whereas the push factors isolated by the labor market model appear to operate primarily at a national or sometimes regional level the factors isolated by the Industrial Economics model seem to be much more sectorally specific. Political choices made by different Eastern European states, particularly those made since 1989, have had an important bearing upon the degree of 'push' being currently experienced within each of the four countries covered by our analysis. But even where a considerable degree of push exists barriers to entry in some industrial sectors remain considerable. A number of factors appear to conspire against entry into sectors where the capital intensity of production is high. As a consequence, as we shall see in subsequent sections, small firm development in all four countries has been most rapid in capital non-intensive branches of production, particularly trade and services.

3. Initial conditions in 1989

3.1 Early experience with the development of small firms

Within the former Yugoslavian Federation, the economic system in Slovenia and Macedonia was based upon the idea of decentralization of management responsibility to individual enterprises within the system of autonomous 'self-managed' firms. The experience with market-type mechanisms was therefore far more extensive than in either Hungary or Bulgaria. Yugoslavian firms traded extensively in Western markets, and the managers of enterprises built up many overseas networks and connections through their export activities. In addition to being the most developed and prosperous East European economy, Yugoslavia, before the war between Serbia and Croatia, was well placed to make the transition to a capitalist market economy. A large proportion of the workforce had worked in Western European countries as migrant workers, and knowledge of how those economies operate was widespread. In addition the population had accumulated large amounts of foreign currency, and the balance of payments was heavily financed from emigrant workers' foreign currency remittances, as well as by a highly developed tourist industry.

Equally important was the experience with independent private firms, especially in crafts, tourism, trade and transport sectors. Indeed, in many instances, emigrant workers' remittances formed a significant source of start-up capital for private enterprise, especially in tourism. In both Slovenia and Macedonia there was an even greater level of experience with the development of private enterprise than had been achieved in Hungary. Private enterprise was permitted as 'craft enterprises' in both Republics of the former Yugoslavia. Although they were regulated in the number of workers they could employ (restrictions which were less onerous in Slovenia), in 1988 there were 247 424 small firms in the private sector in Yugoslavia as a whole, of which around 40 000 were operating in Slovenia and 20 000 in Macedonia. They were, however, mainly one-man firms and generated a total employment of only 71 500 in Slovenia and 32 700 in Macedonia (including owner managers). In addition there were a number of enterprises with mixed social and private ownership, but these never really got off the ground as the owners investment in them could be appropriated by the state which could transform them into socially owned enterprises after a fixed period of activity.

Table 11.1 Employment in small firms in Slovenia and Macedonia 1988

	Employment		Employment share (per cent)	
Sector	Slovenia	Macedonia	Slovenia	Macedonia
Transport	7 611	3 870	13.6	13.0
Trade	855	1 709	1.1	3.3
Tourism	6 602	3 200	19.9	23.8
Crafts	56 446	23 887	67.2	82.5
Total	71 514	31 666	28.4	26.2

Note: Includes both owners and employees.

Source: Statisticki Godisnjak Jugoslavije 1990.

As Table 11.1 shows, the proportion of employment in private firms in these four sectors reached 28 per cent in Slovenia and 26 per cent in Macedonia. Given that these sectors accounted for 22 per cent of total employment in Slovenia and 18 per cent of total employment in Macedonia in 1988 overall the private sector probably accounted for over six per cent of employment in these two countries (or republics as they were then).

Expansion of the small scale private sector began in Hungary in 1982, with a series of government decrees which opened the door for certain types of semi-private business and raised the ceiling on the number of workers which could be employed by small businesses in the craft or artisan sector. The most important of the newly permitted business forms was the so-called Enterprise Economic Work Partnership (EEWP), and the Economic Work Partnership (EWP). These partnerships were formed from groups of employees or ex-employees of a state enterprise and could either work for the enterprise in their spare time using the enterprises own assets (the EEWP), or they could work outside the state enterprise (the EWP). The EWP was essentially a private business, which had, however, to be formed by at least two persons (but with a maximum of 30) to give the appearance of a 'collective' organization (Mizsei, 1992). People often worked in them on a part-time basis, keeping a part-time state sector job for security. The EEWP became popular partly because it enabled people to avoid central wage controls (Mizsei, 1992).

Other business forms which could be established included Subsidiary Enterprises, Small Cooperatives and so-called Specialist Groups. Of these, only the latter two caught on to any significant extent. By 1985 about 35 000 new private businesses of all types had been established (see Table 11.2).

Table 11.2 Evolution of new forms of economic unit introduced in 1982 in Hungary

	1982	1984	1986	1988
Enterprise EWP	3 531	17 770	21 490	16 978
EWP	2 289	7 316	10 941	11 815
Specialist Group	536	2 335	2 768	1 838
Small cooperative	140	356	1 185	2 890
Subsidiary enterprise	-	44	102	136
State enterprise	n.a.	n.a.	2 285	2 377

Sources: Tibor (1992); Hoggett and Kallay (1993); Marrese (1992).

The development of this sector was an important precondition for the subsequent development of private enterprise in Hungary and provided a training ground for the first generation of independent Hungarian entrepreneurs (Hoggett and Kallay, 1993). However, in themselves they were essentially dependent upon the existence of the state enterprise sector, acting as subcontractors filling in some of the gaps in the existing structures.

A similar 'intrapreneurial' strategy (i.e. the development of entrepreneurial opportunities within a state firm) was also implemented in Bulgaria in the early 1980s, although on a much smaller scale than in Hungary and strictly on the basis of state ownership (Jones and Meurs, 1991). The policy was implemented through Decree 12 of 1982, which promoted the development of a small and medium-sized enterprise sector to exploit new technologies based on the use of highly automated machinery. The Bulgarian Industrial Association was established to encourage small and medium sized state-owned firms to be set up as spin-offs from large firms to produce high quality consumer goods.

However, by June 1989 only 650 of these firms had been established in all sectors of industry. They were concentrated in food processing (17.1 per cent), machine building and metal processing (15.4 per cent), textiles and knitwear (13.8 per cent), light industry (13.8 per cent), electrical engineering and electronics (12.9 per cent) and construction materials (10.2 per cent) (Puchev, 1991). Some of these firms were established and owned by local municipalities (34 per cent in 1985), and some (35 per cent in 1985) were engaged in the production of consumer goods. Between 1984 and 1988 mean labor productivity in these small firms was estimated to be between 1.4 and 2.7 times greater than in their large scale counterparts (Puchev, 1990).

Despite this limited success, state support for the Bulgarian Industrial Association was discontinued in 1986, and the experimental program to create a small firm sector under state, municipal and cooperative ownership virtually ground to a halt. By the beginning of the 1990s there were only around 500 small firms employing 50 or fewer workers in the state and cooperative sectors. Although an improvement over the earlier position of almost exclusive industrial gigantism before the program was introduced, the Bulgarian program was not nearly as successful as the Hungarian approach to intrapreneurship on the basis of semi-private and autonomous work groups.

By the end of the 1980s there were already substantial numbers of small firms active in the economies of Hungary, Macedonia and Slovenia. As Table 11.3 shows, 84 per cent of firms in Slovenia and 88 per cent of industrial firms in Macedonia employed fewer than 500 workers in 1989; and the corresponding figures for industrial firms employing fewer than 250 workers were 62 per cent and 74 per cent. In Bulgaria on the other hand nearly 25 per cent of employees were working in firms employing over 500 workers. Comparable data for the size distribution of all firms are given in the Appendix, which show that even in Hungary there was a surprisingly large proportion of small sized firms in 1989, when as many as 37.6 per cent of firms employed fewer than 20 workers.

Table 11.3 Firm size distribution - industrial firms Slovenia, Bulgaria, and Macedonia 1989/90

Employment size group	Slovenia[a]	Bulgaria[b]	Macedonia[a]
1-6	3.6		11.2
7-15	2.2		11.8
16-29	3.7		10.2
30-60	8.6		12.3
61-125	19.6		14.2
126-250	25.0		14.4
251-500	21.0		13.6
<500	83.8	75.6	87.7
501-1 000	10.5	14.4	8.1
>1 000	5.7	10.0	4.2
Total	1 227	2 431	n.a.

Notes: a: 1989, data for Macedonia refer to all registered firms.
b: 1990, data not available for these size categories.

Sources: Statisticni Letopis Republike Slovenije 1991, Table 8-4; Staticheski Godishnik Bulgaria, 1991; Statistical Office of Macedonia, 1993.

Thus, whereas in Bulgaria there was virtually no private sector at all in 1989, in Hungary a new and mainly young entrepreneurial class had emerged during the 1980s.

Both the Hungarian reforms and the Yugoslavian arrangements, created a legacy of decentralization and of some decision making rights to enterprise managers. The educational level and business culture of managers was, therefore, greater in Hungary, Macedonia and Slovenia than in Bulgaria. In Hungary, Slovenia and Macedonia there was also a legacy of small craft firms, some fairly long standing. However the contribution of this sector to the prevailing business culture is more difficult to ascertain. Research in existing capitalist economies (Marceau, 1990) tends to suggest that artisan based forms of entrepreneurship are more embedded in family and community and lack a concern for growth as opposed to continuity and survival.

4. Subsequent developments and outcomes

4.1 Macroeconomic conditions since 1989

During the 1980s the economies of Eastern Europe had experienced a lengthy economic crisis even before the break-up of the Soviet block. Various attempts at enterprise reform within central planning had been adopted in Hungary, giving greater autonomy to managers and permitting various forms of independent enterprise linked to the existing large-scale state firms. In Bulgaria a much more limited experiment with small firms under state ownership had been undertaken. Only in Yugoslavia was there an attempt to introduce a full scale (but unsuccessful) stabilization program and the beginnings of the emergence of a really independent private sector prior to 1989 (Bartlett, 1992). Conditions deteriorated rapidly after 1989 with the disruption of trading arrangements within the CMEA block, and in South East Europe following the outbreak of the Yugoslavian war and the imposition of sanctions by the UN on the rump Yugoslavia (a process which has had a major impact upon all four economies).

Table 11.4 GDP growth rates (per cent)

Year	Bulgaria	Hungary	Macedonia	Slovenia
1988	2.5	–0.1	n.a.	–1.7
1989	–1.9	–0.2	n.a.	–1.8
1990	–9.1	–4.0	–10.6	–4.7
1991	–11.7	–12.0	–11.4	–9.3
1992	–7.7	–4.6	–15.1	–6.5
1993[a]	–4.5	–1.5	–7.0	–1.0

Note: a: projection.

Source: EBRD Current Economic Issues, July 1993, small privatization.

All of the four countries experienced severe macroeconomic difficulties after 1989. The economic recession seems to have bottomed out in 1991 in Bulgaria, Hungary and Slovenia, although it is still continuing in Macedonia, where GDP declined by 15 per cent in 1992.

Corresponding to the economic recession, there was a huge rise in unemployment in all four countries. Again Macedonia stands out as already having high initial levels of unemployment in 1989. However, the definition of unemployment used can be disputed: it is measured on a basis of officially registered employment in the socialized sector alone. Nevertheless, in Macedonia too, unemployment increased continuously up to 1992.

Table 11.5 Unemployment rates (per cent)

Year	Bulgaria	Hungary	Macedonia	Slovenia
1989	n.a.	0.3	22.1	2.9
1990	1.5	2.5	23.0	4.7
1991	10.4	8.0	24.5	8.1
1992	15.2	12.3	26.3	11.3

Source: EBRD Current Economic Issues, July 1993; Statistical Office of Macedonia.

Between 1989 and 1992 employment in state and socialized sector enterprises in all countries fell markedly. In Macedonia, employment in socialised sector enterprises fell from 530 385 in 1989 to 481 284 by 1992, a decrease of over 49 000. In Slovenia, employment fell from 652 176 to 530 448 over the same period, a decrease of over 121 000. The much greater fall in employment in Slovenia accounts for the steeper rise in unemployment there. In Macedonia, owing to the already high levels of unemployment, strenuous attempts have been made to maintain employment in at least the largest socialized enterprises. Indeed, the share of employment in the largest enterprises in Macedonia, (i.e. those employing over 2 000 workers), actually increased from 14.9 per cent to 29.6 per cent. This illustrates the political difficulties in some Eastern European economies in managing the economic transition. Where the democratic alliances are weak and where governments are managed by 'hung' Parliaments (as also in Bulgaria), the political costs of restructuring the large state-owned enterprises outweigh the economic benefits. Where votes and the political legitimacy of the government depend on maintaining the social security of the industrial working class, and in the absence of an effective social security system, this means a political predisposition to maintaining employment in the large firm sector.

4.2 New firms in the private sector

That the economic downturn and the increases in registered unemployment were not even more severe in the four countries can be accounted for to some extent by the progress made in creating conditions for the development of the private sector. In all the countries, enabling legislation has been passed to permit the entry of new private firms. The former Yugoslavia was the first to introduce this new legislation with the Markovic government's Enterprise Law, implemented in 1989. This permitted enterprises to register as limited liability companies and all other forms of companies. Tables 11.6a and b show the rapid development of the small firm sector in Slovenia and the increase in the number of new firms in Macedonia.

Table 11.6a Share of new small firms in Slovenia

Year	Total	Small firms	percentage (small/total)
1990	7 935	6 349	80
1991	13 309	11 582	87
1992	16 141	14 428	89

Note: Small firms are those companies employing 50 or fewer workers.

Source: Prasnikar and Valencic (1992, Table 1).

Table 11.6b The growth of new firms in Macedonia

Year	Private	Cooperative	Mixed
1991	12 987	520	746
1992	34 138	795	1 073

Source: Statistical Office of Macedonia.

Between 1991 and 1992 the number of registered private companies increased from nearly 13 000 to over 34 000 in Macedonia. Although not all registered firms actually operate, this still represents a substantial increase in private economic activity. As yet, however, there is no overall strategy for the development of the small enterprise sector, and the precarious economic position of the Macedonian economy does not lead to an expectation that the private sector is capable of absorbing large numbers of unemployed workers. Nevertheless, the adaptability and innovativeness of the new private sector has probably been important in helping Macedonia to overcome some of the worst effects of economic blockade (by Greece on its southern border and by UN sanctions against Serbia to the north). It is estimated that the private sector in Macedonia now accounts for 94 per cent of registered enterprises, 22 per cent of GDP and 17 per cent of employment.

The majority of legislation necessary to provide an institutional and legal structure for private enterprise, foreign partnerships, a modern banking system, capital markets, etc. was put into place in Hungary between 1988 and 1991. Since 1990 there has been a spectacular growth in the number of legally registered economic organizations, particularly private limited liability companies, in Hungary. Probably many of these were developed out of or directly converted from the previously developed Economic Work Partnerships, or as spin-offs from state-owned enterprises. Table 11.7 shows the development of the number of economic organizations with a legal entity in Hungary after 1989. The totals include enterprises under all forms of ownership, including state firms, associations, joint companies, limited liability companies, corporations, cooperatives and water management companies, but excluding sole proprietors.

Table 11.7 Share of new small firms in Hungary

Year	Total	Small firms	percentage (small/total)
1989	15 169	7 492	55
1990	29 405	20 594	74
1991	52 694	42 978	85
1992	65 054	55 864	88

Notes: (i) Small firms are defined as firms employing 50 or fewer employees, percentage figures are calculated from totals which exclude housing and garage cooperatives and those with an unknown number of employees.
(ii) Data are for December of each year, except for 1992 which are for September.

Source: Central Statistical Office, 1993, Table XV/1 and XV/4.

As can be seen in Table 11.7, the most rapid increase occurred amongst small firms employing fewer than 50 workers. The proportion of small firms increased from 55 per cent of the total number of economic organizations at the end of 1989, to 88 per cent by September 1992. Most (88 per cent of all of these small firms) employed 20 or fewer workers. These figures suggest that increasing numbers of workers are being employed in small firms. Already by 1990, it was estimated that firms employing fewer than 100 workers employed around 20 per cent of the workforce (Tibor, 1992). According to Kiss (1992), the major source of the emerging class of new private entrepreneurs is from ex-employees of the declining state sector, where, as we have seen, it was previously customary to engage in second jobs in the Economic Work Partnerships.

In addition it has been estimated that the number of sole proprietors increased from 221 794 in 1989 to 339 866 in 1991 (Acs, 1992). These businesses were probably mostly either one-man businesses or had only a few employees, and the majority of them operate on a part-time or second-job basis, and have no legal status.

In Bulgaria Decree 56 (1989) permitted small private firms to hire labor for the first time (but only up to a limit of 10 workers). The introduction of the Commercial Law in 1991 eliminated these artificial limits and enabled firms to become limited liability companies. The new law regulates the registration of sole proprietors, unlimited partnerships, limited partnerships and private limited companies.

Following the introduction of these measures there was an upsurge in the number of new firm registrations. At the end of 1989, 14 011 private firms had been registered under Decree 56 and registrations rose rapidly to 69 000 in 1990, and to 130 000 by the end of 1991. Registrations continued to increase following the introduction of the new Commercial Code, reaching a figure of around 200 000 by February 1992 (although it is estimated that only about 120 000 were actively engaged in production).

However, the development of the small firm sector in Bulgaria has been very shallow. On the basis of aggregate information on 24 744 sole traders and partnerships, and 17 241 private craftsmen, one recent study conducted by the Institute of Small and Medium-Sized Businesses with support from PHARE concluded that in 1990 private enterprise accounted for only 1.8 per cent of GDP, less than 1 per cent of exports and employed only 4.3 per cent of the workforce. The study also showed that most of the new private firms in Bulgaria are very small: the average size of firm was 3.4 persons, which varied from 3.0 persons in industry to 9.3 persons in construction. Other studies carried out by the Bulgarian Agency for Economic Coordination and Development show that since 1990 the private sector has increased its share of output. By the end of 1992, the Agency reported that the private sector actually accounted for at least 10 per cent of GDP in 1992, including 50 per cent of retail trade turnover and for around 20 per cent of household incomes (AECD, 1992, 10). However, this apparent increase in the share of private sector activity probably reflected the virtual collapse of the state sector more than anything else.

4.2 Ownership structure

In Hungary, a major source of growth in the number of registered firms has been in the creation of new limited liability companies. Between the end of 1989 and September 1992 the number of such companies had increased from 4 485 to 53 293, and comprised 82 per cent of all economic organizations other than sole proprietorships. In contrast, as privatization progressed, the number of state-owned enterprises began to diminish, falling from 2 399 at the end of 1989 to 1 873 by September 1992. Apart from limited liability companies and state-owned firms, the most important alternative type of economic organizations were sole proprietorships of which, as we have seen, it has been estimated that there were around 300 000 in 1991, and cooperatives, of which there were 5 743 in 1989 (including 3 233 so-called 'small cooperatives'). However, there was little growth in the number of cooperative enterprises: in 1992 there were only 221 more than there had been in 1989.

The private sector in Bulgaria has so far developed mainly through the mechanism of sole proprietorships than through the establishment of limited liability companies. Of the 130 000 firms registered by the end of 1991, some 87 876 (66 per cent) were sole proprietorships (UPEE, 1992). Excluding these firms enables a comparison with the ownership structure of the Hungarian enterprise sector.

The Table 11.8 shows a striking contrast between the development of private enterprise in Bulgaria and Hungary in terms of the legal ownership structure. Not surprisingly, since the Hungarian Company Law was introduced in 1989, while the Bulgarian Commercial Code was introduced only in 1991, the Hungarian private sector has developed a much larger base of incorporated limited liability companies than in Bulgaria.

Table 11.8 Legal form of ownership of the enterprise sector in Bulgaria and Hungary, 1991

Legal form	Bulgaria	Hungary
Limited liability companies	613	41 206
Partnerships and cooperatives	38 718	5 811
State and municipal companies	2 510	2 233
Cooperative farms	1 103	1 421
Joint ventures	412	5 642
Sole proprietorships	130 000	339 866

Sources: UPEE, 1992; Central Statistical Institute, SHK, 1992, Table XV/1 and Table XV/5; Acs, 1992.

However, the Hungarian example shows that the development of the incorporated limited liability sector can be quite rapid once the legal opportunity for incorporation is available.

4.3 Sector distribution

Table 11.9 shows the sector composition of small firms in Bulgaria, Hungary and Slovenia. In the Hungarian case the data refer to all registered firms employing up to 50 workers, of which there were 43 thousand in 1991 (excluding sole proprietors). In the Bulgarian case the data refer to all registered private firms, of which there were 130 thousand in 1991. But since the great majority of these firms are very small indeed, the data probably provide some broad comparability with those for Hungary, although it should be emphasized that the Hungarian data do not include any information on sole proprietors.

On this basis, there may be some evidence to assume that there was a far greater proportion of firms identified as operating in the industrial and manufacturing sector in Hungary than in Bulgaria. In both countries, the service sector accounts for around 20 per cent of all registered small firms accounted for by these data.

An important feature of this sectoral economic structure is the role played by the trade sector in each country, accounting for as much as 20.5 per cent of all registered small firms in Hungary and 25 per cent of all registered private firms in Bulgaria. The high proportion of firms engaged in trade activities indicates that they play an important role in the development of the emerging market structure, responding to the breakdown of the central planning system as a method of coordinating commodity flows. As such they provide a mechanism to overcome the high transactions costs involved in exchange of goods and services in an imperfectly developed market.

Table 11.9 Sector distribution of registered small firms in Hungary and Bulgaria, 1992 (per cent)

Sector	Hungary[a]	Bulgaria[b]	Slovenia[a]
Industry	20.8	7.0	15.1
Construction	13.6	3.6	5.4
Agriculture	3.3	7.3	1.9
Transport	2.9	14.3	2.1
Trade	38.9	25.4	23.8
Services	20.5	19.3	52.3
Other[c]	0.0	23.0	0.0
Total	100.0	100.0	100.0

Notes: a: Registered firms employing fewer than 50 workers.
b: All private firms.
c: This refers to 'other material production' except for Bulgaria where the category specifically refers to 'other manufacturing'. This reflects the weak basis of registration and collection of data on small firms in Bulgaria. Firms often register as engaging in a variety of activities which are actually never undertaken.

Source: Derived from Table 2.3 of Kallay (1992); 168 Hours 2 (29), July 20-26, 1992, 8; Prasnikar and Valencic (1992), Table 2.

An indication of the pace and structure of change is revealed by the percentage increase in the number of small firms by sector between 1991 and 1992. Overall, the pace of new firm registration was high in both countries, with the rate of growth being higher in Bulgaria (at 44 per cent) compared to Hungary (at 24 per cent), possibly due to its later start, but probably also due to the inclusion of sole proprietorships among the data which are easier and less costly to register. Of significance is the above average rate of increase in new firms registered in the trade sector, a phenomenon which occurred in both countries. In view of the large share of this sector in the overall distribution of firms, this suggests that the dynamics of the evolution of this small firms sector reflect some common features of the transition process in both Hungary and Bulgaria, and reinforces the points made previously concerning the important role of small scale firms engaged in commercial trade activities in an imperfectly developed market structure. But perhaps one of the most crucial characteristics of the trade and services sector is its low capital intensity which, given our remarks about barriers to entry made in section 1 of this paper, is precisely the kind of pattern that existing models of new firm entry would lead us to expect when placed in the context of the transformation process.

5. Conclusions

Prevailing economic models of small firm entry highlight two sets of determining factors - one set relates to conditions which motivate and equip individuals for choosing self-employment, the other set refers to conditions which constitute potential barriers to entry which have to be overcome or bypassed in some way. We have seen how our four case-study countries differ substantially in terms of such conditions.

Considering first of all those conditions which motivate and equip individuals to choose the path of entrepreneurialism we have seen how the four countries vary in terms of the appearance and magnitude of both formal and disguised unemployment, previous experience of market type behavior, traditions of small scale domestic enterprise, and so on. The absence of any real previous experience of markets or small enterprise in Bulgaria is striking compared to Hungary, Slovenia or Macedonia. In all countries both formal and disguised forms of unemployment have been increasing rapidly and while this has certainly provided a spur towards self-employment the motivation primarily concerns survival rather than a positive embrace of the 'ethic of enterprise'.

The data we have provided indicate a striking growth in the development of new forms of small enterprise in all four countries, however, the figures need to be treated with some caution. There is a considerable difference between the number of enterprises registered, even where these assume the form of private limited liability companies as in Hungary, and the number actually engaged in economic activity. On the other hand it is also true that in all countries the informal economy is rapidly growing. What is clear is that the vast majority of new enterprises is in fact very small and tends to focus on the area of trade and services.

We can begin to understand the bias of the small entrepreneur towards trade and service sectors if we consider the conditions prevailing in these four countries which constitute barriers to new firm entry. Existing models based upon the experience of Western market economies include conditions such as the existence of restrictive legal frameworks, the degree of industrial concentration and the capital intensity of production within particular sectors. In the context of Eastern European economies we also have to add factors such as the linkage between political and economic elites in the governance of sectors of the economy. Moreover, the impact of the capital intensity of production within different sectors is exaggerated because of the great difficulty potential entrepreneurs face in raising any kind of capital for business development. In fact prevailing conditions relating to entry barriers in our four case study countries were remarkably similar - restrictive legislative frameworks had all largely been removed (though most slowly in the case of Bulgaria) by 1992, linkages between old and/or new economic and political elites appeared to exist in all four countries, also industrial concentration was considerable in the majority of sectors while, paradoxically, trade and commercial and industrial services were scarcely developed at all.

The four countries differed, however, in terms of the existence of conditions which would facilitate the overcoming or bypassing of these barriers to entry. To some extent, because of their geographical location, both Slovenia and Hungary had sound past experience of trading relationships with Western European firms. Moreover, in both instances the quality of business management was higher than elsewhere in Eastern Europe because of their previous experience either with forms of decentralized, internal market arrangements (Yugoslavia) or with forms of intrapreneurship (Hungary in the 1980s). Evidence is beginning to emerge that both of these factors have been important in attracting the relatively high levels of foreign investment, particulary via joint ventures, to these countries since 1990 (Rojec and Svetlicic, 1993; Wang, 1993). Given the problem of raising capital for business development the joint venture route has become a crucial means for raising the capital intensity of the small business sector once denied to entrepreneurs in both Bulgaria and Macedonia either because of their lack of market and business experience (Bulgaria) or because regional political instability makes inward investment too risky (Macedonia).

The process of transformation towards a more market-type of economy has, therefore, proceeded from somewhat different starting conditions in Hungary, Bulgaria, Slovenia and Macedonia. The development of the small business sector has, however, also been strongly influenced by the presence or absence of policy interventions which could facilitate the development of this sector. There is an important difference to be grasped here between the creation of policies and their implementation. While the inflow of foreign aid through PHARE and other programs to the small business sector is greatest in Hungary and Bulgaria the impact of these programs in Bulgaria so far appears to have been minimal as constant ministerial changes have undermined the implementation of any kind of strategic application of these programs. In both Hungary (through the PHARE program in conjunction with the Hungarian Foundation for Enterprise) and Slovenia (through the Ministry for Small and Medium-Sized Enterprise) loan guarantee and micro-credit schemes are being developed but certainly our experience of Hungary suggests that so far such schemes have only scratched the surface in terms of the actual need entrepreneurs have for cheap and easily available credit. With the possible exception of Slovenia, it is striking about our four case study countries that there is a lack of positive policies to promote small enterprise given the scale of the problems to be faced. This partly reflects a more generalized policy vacuum produced by the shifting forms of coalition politics in countries like Bulgaria and Macedonia, but partly it also reflects an understandable, yet in this case dysfunctional, suspicion of any positive role for the state in economic development.

Given the continuing and chronic lack of capital for the development of both large and small enterprises it is perhaps not suprising that the capital of 'connections' plays a crucial role. Two primary forms of network capital exist which have quite different origins: one relates to the household survival networks which provided the backbone of the informal sector within shortage economies; the other relates to the elite networks of the old nomenklatura. The former flourished in most communist societies, particularly in Hungary where it merged into a semi-legalized second economy (Sik, 1993), and now provide the means whereby many ordinary people obtain the capital and other resources to take the entrepreneurial path. While in Bulgaria and Macedonia elite networks are built primarily around the old nomenklatura, in countries such as Hungary the new political elites have not proved backwards in the development of new forms of linkage between actors in the political and economic sectors. Finally, in Slovenia and within the Albanian minority within Macedonia, previous accumulations of capital derived from emigrant worker remittances constitute a small but important source of capital for business development.

In this paper we have tried to examine the importance of initial starting points and formative early policy decisions for the development of the small business sector. We do not wish to deny that in a vital way the fortunes of the small business sector in Eastern European countries are inevitably bound with the fortunes of the economy as a whole. Many of the factors inhibiting the development of the national economies - the collapse of Eastern European markets, the disastrous state of many branches of industry which had previously received state subsidies, protectionist measures taken recently by Western European nations against so-called 'dumping' of Eastern European products - have an impact which consequently trickles down to the small business sector in terms of high interest rates, falling GDPs, stagnation or collapse of domestic markets and so on. But on the other hand we wish to avoid an overly deterministic analysis which gives too much weight to general as opposed to specific influences. Initial starting points and early decisions do make a difference and, when one considers the probably chaotic and indeterminate path that transformation will follow, these differences in the long term could prove to be crucial.

Acknowledgements

This paper was produced as part of the ESRC funded research project on 'Small Firms in South East Europe: New Forms of Ownership and Control', which is part of the UK Economic and Social Research Council East-West Research Program. Financial assistance from the ESRC is gratefully acknowledged. We are also grateful to Rossitsa Rangelova, Taki Fiti, Laszlo Kallay, Gyorgy Lengyel, Janez Prasnikar and Peter Futo for their advice and assistance during the course of the research project, although we are solely responsible for any errors or ommissions in this paper.

References

Acs, Zoltan J. (1992) *The development of the small business sector in Central and Eastern Europe*, Montreal: Paper presented at the International Conference on Small Business, May 24-27.

Acs, Zoltan and David Audretsch (eds.) (1993) *Small Firms and Entrepreneurship: an East-West Perspective,* Cambridge: Cambridge University Press.

AECD (1992) *Annual Report on the State of the Bulgarian Economy, December 1992,* Sofia: Agency for Economic Coordination and Development.

Bartlett, Will (1992) Foreign trade and stabilization policy in a self-managed economy: Yugoslavia in the 1980s, in Ailcock, John B., John J. Horton and Marko Milivojevic (eds.), *Yugoslavia in Transition: Choices and Constraints,* Oxford: Berg.

Bartlett, Will (1993); A comparison of the development of small firms in Bulgaria and Hungary; *Moct-Most,* 2, 73-96.

Central Statistical Institute (1992).

Central Statistical Office (1993).

Chavance, Bernard (1991); What kind of transition and what kind of market in Eastern Europe?; *Moct-Most,* 2, 9-18.

Clague, Christopher and Gordon C. Rausser (eds.) (1992) *The Emergence of Market Economies in Eastern Europe,* Oxford: Blackwell.

Curran, James and Robert Blackburn (1991) *Path of Enterprise: the Future of Small Business,* London: Routledge.

EBRD (1993) *Current Economic Issues*, July.

Gleick, J. (1988) *Chaos: Making a New Science,* Heinemann.

Hoggett, Paul and Lazlo Kallay (1993) *The Development of the Small Business Sector in Hungary*, Bristol: School for Advanced Urban Studies, Working Paper 117.

Jones, Derek and M. Meurs (1991); On entry of new firms in socialist economies: evidence from Bulgaria; *Soviet Studies,* 312-27.

Kallay, Laszlo (1992) *Small Business Development through Privatization,* Budapest: Foundation for Market Economy.

Kiss, Yudit (1992); Privatization in Hungary - two years later; *Soviet Studies,* 44 (6), 1015-38.

Kuczi, T. and A. Vajda (1990); The Social Composition of Small Entrepreneurs; *Acta Oeconomica,* 42, 329-46.

Lengyel, G. (1989) Entrepreneurial Inclinations, in Toth, A. and L. Gabor (eds.); Hungary under the reform; *Research review,* 3, Budapest.

MacDonald, R. (1991) *A Culture of Enterprise or a Culture of Survival? Being Your Own Boss in Cleveland,* paper presented to the British Sociological Association Conference, April, University of Surrey.

Marceau, M. (1990) The dwarves of capitalism, in Clegg, S. and G. Redding (eds.), *Capitalism in Contrasting Cultures,* Berlin: Walter de Gruyter.

Marrese, Michael (1992) *The growth of the private sector in Hungary: establishing new firms and privatising state firms*, Northwestern University: mimeo.

Mizsei, Kalman (1992); Privatization in Eastern Europe: a comparative study of Poland and Hungary; *Soviet Studies,* 44, 283-96.

Monthly Bulletin of Statistics (1993) *Kozponti Statisztikai Hivatal*, Budapest.

Prasnikar, Janez and Dusan Valencic (1992) *The small scale economy in Slovenia: a general overview,* Ljublana: mimeo, CISEF.

Puchev, Plamen (1990); A note on government policy and the new 'intrapreneurship' in Bulgaria; *Small Business Economics,* 2, 73-5.

Puchev, Plamen (1991) *Development of the 'small business' sector in Bulgaria,* conference paper, 36th Annual World Conference, ICSB, Vienna, June 1991.

Richter, Sandor (ed.) (1992), *The Transition from Command to Market Economies in East-Central Europe,* Boulder: Westview Press.

Rojec, M. and M. Svetlicic (1993); Foreign Investment in Slovenia: Prospects and Policy Options; *Communist Economies and Economic Transformation,* 5, 103-14.

Siebert, H. (ed.) (1992) *The Transformation of Socialist Economies,* Tübingen: J.C.B. Mohr (Paul Siebeck).

Sik, E. (1993); From the Second to the Informal Economy; *Journal of Public Policy,* 12, 153-75.

Smith, Alan H. (1991) The implications of change in East Central Europe for the Balkan socialist economies, in Sjoberg, Orjan and Michael Wyzan (eds.), *Economic Change in the Balkans: Albania, Bulgaria, Romania and Yugoslavia,* London: Pinter.

Staticheski Godishnik Bulgaria (1991).

Statistical Office of Macedonia (1993).

Statisticki Godisnjak Jugoslavije (1990).

Statisticni Letopis Republike Slovenije (1991).

Storey, David and John Atkinson (eds.) (1993) *Employment, the Small Firm and the Labor Market*, London: Routledge.

Tibor, Agnes (1992) *Small- and medium-scale business promotion in Hungary*, Paper presented to the International Seminar on Privatization of Bulgarian Economy, Varna, 18-28, June 1992.

UPEE (1992) *Union for Private Economic Enterprise,* Sofia: Union for Private Economic Enterprise.

Uvalic, Milica (1992) *Investment and Property Rights in Yugoslavia: the Long Transition to a Market Economy,* Cambridge: Cambridge University Press.

Wang, Z. (1993); Foreign Investment in Hungary: A Survey of Experience and Prospects; *Communist Economics and Economic Transformation,* 5, 2, 245-54.

Ward, Robin (1991) Economic development and ethnic business, in Curran and Blackburn (eds.), *Path of Enterprise,* op. cit.

Weiss, Linda (1989) *Creating Capitalism,* Cambridge: Cambridge University Press.

168 Hours (1992), July 20-26.

Appendix: changing size distributions of firms in South East Europe

A1 Macedonia

Table 11.A1 Changing structure of enterprise, Macadonia (per cent)

	Firms		Employment	
Employment Size Group	1989	1991	1989	1991
1-6	11.2	72.6	0.1	2.2
7-15	11.8	7.4	0.5	1.1
6-19	10.2	3.8	0.9	1.3
20-60	12.3	3.9	2.2	2.8
61-125	14.2	3.9	5.4	5.7
126-250	14.4	3.4	11.2	10.5
251-500	13.6	2.6	21.0	16.5
501-1 000	8.1	1.3	23.8	15.8
1 001-2 000	3.2	0.7	20.0	14.5
>2 000	1.0	0.4	14.9	29.6

Note: Data refer to all new firms registered as companies.

Source: Statistical Office of Macedonia, Skopje.

A2 Slovenia

Table 11.A2 Changing structure of enterprise, Slovenia (per cent)

	Firms		Employment	
Employment Size Group	1990	1992	1990	1992
0	40.6	37.2	0	0
1-10	31.0	45.0	0.9	3.4
11-50	8.0	7.1	2.6	5.5
51-250	12.7	7.6	19.1	27.6
>250	7.7	3.1	77.4	63.5

Note: Data refer to registered companies.

Source: Prasnikar and Valencic, 1992.

A3 Hungary

Table 11.A3 Changing structure of enterprise, Hungary (per cent)

	Firms			
Employment Size Group	1989	1990	1991	1992
<20	37.6	59.5	72.5	78.3
21-50	17.6	14.9	12.2	10.3
51-300	25.5	16.2	10.6	8.6
>300	19.3	9.4	4.7	2.9

Note: The table refers to 'enterprises with legal entity'.

Source: Monthly Bulletin of Statistics, 1993/1, Kozponti Statisztikai Hivatal, Budapest.

Table 11.A4 Changing structure of enterprise, Bulgaria (per cent)

	Firms			Employment		
Employment Size Group	1989	1990	1991	1989	1990	1991
f<51	0.18	0.20	0.21	0.01	0.01	0.02
51-140	0.19	0.21	0.27	0.04	0.05	0.07
141-200	0.11	0.10	0.10	0.04	0.04	0.05
201-500	0.26	0.25	0.25	0.19	0.20	0.24
501-1 000	0.15	0.14	0.10	0.22	0.23	0.20
1 001-3 000	0.09	0.09	0.07	0.32	0.33	0.31
3 001-5 000	0.01	0.01	0.00	0.07	0.06	0.03
5 001-10 000	0.00	0.00	0.00	0.06	0.05	0.06
>10 000	0.00	0.00	0.00	0.05	0.02	0.03

Note: State industrial enterprises only.

Source: Statisticheski Godishnik Bulgaria.

12 Poland and the Czech Republic: Privatization from above versus privatization from below or mass privatization versus generic private enterprise building

Krzysztof J. Ners

Motto:

> 'It is too early to judge effects of privatization where it actually occurred, but it is not too early perhaps to observe that not much of it is occurring in most places, and that what does occur is much more ambiguous than originally expected.' (Frydman and Rapaczynski, 1993, 10)

1. Introduction

The fall of communist governments has not brought about an immediate reemergence of liberal societies in Eastern Europe. Nor does it imply that a market economy will immediately flourish and restore economic equilibrium after merely temporary difficulties.

Macroeconomic stabilization has to go hand in hand with a complex process of structural and institutional transformation. These have to be mutually reinforcing. Stabilization must be the first step, the key to improved macroeconomic management. However, serious tensions have arisen between demand-management stabilization programs and supply-focused structural adjustment programs, in which due to the rigid structure inherited from the command economy an oligopolistic economic environment faces great difficulties.

Since the beginning of stabilization programs in the post-communist Central Eastern European countries, privatization has been assigned an important role in accomplishing both the transition from centrally planned economies to market friendly systems, and from quasi-totalitarian political system to pluralistic democracy and civil societies.

In view of the property rights debate which takes place on theoretical and political levels privatization has gained special attention. As a rule, socialism implies public ownership while capitalism implies private ownership of most of the material means of production and distribution. In fact, as stated by I. Grosfeld, we have been observing an axiomatic approach to privatization: 'we should take it for granted that privatization is desirable' (Grosfeld and Hare, 1992, 131).

Privatization has been seen as a way of improving the economic performance of the former state-owned enterprises (SOEs). It is also considered to be a fundamental element in the process of creating a competitive market environment. The assumption that progress in privatization, especially in mass privatization, is one of the most important criteria of progress in transition has had very practical consequences. It was accepted as an important element of conditionality by international financial institutions.[1] Even more so, it was in line with the importance attached to the formal transfer of ownership rights.

As the Czech Prime Minister Klaus stated: 'the Czech Republic is far outpacing other nations in the region'.[2] The main reason for his assessment, which is shared by many experts both in the West as well as in post-communist countries, is the simultaneous implementation of an ambitious program of mass-privatization and the macroeconomic adjustment initiated three years ago. The Czech voucher scheme has been advertised as the quickest way to build a market economy.

The very specific feature of the Czech Republic has been the political domination by Klaus' party (ODS) which, to a large extent, had built its electoral success on the popular expectations about mass privatization. The relatively conservative macroeconomic policy and formal transfer of ownership rights by means of the voucher scheme are major features of this party's rhetorics. Thus, thanks to political determination and a relatively balanced economy, the Czech mass privatization program was implemented in an environment no other post-communist country could even dream of. Hence, in other transforming economies privatization schemes were more diversified, and, in fact, voucher privatization has been the subject of time-consuming political debates and has delayed implementation.

It appears important to bear in mind these very specific political and economic conditions of the Czech Republic when assessing the results and the implementation process of mass privatization. If we consider the additional elements of a most advanced technical infrastructure we may assume it to be unrealistic to expect other post-communist countries to achieve better results in mass privatization.

The political struggle in Poland, and the logical focus on macroeconomic stabilization and adjustment on the basis of a very high initial inflation and other inherited macroeconomic imbalances, has caused the privatization process to be slower than expected and the voucher scheme implementation unfortunately delayed. The Polish privatization schemes have evolved into highly differentiated multidimensional arrangements with assets sales by auctions, leasing arrangements for state assets, manager/employee buyouts, direct sales or public share offering and restitution or mass privatization by voucher schemes. So far, privatization by liquidation has been most

1 For example, the World Bank has delayed its $450 million loan until the mass privatization bill is passed by the Polish Parliament.

2 Prime Minister Klaus emphasized this several times. In October 1993, during his visit to the US, he said in New York: 'the reform-oriented and coherent economic policy with by far the lowest inflation rate, the lowest unemployment rate, a balanced state budget and a stable exchange rate of the currency, together with the fastest pace of deregulation, liberalization and privatization, are the factors which put us visibly apart from other countries of central and eastern Europe.' Quoted by Central European Business Weekly, October 22-28, 1993.

successful.[3] The goals of such approaches have been to prevent sales at unduly low prices, to enhance corporate governance and the efficiency of labor, capital and management and to improve the financial stance of companies.

Although privatization in Poland has not been spectacular, the expansion of private, small and medium-sized new businesses has proven to be a very positive trend. Among Central and Eastern European countries, private enterprise in Poland is most advanced. The private sector has a 50 per cent share in Polish GDP with more than 60 per cent of labor currently being offered by some 1.7 million private enterprises. These figures indicate that Poland has passed a significant threshold on its road to a true market economy.

The resources (financial and technical assistance, legal and administrative expertise) being absorbed by the privatization process, the current emphasis on privatization deviates from the development of the new, generic, private entrepreneurship. As a result, the expansion of a new private sector is relatively slow in the Czech Republic, a country which enjoys the strongest profound industrial tradition in the region. The new private sector[4] in the Czech Republic currently accounts for some 20 per cent of GDP.[5]

The comparision of two actual paths of transition - one based on the formal transfer of ownership rights through the voucher scheme in the Czech Republic and another on slower and more diversified paths of privatization accompanied by a quick expansion of new private enterprise in Poland[6] - led to several conclusions.[7] Assuming that the short

---

3 'The most successful privatization path was through liquidation, which in effect allows workers to buy their firm at a discount.' (Blanchard, 1993, 273-274.)

4 It is important to distinguish the generic private sector from the 'privatized' one. According to the Czech Minister for Industry and Trade, V. Dlouhy, since August 1991 55 per cent to 60 per cent of assets of 2 237 enterprises representing a value of some 20 billion dollars have been privatized. See: Wall Street Journal, October 26, 1993.

5 There is limited information available on the private sector, especially on small and medium-sized enterprises in Central and Eastern Europe because entrepreneurs are reluctant to provide information on their activities while the statistical services lack experience. Thus, there are very diversified statistical data. While there is major agreement about data concerning the Polish private sector, opinions on Czech private enterprise diverge. G. Schwartz and P. Silva Lopes estimate the Polish private sector to have accounted for 45 per cent of GDP in 1992, and in former Czechoslovakia for 16-20 per cent of GDP compared to about ten per cent in 1991 (see IMF, 1993, 14). According to the Czech Statistical Office at the end of the first quarter of 1993 29.9 per cent of GDP originated from the private sector (19.5 per cent in 1992), 15 per cent of which in industries where 'the effect of voucher privatization is to be observed later'. Quoted in Mladek (1993).

6 To a large extent, the 'Polish path' is not the result of a conscious strategy of transition. In fact, it is rather the result of a political inability of the first four post-communist governments to vote and implement the voucher scheme which was originally elaborated in Poland much earlier than in the Czech Republic. Another characteristic of privatization in Poland was that a lot less emphasis was placed on the voucher scheme as only one of several possible paths of privatization.

7 Such a comparison should be possible without a very competitive approach assessing the progress in transition. This approach so familiar among the transition countries is understandable as a part of a marketing strategy competing for foreign investment, and because of political reasons. 'Comparison is a source of insight and understanding. It kills static certitudes of isolation; it breeds abilities of relative orientation.' (Holesovsky, 1977, 11).

and medium-term results of these strategies determine the successful accomplishment of transformation we observe these results in terms of impact on industrial restructuring, clear ownership relations, unemployment and job creation, restoring economic growth, improving productivity and transition politics. This issue is not only of theoretical relevance. There is a consensus on building a market economy as an ultimate goal of transition. However, consensus does not exist on sequencing and methods. The harsh discussion about the voucher schemes in Poland, Hungary, the Slovak Republic, Romania and Bulgaria during the last two to three years is empirical evidence of this disagreement and demonstrates how important this issue is for the transition politics.

2. Mass privatization is time consuming and thus delays economic restructuring

There is some controversy about small, spontaneous privatization. Although accusations about the nomenclature and even corrupted privatization exist, the process has been accomplished with impressive speed as retail trade, shops, restaurants and services are predominantly private in all Central and Eastern European countries. It was successful in terms of a transfer of previously state-owned assets to the private owners.

The real problem is the privatization of the big state-owned enterprises. The process of selling off large industrial firms has proven to be much slower than originally anticipated. There has been an assumption that the state-owned enterprises are not able to adjust to the market economy. Even more so, they are (with their labor well organized in trade unions) the main threat to the continuity of radical economic reforms. Because of their rigidity, conservative product mixture and their very often oligopolistic position in the market, they constitute - in simple economic terms - the main impediments to the supply response to price and trade liberalizations. The problem with these dinosaurs of the so-called socialist industrialization is that they are usually unattractive for foreign capital and, due to the regional trade collapse, some of them have lost their markets.

Most privatization experts agree that large-scale privatization in Central and Eastern Europe cannot be accomplished by traditional methods (see Borensztein and Kumar, 1991). The Chilean example, often quoted as the most successful case of privatization in the less developed countries, required a period of 15 years for a divestiture of about 15 per cent of GDP (see Luders, 1990). Chile's total effort over a 20-year period involved the privatization of approximatively 550 firms employing five per cent of the country's workers (World Bank, 1992). Privatization in Central and Eastern Europe at the speed achieved under former Prime Minister Thatcher would require more than 50 years (Scott, 1993). If speed of privatization (formal transfer of ownership rights) is considered the main criterion of progress in transition, the coupon privatization method is a natural, and thus the most obvious, technique.[8]

---

8 We do not deal with re-privatization, which is surprisingly so successful, especially in the Czech Republic.

Poland is transforming its economy utilizing different privatization techniques. The Polish perception of privatization understands it as a tool, i.e. a means of restructuring the economy by making companies competitive and economically viable. For this reason the unemployment rate is high, at an average level of 13 to 15 per cent and even higher in those regions most affected by restructuring.

In fact, in addition to showing that macroeconomic measures have been successful, the single-digit unemployment figures for the Czech Republic at this stage of transition prove that the privatization and restructuring process is not yet concluded. The slowness of the actual transfer of property rights, and the lack of better allocation and microeconomic efficiency on the part of both state-owned companies and those being privatized, were responsible for the economic decline in 1992-1993. The disproportion between the drop in economic income and employment illustrates the situation. This issue is extremely important; according to several estimates about one-fourth of industrial enterprises in the Czech Republic are economically unviable under the new conditions or show negative value added at world prices (see, for example, Hughes and Hare, 1991). Improvements in efficiency do not follow from privatization per se, but from the benefits that increased competition can bring to the market place if it is accompanied by industrial restructuring. The danger of delayed restructuring - waiting until privatization is accomplished - is that all economic and social costs of the economic restructuring will appear only in the third or fourth year of transition and will be associated with a market economy, not with the transition itself. We can assume that the population's willingness to accept the costs of economic transformation is decreasing as time passes from the collapse of communist governments in Central and Eastern Europe.

An additional factor is that, due to an aggressive advertisement for investment funds, the people's expectations were growing during the first and second waves of privatization as far as the immediate and medium-term results were concerned. As several investment funds promised a ten times return for 1 000 Crowns 'invested' in purchasing the privatization voucher, a quick return is often taken for granted.[9]

The Czech privatization process has been a great organizational and political success, as more than eight million Czechs and Slovaks signed up during the first round of privatization instead of the originally anticipated three million. Almost 1 500 companies took part in the first round of privatization (of 2 270 approved). The goal to have more than 90 per cent of assets privatized by the end of 1994 is considered very ambitious.

The Polish mass privatization program was a victim of the political struggle going on after 1989. In fact, Poland has been harshly criticized for its lack of progress in this area. On the other hand, the Polish mass privatization program was less ambitious. Originally 600 state-owned companies were eligible, however, this number was reduced to 200 because of the fact that companies have to be economically viable to be eligible

9 There is always a trade-off. After almost four years of transition in Poland led by Solidarity-rooted parties, the left wing parties won the parliamentary majority; to a large extent this was a reaction to the social and economic costs of radical economic transformation. Simultaneously, in the Czech Republic, public support was gained for mass privatization as a vehicle of transition. The real question is how to exploit these to make the transition process irreversible.

for mass privatization. 28.3 per cent of Polish companies have been privatized during the last three years. There were 8 441 SOEs at the end of 1990; 2 385 companies have been privatized, while 1 013 have been privatized by liquidation. The new government hopes that another third will be privatized by the end of 1996 (Rzeczpospolita, 1993).

In the Polish approach to privatization the most important feature is that privatization is linked with restructuring. This is the goal of 'sectoral privatization' as well as the goal of the Polish mass privatization program passed by the parliament in mid-1993. The aim of this program is to privatize some 600 state-owned firms from different industrial sectors, representing between 8 and 14 per cent of total state assets. These companies will be comprised together into about 20 National Investment Funds. 'The goal is to restructure the companies within the limited financial resources of the country'.[10]

In the Czech Republic, the government's main objectives in microeconomic policy presently are to accomplish the first and second privatization waves and simultaneously prevent bankruptcies of those companies being privatized. Anti-bankruptcy measures have prevented the bankruptcy restructuring. Only 30 of the 993 companies with bankruptcy filings had actually been declared bankrupt by mid-October.[11] The Czech ease for anti-bankruptcy policies is understandable since privatization was expected to occur in a short period of time, and not be unhealthy for the economy. There was a prevailing consideration that the post-communist state could not carry out effective liquidation of enterprises, and that only liquidation decided by private owners under market conditions would be effective. If the government is not able to take responsibility for closing large SOEs, it is unrealistic to expect private owners to take over such companies and eventually restructure them while exposed to great political pressure (especially if the owner is a foreigner). Many of the enterprises now going through bankruptcy proceedings are included in the second wave of privatization, which means that the Czech privatization has not been rapid enough.

Under the Polish privatization law the founding body is responsible for ensuring that any monopolistic enterprise is broken up and non-viable or non-performing enterprises are liquidated before they are considered for privatization. Privatization is often seen as the best means to enforce market discipline and promote an efficient allocation and use of resources. This is true when accomplished in the competitive macroeconomic framework and tough budgetary discipline. Both countries run very tough monetary policies. The differences are rather in the level of corporate control and the financial as well as managerial autonomy of state-owned enterprises ('commercialization') in Poland and the level of trade liberalization, often considered excessive in Poland, but certainly important as an element of competitive environment. Another important difference is the vitality of the Polish private sector as a competitor. These differences are illustrated

10 J. Thieme, chief adviser to the Ministry of Privatization; quoted by Central European (1993, 44).

11 Hospodarske noviny, 18 October 1993. Quoted in Brom and Orenstein (1993, 9-10). The same reported for the period November 1992-September 1993 by Central European Business Weekly supplement 'Banking Review', December 1993.

by the fact that, beginning in March 1994, there will be no governmental wage control in Polish SOEs (private firms are already excluded), whereas the Czech government had been forced to re-introduce wage control for all companies over 25 employees, including private ones in 1993.

The Polish state sector has done much better than expected, but its restructuring is still very slow, even under the very hard budgetary constraint. There is however, evidence that the SOEs have become increasingly convinced that they will have to adjust on their own. As the recent World Bank empirical study on Polish industrial transformation (see Pinto, Belka and Krajewski, 1993) shows, some state-owned enterprises are adapting to new realities with considerable vigor. Monitoring a sample of 75 companies the World Bank study found that the companies reduced their labor force on average by 27 per cent during three years, they improved labor and unit costs management; all firms managed to reduce the consumption of materials and energy per unit of sale and also improved their product-mix as well as marketing. This study was important as it provided some solid empirical evidence against common belief which considers the SOEs unable to restructure and adjust to the market environment. It could be used as an argument against speed as a main criterion of successful privatization/restructuring. SOEs' behavior and reform remain vital for medium-run growth in Poland, where the state manufacturing sector still accounts for a high share of GDP, employment, taxes and exports.

Thus the management of SOEs remains an important objective. It has too long been underestimated, as the expectations about rapid transition prevailed (Rolland, 1993, 275-277). It again raises the discussion about sequencing: privatization and then restructuring versus restructuring and then privatization through suitable privatization paths. One might argue that rapid/mass privatization in fact delays restructuring, while successful restructuring, possible under the right conditions (clarified managerial accountability, more diversified privatization paths, participation of strategic investor, increasingly competitive environment), may facilitate privatization.

These questions are crucial as far as the medium-to-long term development potential is concerned, which itself depends on the speed and depth of sectoral and microeconomic adjustment and an improved economic efficiency. In the short term the supply response[12] is directly linked with ongoing restructuring and clarifying managerial accountability. Long-term successful restructuring allows privatization through a suitable privatization path.[13]

---

12 It perhaps gives a new emphasis to the importance of macro-economic discipline and increasing competitive environment. This last factor depends on the level of trade liberalization and the vitality of the generic private sector.

13 There are numerous foreign assistance programs supporting privatization in the Czech Republic and in Poland. In Poland we should also mention the EBRD program established to finance the restructuring and privatization of potentially viable but not necessarily creditworthy enterprises - 'Special Restructuring Programme'; and the World Bank ESAL Program of support of restructuring in the regions with a high unemployment.

3. Mass privatization does not clarify ownership structure

Instead of clarifying the property ownership structure and establishing a system of economic incentives characteristic for the market economy, the Czech mass privatization 'resulted in a maze of complicated economic and legal relations'.[14] Over 70 per cent of the voucher recipients decided to place their vouchers with the investment funds. From 436 registered investment funds, the 12 largest collected 93 per cent of vouchers invested in mutual funds. This concentration could be considered a positive sign,[15] but the Federal law prevented an Investment Privatization Fund from owning more than 20 per cent of any one company, or from investing more than 10 per cent of its own capital in any one individual company. Thus the problem of strategic investors will be another impediment to the companies' restructuring. As stated by Raiser and Nunnenkamp, 'a new ownership structure of former SOEs is not necessarily conducive to cost efficiency and restructuring' (Raiser and Nunnenkamp, 1993, 20).

Investment funds have gained control of a large part of the Czech economy (according to Mladek, 1993). Will they turn out to be industrial investors or short-term profit-seekers? It is still unclear 'who' owns 'what', as the funds have not disclosed their portfolios. The investment funds co-owning the Czech enterprises belong to big commercial banks which are often owned by each other.

The Czech Republic did not experience spontaneous privatization. Two state institutions play a significant role in most privatized companies: the National Property Fund still owns as much as 20 per cent of the book value of enterprises. The Konsolidacni Banka is a major creditor to virtually all privatized enterprises as a result of an enormous loan consolidation effort (Brom and Orenstein, 1993, 32). Both have played key roles in preventing the bancruptcy of companies undergoing privatization. The Czech state-owned enterprises have outstanding bank loans of some 130 billion Czech crowns (4.4 billion US$) with inter-company debts of another 140 billion crowns (4.7 billion US$).[16] According to The Economist (June 19th, 1993) estimations one third of privatized companies are technically bankrupt.

Clearly, mass privatization may lead to growth in bank power. In the Czech Republic, the three major commercial banks accounted for 13 per cent of the total book value of privatized firms.[17] One should remember that banks not only control the major investment funds but also provide credits increasing the level of their control over the enterprises. Taking into account the weakness of the Czech capital market we are close

---

14 See Frydman and Rapaczynski (1993, 13). According to the authors this unclear situation 'may sometimes even impede a speedy transition to a system in which the rights of capital are clearly delineated and protected'.

15 It would be difficult to argue that the dispersion of SOEs' shares across a wide spectrum of the public would provide a more coherent structure of corporate governance.

16 The Economist, November 13, 1993. The Economist estimates that four-fifths of the debts to commercial banks may never be repaid.

17 PLANECON Monthly Economic Review Washington 1993, various issues, quoted by Raiser and Nunnenkamp, 1993.

to the German system of 'corporative banking ownership'.[18] One should remember that the Czech government still owns approximately 40 per cent of the largest banks. Bank concentration in the Czech Republic is very high: two banks control three-fourths of the market (Ickes and Ryterman, 1992, 335). From the beginning of 1992, when the enterprises were transformed into joint stock companies owned by the National Property Fund, to mid-1993, when the first shareholder meetings were held in privatized companies, many enterprises had no effective owner at all, not even a government ministry (Brom and Orenstein, 1993, 34).

In the Eastern European region, the state is generally not the effective owner of socialist enterprises, free to distribute them as it wishes. Various 'stakeholders' exercise a degree of de facto ownership in the sense of being able to exert some influence over enterprise assets in their own interests (Frydman, Phelps, Rapaczynski and Shleifer, 1993, 180). In the absence of real owners of assets the companies lack clear economic goals and are not subject to any effective corporate governance. Whenever possible, privatization should be organized in such a way that active owners can be established and a framework for corporate governance can be put in place instead of laying emphasis on speed and the formal transfer of ownership.

The Polish plan mainly focused on providing a framework for corporate governance through National Investment Funds in which foreign investment banks, consulting firms and individuals should participate. Rapid commercialization of the majority of state-owned companies is an essential first step that would distance firms from state control and establish incentive structures without any protection for poor economic performance. The way is to transform the firms into joint stock companies with shares initially held by the state.[19]

In general, one can say that the costs of transition are higher than expected (high level of unemployment, poor distribution of income and the collapse of state supported social safety net, education and health care). They put pressure on governments to slow down the pace of reform. Thus, restoring economic growth and creating a new entrepreneurial class ready to support the continuation of market friendly reforms are the major factors of transition politics.

4. Privatizing economy versus privatizing enterprises or bottom up building of market economy

At present, one of the most characteristic features of the industrial structure of Central and Eastern European countries is a large gap created by the weakness of the small business sector.

---

18 See Mladek (1993). Ickes and Ryterman (1992, 334) noted: 'the current emphasis on privatization obfuscates the institution that is truly at the core of properly fuctioning market economy - the capital market'.

19 The important factors are convictions that there will neither be a bailout of firms, nor a realistic price system, nor a competitive environment.

Small enterprises constitute the 'backbone' of any market economy. Thanks to their flexibility, their familiarity with market conditions and their unbureaucratic structure they constitute a driving force for economic growth. At the same time they create a considerable number of new jobs (cf. the contributions in Acs and Audretsch, 1993). Innovation, change and vitality in an economic system are associated with vigorous new small and medium-sized companies. This role is even more important during the transition process in which capital mobility is concerned. It explains the primacy of home-grown entreprenerial activity.

New Polish firms are the primary source of economic vitality. The growth rate of the Polish private sector was 7.1 per cent in 1990, 33.3 per cent in 1991 and 12 per cent in 1992. The Polish private sector responded with alacrity to the new business environment. The share of the private sector in Polish GDP rose from 28 per cent in 1989 to 48 per cent in 1992 and passed the threshold of 60 per cent share in employment and 50 per cent share in GDP in 1993 (see Wyznikiewicz, Pinto and Grabowski, 1993a, b). The growth of a new private sector and the restructuring of some state-owned enterprises were responsible for a 10 per cent increase of labor efficiency in Poland from 1991 to 1992, as opposed to a similar drop of 10 per cent in the Czech Republic.

The OECD expects Poland's GDP to expand by a real four per cent in 1994, after three per cent in 1993 and one to two per cent in 1992. These rates make Poland the fastest-growing economy among the post communist countries within the past three years. Moreover, even under the left-wing government in power after September 1993, the 1994 budget deficit is expected to be about four per cent of Poland's GDP. This fact and the very tight monetary policies let us expect that the government's target to slow down inflation to 23 per cent in 1994 from 35 per cent in 1993 is realistic. This means that the adjustment mechanisms, including restructuring, are operating. The prevalent worry is a high level of unemployment, that seems to be the painful cost of restructuring. We can only express the hope that economic growth is the best opportunity to create new jobs that are economically viable.

The private sector in Poland is the biggest in the region but consists of the smallest firms.[20] Private employment in the non-agricultural sector has increased by more than two million over 3.5 years. But this is to a large degree a stock adjustment process - the provision of those trade and services activities which were not supplied under the previous regime. The picture here is one of very small businesses, financed by internal funds, with high rates of closure as well as low wages and high rates of turnover. Some 90 per cent of private firms were established without any financial support from the banks. To sustain its growth, the private sector will require an increase in the firms' sizes to an efficient scale and a development in manufacturing and sophisticated services.

20 On average Polish private firms employ fewer than three workers.

Too much effort is being invested in privatization and too little in creating and fostering the development of new private firms.[21] While the government and human and financial resources are preoccupied with a succesful accomplishment of the privatization process, privatization reflects government attention and resources from the growth of new, generic private enterprises. However, the introduction of small and medium enterprises allows the enhancement of a supply response, the provision of new goods and services, wealth-creating opportunities and the absorption of redundant labor from state enterprises. Small businesses do not need a huge amount of capital. Their key resource is creativity and information. Money becomes important at a certain level. The collateral, required to access funds rather than interest rates, is a big barrier. The required collateral ranges from 150 to 300 per cent of a credit, and certain assets cannot be put up. Some Czech entrepreneurs complained that 'they commonly have difficulties obtaining the quantity of inputs and raw materials they need at the time they need them. They purchase most inputs from state firms whose managers are uninterested in satisfying their needs' (Webster, 1992).

Stimulating any sector requires the provision of funds, technical assistance and an enabling environment. There is a need for a new orientation in the strategy since SMEs are being reached neither by domestic governmental agencies nor by international institutions. The recent IFC study noted that 'local banks accustomed to lending to state companies that offer their assets as collateral are reluctant to switch to untried private clients, who have no track record or security to offer' (Wyznikiewicz, Pinto and Grabowski, 1993a, 6).

Three types of SMEs should be addressed: start-ups, expansion-stage SMEs and spin-offs from SOEs. There are three stages of support:

- preinvestment, inclusion of business plans, advisory services and the strengthening of local institutions;
- the start-up, where equity financing and leasing is very important, as well as incubators, training and business associations;
- and the early growth phase, necessitating international contacts, working capital, venture capital funds, training and advisory services.[22]

5. Conclusions

Private property is crucial whether achieved by the transfer of property rights through 'privatization' of state-owned enterprises or by the development of new private firms. The discussion should emphasize each of these two ways, the speed and 'technology' of privatization, providing the environment and support for private enterpreneurship

21 The ministries of privatization in Poland and Czech Republic are big and powerful. The Polish Ministry for Support of Small and Medium Enterprises operated only for several months in the Suchocka government with only few employees.

22 The medium-sized enterprises are often forgotten as small enterprises mushroom.

building and the consequences for the transition process in Central and Eastern Europe.

There are usually two expectations about privatization: the economic and the political one. Privatization is perceived as the best means to enforce market discipline and to promote an efficient allocation and use of resources. But privatizing enterprises alone does not suffice; rather, entire industries have to be restructured to ensure competitiveness if efficiency gains are to materialize themselves. Improvements in efficiency do not follow privatization *per se*, but from the benefit that increased competition can bring to the market if accompanied by industrial restructuring.

The political expectations concern the building of the entrepreneurial class as a result of the transfer of the assets from the state sector. This task is very important as the weakness of the middle class is perceived as the main obstacle in building a stable civil society and, thus, a pluralistic democracy. A different argument is that such a transfer could secure the support for the building of the capitalist economy, so important during the socially painful transition period.

However, there is no single panacea and we argue against considering mass privatization as such. This has very practical implications. The axiomatic emphasis on privatization of the large state-owned enterprises has delayed their restructuring. It also redirected government energy, Western assistance and the decision makers' attention from the new enterpreneurship emerging in the region. Assuming that progress in mass privatization is one of the main criteria of good performance has practical consequences in the international arena. In the same approach some Russian reformers argue about the reforms in Russia emphasizing the progress in different mass privatization schemes.[23]

Once a significant private sector appears, the success of its further development depends as much on the change in the general economic environment as on the completeness of the privatization process.[24] Because of their time-consuming nature and the problems with corporate governance, mass privatization schemes should not be given emphasis in the beginning phases of transition. For political reasons it is difficult to have such general acceptance for the mass privatization program as it was possible in the Czech Republic. On the other hand it does not mean that voucher privatization should not be considered, as a very important path of privatization, especially useful in privatizing big and medium-sized companies which are relatively less attractive to foreign capital or to capital privatization. Thus, the question is rather about suitable sequencing and not about paying too much attention to one specific path of privatization that takes too much time to accomplish and diverts attention from other ways of building private ownership.

---

23 Chubais is even arguing that privatization is the most important step and should anticipate the macroeconomic libaralization and stabilization.

24 As we argued in favor of SOEs to be considered for restructuring as quickly as possible and then for privatization, we should once again refer to the World Bank study: 'while the new private sector and foreign investors have a crucial role, this must be in conjunction with the energy flowing from a reformed state sector. The state sector can achieve this in two ways: directly, as a result of the benefits flowing from a more efficient sector; indirectly as a result of resources released for use by new entrants' (see Pinto, Belka and Krajewski, 1993, 37).

The coupon/voucher schemes may play an important role in the privatization process but it cannot be a 'panacea' for successful transition. Concentrating solely on mass privatization as a single means diverts attention and resources from other equally important means of privatizing and restructuring post-communist economies, as for example, developing a new private sector and corporatizing and restructuring some state-owned companies that are not immediately ready for privatization. The real challenge the governments of post-communist countries are coping with in the short to medium-term is to find the right, pragmatic mixture of different means to increase the efficiency of the entire economy, to improve microeconomic efficiency, resource allocation and the corporate control over companies, to create new jobs and to restore economic growth and competitiveness.

References

Acs, Z.J. and D.B. Audretsch (1993) (eds.) *Small firms and entrepreneurship: an East West perspective*, Cambridge: Cambridge University Press.

Blanchard, O.J. (1993); On the dynamics of transformation and restructuring; *Economics of Transition*, 1 (2), London: EBRD, 273-74.

Borensztein, E. and M.S. Kumar (1991); Proposals for Privatization in Eastern Europe; *IMF Staff Papers*, 38, No.2, June.

Brom, K. and M. Orenstein (1993); The 'Privatized Sector' in the Czech Republic: Government and Bank Control in a Transitional Economy; *IEWS Working Paper*, Prague November 23, 9-10, 32.

Central European (1993), November, 44.

Central European Business Weekly (1993), October, 22-28.

Central European Business Weekly supplement 'Banking Review' (1993), December.

The Economist (1993) November, 13.

Frydman, R. and A. Rapaczynski (1993); Privatization in Eastern Europe: Is the State Withering Away?; *Finance and Development*, IMF June, 10,13.

Frydman, R., E.S. Phelps, A. Rapaczynski and A. Shleifer (1993); Needed mechanisms of corporate governance and finance in Eastern Europe; *Economics of Transition*, 1 (2), 180.

Grosfeld, I. and P. Hare (1992) *Privatization in Hungary, Poland and Czechoslovakia*, 131.

Holesovsky, V. (1977) *Economic Systems: analysis and comparison*, New York: McGraw-Hill Book Company, 11.

Hughes, G. and P. Hare (1991); Competitiveness and industrial restructuring in Czechoslovakia, Hungary and Poland; *European Economy*, 2.

Ickes, B. and R. Ryterman (1992) *Credit for Small Firms, Not Dinosaurs*, Orbis, Summer 1992, 334.

IMF (1993); Privatization: Expectations, Trade-offs and Results; *Finance and Development*, June, 14.

Luders, I. (1990) *Chile's Massive SOE Divestiture Program*, Washington: World Bank.

Mladek, J. (1993) *Nine banks, two insurance companies, PPF and the Harvard Group were basically capable to control voucher privatization*, in Czech Privatization Process-Time for Corporate Governance, Paper presented at the IIASA-Austria Conference, 18-20 November.

Pinto, B., M. Belka and S. Krajewski (1993) *Transforming State Enterprises in Poland*, World Bank Working Paper, 37.

Raiser, M. and P. Nunnenkamp (1993) *The Role of Incentives Before, During and After Privatization*, Paper presented at the IIASA, Austria conference, 20.

Rolland, G. (1993); Structural Adjustment; *Economics of Transition*, 1 (2), London, 275-77.

Rzeczpospolita (1993), December 15.

Scott, Thomas (1993); The Politics and Economics of Privatization in Central and Eastern Europe; *Columbia Journal of World Business*, Spring 1993.

Wall Street Journal (1993), October 26.

Webster, L. (1992) *Private Sector Manufacturing in CSFR*, Washington: World Bank.

World Bank (1992) *Privatizing Eastern European Economies: A Critical Review and Proposal*, World Bank Internal Discussion Paper, December 1992.

Wyznikiewicz, B., B. Pinto and M.Grabowski (1993a) *Coping with Capitalism. The New Polish Entrepreneurs*, Washington: IFC Discussion Paper.

Wyznikiewicz, B., B. Pinto and M. Grabowski (1993b) *Investing in the Future, Report of the Task Force for Small and Medium Enterprise*, Warsaw 1993.

13 The entrepreneurial sector and its role in industrial transformation in East Germany and Poland

Hans-Peter Brunner

1. Introduction

In the early process of adjustment from centrally planned to market guided economies, Eastern Europe has seen its industries dwindle and disappear. Correspondingly industrial employment by firms with more than 19 employees has declined by 45 per cent from 3.23 in 1989 to 1.76 million people at the end of 1991 in East Germany. In Poland firms with more than 5 employees experienced an overall decline from 4.02 to 3.32 million people between 1989 and 1991 (see Table 13.1). Only the recreation of a culture of small and medium-sized enterprises, the entrepreneurial sector that was subdued during the post World War II era, will provide employment for a large part of the presently un- or under-utilized industrial workforce of Eastern Europe.

An emergent entrepreneurial sector creates the much longed for employment on the basis of its increasing innovativeness, productivity, and growth. In their long list of stylized facts, Dosi et al. (1993) enter the strong correlation between a country's industrial capabilities of innovating and its international trade and growth performance in the 1970s and 1980s. If anything, in those two decades that positive correlation has become stronger. In the U.S. economy large and small firms coexist within many industrial sectors, but small firms apparently are the ones that specialize in the innovation of new products (Acs and Audretsch, 1990). Other studies show this to be the case in other countries as well. In the case of the Indian computer industry, small- and medium-scale enterprises played a substantial role in the acquisition of international computer technology. Moreover, the entry of a large number of firms in the early 1980s provided a seed-bed from which some successful firms grew to considerable employment size (Brunner, 1991). If small firms can function as innovative agents, then they can thrive in transition economies that need to find appropriate new products to sell in international markets.

The privatized and the nascent entrepreneurial industrial sector is considered the growth node for transforming economies, since it produces competitive tradable goods (see Keren, 1995). This observed pattern of economic development has emerged across a wide variety of countries adopting different reform strategies. Empirical studies, for example in the former West Germany, have established a close connection (positive spillover effects) between high industrial growth (tradables) and above-average growth in service sectors (to a large extent non-tradables) on a regional basis (e.g. Hall, 1991). In the case of West Germany the intraregional spillover was strongly positive from industry to services and trades, and a relatively weak relationship existed from the construction sector to the trade sectors.

Table 13.1 Size distribution of industrial firms in Poland and East Germany compared with West Germany

Firm size (plant)	Enterprises (no. of firms)			Employment (no. of employees)		
	Poland					
	1989	1991	per cent	1989	1991	per cent
-5		314 777	97.8	-	608 823	15.5
6-100	1 203	2 119	0.7	56 175	132 100	3.4
101-1 000	3 805	4 234	1.3	1 337 512	1 329 000	33.9
1 001-	1 000	696	0.2	2 623 436	1 850 700	47.2
Total	6 008	321 826	100.0	4 017 123	3 920 623	100.0

	East Germany					
	1987	1992	per cent	1987	1992**	per cent
-19	-	928	14.7	-	10 449	1.0
20-100	642	3 669	58.0	33 821	173 146	17.1
101-1 000	1 938	1 623	25.7	748 524	622 032	61.5
1,001-	843	104	1.6	2 448 348	207 195	20.4
Total	3 423	6 324	100.0	3 230 693	1 012 822	100.0

	West Germany industry*							
	1987	per cent	1992	per cent	1987	per cent	1992**	per cent
1-19	5 563	12.7	5 809	12.3	56 247	0.8	59 247	0.8
20-99	25 984	59.3	28 015	59.5	1 197 441	17.3	1 295 180	18.1
100-999	11 329	25.8	12 289	26.2	3 015 356	43.7	3 279 336	45.7
1,000-	952	2.2	957	2.0	2 638 471	38.2	2 540 677	35.4
Total	43 828	100.0	47 070	100.0	6 907 515	100.0	7 171 404	100.0

Notes: * Including apprentices for firms > 20 employees, excludes employment in energy producing industry.
** As of Sept. 30, 1992.

Sources: Industry Statistics, Central Statistical Office, Warsaw, 1990 and 1992. Statistisches Jahrbuch der DDR, Berlin (East), 1989; Statistisches Jahrbuch der Bundesrepublik Deutschland, Wiesbaden, 1989 and 1992.

The construction industry did respond strongly with growth in regions of strong industrial growth, however. Experience in newly industrializing economies suggests as well that the service and trade sector is dependent on a well-developed industrial sector, not vice versa. The overemphasis on heavy manufacturing goods sectors in the former German Democratic Republic (GDR), made superfluous an extensive and well-defined service and trade sector. Before 1989, the services and trade sectors employed only 25 per cent of the East German workforce, compared to 42 per cent in West Germany (Sinn and Sinn, 1992, 52-3).

Certain economic conditions, such as short-term and long-term interest rates - themselves a reflection of investment risks; the hardness of government budget constraints and the level of taxes, decisively influence the behavior of entrepreneurs and the processes of innovation. For competitiveness the entrepreneurial decision whether to locate in the tradable or non-tradable sectors of the economy looms particularly large. In the last few years analytical and empirical work in the area of economics of innovation has demarcated the avenues by which certain economic conditions influence the processes of innovation, which provide the basis for growth and competitiveness (Foray and Freeman, 1993; Dosi et al., 1993). Elsewhere, I interpret the mass of information and stylized facts generated by the economics of technical change and industrial innovation with the help of a process model (Brunner, 1994). In that model innovation is driven by new technology absorption and creation, the diffusion of such new information among a technologically diverse population of firms of different size (small, medium and large), and economic selection via entry, exit and appropriation of benefits from technology creation. Governmental institutions can accelerate or slow down the processes of innovation.

The focus of this study is the transforming industrial sector in two Eastern European cases, East Germany and Poland. So far the transformation processes in Eastern Europe have *not* been observed to take place along the nexus of productivity (branch composition of industry), market competition (size structure or industry concentration), and the survival rates of various kinds of firms (turbulence) combined with the intensity of entry and of entrepreneurial activity. In the following two sections I present recently available empirical evidence as to structural shifts in branch composition, size structure, and entry and exit dynamics in the early transforming industrial sectors of first East Germany, and second, Poland. The observed structural changes are indicative of the utilization of those economies' entrepreneurial potential, for their productivity and growth and for their competitiveness on world markets. A section comparing the recent experience of East Germany with the Polish experience highlights differences in strategies and similarities and differences in outcomes.

This paper will then propose an 'evolutionary' strategy of transformation as the best way to unleash the entrepreneurial potential of Eastern Europe. The evolutionary strategy has to be modelled mainly on the experience of those economies in the OECD and East Asia, whose success hinged substantially on the utilization of their entrepreneurial potential. To exploit this potential these economies relied on a continuous reorganization of industrial structures, through a sequence of random trials by firms and systematic, competitive elimination of errors. Government agencies and parastatals supported these acts of creative destruction by casting an extended, effective network of firm support structures over the whole industrial economy. As a result these newly industrialized nations of East Asia are now characterized by industrial diversification, a high degree of turbulence, and localized inter-firm networks that have informational properties conducive to entrepreneurial activities (i.e. the mastery of innovation).

2. The high-tech-high-wage strategy of structural transformation in the new 'Länder' of Germany

With the economic union of the former German Democratic Republic (GDR) and the Federal Republic of Germany (FRG), virtually overnight an Eastern economy switched from a command system to a strategy of compressed transformation of an economy based on social market principles. The major macroeconomic and social changes of July and October 1990 were most prominently the introduction of a stable new currency, the Deutschmark, and the copying of the West German legal system, which meant the recognition of private ownership and of West German social security arrangements. Furthermore, the transfer of West German labor market regulations and extension of the federal financial structure as well as the western banking system meant the overnight establishment of labor and capital markets. Economically this overnight shift meant the complete and immediate opening of the domestic market of the former GDR to foreign competition, particularly to West German and Western European competition. It also meant the rapid introduction of high West German working standards, pay-scales and social security benefits in an economic system that utilized its productive resources at a third of Western efficiency.[1]

The aim of Germany's radical transformation is to set the productivity mark for the East German economy as high as it is for West Germany in the hope that all privatized, surviving production units and those that are newly entering the market will immediately aim for that high mark. The rapid build-up of capital intensive production sites, employing locally abundant personnel at high Western wage levels, then presumably induce high rates of economic growth.[2] That strategy however has not succeeded.

On the one hand, the introduction of stable West German economic conditions, such as the banking and currency system and the federal financial structure, has reduced the uncertainty for long term investments. This has induced 16 per cent of all new East German entrepreneurs to emerge in the manufacturing sector between 1989 and October 1992 (see Table 13.2). The respective percentages for the service sector are 21, for the

---

1 For an early extensive, neoclassical analysis of these changes see George Akerlof (1991). Sinn and Sinn (1992) put East German productivity as low as one sixth of West German.

2 Sinn and Sinn (1992) call this the 'high-wage-high-tech' strategy. They put the analogy as follows: East Germany was famed for the homegrown inefficient car, called Trabbi. This strategy applied to the Trabbi means that from now on those old cars are no more allowed on the road. Unless one drives a new Mercedes, one has to stay home. Extensive transitional periods, which ease out one car to gradually introduce another, are largely absent in such a model.

trades 36, and for construction businesses 18. The comparable distribution of the newly founded firms in West Germany for 1991 is: industry 13 per cent, services 35 per cent, trades 34 per cent, and construction 11 per cent. Relatively to West Germany, entry into the industrial sector is satisfactory in East Germany. Surprisingly the shares of entry into services are considerably lower in the East than in the West. However, the service share is much higher than the initially low share of firms in the sector. Thus the service entry is slowly correcting the imbalance between construction and services, so prevalent in Eastern Europe. The difference in construction entries can simply be explained by the enormous public sector investment in infrastructure and housing since 1989.

Table 13.2 Sectoral distribution of firms, East Germany (per cent)

Sectors	Industry	Services	Trades	Con-struction	Transport	Energy	Finance	Total
Distribution 1989	28.90	9.30	26.70	29.20	5.40	0.01	0.03	100
Entrants	16	21	36	18	6	0	2	99
Distribution October 1992	19.30	19.10	34.50	19.10	6.30	0.03	1.50	100
No. of firms	15 650	15 460	28 000	15 470	5 000	200	1 250	81 030
West Germany compared								
Entrants 1991	13	35	34	11	5	0	2	100

Source: Harhoff and Stahl (1993, 8).

On the other hand, the introduction of West German economic conditions and the rapid opening of the protected, controlled East German economic system to the world market led to the demise of the old industrial sector. Whereas during the Great Depression of 1932 German industrial production reached 59 per cent of its previous peak of 1928, East German industrial production in December 1990 fell to a level of 45 per cent of production in 1989. And according to estimates by the German Ifo-Institute, in December 1991 that level was as low as 33 per cent of the 1989 productive output (Hübner, 1991). It is only through massive infusion of capital into East Germany by West Germany, for the benefit especially of the construction sector, that great human hardship is being avoided.[3]

3 It is estimated that between 1990 and 1995 the public subsidization of, and investment in, the eastern part of Germany will amount to about 500 billion dollars. On a per capita basis each East German is supported by $31 250. If a developing country like India were to receive equivalent per capita aid, lets say over the next decade, this would mean the investment of approximately $26 trillion (26 000 000 000 000). Obviously such a strategy is unrealistic for most parts of the world that would need it. And here I point

If one only considers the stable economic conditions which guide the East German transformation process, the share of entry of new industrial firms can be considered as too low. The underrepresentation of the manufacturing sector may also slow down the rate of entry into the industry related service sector. However, the high wage levels associated with high social security benefits and taxes combined with the low productivity in an open economy, have a strong disincentive effect on long-term investment in the manufacturing sector. Under the circumstances the high-tech-high-wage strategy of transformation can succeed only if East German industry specializes in those sectors, which effectively use expensive skilled labor.

From detailed historical descriptions of the economic development process in the newly industrialized countries (NICs) of East Asia it has been shown that the sectoral production structure of the NICs has become more similar to those of the developed market economies, or OECD countries.[4] Between 1963 and 1989 the growth rate of production in developed market economies was strongest in those (3-digit ISIC) manufacturing sectors which generally are considered as having a high degree of technological intensity: electrical machinery, instruments, chemicals, machinery and transport goods. The newly industrializing countries of East Asia were able to narrow their gap to the developed market economies, by growing even faster in precisely these sectors. In the centrally planned economies the share of sectors that were very capital intensive - heavy machinery and heavy manufacturing - were overrepresented in the production structure. The socialist economies did not succeed to shift resources from these capital intensive sectors to more skill intensive production. Thus they did not experience the growth rates necessary to close the competitive gap to the developed market economies and to the newly industrializing countries. By 1989 Eastern Europe had become, after Africa, the least competitive region in skill intensive industrial sectors.[5]

The challenge for the transforming industrial sector in East Germany consists essentially in establishing a competitive market structure in manufacturing branches that exhibit high skill and high capital intensity. It means ultimately the convergence of the eastern industry structure towards OECD patterns. What is necessary to gauge the potential (emerging) problem of the missing innovative entrepreneurial sector, is thus an evaluation of developments in industry structure, branch composition, and firm turbulence. This then gives a better indication of the potential of the high-tech-high-wage strategy for promoting the existing narrow entrepreneurial basis.

---

again to the uniqueness and to the essence of the East German strategy: it has at its core the rapid transfer of western standards to centers or nodes of excellence in a sea of mediocrity. These centers, established at high cost, are then stimulated to infuse the entire economy within a short time with high standards of production and productivity.

4 Verspagen (1992, 68). Brunner (1993) points to the increasing relative capital and skill-intensity of those industrial sectors in NICs and newly industrializing economies, which figure as the most important (higher-tech) growth sectors of OECD countries. For the study of detailed data on the structure of world industrial growth and trade, see Summers and Heston (1991, 1-41); Moore (1985); Leechor et al. (1983).

5 Dosi et al. (1993) define competitiveness as 'dynamic efficiency', which is the ratio of market shares in OECD imports in dynamic (technologically progressive) versus declining commodities.

OECD countries such as former West Germany also display a pyramid of firm sizes, with a large base of small firms carrying a well-developed layer of medium-sized firms, topped by a few large corporations. Lesser industrial economies display top-heavy firm size distributions. In the process of narrowing their development gap, East Asian newly industrializing economies increasingly relied on the growth of small and medium-sized manufacturing firms precisely in those sectors assumed to produce with relatively high capital and skill intensity (Brunner, 1993). In the process of this economic transformation newly industrializing economies approached firm size distributions prevalent in OECD countries.

Turbulence as a combined measure of entry and exit of firms is increasingly used as an indicator for technological renewal. Studies by Baldwin and Gorecki (1991) have shown that entrants into an industry, regardless of their size, exhibit above average productivity or technological know-how, whereas firms that leave a sector generally produced at below average productivity. This confirms that in a world of rapid changes in the international economic environment, and in competitive relations, the replacement of outmoded organizations by new, more often small firms appears to be a change in favor of innovation.[6]

Do we see a convergence towards OECD (West German) patterns of market structure, branch composition and turbulence since 1989/90? To analyze changes in industrial structure and composition in East Germany I will use a) the firm database of the German Treuhandanstalt (or more simply 'Treuhand'), the agency responsible for privatizing the heritage of the East German economy, and b) other statistical surveys of the overall firm base, which include firm start-ups and closures not included in the decreasing Treuhand population.[7]

Initially, around mid-1990, the Treuhand had a stock of slightly over 10 600 firms (including 5 600 in industry), of which it has privatized about 55 to 60 per cent by July of 1992, that is around 5 600 (including fewer than 2 500 industrial firms). At the beginning of the privatization process, *industrial capacity* (number of firms) of the Treuhand is estimated to have been around 90 per cent of the total. By mid 1992 the Treuhand's stock of firms of 4 340 is estimated to include less than 20 per cent of the total of industrial firms of East Germany (2 445 of an estimated 15 000 for July 1992; see Table 13.3). In July 1992 the already privatized Treuhand firms plus those in Treuhand stocks accounted for about 40 per cent of 'industrial firms' in East Germany. That is, another estimated 10 000 industrial firms may have sprung up in the new 'Länder', which were not part of the original stock of Treuhand plants but which are start-ups and investments. The vast majority of those non-Treuhand start-up firms, around 8 500, are very small (less than 19 employees).

Tables 13.1 and 13.3 reveal the convergence of the East and West German size structure in industry. Over two thirds of the firms are small in the new Länder of

---

6 Peter Murrell (1990, 223) makes this point very clear: 'the socialist countries perform less well on product innovation than on process innovation and have a comparative disadvantage in sectors in which there is a large amount of entry of new firms'.

7 Harhoff and Stahl (1993); German Institute for Economic Research (DIW) (1992).

Germany (67.2 per cent as compared to 71 per cent in the old Länder). However, in absolute terms industrial capacity in the eastern part is only one tenth of that of the western part of Germany. Notable is the relative abundance of very small firms with less than 20 employees in comparison to West Germany.

Table 13.3 Industry structure in East Germany

	Firms					
	All (10-15-92)		With Treuhand (6-30-92)		Non-Treuhand (10-15-92)	
Firm size (employees)	nos	per cent	nos	per cent	nos	per cent
-19	63 377	79.2	937	21.6	62 440	82.5
20-100	11 609	14.5	1 619	37.3	9 990	13.2
101-500	3 824	4.8	1 094	25.2	2 730	3.6
501-1 000	460	0.6	160	3.7	300	0.4
1 001-	326	0.4	126	2.9	200	0.3
unclassified	404	0.5	404	9.3	0	0.0
Total	80 000	100.0	4 340	100.0	75 660	100.0
	Industrial firms					
	All (7-92)*		With Treuhand (6-30-92)		Non-Treuhand (7-92)*	
Firm size (employees)	nos	per cent	nos	per cent	nos	per cent
-19	9 209	61.4	409	16.7	8 800	70.1
20-100	3 808	25.4	963	39.4	2 845	22.7
101-500	1 474	9.8	724	29.6	750	6.0
501-1 000	222	1.5	122	5.0	100	0.8
1 001-	161	1.1	101	4.1	60	0.5
unclassified	126	0.8	126	5.2	0	0.0
Total	15 000	100.0	2 445	100.0	12 555	100.0

Note: * Estimated.

A closer look at the dynamics in the sub-sample of Treuhand privatized and owned firms, which in mid-1992 still accounts for two fifths of East German industrial potential and considerably more than half of its industrial employment, leads to a more differentiated evaluation of structural convergence. Particularly during its early period of operation, the Treuhand arranged for spin-offs of smaller or medium size operational productive units from the huge sector-oriented combines which formed the industrial base of the former GDR. Several thousand such firms were thus coming into existence during 1990 and the earlier part of 1991. Table 13.1 showed that there existed 3 423 industrial 'enterprises' in the GDR in 1987. The Treuhand stocks of firms swelled to 5 600 by the mid 1991 peak.

So, to a small degree the high percentage decline of large firms (–70 per cent; see Table 13.4) and of medium size firms (–60 per cent) between mid 1991 and mid 1992 is still a result of spin-offs. A recategorization of firms occurred from large to medium, and medium to small size, although there was no change of ownership: they stayed with the Treuhand for sale or dissolution. The largest part of this shift down to the smaller size categories was simply the result of the steep decline of industrial employment, visible also in Table 13.1.

Table 13.4 Changes in stock of firms with Treuhand, 1991-1992 (all sectors)

Firm size	net stock (6-30-91)	adjust-ments	priva-tized	repri-vatized	public	liqui-dated	new net	size reclassifications		
unclassified	216	75	40	28	0	16	57	–2	1	1
-19	456	13	116	22	3	119	183	2	–5	3
20-100	1 499	12	447	75	12	272	681	7	125	–139
101-500	1 550	13	434	30	4	256	813	6	39	306
501-1 000	344	5	71	0	2	59	207	0	2	17
1 001-	339	19	40	0	10	41	229	0	2	3
Total	4 404	137	1 148	155	31	763	2 170	13	164	191

Firm size		size reclassifications		net change	still net	adjust-ments	end stock (6-30-92)
unclassified	0	0	0	13	70	56	126
-19	0	0	0	164	347	62	409
20-100	7	0	0	191	872	91	963
101-500	-351	0	0	-143	670	54	724
501-1 000	149	-168	0	-89	118	4	122
1 001-	52	79	-136	-136	93	8	101
Total	-143	-89	-136	0	2 170	275	2 445

Note: Adjustments relate to firms previously not in stock, statistical changes, inputs to mergers. Reprivatized firms are those returned to their pre-socialist owners. Public firms are those given to states or cities.

High employment losses of large firms are somewhat counterbalanced by a lower rate of liquidation (12 per cent). Treuhand firms with less than 20 employees faced the highest liquidation rate of 26 per cent per year. However, these figures are somewhat misleading, since they do not reveal how many of the down-sized large firms (recategorized as small and medium) are liquidated by parts. Clearly the elimination of very large firms en bloc creates a more visible unemployment push, which is politically less justifiable by the Treuhand. Smaller and medium firms can be dissolved in greater numbers with less publicity. It is interesting to note here that for the entire East German firm population, insolvencies per year for 1991 and 1992 are estimated as low as 800-900 firms.[8] Although I think this is a statistical underestimate, it is clear from the Treuhand figures that a good part of the insolvencies occur among Treuhand stocks. The process of creative destruction, the continuous elimination of unproductive firms in favor of more competitive ones, has not yet taken hold sufficiently in East Germany. The convergence towards West German size structure is largely a result of employment losses of larger firms. As the still continuing overall decline in industrial employment indicated, the decline of large firm employment is not compensated so far by entry of very small firms.

The essence of the high-wage-high-tech strategy is rapidly to shift the economy into the capital and technology intensive industrial sectors.[9] Data on the precise sectoral distribution of the 9 200 small and potentially entrepreneurial firms is not yet available. Given the lack of entrepreneurial opportunity until 1990 and the technological backwardness of the former East Germany, it is an untenable assumption that the newly established small firms would produce in high proportions in the high-tech sectors.

The Treuhand is not primarily involved in reforming state enterprises. Rather the agency is committed to selling off potentially viable firms to private bidders who have a direct stake in making their investments pay off. In the framework of the East German transformation strategy one would expect a priori that firms in high-tech sectors are sold off more rapidly by the Treuhand, or those that seem a priori not viable in those sectors will be closed down more rapidly as well. An analysis of the changes in the stocks of Treuhand firms by firm size *and* branch from June 1991 to July 1992 (Table 13.5) makes apparent that dynamic or so-called high-tech industry sectors are *not* sold off at a much higher rate than is the overall industry average (44.5 per cent). Of particular interest are machinery (37 per cent), electronic and electrotechnical (50 per cent), precision and optical instruments (44 per cent), as well as transport industries (44 per cent).

The average annual liquidation rate for all industries is 17.5 per cent (Table 13.5). High-tech sectoral rates are: machinery 13 per cent, electronic and electrotechnical 23 per cent, precision and optical instruments 18 per cent, and transport industries 10 per cent.

---

8 Estimates by the Halle Institute for Economic Forecasting (IWH) put the number at around 2500 for manufacturing.

9 The German ifo-Institute classifies the following sectors as dynamic: machine tools, electric and electronic, chemical, transport, communications, fine ceramics and porcelain, precision instruments.

Table 13.5 Transformation rates by Treuhand (per cent change)

Industry sector	net stock (6-30-91)	adjustments		privatized	reprivatized	public ownership	liquidated	adjustments		end stock (6-30-92)
Power production and water supply	100	3	0	16	0	9	3	7	4	79
Mining	100	3	5	18	0	3	5	0	0	66
Chemical industry	100	1	0	36	4	1	14	5	2	51
Plastic, rubber and asbestos	100	3	0	27	3	0	19	3	3	53
Mineral and mineral processing	100	3	2	34	4	0	14	6	1	49
Iron and non-ferrous basic industry	100	2	1	28	1	0	15	3	3	60
Steel and light-metal working	100	1	0	28	6	1	8	3	0	59
Machine-tools and mechanical engineering	100	1	0	28	3	0	13	6	2	63
Transport vehicles	100	1	1	39	0	0	10	6	2	56
Electronics and electrotechnical industry	100	1	6	24	3	0	23	4	2	50
Precision and optical instruments	100	2	0	22	4	0	18	2	0	56
Ironmongery, musical instruments, sports equipment	100	2	0	21	6	0	26	4	4	52
Wood production	100	3	0	19	6	0	22	3	2	55
Paper and printing	100	4	0	30	3	0	19	2	1	47
Leather and shoes	100	1	0	10	3	0	36	1	2	52
Textiles and clothing	100	3	1	10	5	0	26	3	2	59
Food	100	2	0	35	4	2	14	2	5	49
All sectors	100.0	2.2	0.9	26.1	3.5	0.7	17.3	3.8	2.4	55.5

Note: Adjustments relate to firms previously not in stock, statistical changes, inputs to mergers. Reprivatized firms are those returned to their pre-socialist owners. Public firms are those given to states or cities.

If anything becomes clear from Table 13.5, it is that sectoral privatization and liquidation rates by the Treuhand are clustered around the mean (maybe with the exception of leather, textiles, power, mining and communications industries, which are divested at a slower pace than average). Up to now the industrial transformation in East Germany takes place without particular consideration of dynamic sectors (or for that matter any sector) and technological opportunities. The fact that it has not been seriously debated as yet in Germany which sectors should and could receive special attention under these criteria underlines this point.

Germany's high-wage-high-tech strategy of transformation has the visible result of first eliminating large and even medium-sized production units taken over from socialist East Germany. The few larger investments of Western companies will for the time being remain cathedrals in a deserted industrial landscape, which are waiting for the emergence of a constituency from the heap of newly established very small enterprises. A dramatic downsizing and deindustrialization across sectors is unlikely to provide a fertile ground for the establishment of innovative medium-sized, regionally anchored and integrated companies in internationally competitive high-wage, capital intensive, high-tech sectors. Given this already infertile industrial ground one would now hope for an economic incentive structure that attracts resources of potential start-up firms from the less competitive to the more competitive high-tech sectors. Such an effort would in fact mean the adoption of a transformation strategy that significantly differs from the ongoing strategy. A different strategy could considerably shorten the time necessary for the process of creative destruction to begin to function properly in an internationally competitive environment. Thus a switch in strategy should reduce the future costs of the transformation considerably.

3. Entrepreneurship and structural transformation in Poland

Poland was the country which initiated the wave of economic transformation in Eastern Europe. On January 1, 1990 the so-called Balcerowicz Plan was launched. The plan primarily intended to stabilize the macroeconomy, and included monetary policy reform, currency reform, trade reform, as well as fiscal policy reform. It included a call for an end to the protection and subsidization of state-owned enterprises.

The aims of these adjustment programs are magically to improve the workings of markets by liberalizing prices, reducing subsidies and opening up the economy to world market competition. Efficient markets, however, operate only under conditions of stability. Thus adjustment programs in Eastern Europe also proceeded to stabilize economies by reducing budget deficits, controlling wage inflation and improving the trade balance. I argue here that these programs may well have been successful or may yet be successful in stabilizing an economy in the short run, but that the miraculous emergence of entrepreneurship can not be assumed to be an automatic occurrence. According to Allsopp et al., 'a microeconomic strategy is in an imperfectly functioning economy, not only important in its own right, but a necessary condition for macroeconomic credibility as well.' (Allsopp et al., 1991, 5).

Economic structures and institutions form and shape the extent and the efficiency of markets. Furthermore economic institutions determine the degree of uncertainty of the environment in which the entrepreneur applies his or her skills (North, 1990). It would be unfair not to mention the efforts of Eastern European Adjustment programs to introduce structural changes as well. As such the changes in financial, legal and ownership structures (privatization) are a significant attempt at setting the microeconomic parameters for markets. But, as we see particularly in the case of Poland, the absence of institutions that further domestic price and quality competition, and thus discipline firm behavior, can threaten the entire transformation process.

With the undervaluation of the Polish currency in the first half of 1990 (due to the devaluation in combination with stiff wage controls and price liberalization), the profitability of labor-managed firms increased dramatically. The absence of a credible competitive threat in the domestic markets, however, presented Polish enterprises with a soft price and quality constraint (Allsopp et al., 1991, 2). Instead of improving products and selling them at lower prices in the face of competition, Polish labor-managed enterprises became preoccupied with preserving employment. Notwithstanding the fall in enterprise profitability in the beginning of 1991 and the resulting increase in exits from industries, the absence of a policy that would diversify industrial structures particularly through entry of small and medium-sized firms continues to hinder macroeconomic structural adjustment and produces stagnation.

Another indicator of the persistence of old structures is the level of turbulence, that is the combined entry and exit of firms. Unfortunately for Poland, no reliable data on entry and exit behavior of firms are available for the last three years. For 1990 rough estimates indicate high volatility among *unincorporated* firms.[10] In that year on average 40 000 new enterprises were established each month, while on average 16 500 per month were closed. The overwhelming number of private unincorporated enterprises are, however, crafts and trade and service establishments. Only about 250 000 of nearly 1.5 million unincorporated enterprises can be associated with manufacturing activities. Thus absolute proportions of entry and exits of manufacturing firms should be considerably smaller.

Poland has had the good fortune that its statistical apparatus was largely preserved in the early period of the economic transformation process. Hence a classification of firms and establishments by industry branch and size is, while incomplete, already available for the years 1989, 1990, and 1991. Several aspects are worth explaining to better understand Table 13.6a. The stock of industrial firms in 1991 is estimated to be 18 000 for all of Poland, excluding those that have up to 5 employees.[11] Only 7 049 of these 18 000 are classified in the statistics by branch and firm size. 30 per cent are small, 60 per cent medium sized, and 10 per cent are large (figures in Table 13.1 relate to absolute figures in Table 13.6a).

---

10 Until 1991 private sector enterprises in Poland were legally classified into three categories: (i) *unincorporated* firms - sole proprietorships and partnerships - also known as 'natural persons'; (ii) *incorporated* firms, which are joint stock and limited liability companies, and (iii) joint ventures and 'Polonia' firms, enterprises involving foreign investment or SMEs owned by non-residents.

11 Privatization of State Enterprises 1.08.1990-31.12.1991 (Prywatyzacja Przedsiebiorstw Panstwowych), Central Statistical Office (Warsaw 1992, table 1).

Table 13.6a Poland: industrial enterprise population

Sector	Number of firms and plants by size of employment									
	1990					1991				
	Total 6+	6-100	101-500	501-1 000	1 001-	Total 6+	6-100	101-500	501-1 000	1 001-
Coal	95	8	6	2	79	85	2	5	2	76
Fuel	37	1	7	11	18	41	2	8	11	20
Energy	82	6	11	13	52	84	5	11	15	53
Steel production	47	9	11	3	24	50	9	13	2	26
Non-ferrous metals	33	2	8	5	18	25	1	4	11	9
Metal working	494	169	236	37	52	512	205	230	63	14
Machine tools	640	147	295	107	91	689	171	351	84	83
Precision tools	157	51	68	17	21	162	52	85	11	14
Transport equipment	306	69	131	46	60	350	97	157	44	52
Electronics	319	61	150	50	58	346	76	177	45	48
Chemical	396	90	196	52	58	460	139	222	45	54
Construction material	410	131	200	61	18	470	137	276	47	10
Glass	84	15	39	18	12	92	29	37	16	10
Ceramics	33	2	14	10	7	38	4	19	10	5
Wood production	509	225	206	39	39	598	304	225	38	31
Paper	65	13	30	6	16	90	26	45	8	11
Textile	402	73	152	72	105	417	101	163	84	69
Clothing	469	106	292	43	28	682	265	354	42	21
Leather	245	55	139	27	24	307	117	141	28	21
Food	955	142	569	160	84	1 182	248	705	169	60
Other	389	106	225	46	12	369	129	201	30	9
Sum	6 167	1 481	2 985	825	876	7 049	2 119	3 429	805	696

Table 13.6a (continued)

	Employment 1991					
	Classified industrial firms	Other firms			Polish industrial sector	Difference unaccounted
Sector	–5	–5	6+	Total		
Coal	0	0	387 300	387 300	387 300	0
Fuel	32	73	54 700	54 773	54 773	0
Energy	221	546	120 300	120 846	120 846	0
Steel production	0	0	125 400	125 400	126 100	700
Non-ferrous metals	0	0	52 100	52 100	52 800	700
Metal working	38 900	78 591	188 400	266 991	254 000	–12 991
Machine tools	6 302	13 443	325 200	338 643	345 700	7 057
Precision tools	7 873	16 086	54 300	70 386	68 100	–2 286
Transport equipment	33 937	57 807	254 100	311 907	286 500	–25 407
Electronics	29 774	49 218	177 900	227 118	205 800	–21 318
Chemical	12 992	30 491	236 500	266 991	267 200	209
Construction material	15 851	35 646	120 300	155 946	152 700	–3 246
Glass	4 066	7 723	41 600	49 323	47 500	–1 823
Ceramics	819	1 750	20 800	22 550	21 700	–850
Wood production	43 673	76 758	141 600	218 358	198 300	–20 058
Paper	1 121	2 511	38 600	41 111	41 800	689
Textile	14 648	24 581	221 200	245 781	235 900	–9 881
Clothing	48 154	88 308	158 400	246 708	222 900	–23 808
Leather	20 727	37 441	100 800	138 241	123 400	–14 841
Food	16 152	49 653	406 800	456 453	472 600	16 147
Other	19 535	38 197	85 500	123 697	111 500	–12 197
Sum	314 777	608 823	3 311 800	3 920 623	3 797 419	–123 204

Sources: Industry Statistics, Central Statistical Office, Warsaw, 1991 and 1992. Complete Statistic of Tiny Firms of up to 5 employees. Central Statistical Office, Warsaw, May 1992.

Presumably the difference consists of firms with 6 to 100 employees, since they are the ones that more easily escape statistical scrutiny.[12] The classified firms and plants account for the bulk of Polish industrial employment: 3 312 million (down from 3 663 million in 1990) out of a total of 3.8 million for the country in 1991. In additon 608 823 people are employed by the very small firms with 5 or fewer employees at the end of 1991. The comparable employment figure for very small firms at the end of 1990 was only 435 994. The increase in very small firm employment in 1991 did not yet compensate for the employment losses in larger industrial firms. Employment accounted for by all firm sizes adds up to 3.92 million, roughly 123 000 more than the statistics show for total industrial employment in Poland. The difference is an indication of the unreliability of the statistics, particularly for firms with less than 100 employees. It is very likely that for 1991 employment for start-up small firms in Poland has been considerably overcounted. The overall trends, however, are clear.

Placing these numbers again in the context of East and West Germany and of employment in these two economies, one notices that a firm stock of 18 000 is a very realistic number. Poland's industrial economy was larger than East Germany's in 1990/91, and a fraction of the one of West Germany. What seems unrealistic in Poland when compared to West Germany, is the high number of very small industrial firms (315 000 compared with 56 000 in West Germany). In Poland it is very easy to register as a business with the local state organization. One simply has to enter the firm into the 'records of business activity' for a minimal fee. Many of these registrations are not serious, as is the case in East Germany where speculative numbers of 350 000 registrations in 1991 circulate. Only a small percentage of these registered very small firms are really engaged in manufacturing, and thus one cannot take the Polish number of 315 000 tiny industrial firms (and also the small firm employment numbers) very seriously for the analysis of utilized industrial and entrepreneurial potential.

What is significant about the firm size distribution in 1991 is the dramatic change in percentage points from 1989. The 1991 distribution resembles more closely the one in West Germany (refer to Table 13.1), with 67 per cent of small firms, and 26.8 per cent medium-sized firms. The one major difference is that large firms are still more dominant in the Polish industrial economy than in the West German economy. This is particularly so when one measures the share of large firms in terms of persons

12 Adding those unaccounted firms to the previous number of 2 119 of small firms, I arrive at a rounded estimate of the small firm sector of 13 000 entities. Allowing for a small addition of firms to the other two size categories, I can rewrite the enterprise column of Table 13.1 for 1991:

Firm size (plant)	numbers	per cent
6-100	13 000	72
101-1 000	4 300	24
1 101-	700	4
Total	18 000	100

employed. Large Polish industrial firms in 1991 still employed almost 56 per cent of the workforce, as compared to a little over one third in West Germany (38.3 per cent). This is an indicator of the persistence of old structures which has led to the Polish enterprises' price raising behavior referred to before.

Table 13.6b Poland: industrial enterprise population

	Number of firms and plants by size of employment									
	1989					1991				
Sector	Total 6+	6-100	101-500	501-1 000	1 001-	Total 6+	6-100	101-500	501-1 000	1 001-
Coal	103	1	12	1	89	85	2	5	2	76
Fuel	37	2	6	10	19	41	2	8	11	20
Energy	70	2	5	10	53	84	5	11	15	53
Steel production	47	10	11	2	24	50	9	13	2	26
Non-ferrous metals	33	3	5	7	18	25	1	4	11	9
Metal working	507	126	277	49	55	512	205	230	63	14
Machine tools	619	121	285	106	107	689	171	351	84	83
Precision tools	150	46	68	13	23	162	52	85	11	14
Transport equipments	299	51	127	59	62	350	97	157	44	52
Electronics	313	59	132	59	63	346	76	177	45	48
Chemical	403	84	208	48	63	460	139	222	45	54
Construction materials	355	94	170	63	28	470	137	276	47	10
Glass	82	9	42	18	13	92	29	37	16	10
Ceramics	31	2	12	9	8	38	4	19	10	5
Wood production	511	190	238	35	48	598	304	225	38	31
Paper	63	12	26	9	16	90	25	45	8	11
Textile	393	57	152	57	127	417	101	163	84	69
Clothing	488	96	302	57	33	682	265	354	42	21
Leather	240	22	156	35	27	307	117	141	28	21
Food	850	125	465	162	98	1 182	248	705	169	60
Other	414	91	247	50	26	369	129	201	30	9
Sum	6 008	1 203	2 946	859	1 000	7 049	2 119	3 429	805	696

Sources: Industry Statistics, Central Statistical Office, Warsaw, 1990 and 1992.

Table 13.6b provides the basis for an analysis of the change in branch and size distribution of industrial firms from 1989 to 1991. It has to be kept in mind that this was the period in which the Balcerowicz Plan was introduced and the 'big bang' began in earnest. Within a year, from beginning 1990 to beginning 1991, real net material product fell by about 20 per cent and employment of classified industries decreased by 10 per cent (from just over 4 million persons to 3.66 million). The decrease in employment continued to 3.31 million by the end of 1991 (see Table 13.1 and Table 13.4). The deconcentration of industry proceeded: a 'loss' of 304 large firms was compensated for by an increase in small and medium-sized enterprises of 916 and 429 respectively (Table 13.6c). The highest absolute increases in the number of firms were registered in the food, clothing and construction materials sectors. In both these industry branches a marked shift towards small and medium scale occurred. In terms of percentages, shifts towards smallness were particularly noticeable in the clothing, leather, glass, ceramics and paper sectors (excluding the somewhat peculiar coal and energy sectors).

When compared to the experience in East Germany since 1990, the size of the Polish privatization effort still appears to be small. In a period where the Treuhandanstalt reduced its stock of firms by over 2 000, Poland privatized and liquidated about 750 of its state-owned enterprises.[13] Privatization thus is likely to account for a much smaller part of the described shifts in firm size distribution and entry and exit movements in various sectors than is the case in East Germany with its overall smaller (and rapidly diminishing) industrial base.

Overall these shifts demonstrate a movement towards a size distribution familiar to OECD countries. However, Poland continues to reveal strength in those sectors in which centrally planned economies concentrated their capital-intensive production in the past: machinery and machine tools, textiles, clothing, leather, food, and mineral products.[14] A story about the qualitative, technological transformation of particularly the promising machinery and machine-tools sector cannot be told on the basis of Tables 13.6a to c.

Table 13.7 reveals that the index of industrial production in terms of value added has fallen from 96.5 in 1989 (1988 = 100) to 60.3 by the end of 1991 (a drop of about 40 per cent; for comparison the East German index has dropped by nearly 70 percentage points). If one combines the promising so-called high-tech sectors, chemical industry, electronics, transport equipment, and precision and machine tools, their index dropped to about 63 in 1991, which is marginally above average.

Hence, it is difficult to discern a clear pattern of a structural, sectoral shift without more detailed analysis.

---

13 For details refer to Privatization of State Enterprises 1.08.1990-31.12.1991, and Privatization of State Enterprises 30.06.1992, tables 4.

14 For a detailed presentation of material on relative specialization of manufacturing output of Centrally Planned Economies, LDCs, and Developed Market Economies, 1965-1980, see Chad Leechor et al., annex 3.

Table 13.6c Poland: industrial enterprise population

	Changes in population of firms and plants 1989-1991									
	Numbers					Per cent				
Sector	Total 6+	6-100	101-500	501-1 000	1001-	Total 6+	6-100	101-500	501-1 000	1 001-
Coal	–18	1	–7	1	–13	–17	100	–58	100	–15
Fuel	4	0	2	1	1	11	0	33	10	5
Energy	14	3	6	5	0	20	150	120	50	0
Steel production	3	–1	2	0	2	6	–10	18	0	8
Non-ferrous metals	–8	–2	–1	4	–9	–24	–67	–20	57	–50
Metal working	5	79	–47	14	–41	1	63	–17	29	–75
Machine tools	70	50	66	–22	–24	11	41	23	–21	–22
Precision tools	12	6	17	–2	–9	8	13	25	–15	–39
Transport equipment	51	46	30	–15	–10	17	90	24	–25	–16
Electronics	33	17	45	–14	–15	11	29	34	–24	–24
Chemical	57	55	14	–3	–9	14	65	7	–6	–14
Construction materials	115	43	106	–16	–18	32	46	62	–25	–64
Glass	10	20	–5	–2	–3	12	222	–12	–11	–23
Ceramics	7	2	7	1	–3	23	100	58	11	–38
Wood production	87	114	–13	3	–17	17	60	–5	9	–35
Paper	27	14	19	–1	–5	43	117	73	–11	–31
Textile	24	44	11	27	–58	6	77	7	47	–46
Clothing	194	169	52	–15	–12	40	176	17	–26	–36
Leather	67	95	–15	–7	–6	28	432	–10	–20	–22
Food	332	123	240	7	–38	39	98	52	4	–39
Other	–45	38	–46	–20	–17	–11	42	–19	–40	–65
Sum	1 041	916	483	–54	–304	17	76	16	–6	–30

Sources: Industry Statistics, Central Statistical Office, Warsaw, 1990 and 1992.

*Table 13.7 Poland: value added in industry**

	Year				Year (Index % 1988=100)					Qual. adj. (1988)
Sector	1988	1989	1990	1991	1989	1990	1991	Rank	DRCs	Rank
Coal	222.9	199.7	120.0	117.6	89.6	53.8	52.8		-	
Fuel	216.9	200.0	115.7	92.9	92.2	53.3	42.8		-	
Energy	110.2	83.0	57.5	38.2	75.3	52.2	34.7		-	
Steel production	122.7	104.1	93.2	63.7	84.8	76.0	51.9	10	1.90	9
Non-ferrous metals	81.1	73.4	47.6	24.1	90.5	58.7	29.7	15	2.83	13
Metal working	209.7	230.3	188.2	163.9	109.8	89.7	78.2	3	1.85	8
Machine tools	465.3	546.1	511.6	390.8	117.4	110.0	84.0	2	2.54	11
Precision tools	94.4	97.4	91.6	71.3	103.2	97.0	75.6	4	1.34	2
Transport equipment	365.9	305.5	228.9	109.8	83.5	62.6	30.0	14	5.00	15
Electronics	290.7	292.4	274.9	219.7	100.6	94.6	75.6	4	2.82	12
Chemical	316.5	265.4	198.4	161.1	83.9	62.7	50.9	12	3.48	14
Construction materials	112.4	125.0	110.0	100.0	111.2	97.9	88.9		-	
Glass	43.2	35.8	25.1	23.4	82.9	58.1	54.2	8	1.63	7
Ceramics	21.6	19.8	15.0	11.3	91.7	69.4	52.3	9	1.42	4
Wood production	139.1	166.8	107.0	97.5	119.9	76.9	70.1	6	1.55	6
Paper	33.4	33.9	17.8	17.2	101.5	53.3	51.5	11	1.38	3
Textiles	348.3	346.1	183.2	144.9	99.4	52.6	41.6	13	1.45	5
Clothing	119.0	145.3	111.4	103.9	122.1	93.6	87.3	1	2.12	10
Leather	103.8	85.7	61.9	57.0	82.6	59.6	54.9	7	1.29	1
Food	547.1	422.8	328.3	368.4	77.3	60.0	67.3		-	
Other	96.4	138.8	93.7	73.1	144.0	97.2	75.8		-	
Total	4 060.6	3 917.3	2 981.0	2 449.8	96.5	73.4	60.3		2.07	

Note: * In billion złoty at 1984 constant prices. Spearman's rank correlation coefficient = 0.21.

Sources: Industrial Statistics, 1990, 1991 and 1992, Central Statistical Office (Warsaw). Hughes and Hare (1992).

The hesitant privatization, liquidation and restructuring process of state-owned and managed firms in Poland puts a much higher burden on start-up firms for effecting a gradual orientation of the industrial economy from socialist and uncompetitive to internationally competitive. Not only is there no discernable shift of resources from low-tech to more skill intensive sectors, but there is no substantial transfer of resources from internationally uncompetitive to a priori more competitive sectors as well, as I will now show. For 1988 Hughes and Hare (1992, 82-104) calculated quality adjusted ratios of domestic inputs valued at world prices relative to one unit of GDP produced at world prices (so-called Domestic Resource Costs, or DRCs) for Poland's industry sectors on a 3-digit (ISIC) level. The authors found that, among those sectors listed in Table 13.7, leather, precision tools and paper had DRC values close to one, and were thus relatively competitive.[15]

A ranking of sectors according to the 1991 index of value added at domestic prices, which in post big-bang times were presumably closer to world prices than before, leads to a low rank correlation coefficient of 0.21 with 1988 DRC ranks. This shows that the more competitive sectors did not contract significantly less than the a priori relatively uncompetitive sectors. This result coincides with my analysis of shifts in firm size distribution, where firm entries and exits were not significantly different in low-tech and high-tech sectors.

4. The recent experience of industrial transformation in East Germany and Poland in comparison

Although both Poland and the former GDR experienced radical changes in the macro-framework, it is only the latter country which saw its currency and its legal and institutional framework dissolved. Economically this overnight shift meant the complete and immediate opening of the domestic market for the former GDR to foreign competition. The result had to be the rapid decline of the existing very centralized industrial basis. The Treuhand was formally put in charge of breaking up the large conglomerates to sell or liquidate the smaller pieces. The overall result was, as I have shown, a dramatic convergence of the East German firm size distribution towards the one existing in West Germany, albeit largely as a result of the disappearance of large and even medium-sized production units. Neither the entrepreneurial potential nor the required time for this potential to unfold was there to stem this dramatic industrial decline in any significant way.

Before the beginning of the radical transformation process in Poland and the former GDR, a creeping liberalization of the private sector in Poland and a rapid socialization drive for East German private enterprises created distinctly different starting conditions for entrepreneurs in the two countries. In Poland a large group of private entrepreneurs had accumulated some small business experience which they could put to use when the

---

15 High positive DRC values means a low level of competitiveness for the respective sector.

Balcerowicz plan took effect. No such potential was available in the GDR. In turn this different initial position may have advantaged Poland for establishing a large basis of small firms for the transformation of its industry.

The aim of Germany's radical transformation was to set the productivity mark, and correspondingly the wage level, for the East German economy as high as it is for Western Germany in the hope that all privatized, surviving production units and those that newly enter the market would immediately aim for that high mark and thus become internationally competitive. Within a stable macroeconomic framework and generous investment subsidies (see Haus, 1992 for details), combined with a free inflow of western expertise and market know-how, were supposed to compensate for the initial lack of any entrepreneurial experience. Although the figures show a movement of size structure and turbulence measures in the direction of West German levels, this 'nucleus' strategy is not producing the expected rapid structural transformation of industries. From the data a shift of economic resources towards those sectors requiring highly skilled labor to be internationally competitive is not apparent. Surprisingly, the structural transformation in East Germany seems to be occurring no faster than in Poland.

One reason is the absence so far of any significant discussion based on thorough economic analysis about feasible and desirable sectoral (branch) transformations. Such a discussion is a prerequisite for the development of a direction and strategy for industrial policy. The absence of any such policy direction not surprisingly led to an East German privatization program which did not *de*emphasize branches with relatively undifferentiated, homogenous product markets and where technological change and labor productivity growth is rather slow, in favor of sectors that would utilize highly productive but expensive labor.

A second reason for the retarded transformation is the extreme emphasis on indiscriminate promotion of capital-intensive 'foreign' subsidiaries to replace the collapsing 'domestic' base with the help of substantial subsidies. The extensive Treuhand privatization led to a significant number of takeovers by western firms of former and by now broken-up combines. In many cases 'raiders' have either liquidated remaining pieces of combines in favor of a 'cathedral in the desert', or have used the acquisition as the foundation for such an edifice. As Grabher notes:

> 'A smooth integration of these enclaves into the production chain of the large corporation presupposes a far-reaching paralysis of the pre-existing economic and social relations both within the old plant as well as its linkages with former suppliers. ... The resulting truncated functional repertoire of the 'cathedrals in the desert' has an important further impact on the host economy's potential, especially for the stimulation of entrepreneurship. The lack of decision-making corporate functions, especially those of qualified engineering and management functions, is also a lack of those 'seedbeds' that produce entrepreneurs.' (Grabher, 1992, 10-1)

The aim of Poland's transformation strategy was to 'get prices right' with the help of macroeconomic adjustment and to reverse the concentration of productive resources in state hands. Poland has partly achieved its transformation goals, although, as I have shown, the size distribution of firms in industry has not yet reached those common in OECD countries. Privatization and liquidation is proceeding more gradually than in East Germany. As in East Germany the Polish 'privatization' strategy did not include a comprehensive microeconomic strategy. As a result Poland displays a continued strength in those sectors on which former centrally planned economies focussed their efforts. A notable shift in sectoral composition towards industries where Poland is likely to have existing comparative advantages has not occurred.

Poland right from the beginning saw the necessity of pursuing the path of a low wage, low productivity economy in becoming internationally competitive. But the country lacked the institutional structure and determination to chart a path that would transform its existing productive capacities gradually in the direction of higher value-added products in competitive industries. Poland has not yet clearly determined which enterprises or industries are in the most favorable starting position. Through overly ambitious program of liberalization Poland may risk the elimination of know-how and entrepreneurial talent which is needed later on in the transition process. Once existing advantages are identified and targeted it will be possible for Poland to stimulate production with a selective industrial and technology policy geared to productivity and technology-driven growth. Thus the already existing examples of East Asian economic transformation loom all the larger for Poland. Those countries have managed a process of gradually shifting away from low wage, relatively low productivity, towards the well-known high-tech sectors. Along the way real incomes and wages have increased substantially (Wade (1990) has become a milestone in the literature for presenting this story in detail). The evidence presented in this paper showing that Poland thus far has failed to shift at all, is disconcerting.

Two additional remarks here. In East Germany and in Poland little distinction is made, both in terms of policy intervention and in terms of the statistical data basis, between trades and service establishments and industry structure. The empirically established interdependencies between the industrial, trade and service sectors warrant a cleaner distinction for better analysis. Finally, I have to note that the monitoring efforts regarding the industrial transformation process focus too much on static changes (e.g. number of firms existing or number of firms privatized) and too little on the dynamics such as entry and exit rates or changes in firm population and sectoral composition.

5. Making the entrepreneurial phoenix rise in Eastern Europe: industrial policy recommendations

It is clear that changes in Eastern Europe have been very dramatic indeed over the last three years. Economically they could spell a better future for the countries concerned, depending on whether it will be possible to promote the existing entrepreneurial potential which to a large extent laid dormant so long in socialist centralized economies. The as yet incomplete statistical evidence of the ongoing structural transformation of the industrial sectors of East Germany and Poland highlights that both the high-tech-high-wage, the low-tech-low-wage liberalization and privatization strategies have not sufficiently induced structural transformation of the productive sector. A switch in transformation strategy is advisable, both in the case of East Germany's pursuit of a high-wage-high-tech path and in the case of Poland's pursuit of its low-wage-low-tech path.

Transforming a manufacturing sector with a large share of capital-intensive, relatively low technology products to one which produces a large proportion of products using more capital and much higher skills (but relatively fewer lesser skilled labor) generating higher value added, is a major development challenge. First the existing structure of manufacturing has to be understood in terms of actual competitiveness. Then directed policies to transform it in the direction of higher skill and capital-intensive sectors can be implemented. A limited period of gradual trade liberalization safeguards the learning process during transition which is necessary for innovative and increasingly technology-intensive sectors to lower costs and improve productivity at an international level.

One of the conundrums of systemic transformation in Eastern Europe is that there is so much to do at once, and that doing everything is not possible. Therefore, the various reform efforts have to be integrated into a *mutually reinforcing* set of policies for building industrial competitiveness in a *sequenced* fashion. However, questions of sequencing have not featured much in traditional economic policy research. I can only draw on a good number of actual experiences with substantive policy reform in countries of the economically developing world, and particularly in Asia.[16] There experience has shown that no comprehensive reform is possible without first eliminating macroeconomic imbalances in the short-term. Also, a sound macro framework continuously maintains the real exchange rate at a level at which international competition remains a real and credible threat to domestic enterprises if they do not adjust to new market conditions in due time. But it has happened in all too many economically developing economies that longer-term fundamental economic adjustment has had to take second place to short-term macro-stabilization.[17] The consequence has been that industries with a high value-added *potential* have been eliminated, before macroeconomic and structural condition could bring that potential to bear fruit.

An evolutionary strategy of economic transformation does have a vast, unused potential for tapping the creative forces of Eastern Europe's entrepreneurs. In principle such a strategy should contain elements which address the needs of the sub-sectors and the producer firms, the institutions and support infrastructure, and the mechanisms of resource (financial) flows to manufacturing. The policies have to be timed and sequenced to sustain the efforts of firms, while at the same time they have to address the pressing issue of unemployment as witnessed by the dramatic reduction of the industrial workforce both in Poland and more dramatically in East Germany.

---

16 An extensive empirical literature exists about structural adjustment programs of the type the World Bank and the International Monetary Fund have advocated and implemented.

17 Hungary in the 1980s is a prime example.

Specifically in the case of East Germany, such an alternative transformation strategy should focus on the transfer of knowledge and technology through joint ventures arranged between 'foreign' investors and 'domestic' producers. Such transfers must focus on those industrial sectors which are judged to be of future significance for the region in question. Equity investments should be tied to 'local content' rules, and government should support small and medium-sized firms through preferences in procurement for public investments. An evolutionary strategy puts emphasis on the development of the administrative and information infrastructure supportive to entrepreneurs and accessible to smaller firms, such as localized consulting, R&D centers and training facilities, or specific market information provided by industry associations.[18]

In the particular case of Poland an evolutionary strategy of transformation needs to build on the present comparative advantage of the economy. Initially it would attempt to shift resources into these competitive sectors. This means setting priorities in the selection of enterprises to be privatized according to their actual and potential competitiveness in world markets. A world price-based analysis would furnish the necessary information for public or private agencies. With this initial structural change an acceleration of growth should occur, making available new economic resources. Next, the strategy would identify entry points into the world market in industries where the country had a potential comparative advantage. Entry points are typically in markets close to those with present comparative advantage and which offer an opportunity of flexible specialization. That means an option for strategies of 'following closely' the economically more advanced nations and of 'creative imitation' of technology policies.[19] A potential comparative advantage matures into an actual advantage if directed incentive and institutional adjustments lead to an adoption of a different industry structure.[20]

As a consequence of the evolutionary strategy, growth centers emerge gradually from the existing industrial base. These centers then become interconnected and linked through strategic intervention by public-private coalitions. The economic incentive structure is directed to integrate local investment by entrepreneurs into regional, national and at times international information and technology networks. Typically, firms which have their center of gravity in regions going through the process of economic transformation are promoted by policies that favor innovation, such as research and development aid, subsidies for the creation of company think-tanks and training efforts, as well as institutional development of technological advisory bodies. Not surprisingly, as a result of an implementation of the evolutionary strategy, centers

---

18 A very extensive list of such programs is given by Albach et al. (1992).

19 For more elaboration of this point see for example Velloso (1991).

20 This point needs emphasizing with quotes from Dosi and Freeman (1992, 11, 14): 'one of the major points to ... merge of the long-term trends in world exports of manufactures was the huge change in the commodity composition....forging ahead tends to be associated with leadership in new technologies and competence in basic science (although not necessarily with leadership in basic science). It is also associated with institutional changes in the generation and diffusion of new pervasive technologies and with the rapid expansion of education and training.'

of growth tend to emerge in those industrial sectors that serve markets of technology-intensive, heterogeneous products (flexible specialization). The timing of macro-economic policies and of privatization efforts,[21] depends in this strategy greatly on the appearance of competitive growth centers.

It is this general strategy of evolutionary development or transformation of an emerging economy which resembles that of the newly industrializing economies of Asia. Successful East Asian economies have shown that industrial and regional policy programmes are a necessary part of a strategy that does not rely on a belief in a spontaneous rise of the entrepreneurial phoenix. From past experience it is clear that functioning markets and capable market agents have to be created and sponsored by conscious institutional design and public policies.

References

Acs, Zoltan and David Audretsch (1990) *Innovation and Small Firms*, Cambridge MA: MIT Press.

Akerlof, George A. (1991) *East Germany in From the Cold: The Economic Aftermath of Currency Union*, Working Paper, Washington: Institute for Policy Reform.

Albach, Horst, Holle Grünert and Rainer Schwarz (1992) *Technologiepotential des Landes Brandenburg - Analyse und wirtschaftspolitische Empfehlungen*, Berlin: WZB Discussion Paper FS IV 92-11.

Allsopp, Christopher, et al. (1991) *Economic Adjustment in Poland: Options for 1991 and Beyond - Interim Report*, Oxford: Oxford University, January (unpublished).

Baldwin, John R. and Paul K. Gorecki (1991) Entry, Exit and Productivity Growth, in Geroski, P.A. and J. Schwalbach (eds.), *Entry and Market Contestability: An International Comparison*, Oxford: Basil Blackwell, .

Brunner, Hans-Peter (1991); Small-Scale Industry and Technology in India: The Case of the Computer Industry; *Small Business Economics,* 3, 121-29.

Brunner, Hans-Peter (1993) The development experience and government policies: lessons for Eastern Europe?, in Acs, Zoltan and David Audretsch (eds.), *Small Firms and Entrepreneurship - An East-West Perspective*, Cambridge: Cambridge University Press, 208-26

Brunner, Hans-Peter (1994) Technological Diversity, Random Selection in a Population of Firms, and Technological Institutions of Government, in Leydeschorff, L. and P.v.d. Berselaar (eds.), *Evolutionary Economics and Chaos Theory - New Directions in Technology Studies*, London: Pinter, 33-43.

Dosi, Giovanni and Christopher Freeman (1992) *The diversity of development patterns: On the processes of catching-up, forging ahead and falling behind*, Paper prepared for the International Economic Association Meeting, Varenna, Italy, October.

21 Privatization should occur when public sector reform agents are less likely than private sector agents to lead a firm to international competitiveness.

Dosi, Giovanni et al. (1993) *On the Process of Economic Development*, Rome, January (unpublished).

Foray, Dominique, and Christopher Freeman (eds.) (1993) *Technology and the Wealth of Nations*, London: Pinter.

German Institute for Economic Research (DIW) (1992); Gesamt- wirtschaftliche und unternehmerische Anpassungsprozesse in Ostdeutschland (Macroeconomic and entrepreneurial adjustment in East Germany); *Weekly Report*, 52.

Grabher, Gernot (1992) Eastern Conquista - The 'Truncated Industrialization' of Eastern European Regions by Large West European Corporations, in Ernste, H. and V. Meier (eds.), *Regional Development: A Contemporary Response*, London: Bellhaven.

Hall, John B. (1991); Sectoral transformation and economic decline: views from Berkeley and Cambridge; *Cambridge Journal of Economics,* 15, 229-37.

Harhoff, Dietmar and Konrad Stahl (1993) *Firm Dynamics in Eastern Germany - First Empirical Results*, Mannheim: ZEW, March (unpublished).

Haus, Matthias (1992) *Aufbau mittelständischer Unternehmen in den neuen Bundesländern durch Investitionsförderung*, Bonn: IFM Report no. 95, Dec.

Hübner, Kurt (1991); Das Kopieren des Westens ist ein Weg in die Sackgasse; *Der Tagesspiegel,* 13 December.

Hughes, Gordon and Paul Hare (1992); Industrial Policy and Restructuring in Eastern Europe; *Oxford Review of Economic Policy*, 8, 1, 82-104.

Keren, Michael (1995) *A Dynamic-Evolutionary Perspective on Transformation*, in this book.

Leechor, Chad et al. (1983) *Structural Changes in World Industry: A Quantitative Analysis of Recent Developments*, World Bank Technical Paper, Washington DC: World Bank.

Moore, Lynden (1985) *The Growth and Structure of International Trade Since the Second World War*, Brighton, Sussex: Wheatsheaf Books.

Murrell, Peter (1990) *The Nature of Socialist Economies: Lessons from Eastern European Foreign Trade*, Princeton: Princeton University Press.

North, Douglass C. (1990) *Institutions, Institutional Change and Economic Performance*, Cambridge: Cambridge University Press.

Sinn, Gerlinde and H.-W. Sinn (1992) *Jumpstart: the economic reunification of Germany*, Cambridge: MIT Press.

Summers, R. and A. Heston (1991); The Penn World Table (Mark 5): An Expanded Set of International Comparisons (1950-1988); *The Quarterly Journal of Economics,* 16, 1-41.

Velloso, Joao Paulo dos Reis (1991) International Competitiveness and the Creation of an Enabling Environment, in Irfan ul Haque (ed.), *International Competitiveness - Interaction of the Public and the Private Sectors*, Washington DC: Economic Development Institute of the World Bank.

Verspagen, Bart (1992) Uneven growth between interdependent economies - an evolutionary view on technology gaps, trade and growth,. Ph.D. dissertation, University of Limburg, Maastricht: University Press.

Wade, Robert (1990) *Governing the Market*, Princeton: Princeton University Press.

14 Small entrepreneurs in the society of employees

Richard Růžička

1. Introduction: retrospect and prospects

Privatization in the Czech Republic started from the very bottom, at least in terms of an absolute lack of private economic involvement in the social structure. The Czechoslovakia of the end of the past decade was a pure society of employees, possibly the purest one in Central Europe. In effect, at the beginning of the 1960s there were clear symptoms of a rapid extinction of the consciousness and culture of direct and full-life responsibility. Only 2.5 per cent of the economically active population were private owners[1] of the means of their economic activities.

Figure 14.1 Structure of employment

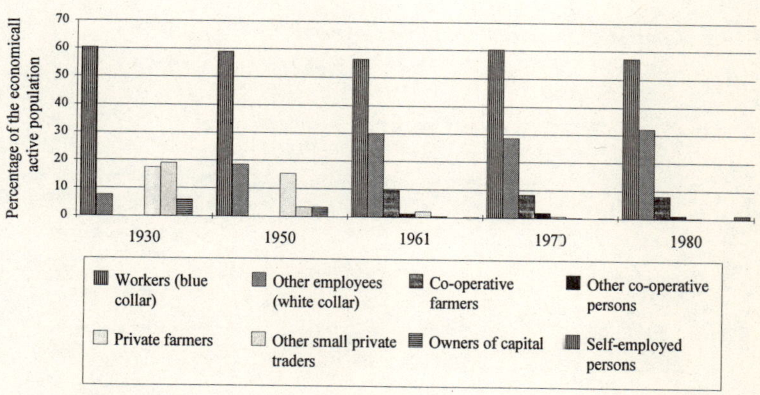

The remainder of private farmers and small traders had vanished completely after another twenty years. The profundity and misery of this change was mainly due to the fact that the Czechoslovakian society did not allow for a feeling that an individual possessed an enterprise as his or her own economic unit, or even as being a worthwhile environment for his or her economic life.

1 The following data are the result of the comparison and recalculation of data from the archives of the Federal Statistical Office, Czechoslovakia.

Of course, such an experience of ownership might be achieved within a collective. But in post-war Czechoslovakia the future was planned only for cooperatives, especially in agriculture, and to a certain degree in the services or in industry which held the vacant space left by the former private and/or collective enterprises. But, unfortunately, this way of economic organization was also based on discontinuity. In fact, the cooperative farms started as a very new form of ownership and organization, without any possibility of resisting state power and paternalism. This was the reason for the approximation of the cooperatives towards the state economic sector and for the approximation of farmers (members of the cooperatives) to the unspecified position of employees with their special mentality.

Table 14.1 Structure of employment in 1980

Year of census	1980
Employees (state)	89.5
Members of cooperatives (original owners, new members)	9.2
Private persons (economically active)	0.1

Figure 14.2 Change in the structure of employment

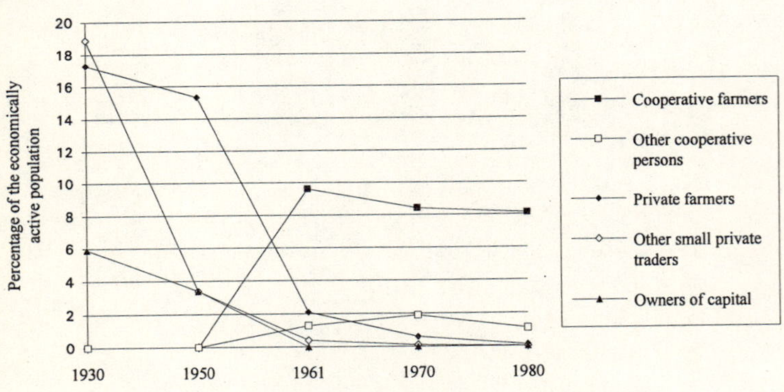

After a relatively long period of forty years the resumption of continuity is taking on the shape of reconstruction rather than of the revitalization of suppressed economic elements. This applies to the fundamental socioeconomic relations as well as to their expression by the various forms and facets in all individual behavior and consciousness. At a first glance the start-up situation of private and especially of small and medium-sized enterprises does not seem too bad. But being first in privatization, i.e. to be the subject of the first wave of privatization, is not necessarily an advantage, not even in the Czech Republic where the process is a relatively fast one. Formally, the privatization period is short: by the end of 1994 only a small part (10 per cent to 15 per cent) of the state property is to remain. The ratio of property transformed, i.e. privatized, in proportion to that of remaining state property is shown in Table 14.2.[2]

Table 14.2 Structure of property (per cent)

State property	10
Mass privatization	44
Transformation of cooperatives	17
Restitution of property to municipalities	22
Restitution (personal)	6
Small-scale privatization	1

The process of establishing small and medium-sized enterprises involves a broader group since the majority of newly set up enterprises did not form part of the former 'common' property. The length of time of the privatization process differs for small and for mass privatization measures. This causes a conflict between the various levels of transformation in which the small entrepreneurs are economically weak.

2. General theory

All socio-economic subjects worked and lived in mixed circumstances, as they do now. But the consequences of this situation differ for the various subjects. Frequently, former conditions still exist and, to a certain extent, still prevail in society. This becomes evident when regarding property right structures. The socialist system of ownership was based on common ownership. More than that, formal nationalization and collectivization resulted in a large-scale hidden regressive reprivatization in terms of an increasing possibility of a free and irresponsible use, misuse or failure to use and dismantling of the social wealth.

The nature of this very social ownership is revealed only in two processes of social and individual reproduction: (1) in the ability of ownership structure and its subjects to secure a relatively sustained surplus work as a source of individually and socially usable wealth, and (2) in the ability of the structure and subjects to turn this wealth efficiently into a process of renewal and transformation of life. Both surplus work and its effective use are organic, inherent interests of society, i.e. are interests of peoples' interdependence in the process of the production and reproduction of life. These

2 Preliminary data by the Ministry for Administration of National Possessions and their Privatization: 1993.

properties are the qualities of a system. From the 1940s until the 1980s ownership relations in Czechoslovakia lacked these characteristics. The occurrence of surplus provided only for a chance of misusing it, and this without any profit for the producer of this surplus work. It may be said that surplus work proved to be and was felt by people to be a useless effort.

This was instilled into society by the everyday life of people, by their experience. The elimination of other forms of ownership - even of small independent economic organisms - meant that there was no chance for a regular reproduction and cultivation of other personal and group-life strategies. The inertia of human action is effective even in the case of total and radical metamorphosis into a small private trader's position, let alone the case of people facing slowly changing ownership relations within big enterprises, including their managements (see Růžička, 1990 for more details).

Of course, the people's experience formed the basis for value orientations. On the one hand, the long-term feeling of entrepreneurial hopelessness led to a widespread desire for and belief in a quick, just, and socially supported development of the private (particularly the small private) sector. On the other hand, it produced mass attitudes of resignation and longing for safety. It resulted in a personal strategy of consumption which misused the so-called 'common productive wealth' (e.g. of working time, tools of work and others).

Sociological research showed an increased tolerance of such behavior which ranged from the abuse of working hours to the theft of 'socialist property'. Independent undertaking was found at the bottom of the list of values. Personal initiative was more and more shifted into after-work-hours activities or extra jobs which provided greater ownership sovereignty. As a result people began to subordinate their regular work to their unofficial and outside employment. Society's economic performance was sustained mostly thanks to the unchangingly strong work ethics, which, however, was on the decline, too.[3]

It is not true that so-called socialist ownership did not constitute ownership. It was a real and widespread parasitic way of ownership. Individual owners were workers in the widest sense of the term. They were employers and employees at the same time. In this relationship the worker-employee was decisive. Society's strategy was not production but consumption, however, not consumption by 'the social body' of individuals.

While social transformation is a chance for the independence in people's economic and social life, it also harbors the danger of losing the social independence implied in their 'employer-employee' position.

3. A personal case study

It is difficult to do theoretical and empirical research in this field without having gained some personal experience in entrepreneurship and in the process of privatization. Thus, you will gain additional knowledge. This personal experiment is hard and costly. Yet,

3 See Růžička (1989), Hubáček and Růžička (1988), Linhart et al. (1988).

the reward will not only be a possibility to prove your theoretical and empirical research but also yield a new dimension in understanding and reflecting the complex processes which are quite often beyond your imagination (see Banfield, 1979). The point of view of a participant gives you the possibility immediately to combine the theoretical and macroempirical scientific level with your own personal experience.

In this article we can only show some illustrations related to the small entrepreneur's starting position in the atmosphere of a society in which socialist thinking with respect to property rights still prevails.

1. When you start your business almost nobody understands your entrepreneurial (especially financial) situation. Egalitarianism which existed for decades contributed to the cultivation of envy and hostility against entrepreneurial spirit.[4]

   In addition, there were socialist perceptions about economic life which were regarded as the suitable forms of interpretation of the societal reality. The majority of the population does not want to become entrepreneurs because they are afraid of losing social security; entrepreneurs are regarded to be persons who use apparently superfluous ('probably dirty') money. The perception of the population is based on ignorance. They are not interested in getting precise information which might contradict their prejudice. They are used only to a family economy in which paternalistic conditions prevail. If you charge higher prices (e.g. in your establishment, because you have invested in a better environment, etc.) the majority of the population thinks you to be a thief. It is beyond their way of thinking that prices are determined by supply and demand. People are still used to live in a world where narrow-minded, relatively small patterns of reproduction determine the conditions of economic life. Of course, all of us face the consequences of the internalization of the life-style of economic populism of the former regime. The small and medium-sized private entrepreneurs are the first persons to be confronted with these legacies of the previous socialist society.
2. If you start an enterprise you must also overcome the consequences of the fact that the people working for you are still accustomed to the out-of-responsibility working style of the former ownership system (e.g. to use their working hours not only for you, to use your things for their purposes only, not to respect your time, etc.).

   If you start a company specializing in construction handicraft works and you have no strong financial basis, you are really unlucky because there is a boom for building firms and construction workers at the beginning of the privatization process. Consequently, you cannot choose your partners. You are only obliged to pay for proper work. This, in turn, will reduce your turnover, because you lose orders. You will observe many surprising things: e.g. the same worker, on the same day and in the same field of work, who as an employee of a firm is working

4 Much of the information on the present conditions of small private business has been identified and partially verified or explained in the author's project 'Social Resources, Forms and Relations of Citizen's Independent Economic Action'. This research was done by the method of participation in the entrepreneurial environment (Růžička 1991-1993). See also Růžička (1992).

for you very slowly during the best part of the day, suddenly chang into a very hard working self-employed part-time private entrepreneur without being troubled by these two faces of his work. This is no schizophrenia. He is able to split his personality at work into two different workers. You may observe the same employees - in spite of your rebukes - using your equipment for their moonlighting somewhere else. The distinction between the former (still existing state or cooperative enterprises) 'common property' and the new private property does not exist for many people. On the other hand, you may be shocked when recognizing that some new private companies perform excellently. They work for customers abroad and the workers see a chance of a much higher and output-related pay. In this case the mental barriers have vanished.

3. Small entrepreneurs start at a time in which the state-owned, or those enterprises still controlled by the state, gain additional new sources for their survival without restructuring their internal system. Such new sources are, in fact, only originating in the private sector. The former socialist enterprises try to get these resources by using their monopoly power of old. With small private start-ups, this position often allows them to go to the very core of subsistence. There are many varieties of this behavior, but the typical and perhaps most instructive example is the one from entrepreneurial life depicted below.

   You have taken a credit and you thought that it would be sufficient to start your business. You know that the interest payments amount to 30 per cent of the total credit. The rest is planned for investment. But you do not know that nearly any step in your entrepreneurial investment is a trap: if you bought electric equipment, you probably need more electric power. If you are properly connected in a normal society, the rest, i.e. an adequate electricity supply, is not a problem. Not so in the transforming post-communist society. If you apply for it, the answer by the distributing enterprise is: 'this is not possible, you must build up the new connection to another main line'. It takes you another 20 per cent of the credit. Only after that they will disclose a secret: 'do you know that we have new regulations now? Anybody who needs more kilowatts must pay two thousand crowns per kw.' This is not for some service but just for a stamp on a paper. And that for nearly 40 per cent of your credit. This may be your first chance for a suicide. (When I explained to my Danish colleagues how it is possible to go ahead in spite of this and to stay in the same place, they exclaimed 'this sounds like a story written by Franz Kafka'.) It is important to know why these patterns of behavior still prevail.

4. Empirical research

In 1993 the position of a small entrepreneur was very different from that in 1991, more complicated and harder. First of all there is a mixture of old and new laws and amendments implemented by the new Czech Republic. The majority of these laws and regulations is not well understood and is not adequately handled by the state bureaucracy and the new entrepreneurs. Of course, it is a necessary stage in the development.

The problem is that the present period involves the entirety of systemic changes. All social groups still exist but only the group of small and medium-sized private entrepreneurs are really implementing and internalizing the goals of that systemic change. They really face and implement the restructuring of transformation.

Especially from the point of view of smaller private enterprises we are facing a new period of accumulation of capital. And this period is also the phase of the first accumulation of entrepreneurial experience. An insufficient knowledge of the market situation (of supply and demand, goods and services necessary to start an enterprise, the ethics of work, the troubles caused by immaturity of the state of law, etc.) creates postponements in the setting up of actual operations of the enterprise and consequently causes financial difficulties. Apart from this, there is a strong contradiction between the entrepreneurs' necessity to use efficiently the financial means and the parasitical behavior of a number of de facto monopolistic state companies which are looking for additional financial resources.

The characteristics of the period of transformation and of the smaller entrepreneurs become manifest, for instance, in the results of the research on the new limited liability companies.[5] The question *'Are any of the recently mentioned problems obstacles to a more rapid development of your enterprise?'* reveals the following results:

Table 14.3 Obstacles to enterprise development (per cent; the rest no answer)

	Definitely yes	Rather yes	Rather no	Definitely no
Defective laws, regulations, enactments	37.1	26.4	15.8	2.5
Lack of understanding and no interest by local government	15.5	21	33.1	11.6
State or cooperative sector monopoly	17.1	17	29.1	16.6
Lack of knowledge, skills, contacts	7.4	24.2	33.2	16.1
Difficulties to hire good workers	21.2	22.8	21.3	13.8
Financial problems (credits, interests, taxes, insolvencies)	29.1	26.4	17.9	8.9

The second and probably long-term troubles are connected with the state of capital. Practically nobody was able to accumulate capital during the past forty years. For the majority of tradesmen and other smaller entrepreneurs the shortage of capital means that

5 The following data are the results of the research 'New Generation of Private Entrepreneurs' (the research was directed by Jana Víteèková, the author of this paper was a member of the team) in the Institute of Sociology, Czechoslovakian Academy of Sciences. The field work was done in spring and summer 1992. The research involved 1 005 entrepreneurs (it means also 1 005 'Ltd-companies') [Archives of the research 1993].

nearly all financial means in their families are mobilized for business undertakings. They have no money, they have no time. This means that they have only a small chance of defending their interests. The data below (Table 14.4) show *what sources the entrepreneurs used to collect their own investment share*. It is necessary to keep in mind that the property of entrepreneurs and their relatives is nothing extraordinary. This major source of investment, in most cases, is nothing more than the usual savings of former employees and things usually used for family life, including leisure. Only a small part of the financial means used to found enterprises originated from profits from former business activities (partially or fully only in the case of 15 per cent of our limited liability companies).

Table 14.4 Origins of the financing of enterprise investment

	Principal source	Supplementary source	Not used as a source
Own savings, personal property	68.1	17.9	5.5
Savings, property of parents. relatives	10.0	15.6	49.5
Loans from inland private persons	5.2	9.1	60.1
Loans from foreign private persons	3.5	3.2	66.7
Credits granted by domestic banks	26.1	7.2	44.9
Credits granted by foreign banks	0.7	0.8	40.0
Donations, gifts	1.4	4.7	65.9
Restitutions	1.2	1.4	68.7

Note: Numbers of entrepreneurs answering question (in per cent).

Figure 14.3 Instruments of financing enterprises

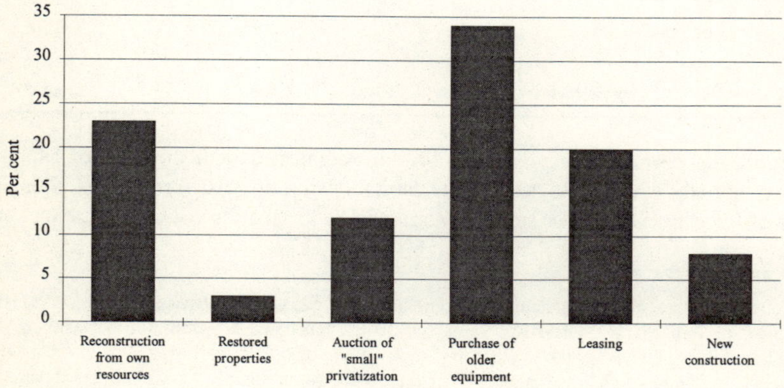

The lack of capital becomes recognizable, for instance, also in the ways in which business premises and other operational means are created (Figure 14.3). Our research showed that for example privatization auctions of 'small enterprises' were used by 13 per cent of the entrepreneurs, purchase of older equipment by 36 per cent, leasing by 22 per cent, start-ups by eight per cent, reorganization by 25 per cent, and restored properties by 4 per cent.

For the first wave of start-ups obstacles most certainly play a different role than for the second wave of setting up small enterprises. The motives for the change of ownership and professional career are shifting the weight of the barriers (Figure 14.4). The leading motive in this case is to overcome long-lasting objective and subjective situations, to become emancipated, i.e. to overcome the hurdles of a one-way (professional, working) career, and to do so of one's free will. Naturally, it also means to separate oneself from an inefficient economic system (both in terms of quality and quantity of work and earnings based on it). It is an immediate solution by the individual or small group, in comparison to the will to reach economic independence. Other motives to start a business have not been so intense or frequent. The interviews of this empirical and sociological study demonstrate that the transition to a market economy based on private entrepreneurs does not only require material resources but also a complete change in lifestyle and values. This process cannot be accomplished by order from above but can only organically develop evolutionarily. This, in turn, necessitates an appropriate environment. Thus, Western assistance in the process of transition to a market economy has to emphasize technical assistance in order to generate the lost entrepreneurial spirit which has contributed to the superiority of a market economy when compared to socialist economies and societies.

Figure 14.4 Motives to start enterprises

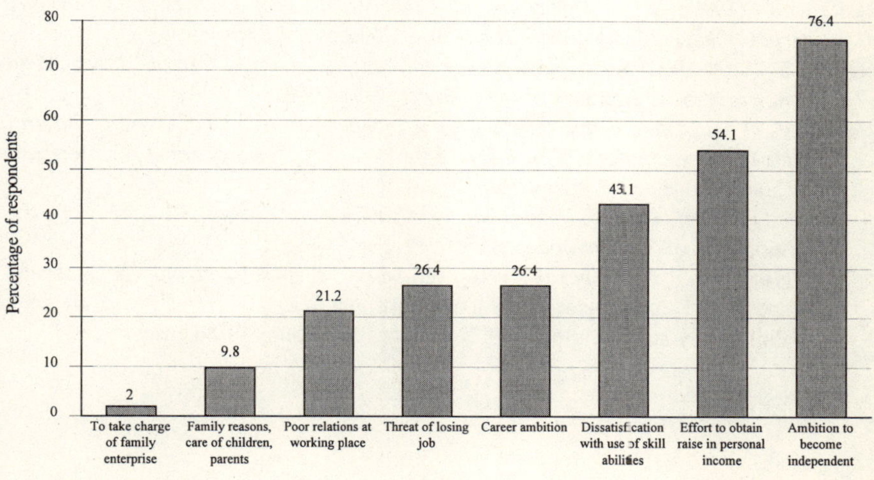

5. Conclusion

The present situation resembles an escape to the New World, including a special kind of homesickness: the remembrance of a quiet working time or family life with an abundance (or sufficiency as a minimum) of spare time is of course very frequent under the pressure of immediate needs or imminent dangers. From an economic point of view the group of small private businessmen will hardly be decisive for the future of society. But from a social standpoint their success is the key to society's economic mentality. It is the matter of cultivation of an individual's self-confidence and flexibility, and consequently of society's self-confidence and trustworthiness. At present the basic interest of this changing society is a certain solicitude about small private businessmen. This strategy may contribute to social stability.

References

Banfield, E.C. (1979) The Moral Basis of Backward Society, in Heidenheimer, A.J. (ed.), *Political Corruption*, Readings in Comparative Analysis, New Brunswick.

Hubáček, O. and R. Růžička (1988) Volný čas v Praze (Leisure Time in Prague), in Vývoj socialistického způsobu života v hl. městě Praze, Prague: Institute for Philosophy and Sociology of Czechoslovakian Academy of Sciences.

Linhart, J., R. Růžička et al. (1988) *Prognóza sociálního rozvoje československé společnosti* (A Prognosis of Social Development of Czechoslovak Society), Prague: Institute for Philosophy and Sociology of Czechoslovak Academy of Sciences.

Růžička, R. (1989) *Vědomí, vlastnictví, technologie* (Consciousness, Ownership, Technology), Prague.

Růžička, R. (1990) *Social Ownership and the Structure of Ownership Behaviour: Czechoslovakia*, Madrid: the XIIth World Congress of Sociology.

Růžička, R. (1991-1993) *Social Resources, Forms and Relations of Citizens' Independent Economic Action*, Archives of the research 1991-1993.

Růžička, R. (1992) *Chances and Barriers of the Independent Economic Action: Cultural Change, Participation, Efficiency*, Santander, 5th International Conference: Cultural Change and Participation.

______ and R. Růžička (1990) *Názory na rozvoj soukromého podnikání* (Opinions on the Development of Private Undertaking), Prague.

______ (1988) *Stav a perspektivy vývoje podmínek a způsobu života* (A State and Prospects of Development of the Conditions and Way of Life), Prague, Institute for Philosophy and Sociology of Czechoslovak Academy of Sciences.

15 How to become an entrepreneur in East Germany: conditions, steps and effects of the constitution of new entrepreneurs

Michael Thomas

1. Introduction

Rather than dealing with the whole process of privatization or constitution of entrepreneurship in East Germany, this paper focusses only on a special issue of that process: the setting up of enterprises by East Germans, former citizens of the GDR, who, in a narrow sense, are to be understood as new entrepreneurs. This article is mainly based on a research project which comprises a period of three years and is now at the end of its first year.[1] The empirical information on social characteristics and potentials of new entrepreneurs has been raised by my own inquiries in the regions of East Berlin and the State of Brandenburg. Responses to a postal questionnaire by more than 900 entrepreneurs in this region and about 30 interviews are the basis of the analyses presented here

In this contribution, I will concentrate on some social issues that might serve as a complement to a pure economic analysis. The focus is on the embeddedness of new entrepreneurship in social and cultural factors, or the 'ongoing systems of social relations' (Granovetter, 1985; see also Bögenhold, 1989 and Thomas, 1993). The concept of embeddedness may be particularly important for analyzing problems of the transformation process and the creation of a new entrepreneurship, in which social and cultural factors are highly influential. The argument presented here focusses on East German businessmen and on how they, as former citizens of the GDR, become entrepreneurs. Because the vast majority (about 80 per cent) of the former socialist firms privatized by the Treuhand are sold to West German or foreign entrepreneurs, our question concerns the nucleus of bottom-up privatization in East Germany, where more than 80 per cent of the start-ups are foundations by East Germans.

For East Germans the way into the market economy has become a new start. This gives a special meaning to the question of the development of market actors. Consequently, this paper will illustrate some of the problems and preconditions relating to the former GDR as well as some global tendencies in the new firm formation process in East Germany since 1989.

1 'New Entrepreneurs in East Germany: Potentials, Characteristics and Steps.' The project is sponsored by the Volkswagen Foundation.

2. The legacy of the past: entrepreneurship in the GDR

The history of private business and entrepreneurship in the GDR has its peculiarities compared to other socialist countries like the Soviet Union. However, this history resulted in the common socialist state-planned economy and was in the same way a reason for the collapse of the GDR as it is disagreeable with regard to the transformation and the constitution of the market entrepreneurs. Notwithstanding such peculiarities and differences with regard to other former socialist countries (especially those of the orthodox or Soviet model of socialism) there was neither the chance nor the place for the development of private ownership in the GDR. After World War II, at the end of the 1940s in East Germany, the share of entrepreneurs in the workforce was higher than average. This rate decreased from 30 per cent in 1949 to 2.2 per cent in 1989; at the end of the 1980s it was 11.2 per cent in West Germany. When the GDR system collapsed in 1989, there were only 185 000 private entrepreneurs left compared to about 2.4 million in 1949. There had never been a complete removal of private entrepreneurs in the GDR, but the remaining private sector (mainly firms in the trade and craft sector) was kept very small and the conditions for private entrepreneurship were quite unfavorable.

The centralization of the economy, the elimination of small firms, the loss of opportunities for entrepreneurship (e.g. to manage a factory autonomously) as well as the growing critique of lifestyles and cultural patterns of the so-called middle class were some of the causes for the lack of modernity in the GDR. The extremely complex process of socialist industrial fordism - central planning, nationalization, domination of large plants and large-scale manufacturing within absolutely dependent enterprises (combines), the missing of entrepreneurship as a factor of permanent innovation, and initiative functioned as a 'modernization trap' with severe consequences for the remaining small private firm sector. Although it cannot be denied that there was some modernization and innovation within the GDR economy, this process was relatively slow and often proceeded in a wrong direction. Many institutions and structures necessary for modern market economies remained absent; chances for individuals to accumulate capital, to get experiences in managing their own autonomous enterprise, and to develop market connections and strategies were the exception only; so called 'behavioral patterns' of the middle class vanished. Even more so, the bureaucratically planned society had effectively damaged creativity, competence, initiative, etc. of individuals as well as of social groups. In the light of these factors, the emergence of entrepreneurship in East Germany is not comparable with processes of business formation in established market economies. One main difference is that East German aspiring businessmen have to develop qualifications such as creativity, initiative, and the ability to bear risks to a higher degree than their West German counterparts.

Just as the socialist system had influenced the existing private sector in the GDR, the continuing dominance of the planned system and its reglementations by state authorities had similar consequences. The assumption, that the remaining private sector - and the entrepreneurs in that sector - could probably be a nucleus or basis for a step-by-step transformation to a market economy (cf. Pickel, 1992) appears to be false not only because of the jump-start conditions of the transformation process in East Germany; the backwardness of an obsolete machinery and product program, capital shortages, the organizational structure of the production process, and the missing of market competition in the GDR also led to serious problems in the transformation process. Nearly half of the old entrepreneurs had to declare bankruptcy during the first two years following Germany's unification. The relatively positive development in the construction sector may be seen as an exemption, but even here the recovery is more a result of new firms entering the market and not based on the 'old' entrepreneurs.

All in all, no favorable preconditions for becoming entrepreneurs existed for individuals who lived within the old GDR system.

3. Setting-up businesses in East Germany

The optimistic expectations about a speedy and successful process of privatization and formation of entrepreneurship in East Germany now appear to be wrong. The 'jump-start' into the market economy, the lack of political support as well as political mistakes have had a negative influence on new entrepreneurs and the minority of incumbent East German entrepreneurs that could survive in the GDR system until Germany was unified.

There was a dramatic rise of private ownership in East Germany in 1990 and 1991, comparable to a so-called *'Gründerzeit'*. In July and August of 1990, two months after the currency-union between East and West Germany was set up, nearly 1 200 new businesses were registered per day. Although the number of start-ups decreased in the following, there were about 350 000 new private businesses at the end of 1992. Many of these new firms failed after only a short period of time and in our sample of East German firms we can well recognize the instabilities of the newly founded firms. As an example 10.6 per cent of the entrepreneurs that participated in our inquiry stated that their business was in an initial stage; 5.6 per cent responded that they expected the crash during the following three months.

This instability appears quite normal, when compared to the development of newly founded firms in West Germany. However, additional instability occured due to the ongoing de-industrialization in East Germany and the poor performance of existing private enterprises. Many regional networks as well as linkages to customers and suppliers in other sectors had been destroyed by these developments. In our sample - and this result equals results from other studies - only about seven per cent of the new businesses originated in manufacturing. In this sector, the share of insolvencies was significantly lower than in the trade and service sectors, which constitute about 73 per cent of all new businesses. The unfavorable environmental conditions in East Germany lead to high instability. While the exit rate was about 9 per cent, in 1990 it increased up to 63 per cent in the first half of 1993. These numbers imply that: nearly two out of three new businesses failed within the first two or three years. In the first half of 1993 about 6 000 newly founded private firms were registered per month. This has lead to a net increase in business-stock of about 19 000 firms in that time period.

4. Processes of the constitution of new entrepreneurs

The new entrepreneurs in East Germany differ from West German entrepreneurs in two respects: East Germans are older (37.2 per cent between the ages of 31-40; 30.5 per cent between 41-50; 18.3 per cent are older than 50) and on average they have a higher qualification (with no significant difference between male and female entrepreneurs). One third of the new entrepreneurs are women. Although the so-called free market is a new experience for them, the majority is convinced that it is endowed with the social and cultural preconditions necessary for its new social role. These preconditions result from experiences in the socialist GDR.

Who of the former GDR citizens becomes an entrepreneur? In general one can say that the new East German entrepreneurs come from all social groups, even though most of them were no underdogs of the GDR society. This hypothesis is reflected in a slogan of a young entrepreneur we interviewed who said: 'he who was nothing in former times, will be nothing now'. Accordingly, 48 per cent of the new entrepreneurs in our sample stated that they had been able to put their ideas of life under the socialist regime into practice, and another 42 per cent answered that this was partly the case.

We thoroughly examined the former social position of new East German entrepreneurs, and the exact position of 'group of origin' in the social sphere of the GDR society, as we expected some relevant social and cultural distinctions between entrepreneurs belonging to different groups like the power elite, the engineers, intellectuals, etc. We concentrated our research on professional biographies of new entrepreneurs, hoping to uncover relevant strategies of action as well as social ties. And these professional biographies may be seen as the key to a the social identity, i.e. a personal 'starting set'. Four groups of origin can be identified:

- the power elite (members of the secret service, the army, employees of political parties and mass organizations);
- engineers and natural scientists working in industry;
- intellectuals (social scientists, artists and other forms of cultural workers); and
- normal workers.

In our sample about 40 per cent of the new entrepreneurs were normal workers, one third belonged to the group of engineers and natural scientists and one fifth were intellectuals. Remarkably, members of the former power elite formed only a small minority of about seven per cent among the new entrepreneurs.

In our representative inquiry we found some interesting information on the connection between the former social group of origin of the East German entrepreneurs and their new businesses. A recurring pattern is that the vast majority (about 90 per cent) of those new entrepreneurs that had been members of the former power elite or of the intelligentsia opened businesses in the trade and services sectors. We found that members of these groups became entrepreneurs more or less by chance; quite often a connection to a certain person or a certain opportunity gave the decisive impulse to start a business of their own. Often they became dependent entrepreneurs, for example working as brokers for insurance companies or real-estate agents.

The majority of the group of engineers (in our inquiry about 52 per cent), however, started their own businesses in fields in which they had worked before; another - smaller - group started a business in high-tech services. Typically, these are markets requiring a considerable know-how and thus have high entry barriers. Due to their qualification, their experience and resources, these engineers have the necessary preconditions for setting up a firm pertaining to their field. We know from our research that a lot of engineers had more than one alternative to further their career and that they consciously chose to start their own business. If they had had a chance under the old regime, they would have elected private ownership years ago. In the privatization process the engineers have acted more rationally and strategically than other groups, e.g. by collecting profound information from banks and lawyers before they start.

When being asked for the main reasons to start their own business, only about one third of the entrepreneurs stated unemployment or problems with the job. In fact, nearly 90 per cent of the new entrepreneurs had been employees before they became employers themselves. For about 56 per cent of them, the chance of realizing their own ideas was 'very important'; nearly half of the respondents found it 'very important' to be independent. As far as the engineers in our sample are concerned the interpretation of these results are rather clear. One of the engineer-entrepreneurs told us - and this is very characteristic - 'We are not the people who were fired or would have been fired!'

The example of engineers shows that people of the GDR often can use their former qualification and experience in their profession as 'capital' or 'key-qualification' for their new existence as entrepreneurs. They are convinced that they are well prepared and have the proper qualifications. And in fact these are important social and biographical preconditions for acting in the new social field. About two-thirds of our entrepreneurs told us that they had had experiences in the field of management and leadership under the old system and that these experiences were more than fruitful for running their own business. As we can conclude from our research, the abilities to deal with persons, to organize, to solve problems, as well as to think and work in a more complex manner are basic qualifications. As one of our entrepreneurs stated: 'he who in former times had the chance to work independently, will follow this path in the future'. This form of leadership seems to be a very important experience and the direct foundation for establishing and using ties of trust. In some of our interviews we could see how these ties of trust developed and which role they played in the process of building up a business. Most of these cases concerned the setting-up of new businesses in cooperation with a friend or with former colleagues as employees. Of course, these personal ties and especially the ties of trust can not be the same over time. Conflicts occur in firms, firing may become necessary. And yet such ties are taken advantage of in the processes of business building and we can observe different forms of interaction and social orders in the new enterprises.

We were most astonished about the fact that in our inquiry 50 per cent of the entrepreneurs stated they had experienced a better living situation, i.e. better working conditions, leisure time activities and income in the former GDR system; 12.4 per cent responded that their standard of living had been worse, 36.7 per cent stated no change of standard. Moreover, 50 per cent of the entrepreneurs stated that the chances to realize their own aims and ideas had been higher. The respective answers differ only insignificantly among the main groups, with the evaluations of the engineers being a little more negative and those of the members of the former power elite and intelligentsia more positive. However, we find much greater differences between the generations in regard to the evaluation of former living conditions, with the younger generation being less satisfied with the old regime. This appreciation of the former GDR system is actually a surprise; particularly because of the fact that the majority of new entrepreneurs cannot belong to the group of citizens of the GDR who were satisfied with social immobility, lack of creativity, etc. and now need to develop their own initiative, creativity, etc.

The relatively positive perception of the old communist system may partly be explained by difficulties and negative experiences with the market economy, particularly the special conditions required of aspiring entrepreneurs in East Germany. Quite often, expectations concerning the situation on free and rationally organized markets have turned out to be wrong; the new entrepreneurs miss a fairness of competition and the reliability of their business partners. Parallel to a relatively positive interpretation of the GDR we often find a negative interpretation of the new economic system. As a side-effect of the complicated situation today there is a tendency to glorify the past. However, we have no indication that the positive perception of GDR-reality is a nostalgia or a sign of backshifting.

Our investigations of new entrepreneurship in East Germany demonstrate that some preconditions formed and required in the GDR are of importance for the new social role as businessmen. Social and biographical facts from GDR-times may indeed be taken into account when analyzing the creation of entrepreneurship in East Germany.

References

Bögenhold, Dieter (1989); Die Berufspassage in das Unternehmertum; *Zeitschrift für Soziologie*, 18, 263-81

Granovetter, Marc S. (1985); Economic Action and Social Structure: The Problem of Social Embeddedness; *American Journal of Sociology*, 6, 481-510.

Pickel, Andreas (1992) *Radical Transitions - The Survival and Revival of Entrepreneurship in the GDR*, Boulder: Westview.

Thomas, Michael (1993); Private Selbständigkeit in Ostdeutschland. Erste Schritte in einem neuen Forschungsfeld; *Soziale Welt*, 44, 223-42.

16 Businesses founded in East Germany: economic activity and capital investment

Thomas Hinz and *Rolf Ziegler*

1. The starting point: the special situation of East Germany

In the month of July 1990 the *Bundesbank* exported hard currency - the *Deutsche Mark* - to the GDR, and the highest number of business registrations in the East German process of transformation was counted. Almost 36 000 entries were recorded according to official statistics. In the whole year of 1990 there were 280 000 entries, and another 270 000 in 1991 (Gemeinsames Statistisches Amt, 1991). This rather impressive figure indicating enormous dynamics is based on a special constellation of the starting point of system transformation in East Germany.

It is widely accepted in the discussion of economists and politicians that the constitution of small business plays a fundamental role in the deconstruction of the planned economy which was mainly orientated towards large-scale plants. After giving a description of the starting point in East Germany (in the first part of the article) we will analyze to what extent the process of creating new businesses has been successful and what economic potential - measured by capital investment - is being expressed by the new firms.

The special situation of the former GDR and - after the unification in October 1990 - of the *Neue Bundesländer* should briefly be depicted in respect to the reorganization of a socialist-planned economy, because there is reason to argue that the observed dynamics of East German business registrations are linked to these special circumstances.

The process of transformation started with conditions assumed to create a relatively high level of *certainty* about the future economic and political development. This means: the goal of the transformation (market economy and political democracy[1]) and the path to reach this goal (unification of both German states) were determined after the elections of the *Volkskammer* in March 1990. The total system of laws and institutions - the frame of economic, legal, and political order was transferred to the *Neue Bundesländer*.[2] Even if the blind transfer created some unfortunate outcomes, and some regulations became obstacles to a dynamic building up of the economy,[3] it has to be

1 Lindenberg (1992) stresses the relevance of a combination of private property rights and political democracy. In states introducing private property without political reforms actors tend to opportunistic behavior. Networks of 'weak solidarity' typical for western economies are hardly built up.

2 Problems of state controlled (exogenous) transference of institutions are discussed by Lehmbruch (1993).

3 The law of restitution property rights in East Germany is vehemently criticized (Sinn and Sinn, 1991).

outlined how a horizon of certain expectations relevant for processes of economic exchange has developed in East Germany. Admittedly, there is still a lot of friction in the building up of an administration (Scheytt, 1992) but in the foreseeable future administration and institutions will be able to carry themselves through laws, to implement the 'frame of order' and to adapt organizational programs and strategies to East German conditions.

The consensus about German unification at the level of foreign politics and the international embeddedness of the process has also brought about a certainty about the future path. There is no way back. The former GDR has fully been integrated into the West European system of economic and political cooperation. The transferred 'frame of order', together with an integration into the Western capitalist system, leads to a favorable environment for investments in the form of setting up new firms. An extraordinary risk-premium for invested captital does not have to be paid. Under certain circumstances, the extension of the West German market into East Germany brought about two other constellations which could not be found in other ex-socialist countries.

In the former GDR supply decifits - with regard to consumer goods - were often articulated and could, therefore, be clearly identified. As a result of the economic union in July 1990, people in East Germany received their purchasing power in hard currency and were consequently urged to catch up with their consumer needs. Western producers were able to sell their products and services on the East German market under riskfree conditions. Thus, the West German economy boomed right after the unification, whereas the East German national product dramatically decreased.[4] Of course, this did not favour the constitution and the consolidation of an orginally East German production; on the other hand, it was the basic precondition for numerous opportunities for West German enterprises to open up branches and subsidiary firms in East Germany.

By joining the Federal Republic of Germany, the former GDR received an immediate and gigantic transfer of capital. With the focus on the creation of new business organizations it has to be mentioned that several funding programs and tax reductions were established for the purpose of supporting activities known to lead to a higher degree of self-employment and entrepreneurship. German social policy programs have lessened the shock of changing the system. Labor market programs aiming at a requalification of labor force led to an investment in human capital which has not been reached in other former socialist countries of Eastern Europe. An enormous amount of courses in professional education are being held to prepare the citizens of the former GDR for changing requirements on the labor market. Numerous courses for becoming an entrepreneur are also being offered.[5]

---

4 A brief description of economic trends in the transformation of East Germany is given by Büchtemann and Schupp (1992).

5 Large qualification companies (ABM) funded by the German labor office have thousands of participants. One purpose of these companies is to stimulate the foundations of new businesses. See Knuth (1992).

A further specific quality of the East German transformation is the mode of the privatization of state-owned plants. In East Germany the *Treuhandanstalt* is engaged in selling large parts of state property to private owners within a limited period of time. The role of the *Treuhandanstalt* has been a matter of controversy in the discussion of transformation politics, but nevertheless it played a key role in economic restructuring. While privatization of large plants goes on rather slowly and is accompanied by enormous amounts of dismissals, the constitution of small businesses is characterized by split-offs of state-owned plants: small units are sold separately - quite often to former employees.

These characteristics of the East German development appear to be a favorable starting point for the building up of new businesses when compared to other East European economies. If we have so far emphasized the degree of relative certainty in environmental conditions, we have to also mention impediments and imponderabilities of the transformation period with regard to a Western economy:

- The conditions for the accumulation of capital by private entrepreneurs in the communist system were not comparable to those required in a capitalist society. Most of all, the expropriations in the first years after 1945 destroyed values of private property in a remarkable way. The regulation of restitution titles of property - now a law within the unification - treaty has only hesitantly created private property, primarily on account of the fact that the bureaucratic administration is so complex. Anyone searching for data on the distribution of property in East Germany will have difficulties finding meaningful statistics, although it is indisputable that state intervention has led to a levelled-out distribution of private property in toto (Geißler, 1992).

  Privately-owned firms exist only in a small remaining stock (Bannasch, 1990; Schrumpf, 1990). These firms were hardly able to accumulate capital on their own. This is to higher degree true for the state-owned plants due to their more direct mode of integration into the planning system. The timid efforts of reform to leave a part of the surplus to the management of the state-owned plant for purposes of reinvestment were not able to spread distinctly (e.g. Cornelsen, 1989).

  The lack of consumer goods was responsible for the emergence of considerable bank deposits, as long as earned money could not be spent in the shortage economy. This surplus of spending power has created a widely diffused fundament of financial capital in the early morning of transformation but the scale and relevance of this sort of potential investment capital is difficult to estimate.
- The usability of human capital gathered in times of the socialist planned economy is restricted under the altered conditions of a market economy.[6] However, we can expect experiences made by the founders of the firms in work biography to play a dominant role in raising new businesses.

---

6 In a shortage economy, quite different qualifications are required compared to those in a competitive economy. Especially older workers are faced with devaluation of human capital (Bird et al., 1992).

- The law to clear up titles of property causes a serious delay in constituting new firms. A second intensively discussed problem is the shortage of business area. Furthermore, the bad equipment of the infrastructure has been claimed an important obstacle for newly founded firms (Friedrich, 1990).

If one tries to rate the factors characterizing the East German transformation, one has to state a quite favorable environment compared to other East European economies - caused by the relative certainty and the transfer of capital from West to East Germany. On the other hand the levelled-out distribution of property limits the chances of investment for citizens of the former GDR. Nonetheless, the problematic conditions have not had a deterrent effect on the willingness to found new businesses: we have already referred to the considerable amount of business registrations. In the following our main interest will be to evaluate the newly founded businesses in view of stability as well as important basic patterns of the new firms indicating their economic potential.

2. Data: Leipzig and Munich founder studies

Our analysis is based on a comparison of newly founded East German firms with West German ones.[7] The East German data were collected as part of the research project *'Leipziger Gründerstudie'* (Leipzig Founder Study). This project combines three different sources of data:

- *First*, the official records of business registrations (including the entries to the 'Handwerksrolle' which is a register for skilled manual workers who are self-employed) from the second half of 1991 form a cohort of 4 162 newly founded firms. The amount of variables is small but the data contains rather important information about some basic characteristics of the registered firms, i.e. the branches of industry and the legal form. We checked the defined cohort with respect to firms deleted from the register once a year. By focusing on the official data it was possible to give evidence of the development of the cohort of foundations[8] as a whole.
- *Second*, anwers to a questionnaire that was sent out in early 1992 to all of the 4 162 business foundations and received a remarkable response rate of 48.3 per cent (N= 2 011).
- *Third*, data gathered by the questionnaires also worked as screening information for a subsequent interview. For these interviews we selected a stratified random sample of 840 new businesses. 742 interviews (average interviewing time was one hour)

---

7 The previous research on East German new firms (May-Strobl and Paulini, 1990, 1991; May-Strobl et al., 1992; Koch and Woderich, 1992) and on the process of reorganization (articles in Heidenreich, 1992) is for the most part based either on case studies or examination of registration data. With reference to these sources of information the estimates of the viability and the economic relevance of the new firms remain rather vague.

8 The term 'foundations' is used for newly founded (at least newly registered) businesses.

were conducted during the summer of 1992, in most cases with the apparent founder of the firm. In the middle of 1994 these firms will be interviewed again.

Data on a comparison of East and West German results was already raised in a similiar project analyzing 1 849 newly founded firms in the region of Munich and Upper Bavaria. Business registration of that sample of new firms took place in 1985 and 1986.

3. Stability and economic activity of newly founded firms

Until now statements about the new business formation process in East Germany have been based on the analysis of aggregated registration data (Liebernickel and Schwarz, 1992). The administrative act of registration is clearly a first step in becoming an entrepreneur. Then the person has at least an idea of the kind of business that would bring him some money. However, the mere registration does not appear meaningful in respect to the economic potential of a newly founded business if one thinks of the financial capital invested or jobs created.

Furthermore it is known from experiences in West Germany that about 20 per cent of the new registrations are either fictitious firms, e.g. made up to receive some tax reduction, or 'still born' firms, which never show any business activity at all (Preisendörfer and Ziegler, 1991). It is estimated that only half of the recorded registrations in East Germany actually go into business (May-Strobl and Paulini, 1991).[9]

The first, most important questions should be: how high is the stability of the cohort of the newly registered businesses, and what economic activity evolves with registration? To answer these questions we will focus on official registrations. After the fall of the Berlin wall and during the subsequent time of rapid political changes a trading license was often applied for. The applicants appeared to base their decision on luck, euphoric feelings and the prospect to earn money easily. For our cohort of registrations the proportion of so called 'nine-day wonders' in business reaches about 20 per cent (Table 16.1a). These registrations were deleted from the register in September 1992, about one year after their entry.[10] Whether these business registrations can be characterized as serious efforts to start a business is difficult to assess. There is a higher rate of deletion from the register in those branches of the industry with a lower market entry barrier. It seems reasonable to assume that a remarkable number of new firms were founded just for a trial or to bridge the waiting time preceding another occupational opportunity. Businesses of skilled manual workers characterized by higher barriers of market entry have been significantly more stable

Business registration is, as mentioned above, only a partial step in the process of founding a business. A crucial issue is whether economic activity actually begins within a certain time after registration or if any impediments prevent starting activity. In East

---

9 Our impressions of the fieldwork indicate, however, that this share of 50 per cent is distinctly overestimated. Only five per cent of the firms on our mailing list could not be found.

10 The value for the West German area is at the same level, though this result is referred to the time period of eight years (1980-1988).

Germany a strong influence of problematic circumstances is assumed to exist (May-Strobl and Paulini, 1990; Friedrich, 1990). In our sample, about 90 per cent of the still registered firms started their business before spring 1992. Five per cent of the business men intended to do so in the near future and the remaining five per cent no longer consider the idea of becoming an entrepreneur (Table 16.1a).[11] In the first interim result we found a considerable but not dramatically high rate of deletion from the register while most of the still registered firms have in the meanwhile started with economic activities.

A further investigation of the economic potential of the foundings was conducted with a West German area (the region of Munich and Upper Bavaria) as point of reference.[12] It is possible to more vividly picture the East German dynamics when looking at a comparative region in West Germany. In East Germany we, to a considerable degree, find firms which emerged from organizations of the socialist past. Almost 10 per cent of the registrations have evolved from a plant of the former planning economy (Table 16.1a), and if one looks at the businesses of skilled manual workers the proportion is 20 per cent. These firms have nominal resources above average but the evaluation of heritage is difficult. A typical example of such a split-off foundation is the privatization of the rather small retail shops of *HO*, the GDR trading organization, often passed on to former employees. This type of foundation naturally does not have a West German equivalent.

Advantages of split-offs might consist of maintaining networks of buyers and suppliers, using fixed assets and a better infrastructure. On the other hand split-offs are risky because old technology may still be in use, and in some cases there are heavy ecological burdens of the past that are very difficult to manage. Complete takeovers are obviously limited to the firms sold by the *Treuhandanstalt*. Accordingly, there is only a small proportion of takeovers (about six per cent) in the Leipzig data, while this share in the West German sample was 20 per cent. We have restricted the following analysis to originally new firms, i.e. firms without a precursor as indicated in the questionnaires.

In contrast to West Germany it should be noted that a striking proportion of new firms starts as branches and subsidiary firms or as firms closely connected to another enterprise. About one third of the Leipzig firms belong to this category. In the region of Munich only 10 per cent of the new firms could be indentified as dependent on other enterprises (Table 16.1b). An important quality of the East German situation has already been mentioned with the higher degree of interfirm connections and dependence.

11 An explanation for this commonly rather low value can be given if we look at two overlapping effects. First, it is clear that firms having serious problems are subject to a negative selection process. They are harder to be reached and motivated to take part in our study. Second, some impediments in the process of founding a new business often occur before the firm is registrated. The influence of the first (selection) effect will be diminished by using a weighted data set. In respect to the relevance of the second effect only speculations can be made.

12 For a meaningful comparison of the two datasets the following analysis has been restricted to firms registered at the Chamber of Commerce (IHK - Industrie- und Handelskammer). New craft businesses of skilled manual workers are not taken in account.

A remarkable number of East German new firms are subsidiaries - we assume - of West German provenence.

Table16.1a Economic activity of registered firms in the region of Leipzig

State of registration one year after entry (cohort of foundations) (per cent)	
Deleted from register	18.3
Still registered	81.7

Note: N=4 162, Registrations of IHK and HWK Leipzig.

Activity-status of firms still registered (per cent)	
Active	89.6
Becoming active in near future	5.4
Not active	3.6
Closed	1.4

Note: N=1 638, Leipzig founder study questionnaire spring 1992, weighted data.

Our data confirm the well-known malaise of industrial production in East Germany. Only three per cent of the newly founded firms come from the industrial sector (Table 16.1b). Trading shows a 40 per cent proportion in Leipzig. This is surely due to the fact that needs of consumer goods are easily detected and supply is not problematic. The majority of new businesses comes from services. The most numerous registrations in services have been recorded for credit and assurance agencies. Other important new businesses in services are hotels and restaurants and services for enterprises.

A distinct difference between Leipzig and Munich can be seen by focusing on the founded firm's character of creating the main source of the founders' income.[13] In Munich about 60 per cent of so called full-time foundations were registered, in Leipzig this number is 70 per cent (Table 16.1b). Accordingly one can conclude that the East German new firms are to a higher degree expected to feed their founders. This information fits well with the fact that East German full-time founders work longer for their business than West Germans do.

The results presented so far spotlight the serious efforts of the East German business organizations to come up with some economic activity. This happens in a remarkable way in connection with other firms. The next question should be whether this attempt seems to be successful in regard to the provision of resources. We ask in detail: measured by the capital invested, are the founded firms smaller in East Germany?

13 A first-job business creates the main source of income for at least one person. Firms founded as a second job are mostly characterized by a low level of economic activity (number of employees, turnover).

Table 16.1b Organizational basic patterns of new firms in the regions of Leipzig and Munich (per cent)

	Leipzig	Munich
Type of business		
Originally new	82.3	76.5
Split-off ('Ausgründung')	11.2	3.4
Reprivatized	0.6	-
Takeover	5.9	20.1
	(N=1 513)	(N=1 845)
Degree of independence (only new firms)		
Completely independent	67.4	90.1
Subsidiary firm (branch)	10.7	1.4
Closely related to another enterprise	21.9	8.5
	(N=1 238)	(N=1 410)
Branch of industry (only new firms)		
Manufacturing	3.4	5.3
Construction	2.7	1.9
Trade (retail and wholesale)	40.7	34.1
Services	53.2	58.7
	(N=1 240)	(N=1 411)
Character of business activity (only new firms)		
Full time businesss	71.1	58.5
Part time business	28.9	41.5
	(N=1 225)	(N=1 411)

4. Capital invested

The start-up capital[14] of new firms is a crucial variable. The amount of financial capital raised by the founder is an indicator of the firm's size and - more indirectly - of its economic potential. It is known from research done in West Germany that the starting size has a strong impact on the chance of survival of a firm (Brüderl and Schüssler, 1990; Brüderl, Preisendörfer and Ziegler, 1992). The capital invested measures the viability of the new business. Having described the limited possibilities of accumulating financial capital during the socialist regime of the former GDR we might expect that the East German founders are equipped with less personal capital than founders in West

14 The start-up capital of a firm consists of both the fixed assets and the overhead expenses at the time of founding. For the different legal forms of capital companies the start-up capital is not only composed of the capital invested in ordinary shares.

Germany. However, when taking into account the organizational environment, a contrary trend should operate. A first layer of small business has to be built up. In Munich, the examined newly founded firms form an additional stream in an established market environment. The special constellation of building up a market structure requires a higher average investment in Leipzig.

Obviously it is to be expected that the start-up capital varies according to some important organizational patterns. For example, new businesses in industry and trade need a higher amount of raised capital compared to services. A decisive point regarding the start-up capital of a firm is the purpose of the foundation: does working in the founded firm create the main income (full-time foundation) or an additional income (part-time foundation)? Does the legal form of the new firm require a certain provision of capital to begin business? How many partners are engaged in providing the capital?

Figure 16.1 Start-up capital of newly founded firms

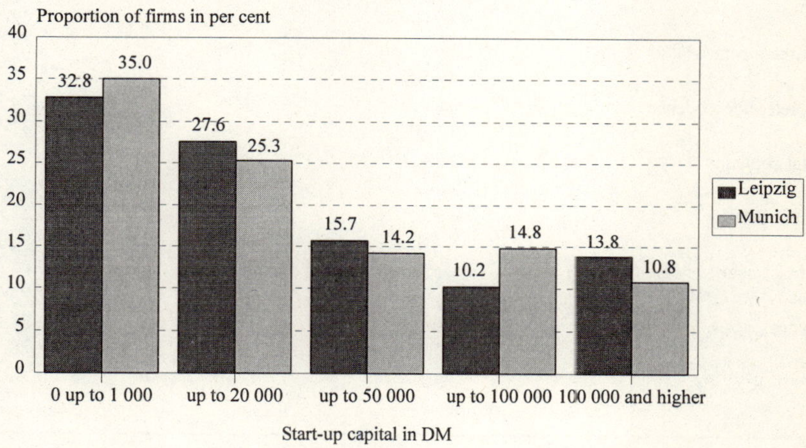

Notes: Leipzig: N=1 191, mean 107 700 DM, median 10 000 DM.
Munich: N=1 411, mean 72 250, median 8 900 DM.

Sources: Leipzig founder study questionaire spring 1992; Munich founder study.
Weighted data; Munich start up capital in addition weighted by inflation index.

Figure 16.1 shows the grouped distribution of start-up capital in East and West Germany.[15] We see that both distributions are very similar. Both he mean (107 700

15 The following analysis is again restricted to actual new firms in East and West Germany. Split-offs, reprivatized firms and take-overs are excluded. This is necessary if one wants to get a meaningful comparision. The considerable share of split-offs in East Germany starts business in completely different circumstances in relation to originally new firms. Fixed assets of the socialist 'mother' are brought in. It seems to be rather difficult to evaluate fixed assets according to West German standard of book keeping.

DM to 72 250 DM) and the median (10 000 DM to 8 900 DM) are higher in the region of Leipzig.[16] About one third of the firms begin with miminum provision of financial capital of less than 1 000 DM. These firms might be mainly new service firms which have no fixed assets and only very low overhead expenses, e.g. assurance agents and salesmen.

Table 16.2 Determinants of start-up capital of newly founded firms in the regions of Leipzig and Munich (organizational variables)

	Leipzig (model 1)	Munich (model 2)	Pooled (model 3)
Manufacturing	1.45	0.90	0.95
	(3.25)*	(3.49)*	(4.24)*
Trade	0.63	1.40	1.06
	(3.16)*	(7.51)*	(7.42)*
Full time business	2.93	1.38	2.05
	(13.38)*	(7.49)*	(14.36)*
Complete independence	2.03	0.96	1.78
	(9.54)*	(3.31)*	(10.37)*
Capital company	2.28	3.09	2.84
	(6.75)*	(13.81)*	(15.11)*
Business partner	–0.09	1.12	0.62
	(0.35)	(5.22)*	(3.69)*
Creating business in East Germany	-	-	0.68
			(4.92)*
Constant	4.08	4.68	3.83
	(16.74)*	(15.33)*	(18.78)*
Adjusted R^2	0.28	0.32	0.28
N	1 118	1 380	2 499

Notes: Dependent variable: logarithm of start-up capital; * significant at the 5 per cent-level; t-values in parentheses; categories of reference: services, part time business, subsidiary firm, no capital company, no business partner engaged, creating business in West Germany.

Sources: Leipzig founder study questionnaire spring 1992, non-weighted data.
Munich founder study, non-weighted data.

The higher average capital of the Leipzig sample may be explained by the lower proportion of second-job foundations there and the higher share of businesses in the Munich sample that were in sectors, where capital intensity is relatively low.

So the West German takeovers can hardly be compared with the East German split-offs.

16 Our analysis takes financial capital of 1985 and 1986 into account, weighted by a factor of 1 107. This value is given by the Statistisches Bundesamt (1992) for an index of inflation in the branch of capital goods.

A separate multivariate estimate arrives at the result (models 1 and 2 in Table 16.2) that the amount of start-up capital in East and West Germany is influenced by the same organizational factors: the branch of industry, full-time or part-time foundation, the degree of independence and the legal form. As expected, a higher amount of start-up capital is raised in the industrial and trading sector (reference: services), and if a full-time foundation is started indepedently from other enterprises, there is a positive impact on the amount of start-up capital. The legal form of the enterprise also matters. However, it is a striking fact that founding a business together with a partner is not related to a higher start-up capital in East Germany. This means here that a business partner does not primarily have the role of a supplier of start-up capital. Pooled data of Leipzig and Munich is the basis for an estimate (model 3 in Table 16.2) identifying a single separate effect of creating new business in the East. If one considers all relevant organizational patterns there is a significant trend towards businesses provided with higher start-up capital in East Germany. The simple hypothesis that new businesses in East Germany are provided with relatively low start-up capital is definitely not confirmed by our data. On the contrary, new businesses in East Germany are characterized by a higher investment of financial capital.

The organizational patterns surely explain the main impact on the amount of start-up capital raised. But in respect to restrictions in the capital market (Büchel and Pannenberg, 1992), factors dealing with the person of the founder have to be taken into account. Most of all - excluding the ownership of houses and land - the chances of founders to accumulate financial capital during the occupational career are important.

Before we look at the additional impact of personal characteristics on raised capital we will provide some insight into the distribution of personal variables. It is very important to note that the comparative description is appropriate only in order to give an impression of the founder's personal characteristics. A reasonable comparison must refer to the whole population of employees in East and West Germany. Otherwise the observed differences could be misleading. However, some illustrative results shall be remarked:[17]

- The share of new firms founded by women does not differ extremely between Leipzig and Munich. In Leipzig one third of the new businesses are started by women, in Munich women account for 26 per cent.[18]
- A clear distinction is observed when focusing on the age of the founder at the time of founding. Founders in East Germany are on average five years older than those in West Germany. The average age in the East is 39 years.
- 75 per cent of East German founders are skilled workers ('Facharbeiter'); in West Germany these employees account for about half that value.
- If one sums up the proportions of precarious labor market positions (unemployment, short time work, participants in qualification programs), one finds 34 per cent of the

17 See the list of means of the variables used in models 4 to 6 in the appendix.

18 Based on the Munich Founder Study, Jungbauer-Gans (1992) presents a detailed investigation of women as founders of new firms.

Leipzig founder population in this category. Only a small proportion of the founders had not been in the labor market before they started the new firm. In West Germany a contrary situation exists: six per cent of the founders were unemployed, 23 per cent never worked in the labor market.

- Almost 16 per cent of the founders in East Germany had had the experience of being self-employed prior to the foundation of the actual firm in 1991. Founders from West Germany were overrepresented in this group. Here about one third had the experience of being self-employed.

In a multivariate model the influences of personal characteristics on the amount of start-up capital will now be estimated together with the organizational patterns.

Table 16.3 Determinants of start-up capital of newly founded firms (organizational and personal variables)

	Leipzig (model 4)	Leipzig (model 5)	Munich (model 6)	Pooled (model 7)
(1) Organizational Variables				
Manufacturing	1.33 (2.77)*	1.37 (2.89)*	0.79 (3.05)*	0.86 (3.72)*
Trade	0.46 (2.19)*	0.48 (2.29)*	1.38 (7.39)*	1.01 (7.16)*
Full time business	2.88 (12.12)*	2.80 (11.94)*	1.31 (7.00)*	1.96 (13.22)*
Complete independence	1.96 (8.43)*	1.97 (8.61)*	1.00 (3.40)*	1.68 (9.27)*
Capital company	1.93 (4.87)*	1.64 (4.16)*	2.59 (11.09)*	2.43 (11.99)*
Business partner	–0.09 (0.34)	–0.12 (0.43)	1.05 (4.91)*	0.63 (3.66)*
(2) Personal Variables of Founders				
Sex (1=female)	0.08 (0.35)	0.16 (0.72)	–0.71 (3.37)*	–0.33 (2.13)*
Age/10	0.07 (0.55)	0.08 (0.77)	0.19 (1.63)	0.08 (1.16)
Schooling				
POS/MR (10 years)	0.17 (0.56)	0.20 (0.67)	–0.00 (0.01)	0.17 (0.97)
EOS/Abitur (12 years)	0.15 (0.38)	0.16 (0.42)	–0.14 (0.54)	0.06 (0.28)

Table 16.3 (continued)

Occupational schooling				
skilled worker	0.23 (0.87)	0.28 (1.08)	0.07 (0.34)	0.15 (0.91)
master, engineer	0.08 (0.26)	0.09 (0.29)	0.14 (0.54)	0.13 (0.64)
university	0.12 (0.34)	0.13 (0.37)	0.39 (1.40)	0.31 (1.42)
Job status prior to creating business				
out of the labor market	–0.52 (1.24)	–0.65 (1.56)	–0.51 (2.16)*	–0.59 (2.88)*
unemployed	–0.15 (0.66)	–0.07 (0.33)	–0.68 (1.72)	–0.15 (0.75)
self-employment experience	0.87 (2.96)*	0.15 (0.47)	0.60 (3.05)*	0.73 (4.39)*
place of residence 1989 GDR	-	-1.99 (5.41)*	-	-
creating business in East Germany	-	-	-	0.61 (3.60)*
constant	3.64 (5.16)*	5.39 (7.03)*	4.41 (9.27)*	3.62 (9.74)**
adjusted R^2	0.27	0.29	0.33	0.29
N	981	981	1 354	2 335

Notes: Dependent variable: logarithm of start-up capital; * significance at 5 per cent-level; t-values in parentheses; categories of reference: services; part time business; subsidiary firm; no capital company; no business partner engaged; male; schooling of 8 years and below; no such occupational schooling; being employed prior to creating a business; no self-employment experience; place of residence 1989 outside GDR; creating business in West Germany.

Sources: Leipzig founder study questionnaire spring 1992, non-weighted data.
Munich sounder study, non-weighted data.

In the separate analyses of Leipzig and Munich (models 4 and 6 in Table 16.3) we find positive non-significant impacts of schooling variables both for East and West Germany. The effect of age is positive but insignificant. It is remarkable that East German women do not start their businesses with a significantly lower start-up capital. The reason might lie in the higher orientation of East German women to be part of the labor force. Women strongly try to maintain their occupational status in East Germany, while founding a firm in West Germany is often a way of returning to the labor market after an interruption, for example a so-called family break. New businesses started by persons coming from outside of the labor market or by formerly unemployed tend to raise lower start-up capital; however, the effects are less distinct compared to West Germany and, in addition, are not statistically significant. This result is astonishing if one looks at foundations coming from unemployment as opposed to foundations grounded on necessity (Bögenhold, 1987).

In comparision to Munich the personal characteristics seem to be of less importance in East Germany. This is a finding which matches our considerations on the levelled-out distribution of private property quite well. The only variable on the individual level that is of statistical significance is the experience of being self-employed. If the founder was self-employed prior to having founded the firm, the start-up capital was higher. As outlined above, opportunities for citizens of the former GDR to have some experience with self-employment were quite restricted. When examining this coefficient by controlling the influence of the variable 'place of residence in 1989', an impressive finding appears: founders from the former GDR raised a significantly lower amount of start-up capital, and the influence of their previous experience of being self-employed lost strength and statistical significance (model 5 in Table 16.3). In other words: on the one hand, firms are founded with a higher start-up capital in East Germany, on the other hand, founders coming from East Germany invest less capital than West Germans starting businesses in East Germany. An estimation based on the pooled data of Leipzig and Munich (model 7 in Table 16.3) confirms the picture of higher capital intensity in East German newly-founded firms. Also the start-up capital is higher in East Germany if one 'brings man back in'. This is true even if the West German founders were excluded from the model.

These results deserve to be interpretated carefully in view of slowly evolving market structures. We could demonstrate again that - contrary to some apprehension - the amount of start-up capital in East Germany is not lower than in West Germany. The crucial question is how the invested start-up capital is raised. How high is the proportion of personal capital, how much money is raised through credits, and who gives the credits to the founders?

The Leipzig newcomers raise less personal capital on becoming entrepreneurs. A comparison of the absolute sums in Figure 16.2 shows that a greater proportion of firms start with a minimum capital in Munich. The median is DM 8 000 in Leipzig and is distinctly higher than in Munich (DM 3 300). However, we find only six per cent of the Leipzig firms with a personal capital of DM 50 000 and above. In Munich this proportion comes to 19 per cent. Measured by personal capital, very small and also rather large firms are opened in Munich. Looking back at the results for the total start-up capital, we can assume that higher values of start-up capital go together with lower shares of personal capital in East Germany. A further difference between Leipzig and Munich exists also with respect to the share of personal capital. In Leipzig only 48 per cent of new firms were founded with 100 per cent personal capital, whereas 7 out of 10 new Munich firms started businesses without raising outside capital (Table 16.4a).

Figure 16.2 Personal capital of newly founded firms

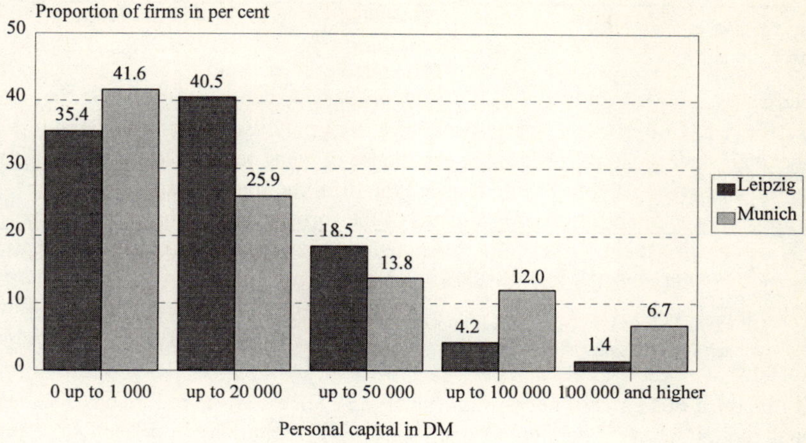

Notes: Leipzig: N=512, mean 19 600 DM, median 8 000 DM.
Munich: N=1 411, mean 38 700, median 3 300 DM.

Sources: Leipzig founder study interviews iummer 1992; Munich founder study.
Weighted data; Munich personal capital in addition weighted by inflation index.

*Table 16.4a Share of personal capital (per cent)**

	Leipzig	Munich
0 per cent-25 per cent proportion of personal capital	34.3	12.8
26 per cent-50 per cent proportion of personal capital	14.3	12.9
51 per cent-75 per cent proportion of personal capital	2.8	4.0
76 per cent-100 per cent proportion of personal capital	48.6	70.3
Total	100	100
No personal capital	13.5	9.6
100 per cent personal capital	48.0	69.6
Average proportion of personal capital	58.7	78.9
	(N=412)	(N=953)

Note: * New firms, if start-up capital existing.

*Table 16.4b Sources of outside capital (per cent)**

Parents, spouse, relatives	8.6	13.4
Friends	4.5	9.9
Bank credit	73.7	76.5
Supplier's credit	5.8	5.0
Funding program	36.6	13.3
	(N=266)	(N=442)

Notes: * New firms, if outside capital existing.

Sources: Leipzig founder study interviews summer 1992, weighted data.
Munich founder study, weighted data.

About one third of Leipzig's new firms with at least some start-up capital has a share of personal capital below 25 per cent (Table 16.4a). The region of comparison's personal capital reaches a share of 13 per cent. There is obviously a correlation between the amount of start-up capital and the share of personal capital: the higher the total start-up capital, i.e. the greater the size at the time of foundation, the lower the share of personal capital. The detected difference concerning the proportions of personal capital between Leipzig and Munich does not change if organizational patterns and the personal characteristics of the founder were controlled. In the pooled model new firms in East Germany are estimated to have a share of personal capital,[19] 16 per cent lower than in West Germany.

Looking at business partners leads to another interesting result: we have already demonstrated that the existence of a business partner does not influence the amount of start-up capital of East German new businesses, but in respect to the share of personal capital, there is a significant positive effect. The share of personal capital on total start-up capital increases by 11 per cent if there is a business partner. In West Germany the existence of a business partner is related to decreases of the share of personal capital by five percent; simultaneously, there is a positive influence of business partners on the total amount of start-up capital. East German business partners increase the amount of personal capital, in West Germany the start-up capital is increased as a whole, however, using higher shares of outside capital.

With Table 16.4b one can easily identify the sources of outside capital. The largest share of founders (74 per cent) receive credit from a bank, and 37 per cent raise capital through an official funding program. This value is considerably higher than the value of 13 per cent in Munich. If one looks at the proportion of the funded foundations one has to state that 16 per cent of the foundations in East Germany are supported by funding programs, while in West Germany only 3 per cent of the foundations are subsidized. A

19 OLS model as used for model 7 with share of personal capital as dependent variable.

multivariate analysis[20] shows that the probability of receiving capital from a funding program is significantly higher for foundations in East Germany. This could imply that supporting programs are actively engaged in building up an economy with small business organizations. Other ways of earning credit play merely subordinate roles. The founders' place of birth is found to have no relevance regarding credit approval. It is remarkable that in East Germany social networks such as family and friends are less important for raising financial capital than they are in the West.

We can conclude that:

(1) East German firms are founded with a higher start-up capital in general;
(2) West German founders going East raise an evidently larger sum of financial capital;
(3) the share of personal capital is lower in the East; and
(4) East German outside capital is raised by a distinctly higher degree through funding programs.

5. Summary

The main aim of this article was to give an overview of the new firm formation process in East Germany - always focusing on a comparable West German region. We began with a description of East German starting conditions in general and stated that the distribution of property levelled-out under the communist regime is unfavorable.

The minimum stability of firms is the most crucial element for a successful transformation. We found that about 20 percent of the registered firms were cancelled from the register one year after their entry, and 90 per cent of the firms still registered have started their business activities - or are planning to do so in the near future. In contrast to West Germany we observed a remarkable share of 'new' firms which are actually not new, for example the split-offs - mostly of very small units - which are different from originally new foundations. The new companies are mainly firms in services and trades. One third of the newcomers are closely connected to other firms or enterprises or act as subsidiary firms - most of all for West German companies. The share of first-job-foundations is significantly higher than in the West German region.

It is a striking fact that the financial capital invested, when correlated with for important variables measuring characteristics of the organization, is higher for East German foundations. We also saw a strong influence of organizational patterns such as 'branch of industry', 'legal form' and 'degree of independence' on the amount of start-up capital. Taking the personal characteristics of the founders into account one has to mention two relevant points. First, persons with an unfavourable position in the labor market tend to found smaller firms, but the effects are less distinct than in West Germany. Second, women do not open up business organizations with a smaller sum of start-up capital.

20 Logistic regression with set of variables of model 7 and outside capital from funding program as dependent variable.

Concluding, we may state that the share of personal capital in East Germany is lower than in West Germany. Most importantly the value of outside capital raised through funding programs is accordingly higher. The weakness of personal capital may cause serious problems for the ability of the new firms to survive - especially in an environment of permanent economic depression.

Appendix

Table 16.A1 Means of variables used in regression

	Leipzig	Munich
Start-up capital (logarithm)	8.22	8.23
Manufacturing and construction	0.05	0.14
Trade	0.44	0.35
Services	0.51	0.51
Full time business	0.71	0.64
Complete independence	0.73	0.90
Capital company	0.10	0.29
Partner in business	0.20	0.28
Sex (1=female)	0.31	0.25
Age	39.45	35.02
Schooling POS/MR (10 years)	0.56	0.28
Schooling EOS/Abitur (12/13 years)	0.25	0.40
Skilled worker	0.75	0.48
Master/engineer	0.13	0.13
University	0.18	0.17
Out of the labor market before founding	0.07	0.20
Unemployed before founding	0.34	0.05
Self-employment experience	0.16	0.30
Place of residence 1989 (1=GDR)	0.88	
	N=1 107	N=1 393
	(not weighted)	(not weighted)

Sources: Leipzig founder study questionnaire spring 1992.
Munich founder study.

References

Bannasch, H.-G. (1990); The Role of Small Firms in East Germany; *Small Business Economics*, 2, 307-11.

Bird, E.J., J. Schwarze and G. Wagner (1992) *The Changing Value of Human Capital in Eastern Europe: Lessons from the GDR*, DIW Discussion Paper 55, Berlin (mimeo).

Bögenhold, D. (1987) *Der Gründerboom - Mythos und Realität der neuen Selbständigkeit*, Frankfurt a.M.

Brüderl, J. and R. Schüssler (1990); Organizational Mortality: The Liabilities of Newness and Adolescence; *Administrative Science Quarterly*, 35, 530-47.

Brüderl, J., P. Preisendörfer and R. Ziegler (1992); Survival Chances of Newly Founded Business Organizations; *American Sociologal Review*, 57, 227-42.

Büchel, F. and M. Pannenberg (1992); 'Neue Selbständige' in Ostdeutschland - Statusentscheidung, Realisierungschancen und materielle Zufriedenheit; *Mitteilungen aus der Arbeitsmarkt- und Berufsforschung*, 4, 544-52.

Büchtemann, C.and J. Schupp (1992) *Repercussions of Reunification: Pattern and Trends in the Socio-Economic Transformation of East Germany*, DIW Discussion Paper 44, Berlin (mimeo).

Cornelsen, D. (1989) Die Volkswirtschaft der DDR: Wirtschaftssystem - Entwicklung - Probleme, in Weidenfeld, W. (Hrsg.) *Deutschland-Handbuch. Eine doppelte Bilanz 1949-89*, Bonn.

Friedrich, W. (1990) *Führungskräfte und Gründungspotentiale in der ehemaligen DDR*, WSF-Studien zur Wirtschaftsforschung, Kerpen (mimeo).

Geißler, R. (1992) *Die Sozialstruktur Deutschlands - ein Studienbuch zur Entwicklung im geteilten und vereinten Deutschland*, Opladen.

Gemeinsames Statistisches Amt (1991) *Monatszahlen 12*, 91, Berlin (mimeo).

Heidenreich, M. (Hrsg.) (1992) *Krisen, Kader, Kombinate. Kontinuität und Wandel in ostdeutschen Betrieben*, Berlin.

Jungbauer-Gans, M. (1992) *Frauen als Unternehmerinnen*, Frankfurt a. M.

Knuth, M. (1992) *Arbeitsmarktpolitische Potentiale und Perspektiven von Gesellschaften zur Arbeitsförderung, Beschäftigung und Strukturentwicklung*, Bonn: Bundesministerium für Arbeit und Sozialordnung.

Koch, Th. and R. Woderich (1992) *Freier Flug oder Fall in die Marktwirtschaft? Existenzgründer in Ostdeutschland*, BISS-Forschungsheft 1, Berlin (mimeo).

Lehmbruch, G. (1993); Der Staat des vereinigten Deutschland und die Transformationsdynamik; *BISS Public*, 10, 21-41.

Liebernickel, W. and A. Schwarz (1992) Neue Gründerzeiten? Die beginnende Konstituierung neuer Selbständiger in Ostdeutschland, in Thomas, M. (Hrsg.) *Abbruch und Aufbruch. Sozialwissenschaften im Transformationsprozeß*, Berlin, 275-91.

Lindenberg, S. (1992); An Extended Theory of Institutions and Contractual Discipline; *Journal of Institutional and Theoretical Economics (JITE)*, 148, 125-54.

May-Strobl, E. and M. Paulini (1990) *Unternehmensgründungen in den neuen Bundesländern*, Bonn: ifm-Materialien Nr. 77.

May-Strobl, E. and M. Paulini (1991) *Laufende Berichterstattung über das Gründungsgeschehen in den neuen Bundesländern*, Bonn: ifm-Materialien Nr. 83.

May-Strobl, E., L. Kokalj and A. Schmidt (1992) *Aktuelle und periodische Berichterstattung zur Entwicklung der mittelständischen Wirtschaft in den neuen Bundesländern*, Bonn: ifm-Materialien Nr. 87.

Preisendörfer, P. and R. Ziegler (1991); Adressenaktualisierung und Feldverlauf einer Studie über Gründung und Erfolg von Kleinbetrieben; *ZUMA-Nachrichten*, 27, 93-108.

Scheytt, O. (1992) Reorganisation der kommunalen Selbstverwaltung, in Rühl, C. (Hrsg.) *Institutionelle Reorganisation in den neuen Ländern*, Marburg, S. 23-43.

Schrumpf, H. (1990); Selbständige in der DDR - ein Potential zur Lösung der aktuellen wirtschaftlichen Probleme?; *Mitteilungen des Rheinisch-Westfälischen Instituts für Wirtschaftsforschung*, 41, 105-16.

Sinn, G. and H.W. Sinn (1991) *Kaltstart - Volkswirtschaftliche Aspekte der deutschen Vereinigung*, Tübingen.

17 The bottom-up strategy to transformation: summary and policy conclusions

Horst Brezinski and *Michael Fritsch*

1. Introduction

Although the studies on the state of the transformation process in the post-socialist countries of Eastern Europe in the previous chapters showed considerable heterogeneity, there are also a lot of similarities and corresponding developments. In this last chapter we will summarize the main results and draw helpful conclusions for policies. We will first give a short overview on some important aspects of the development of the small-firm sector in the post-socialist countries since 1989 (Section 2). Section 3 deals with the legacies of these countries with regard to bottom-up transformation and Section 4 then describes the main prerequisites for a flourishing small and new firm sector. Finally we will give an outline of several guidelines for a policy aiming at stimulating the process of bottom-up transformation (Section 5).

2. The development of the small-firm sector in post-socialist countries since 1989[1]

It is very difficult to determine, how many new private firms have been founded or what share of employment or of GDP is due to private-sector activities in the post-socialist countries. Reasons for this are deficiencies in the statistical recording and reporting systems, problems in identifying new firms (EBRD, 1994) and ambiguities in the classification of activities as 'public' or 'private'. A special issue is the high share of black-market activity for which only rough estimates are available. It is, however, clear that the degree of privatization of the economy differs among the former socialist countries and that the share of the private sector as well as the number of private firms is increasing in all these countries. For example, in Poland the number of private firms rose by more than 219 per cent between 1989 and 1993 (Brunner, 1995), in Hungary the number of private firms by more than 200 per cent between 1989-93. Obviously, the vast majority of these firms represent only self-employment and they created jobs only for the owner and possibly for members of the family. But the number of private firms that are organized in a corporate form rose at tremendous rates in some countries (434 per cent in Poland between 1989 and 1993, 1 450 per cent in Hungary in 1988-93) and started to make a significant impact on employment.

1 All figures in this section were taken from the data collection of Werner (1994).

Looking at the private sector's share of GDP and employment we find Poland, the Czech Republic and Hungary at the upper end of the scale with more than 55 per cent of GDP and employment; at the other end of the scale there are the Southern republics of the former Soviet Union with only about 15 to 20 per cent of GDP (Belarus, Tajikistan, Turkmenistan, Uzbekistan, Georgia and Kazakhstan) produced privately and a private-sector employment share of less than 20 per cent in 1993 (EBRD, 1994). An analysis by sector reveals the highest share of private activity in retail trade, in services and in construction. In some of the post-socialist countries also the agricultural sector is privately operated to a high degree. This is mainly due to previous patterns, e.g. in Poland or to (wild) restitution, e.g. in Romania. Manufacturing and transportation have relatively low private activity shares. Thus, newly established enterprises do not play a decisive role in industry. This may be explained, among other things, by the relatively high need for capital that is characteristic of start-ups in manufacturing, a capital which is not provided by the financial system.

In view of the immense problems of top-down privatization in which the share of the private-sector activity can be taken as an indicator of the intensity, a bottom-up strategy has been pursued in these countries. This becomes obvious when observing that by mid 1994 large-scale privatization has been undertaken in a satisfactory manner only in the Czech Republic (Ners, 1995). Over 50 per cent of state-owned enterprise assets have been privatized by a scheme that allows for external control and reflects support for corporate finance. Enterprise restructuring which substantially improves the corporate governance, may implement strong financial discipline at the enterprise level and is considered to break up large conglomerates, has not taken place in any of the economies in transition (EBRD 1994). However, small-scale privatization has been more or less implemented in countries such as Croatia, the Czech Republic, Estonia, FYR Macedonia, Hungary, Kyrgyzstan, Lithuania, Poland, the Slovak Republic and Slovenia. In these countries the growth of private enterprise during the end of 1992 and mid 1994 has considerably increased. To a large extent this is due to the removal of legal barriers to entry and requirements restrictive to production. However, the official data often tend to overestimate the number of newly-created enterprises; e.g. in Estonia about 30-50 per cent of start-ups are apparently not in operation (Haav, 1995; Ners, 1995; Houbenova-Delissivkova and Puchev, 1995).

It may be expected that the post-socialist countries which are ahead in small-scale privatization will be better prepared for the systemic structural changes which will still have to take place when integrating in the world economy. In these countries comprehensive price liberalization and competition have been introduced. Yet, experience shows that in many cases privatization leads to a severe reduction in employment. As a result, start-ups are urgently needed to compensate for the job losses in the former socialist sector. At least in that respect they can make a significant contribution to the reduction of social tensions caused by unemployment; they may help to create political stability. Although the transformation of the East German economy is a very special case, it is interesting to note that only a few years after this process started, the vast majority of private-sector jobs in East Germany is provided by newly founded businesses. The jobs that are due to top-down privatization constitute only a small share and their number is constantly decreasing (Fritsch and Werker, 1994; May-Strobl and Paulini, 1994).

In general, bottom-up transformation may be considered a way of transition that is likely to be *relatively* successful. However, much can still done to improve the economic performance in those countries that practise such a strategy by making better use of the potential for an increase in welfare.

3. Legacies of post-socialist economies for bottom-up transformation

Bottom-up transformation assigns a key role to private entrepreneurs in the process of transformation and economic recovery. However, for a number of reasons, the small firm sector and entrepreneurship in all socialist countries of Eastern Europe was underdeveloped. This legacy leads to highly problematic starting conditions for a quick development of a dynamic small- firm sector.

At first there were ideological reasons which demanded the reduction or even the abolishing of the private sector (Andreff, 1993). Private initiative was regarded as a bourgeois and contradictory element in a socialist planned economy. Private enterprises were seen as possibly contributing to the revival of 'reactionary' ideas and as opposed to the socialist value system. Moreover, an autonomous private sector constituted a contradiction to an economic system which aimed at the implementation of total central planning and, consequently, had to be suppressed. The state favored the creation of large-unit enterprises with a high degree of vertical integration which seemed to promise economies of scale and which could be more easily commanded and controlled.

Towards the end of the 1960s and during the 1970s there was a revival of the private sector in most East European countries. This development, however, could not be a true base to start from for a market economy based on private property (Brezinski, 1992). These private entrepreneurs enjoyed more or less a monopoly situation. The administration rigorously controlled the number of companies that entered a market, characterized by severe shortages. Moreover, in order to improve the supply for the consumers official access to markets was only granted in specific fields, e.g. services and small trade. In view of the scarcity of goods and services the government fixed prices. In practice this constituted minimum prices. As a result entrepreneurs did not reflect those characteristics Schumpeter attributed to them, namely the desire to be innovative and to take risks. The most important task for private entrepreneurs was obtaining inputs; marketing was not necessary. The insecurity about the future economic policy of the socialist governments towards the private sector and the possibility of private property rights possibly being weakened, caused private entrepreneurs not to be much interested in investing. Moreover, the lack of competition was no motivation to be innovative. Institutionally the private sector was more or less integrated into the state sector, albeit in a subordinate position. In the allocation of supplies, commercial space and market shares, state enterprises were given preference (Pickel, 1992). These conditions; the restrictions to invest in private business and the lacking of incentives and opportunities to accumulate private capital left the previously private sector in post-socialist countries undercapitalized to a high degree and ill equipped to cope with the transition to a market.

Our analysis of the situation of the private sector as it prevously existed applies also to the underground economy in the former Communist Bloc countries. This black economy was centered mainly in those fields where shortages due to the failure of the planning system prevailed or where the fixed price system allowed for gains from arbitrage. The underground entrepreneurs who mainly engaged in speculative operations and constantly risked being detected, were interested only in big short-term profits with no inclination to invest these profits (Andreff, 1993; Arzeni, 1995). To a high degree this was an 'unproductive' form of entrepreneurship (Baumol, 1990). Consequently, the legal and also the illegal private sector of the economy can hardly be seen as an adequate basis for a take-off towards a market economy. On the contrary, those entrepreneurs working in the underground economy may be considered to be obstacles to transition (Arzeni, 1995).

In addition, the old planning system did not contribute to the creation of entrepreneurial skills and ethics. The system of fixed prices together with planned output and allocation of resources did not provide incentives for socialist managers to make efficient use of resources or to be innovative. The bonuses for the fulfillment or the overachievement of the planned targets were small. Since a better performance than planned led to higher targets in the next plan there was a clear disincentive to overachievement. The planning authorities discouraged or even impeded unplanned innovation and any other form of flexibility aiming at increasing efficiency.

The specific foreign economic policies of the socialist countries were highly protectionist. The system of foreign trade monopoly of the state and the inconvertibility of the national currencies isolated the national economies from international competition. Consequently, the change of world-market prices had no impact on entrepreneurial decisions. Therefore, the liberalization of foreign trade from 1989 on resulted in a shock for the previously private enterprises which were not used to engage in competition.

4. Prerequisites for the establishment of an efficiently performing sector of small and new firms

There are a number of prerequisites that have to be fulfilled if private entrepreneurial initiative is to lead to a prospering economy that generates the jobs needed.

The first of these prerequisites is that private production and entrepreneurship is legal and that - if there is price regulation by the government - this regulation allows for some profit. In addition, private enterprises must have access to inputs and be allowed to market their outputs. As to the availability of inputs there are three methods to organize the allocation of inputs for private firms. In the worst case these resources are supplied by the state itself or by a state monopoly. Another possibility would be a government-controlled market, i.e. the state authorities strongly influence the amount of supply or prices. The third and most promising method is a free competitive market in which the government only sets some general rules and leaves the process of exchange to the individuals. All three methods to solve the problem of supplying resources presupposes a certain degree of acceptance of basic property rights necessary for enforceable contracts (Charup and Webster, 1993).

In the post-socialist countries of Eastern Europe one can find a whole variety of methods of resource allocation to the private sector. In nearly all these countries black markets and irregular activities play and have played a considerable role. This applies to inputs and outputs. To some extent this is the extension of the former practice of a society of shortage. Today, this phenomenon is aggravated by the attempt to evade taxes and the knowledge that the risk of detection and of punishment is relatively small. In addition, the dramatic fall of demand has left many resources unemployed and willing - in particular in the case of unemployed workers - to find employment at lower wages than are paid in the regular economy (Ners, 1995). Rapid institutional changes cause regulations to be virtually nonexistent or not to be successfully implemented (Bartlett and Hoggett, 1995; Haav, 1995; Houbenova-Delissivkova and Puchev, 1995; Chepurenko and Vilensky, 1995). Often there is collusion between the local authorities, criminal organizations and the managers of former state-owned enterprises. This general framework has served as a catalyzer for the rise of black market activities in most East European countries (Arzeni, 1995; Brezinski, 1995).

This development has several consequences:

(1) A relatively high share of private sector entrepreneurship is either illegal or is at least legally questionable.
(2) Due to the high risk connected with illegal activities transaction costs are high since property rights cannot be enforced.
(3) A growing underground economy impairs the influx of the much needed foreign capital, because Western investors lack the knowledge, the information and the access to a social network to operate successfully 'in a business climate lacking the basics of a modern economy: business ethics, codes of conduct, and reputation' (Charup and Webster, 1993).

Moreover, corruption and illegal practices are regarded to be rampant and costly. All this impedes a quick transition and reduces the chances for enterprises to be set up as suppliers of large foreign firms or to get access to foreign capital.

A market which is to ensure a viable allocation of resources requires prices which express the degree of scarcity. Scarcity prices and hard budget constraints on the part of the enterprises as well as in the public sector will stimulate a reallocation of resources which are no longer needed. Unless this reallocation takes place, the market supply will be too limited and resource prices systematically will be too high. Under normal conditions one would expect that the opportunity to obtain a return for a resource that is no longer useful for an actor generates an incentive sufficient to sell this resource. Thus, even at an initial market price that is too high, this positive price would induce further supply until the appropriate price is attained. Experience in the post-socialist countries, however, shows that this a very gross assumption which ignores the low level of market transparency and the inelasticities in production. A major reason is that managers of state-owned firms frequently still have a limited incentive to act efficiently because they do not perceive their position or income as depending on profits. Moreover, often horizontal links between entrepreneurs are virtually non-existent, as is shown in the empirical analysis of private manufacturing in St. Petersburg by Charup and Webster (1993).

In addition, what is needed is favorable taxation to create incentives, a functioning banking system which provides for the necessary capital at reasonable interest rates (Meth-Cohn et al., 1994), less government regulation, and transparency of the markets. It may be concluded that in many post-socialist markets adjustment mechanisms are heavily distorted and that it is difficult for investors to obtain credits to finance the investment which is needed.

Other prerequisites of a successful bottom-up transformation are macroeconomic conditions: some stability, especially a stable currency, is desirable for a functioning market mechanism. If inflation is high or highly unpredictable, actors will hesitate to sell resources and will try to save some 'real' value from inflation. Moreover, a frequently discussed issue is how far trade liberalization is desirable at the early stages of the transformation process. The advantages seem to be clear: free or liberalized trade leads to an enlargement of the market on the supply side as well as on the demand side, it stimulates the international division of labor and links national prices to world market prices. This requires a convertible currency and a low degree of protectionism. However, these advantages do not materialize in the reality of post-socialist countries. Given the inelasticity of domestic supply and the gap in technology and know-how, domestic suppliers may not be able to quickly adapt to market conditions. Therefore, cascading tariffs for certain goods may be an appropriate means to protect, for a limited time, the domestic industry and, in particular, the newly emerging enterprises.

Last but not least, a successful bottom-up transformation necessitates the existence of a sufficient number of persons with entrepreneurial abilities and a sociopsychological climate favorable to private initiatives (Arzeni, 1995; Reynolds, 1995). Both factors are not predominant in either former socialist countries or in Western market economies. Creating a culture of entrepreneurial spirit seems to be one of the secrets of our time. Even if we assume that certain qualities that contribute to entrepreneurial success are innate or culturally determined - e.g. a propensity to risk-taking - there is still room for political action (Tyson, Petrin and Rogers, 1994). Some ingredients of entrepreneurship, e.g. management skills, can be learned or improved. The effectiveness of entrepreneurial talent depends in part on the availability of inputs and the implementation of the appropriate legal framework for a market economy. Historical experience shows that some nations or regions have been very successful in fostering entrepreneurial innovation through supportive policies, e.g. Japan and the Republic of Korea. But the same experience also shows that the emergence of an entrepreneurial culture normally takes generations.

5. Conclusions and implications

The discussion allows for a number of conclusions and recommendations for economic policy. It has become obvious that the development of entrepreneurship and a small-firm sector represent dominant components in the transformation process of post-socialist countries. In most of these countries it is the only potential source of economic recovery that can realistically be hoped for. Economic policy should therefore:

- Legalize entrepreneurial activity. As has been argued above, black market activity is not only costly in terms of transaction costs; it also leads to a high proportion of 'unproductive' entrepreneurship (Baumol, 1990). Converting illegal activities into legal ones means creating a stable market. One can expect that this, in turn, will have at least two effects: (1) exchange of goods and services being cheaper because of lower transaction costs, more transactions will take place which induce an increase in the division of labor; (2) many forms of illegal and unproductive entrepreneurship will no longer be profitable, thus decreasing such activities.
- *Implement market conditions conducive to productive exchanges.* The form of the market constitution, i.e. the 'rules of the game' is, to a large extent, decisive for market behavior and performance. We do not know exactly which constitution might be optimal for a specific market since it probably varies from country to country and may rely also on cultural factors. Therefore, the creation of an optimal market constitution may be regarded as an evolutionary process. Yet, still some fundamental guidelines for a market constitution being conducive to productive exchanges are evident:

    - The market constitution must provide incentives for private actors to start new businesses.
    - Market prices should primarily be determined by market forces and not by government authorities.
    - Markets should be open, market positions contestable. There is a need for anti-trust legislation as well as for measures to safeguard fair competition.

- *Generate an efficient financial system.* Since entrepreneurs were not able to accumulate capital in the past, they need access to monetary resources. Therefore an efficiently performing banking system on the national as well as on the local level is needed. In addition, since entrepreneurs do not have collateral, they need institutional guarantees from institutions such as enterprise development funds (Gulásci, 1993, Schlotter, 1994) or international institutions. Moreover, quite often the capital is provided for by family members and friends; i.e. it originates from an informal circuit of capital and fiscal incentives are needed; because the chances of losing the invested money is about 50 per cent (Meth-Cohn et al., 1994),
- *Stabilize the legal, political, and social framework.* A predictable legal, political, and social environment will reduce uncertainty and transaction costs for the actors. In particular, stability will allow for the emergence of more long-term market

relations and 'hybrid' forms of inter-firm cooperation which lead to an increasing division of labor (Brezinski and Fritsch, 1996). This, in turn, can be seen as a precondition for the emergence of a strong entrepreneurial culture.

- *Promote entrepreneurial qualifications and try to increase the number of successful entrepreneurs.* As mentioned above, our knowledge of the number of private firms in post-socialist countries as well as of their quality is limited. But, we do know that many of the entrepreneurs do not have the skills needed for successful entrepreneurship. It is also obvious that a large number of qualified entrepreneurs is necessary to overcome the problems of unemployment caused by the breakdown of the large units of production that once dominated the economic system. Given the widespread lack of understanding of the working of markets, and the non-acceptance of market results still often to be found in the East European countries, it remains unclear, however, where these large numbers of qualified entrepreneurs are to come from. The private firms that existed in the socialist system under central planning cannot be expected to be a nucleus for entrepreneurship and the question which groups of the post-socialist societies might be suited for setting up growing firms is still open.

  Economic policy should stimulate entrepreneurship, provide training of necessary skills, develop an infrastructure to support entrepreneurship, and try to create an entrepreneurial culture. This includes the formation of entrepreneurial self-organizations such as chambers of commerce, workers' unions and employers' associations (Gulásci, 1993).
- *Stabilize macroeconomic conditions.* This, in particular, means that a stable currency is needed and that government economic policy becomes predictable for actors. Otherwise, markets will not function optimally and - what might be even more important - actors will hesitate to (re)invest and take their profits abroad.
- *Integrate the national economy into the World market.* The countries in transition suffer from a wrong division of labor which was imposed upon them in the past and which was conserved by a strict protectionism. Integration can only be achieved by granting market access. This requires access to Western markets, especially to those markets which are heavily regulated, such as agriculture, steel and textiles because the East European countries have comparative advantages exactly in these fields in the short run. The opening of their markets to foreign products should not be achieved by immediately abolishing the tariffs completely, because the vast majority of domestic producers are not internationally competitive. Thus, cascading tariffs are needed. Moreover, the national currencies should be freely convertible in order to generate a capital influx from the West and in order to avoid a capital flight on a massive scale. Exchange rate policy has to be designed in a way that the national currency is undervalued in order to increase exports and to reduce imports of consumer goods.

Considering the problems of top-down transformation, the bottom-up strategy appears to be a promising chance for the post-socialist countries to a market system that should not be missed. Given the limited amount of Western aid available this may even be the only way to prosperity. But this way is long and East European countries are only poorly equipped in terms of new firms and entrepreneurship for a speedy recovery. As has been shown, much can and should be done to speed up the development by supporting the newly founded private firms and by stimulating productive entrepreneurship. Our analysis makes clear that bottom-up transformation cannot be a strategy that yields satisfactory results unless it is profoundly and intensely supported by government policy. So far bottom-up transformation has been observable nearly exclusively in the services and trades. For the future, however, this type of economic transformation will be necessary and practicable in the industrial sector, since reorganizing this sector will virtually mean restructuring the economy.

References

Andreff, W. (1993) *La crise des économies socialistes*, Grenoble: Presses Universitaires de Grenoble.

Arzeni, S. (1995) Entrepreneurship in Eastern Europe: a critical view, in this volume.

Bartlett, W. and P. Hoggett (1995) Small firm policy in South East Europe: the importance of initial conditions, in this volume.

Baumol, W.J. (1990); Entrepreneurship: Productive, Unproductive, and Destructive; *Journal of Political Economy*, 98, 893-921.

Brezinski, H. (1992); Privatisation in East Germany; *Moct-Most*, No.1, 3-21.

Brezinski, H. (1995) Schattenwirtschaft in Osteuropa, in Nohlen, D. (ed.), *Wörterbuch Staat und Politik*, München, Zürich: Piper, 665-670.

Brezinski, H. and M. Fritsch (1996) Spot-Markets, Hierarchies, Networks, and the Problem of Economic Transition, in Brezinski, H. and M. Fritsch (eds.), *The Emergence and Evolution of Markets*, Aldershot: Edward Elgar Publishers (forthcoming).

Brunner, H.-P. (1995) The entrepreneurial sector and its role in industrial transformation in Eastern Germany and Poland, in this volume.

Charup, J. and L. Webster (1993); Constraints on the Development of Private Manufacturing in St. Petersburg; *Economics of Transition,* 1, 299-316.

Chepurenko, A. and A.V. Vilensky (1995) New firms in Bulgaria: the impact of structural and institutional changes, in this volume.

European Bank for Reconstruction and Development (EBRD) (1994) *Transition Report,* London.

Fritsch, M. and C. Werker (1994); The Transformation of East German's Corporate Structure; *East Germany*, 13, 3-7.

Gulásci, G. (1993) The Place of Small Enterprise Development in Contemporary Economic Policy, in Public Policy Institute Foundation (ed.), *Private Sector Development and Local Government in Hungary*, Budapest, 105-17.

Haav, K. (1995) Big problems of small businesses in Estonia, in this volume.

Houbenova-Delissivkova, T. and P. Puchev (1995) New firms in Bulgaria: the impact of structural and institutional changes, in this volume.

May-Strobl, E. and M. Paulini (1994) *Die Entwicklung junger Unternehmen in den neuen Bundesländern,* Stuttgart: Schäffer-Poeschel.

Meth-Cohn, D., K. Kasriel, B. Papp and M. Valencia (1994); Entrepreneurs Bloom; *Business Central Europe,* October 1994, 7-11.

Ners, D. (1995) Privatization from above versus privatization from below or mass privatization versus generic private enterprise building, in this volume.

Pickel, A. (1992) *Radical Transitions - The Survival and Revival of Entrepreneurship in the GDR*, Boulder: Westview.

Reynolds, P.D. (1995) The role of entrepreneurship in economic systems: developed market and post-socialist economies, in this volume.

Schlotter, H.G. (1994) Unternehmenspolitik im Übergang zur Marktwirtschaft, in Hermann-Pillath, C., O. Schlecht and H.F. Wünsche (eds.), *Marktwirtschaft als Aufgabe*, 501-17.

Tyson, A. L., T. Petrin and H. Rogers (1994); Promoting Entrepreneurship in Eastern Europe; *Small Business Economics*, 6, 165-85.

Werner, K. (1994); Zur Entwicklung kleiner und mittlerer Unternehmen in Mittel- und Osteuropa - Ein Überblick; Institut für Wirtschaftsforschung Halle (ed.), *Mittel- und Osteuropa*, 3, 7-21.

Author Index

Acs, Z.J. 2, 5, 12, 32, 131, 148, 151, 164, 166, 170, 184, 187, 189, 214
Agency for Economic Co-ordination and Development (AECD) 118, 122, 130, 134, 148, 165, 170
Akerlof, G. 192, 213, 214
Albach, H. 101, 104, 214
Allsopp, Ch. 200, 201, 214
Anachkova, B. 134, 148
Andreff, W. 255, 256, 261
Angelov, I. 119, 130
Antosenkov, E. 74, 91
Ardishvili, A. 75, 91
Arkadie, B. 94, 104
Armit, R. 72, 91
Arzeni, S. 4, 52, 256, 257, 258, 261
Atkinson, I. 153, 172
Audretsch, D.B. 2, 5, 12, 15, 16, 32, 131, 148, 151, 170, 184, 187, 189, 214

Baldwin, J.R. 195, 214
Banfield, E.C. 221, 226
Bannasch, H.G. 235, 251
Barreto, H. 7, 32
Bartlett, W. 4, 133, 134, 149, 151, 154, 161, 170, 171, 257, 261
Batstone, S. 4, 72, 83, 93
Baumol, W.J. 7, 31, 32, 54, 58, 74, 91, 256, 259, 261
Belka, M. 181, 186 188
Ben-Ner, A. 24, 32
Berliner, J. 36, 46, 47
Best, M. 73, 74, 83, 84, 87, 88, 90, 91
Birch, D. 1, 5, 10, 32
Bird, E.J. 235, 251
Blanchard, O.J. 94, 104, 177, 187
Bögenhold, D. 227, 232, 246, 251
Bogetic, Z. 133, 149
Borensztein, E. 178, 187
Borgomeo, C. 57
Brezinski, H. 1, 5, 253, 255, 257, 260, 261
Brom, K. 180, 182, 183, 187
Broom, G. 19, 33
Brüderl, J. 24, 32, 240, 251
Brunner, H.P. 5, 189, 191, 194, 195, 214, 253, 261
Brzezinski, Z. 101, 104
Büchel, F. 243, 251
Büchtemann, C. 234, 251
Bullock, M. 85, 86, 91

Cardozo, R. 75, 91
Carroll, G.R. 24, 32, 33
CENSIS 58
Central Statistic Office, Warsaw 190, 201, 203, 205, 207, 208
Charup, J. 143, 144, 149, 257, 258, 261
Chavance, B. 152, 171
Chepurenko, A. 4, 59, 257, 261
Cieszynski, B. 90
Clague, Chr. 94, 104, 131, 149, 151, 171
Cooper, J. 82, 91
Costariol, M. 114
Curran, J. 154, 155, 171
Curtin, R. 7, 10, 20, 32

Daianu, D. 109, 114
Daniel, D. 107, 114
Davidsson, P. 10, 15, 32
Debackere, K. 92
Dellenbrant, J.A. 94, 104
Demekas, D. 108, 115
van Dierdonck, R. 75, 92
Dimitrov, A. 130
Dornbusch, R. 104
Dosi, G. 189, 191, 194, 213, 215
Dulev, S. 130

Dumitriu, I. 109, 115
Dutch Research Institute for Small and Medium-sized Business 125, 127, 128, 130
Dyker, D. 95, 104

Earle, J. 113, 115
Economic Commission for Europe 74, 91
Eero, E. 103, 104
Ehrlich, R. 99, 105
EIM 72, 91
Eisinger, P. 74, 84, 92
Estam, J. 94
Estonia National Customs Board and Bank of Estonia 96, 97
Estrin, S. 145, 149
European Bank for Reconstruction and Development (EBRD) 5, 52, 58, 92, 161, 162, 171, 253, 254, 261
European Network for SME Research (ENSR) 33
Expert Institute RSPP 61, 70

Finchman, M. 24, 33
Foray, D. 191, 215
Freeman, Ch. 191, 213, 215
Freeman, J. 24, 26, 33, 34
Friedrich, W. 236, 238, 252
Fritsch, M. 1, 2, 5, 15, 16, 32, 253, 255, 260, 261
Frydman, R. 113, 115, 175, 182, 183, 187

Garofoli, G. 15, 33
Geißler, R. 235, 251
German Institute for Economic Research (DIW) 195, 215
Gibb, A. 75, 86, 92
Gibb, Y. 75, 86, 92
Gleick, I. 153, 171
Gorecki, P.K. 195, 214
Goskomstat 62, 70
Government of Romania 108, 115
Grabher, G. 210, 215
Grabowski, M. 184, 185, 188
Granovetter, M.S. 12, 33, 227, 232
Grayson, L. 75, 92
Greif, A. 36, 47
Grosfeld, I. 175, 187
Grünert, H. 214
Gudgin, G. 15, 33
Guesnier, B. 15, 33
Gulásci, G. 259, 260, 261
Gulubov, N. 130

Haav, K. 4, 94, 101, 104, 105, 254, 257, 261
Hall, J.B. 189, 215
Hannan, M.T. 24, 33
Hansen, J. 94, 95, 96, 102, 105
Hare, P. 175, 179, 187, 208, 209, 215
Harhoff, D. 193, 195, 215
Hart, M. 15, 33
Hauer, A. 3, 5
Haus, M. 210, 215
Heidenreich, M. 236, 251
Heston, A. 194, 215
Hinz, T. 5, 233
Hoggett, P. 4, 151, 157, 159, 171, 257, 261
Holesovsky, V. 177, 187
Houbenova-Delissikova, T. 4, 116, 124, 130, 254, 257, 261
Hubáček, O. 220, 226
Hübner, K. 193, 215
Hughes, G. 179, 187, 208, 209, 215
Hunya, G. 4, 107, 108, 112, 113, 115

Ickes, B. 183, 187
Institute for Philosophy and Sociology of Czechoslovakian Academy of Science 223, 226
International Monetary Fund (IMF) 72, 74, 78, 92, 177, 187

Järve, T. 95, 105
Joeste, M. 94, 105
Jones, D.C. 4, 131, 132, 133, 134, 135, 138, 140, 148, 149, 159, 171

Jowell, R. 100, 105
Jungbauer-Gans, M. 243, 251

Kaevats, Ü. 94, 105
Kahk, J. 94, 105
Kallay, L. 157, 159, 167, 170, 171
Karlsson, M. 94, 104
Kasriel, K. 262
Keeble, D. 15, 19, 33
Kell, K. 94
Keren, M. 4, 35, 41, 42, 47, 189, 215
Khan, M. 108, 115
Kirchhoff, B.A. 10, 24, 33
Kirzner, I. 73, 92
Kiss, Y. 164, 171
Klaamann, V. 102,105
Kleinhenz, Th. 3, 5
Knobl, A. 94, 105
Knuth, M. 234, 251
Koch, T. 236, 251
Kokalj, L. 252
Konsoulov, V. 130
Kornai, J. 35, 44, 47, 85, 86, 92, 94, 105
Kozlov, V. 75, 92
Krajewski, S. 181, 186, 188
Krugman, P. 104
Kuczi, T. 155, 171
Kumar, M.S. 178, 187

LaPlant, D.J. 19, 33
Layard, R. 104
Lazarsfeld, P. 110, 115
Leechor, Ch. 194, 206, 215
Lehmbruch, G. 233, 251
Lengyel, G. 155, 170, 171
Levinthal, D.A. 24, 33
Lewis, J. 19, 33
Liebernickel, W. 237, 251
Lindenberg, S. 233, 251
Lindmark, L. 10, 15, 32

Linhart, I. 220, 226
Liuhto, K. 94, 105
Loogma, K. 100, 105
Loveman, G. 2, 6, 12, 33
Luders, I. 178, 187
Luup, L. 99, 105

Mac Donald, R. 154, 171
Maki, W. 10, 11, 12, 19, 34
Marceau, M. 161, 171
Marrese, M. 159, 171
Marshall, A. 2, 5
Marx, K. 30
Massey, D. 80, 81, 92
May-Strobl, E. 236, 237, 238, 251, 252, 255, 262
Meth-Cohn, D. 258, 259, 262
Meurs, M. 132, 140, 149, 159, 171
Miller, B. 24, 26, 34
Ministry of Administration of National Possession and their Privatization, Czechoslovakia 219
Mizsei, K. 155, 158, 171
Mladek, I. 177, 182, 183, 188
Monck, C. 86, 90, 92
Moore, L. 194, 215
Morgan, J. 7, 10, 20, 32
Moscow State University 76, 91
Müller, D. 148, 149
Murrell, P. 145, 149, 195, 215

National Agency for Privatization, Romania 107,113
National Statistical Office, Romania 125, 126
National Statistics Office 123, 130
National Trade Register Office, Romania 111, 112
Nedzvetsky, S. 66, 70
Nelson, R.R. 45, 47
Ners, K. 4, 175, 254, 257, 262
Norgaard, O. 94, 104, 105
North, D.C. 148, 149, 200, 215
Nove, A. 72, 92
Nunnenkamp, P. 182, 188

Oakey, R. 75, 92
Orenstein, M. 180, 182, 183, 187

Organization for Economic Cooperation and Development (OECD) 9, 33, 92, 94, 105
Olofsson, Ch. 10, 15, 32

Pannenberg, M. 243, 251
Panorama of EC Industry 104
Papp, B. 262
Parchev, I. 148
Parvulov, S. 132, 133, 134, 135, 145, 146, 149, 150
Paulini, M. 236, 237, 238, 251, 252, 255, 262
Petrin, T. 258, 262
Pettai, I. 100, 105
Phelps, E.S. 183, 187
Phillips, B. 10, 33
Pickel, A. 228, 232, 255, 262
Pinto, B. 181, 184, 185, 186, 188
Piore, M. 2, 6, 78, 83, 84, 87, 92
Pollisinski, K. 95, 105
Porter, R. 57, 58, 92
Potter, J. 15, 33
Prasnikar, I. 163, 167, 170, 171, 173
Preisendörfer, P. 24, 32, 33, 237, 240, 251, 252
Puchev, P. 4, 116, 130, 132, 149, 159, 171, 254, 257, 261

Quintas, P. 92

Rahva, Hääl 104
Raiser, M. 182, 188
Rajasalu, T. 95, 102, 105
Rapaczynski, A. 113, 115, 175, 182, 183, 187
Rappa, M. 92
Rausser, G.C. 94, 104, 131, 149, 151, 171
Reiljan, J. 101, 106
Reynolds, P.D. 2, 4, 5, 7, 9, 10, 11, 12, 14, 17, 19, 20, 21, 24, 26, 27, 28, 32, 34, 258, 262
Richter, S. 151, 171
Rocha, R. 94, 95, 102, 105
Rock, C. 131, 133, 149, 150
Rogers, H. 258, 262
Rogova, S. 94, 99, 106
Rojec, M. 169, 172
Rolland, G. 181, 188
Romanian Development Agency 110, 113, 115, 118
Rosati, D.K. 94, 106
Rostow, W. 79, 92
Rowe, D. 77, 90, 91
Rühle, I. 3, 6
Ruutsoo, R. 94, 105
Růžička, R. 4, 217, 220, 221, 226
Ryterman, R. 183, 187

Sabel, C. 78, 83, 84, 87, 92
Sayer, A. 78, 92
Scheytt, O. 234, 252
Schlotter, H.G. 259, 262
Schmidt, A. 252
Schrumpf, H. 235, 252
Schumpeter, J.A. 2, 6, 8, 34, 55, 58, 74, 79, 92
Schupp, J. 234, 251
Schüssler, R. 23, 32, 240, 251
von Schuttenbach, L. 3, 5
Schwarz, A. 237, 251
Schwarz, R. 214
Schwarze, J. 251
Scott, T. 178, 188
Sengenberger, W. 2, 6, 12, 33
Sepp, U. 94, 106
Shleifer, A. 183, 187
Siebert, H. 151, 172
Sik, E. 155, 169, 172
Sinn, G., H.W. 191, 192, 215, 233, 252
Smith, A. 151, 172
de Soto, H. 7, 32
Stahl, K. 193, 195, 215
Standing, G. 137, 141, 149
State Committee on Antimonopoly Policy of the RSFSR 74, 92
Staticheski Godishnik Bulgaria 160, 172

Statistical Office of Estonia 94, 98, 99, 100
Statistical Office of Macedonia 160, 162, 163, 172, 173
Statisticki Godisnjak Jugoslavije 158, 172
Statisticni Letopis Republike Slovenije 160, 172
Statistisches Bundesamt 242
Sterlin, A. 75, 92
Stevenson, H. 55, 56, 58
Stinchcombe, A.L. 24, 34
Storey, D.J. 7, 9, 10, 12, 15, 17, 27, 33, 34, 90, 92, 153, 172
Summers, L. 104
Summers, R. 194, 215
Svetlicic, M. 169, 172
Swanson, D. 143, 144, 149
Sziraczki, G. 149

Tibor, A. 159, 164, 172
Thieme, J. 180
Thomas, M. 5, 227, 232
Tsiganov, A. 72, 74, 92
Tyler, P. 19, 33
Tyson, A. L. 258, 262

Union for Private Economic Enterprise (UPEE) 165, 166, 172
United Nations 74, 92
University of Warwick Science Park Ltd. 73, 77, 91
Uvalic, M. 151, 172

Vajda, A. 155, 171
Valencia, M. 262
Valencic, D. 163, 167, 171, 173
Velloso, J.P. d. R. 213, 216
Verspagen, B. 194, 216
The Vienna Institute for Comparative Economic Studies (WIIW) 109, 115
Vilensky, A. 4, 59, 257, 261
Virág, Z. 113, 115
Voss, T. 24, 33

Wade, R. 211, 216
Wagner, G. 251
Walker, Sh. 15, 33, 78, 92
Wang, Z. 169, 172
Ward, R. 154, 172
Webster, L. 143, 144, 145, 149, 185, 188, 257, 258, 261
Weiss, L. 153, 172
Werner, K. 3, 6, 253, 262
Westhead, P. 4, 7, 17, 27, 34, 72, 90, 92
Wield, D. 92
Willumsen, H. 104
Wilton, I. 133, 149
Windell, J. 149
Winkler, A. 3, 6
White, S. 7, 21, 28, 34
Woderich, R. 236, 251
World Bank 92, 95, 96, 102, 131, 132, 149, 178, 188
Wynarczyk, P. 95
Wyznikiewicz, B. 184, 185, 188
Wyzan, M. 131, 133, 150

Yamin, M. 83, 92
Yotzov, V. 130

Zavrakhanov, I. 75, 93
Zelenograd Science Park 88, 91
Ziegler, R. 5, 24, 32, 233, 237, 240, 251, 252

Subject Index

administration 15, 25, 28, 44, 46, 65-67, 69, 76, 87, 107, 113f., 121, 127, 166, 217-219, 223, 228, 234f., 255
agglomeration 13, 18f., 56, 75, 82
agriculture 11, 40, 55, 59, 99f., 110f., 113, 119, 167, 218, 254, 260
Albania 117, 169
assets → capital stock
auctions 80, 87, 113, 133, 176
Australia 15

banking sector 25, 29f., 43, 52, 60, 65f., 70, 76, 86, 102, 109, 112, 119-121, 123f., 127f., 136, 138, 140, 142, 153, 156, 163, 182-185, 192, 224, 231, 235, 248, 258f.
bankruptcy 39, 56, 107, 113, 121, 126, 180, 182, 198, 223, 229
bottom-up transformation 1, 3-5, 35f., 46, 52, 57, 113f., 150, 227, 253-255, 258, 260f.
Britain → United Kingdom
budget constraint 39, 41-44, 85f., 119, 181, 191, 257
Bulgaria 4, 112, 116-129, 131-137, 141-145, 147, 151, 154-157, 159-162, 164-169, 178
bureaucracy → administration
business associations 28, 58, 66, 69, 102, 128, 132, 148, 159, 164, 185, 213, 260

Canada 15, 29, 97
capital 5, 13, 19, 28, 30, 36, 63-65, 70, 74, 77, 86, 101f., 110-113, 120-124, 128, 136-138, 140-142, 145-147, 155-157, 163, 167-170, 177, 182-186, 192-194, 198, 200, 206, 210, 212, 223, 225, 228f., 231, 233-236, 239-243, 246, 248f., 254, 258-260
- financial 235, 237, 240, 242f., 249
- foreign 70, 88f., 99, 103, 108, 112f., 120, 126, 142, 169f., 178, 186, 201, 257
- intensity 156f., 167-169, 194f., 242, 246
- outside 245, 248-250
- personal 240, 246-250
- start-up 13, 27, 65f., 86, 110, 123, 144, 157, 240-246, 248-250
- stock 100, 113, 136, 138, 140, 144, 147
- venture 26, 84, 128, 185
China, People's Republic 7
Chile 178
CIS 72, 90, 97, 99
collateral 109, 185, 259
communism 38, 40, 42-44, 52-54, 100f., 107, 131f., 153, 155, 169, 175, 179, 228, 232, 235, 249
Communist party 116, 132, 175
construction 9, 11, 19, 29, 59f., 63, 65, 99f., 134, 189, 191, 193, 202f., 205-208, 221, 229, 240, 250, 253f.
cooperation 59, 62, 68, 73, 78, 84, 87, 104, 129, 231, 234, 260
cooperatives 60, 62-64, 87, 98f., 111, 116, 119, 128, 131f., 134-136, 140-143, 145-147, 150f., 159f., 163-166, 218f., 223
corruption 54, 67, 103, 107, 113f., 127, 187, 257
craft sector 29, 65, 66, 107, 116, 154, 157f., 161, 165, 201, 221, 228, 238
creative destruction 2, 8, 78, 191, 198, 200
credits 36, 43, 56, 66, 69, 85, 102f., 109, 114, 120, 123f., 127f., 136, 156, 169, 182, 185, 222-224, 246, 248f., 258

criminal activities 25, 30, 36, 45f., 54, 64-66, 122, 126f., 257
Croatia 157, 254
currency 44, 54, 71, 86, 95, 102, 108, 110, 118f., 156f., 176, 192, 200f., 209, 229, 233f., 256, 258, 260
Czech Republic 4, 52, 117, 143-145, 175-177, 179-186, 217-226, 254

Denmark 98
democracy 3, 52f., 101, 104, 116f., 120, 122, 126, 162, 175f., 186, 233

entrepreneurs 2-5, 9, 13, 16, 19, 23, 25, 28-30, 32, 36-39, 41, 43, 45, 53-58, 64f., 69, 72, 75, 79f., 84-86, 89, 101-103, 108, 110, 119, 123-128, 136, 148, 152, 154-156, 159, 164, 168f., 177, 185, 192, 200, 209f., 212f., 217, 219, 221-225, 227-232, 234f., 237f., 246, 255f., 258-260
- nascent 20-25, 27f., 189
entrepreneurship 4f., 7-9, 11f., 14, 25, 31, 52-57, 59f., 62-69, 73-75, 79, 83, 89, 101, 103, 114, 116, 122f., 151f., 159-161, 168f., 177, 183, 186, 191, 194, 198, 200, 204, 209-211, 214, 220, 227-229, 232-234, 255-261
- and economic development 1-4, 8, 10, 31, 35, 38, 52-54, 74, 90, 163, 178, 189, 253, 259
- destructive 77
- illegal 25, 54, 64, 257, 259
- productive 54f., 73-75, 261
- unproductive 54, 74, 77, 256, 259
entrepreneurial
- activity 7-9, 12, 23, 25f., 30f., 54, 74f., 78, 86, 151f., 191f., 259
- behavior 8, 54f., 74, 191
- culture 14, 21, 55, 57, 116, 120, 129, 155, 256, 258, 260
- processes 8, 10, 12, 14, 17-27, 31, 65
- spirit 76, 100, 221, 225, 258
Estonia 4, 94-104, 254
European Community 72, 96, 98-100, 114, 128
exchange rate 38, 44, 47, 102, 109, 119, 123, 146, 176, 212, 260
exports 38, 44-47, 76, 94, 96f., 100, 102, 110, 112, 114, 127, 137, 139f., 142, 144f., 147f., 157, 165, 181, 213, 260

farming → agriculture
Finland 94f., 97-99
flexibility 3, 13, 38, 45, 83, 116, 129, 154f., 184, 213f., 226, 256
foreign
- aid 53, 114, 120, 169, 225, 260
- capital → capital, foreign
- dept 117, 120, 132
France 15f., 57, 98

Georgia 254
Germany 57, 97, 195, 200, 210, 229
- East 5, 44, 116, 123, 131, 189-196, 198, 200, 204, 206, 209-213, 227-230, 232-246, 248-250, 254
- West 15f., 19, 27, 189-193, 195f., 198, 204f., 209f., 227-230, 234, 236-246, 248-250
government 3-5, 8f., 11, 14, 18, 25-28, 30f., 35f., 39, 43, 45-47, 52-54, 56f., 66-69, 72, 74-76, 79, 81, 84, 88, 101f., 107f., 112f., 116f., 120f., 126-129, 132f., 138-140, 142, 156, 158, 162f., 175, 177, 179-181, 183-187, 191, 213, 223, 255-261
Greece 95, 98, 163

Hungary 4, 52, 94, 110, 112-114, 116f., 120, 131, 143-145, 151, 154-169, 174, 178, 212, 253f.

illegal economy → underground economy
imports 38, 44, 46, 96f., 100, 104,

108, 110, 112, 114, 260
India 189, 193
industry 11-13, 15-20, 27, 29, 37, 39, 42, 44-46, 55-57, 59-61, 63-66, 68, 72f., 75-78, 80f., 83-88, 95f., 98-100, 108, 113f., 119, 124, 131-148, 150, 153, 156f., 159f., 165-168, 170, 178-184, 186, 189-214, 218, 228-230, 236f., 239-244, 249f., 254, 258
inequality 30
inflation 44, 59, 66, 96, 102, 109f., 116-120, 123, 154, 176, 184, 200, 258
infrastructure 7, 14, 25, 28, 31, 52, 77, 83, 89, 108, 127f., 176, 193, 212, 260
innovation 2f., 9, 12, 35, 41, 54f., 57, 66, 72-89, 116, 132, 163, 184, 189, 191f., 194f., 200, 212f., 228, 255f., 258
inputs 13, 19, 28, 38f., 137, 139f., 144f., 155, 185, 209, 255-258
institutions 3, 7, 12, 27f., 30f., 35f., 40f., 56, 65, 72f., 75-79, 82f., 86, 88, 90, 95, 101, 104, 108, 113, 117-121, 126-128, 132f., 137, 145, 148, 154, 163, 175f., 182, 185, 191, 200f., 209, 211-213, 228, 233f., 257, 259
interest rate 66, 86, 102f., 109, 120, 123, 128, 156, 170, 185, 191, 222f., 258
investment 26, 29, 42, 45, 52, 66, 74, 76f., 82, 84, 86, 88, 99, 103, 108f., 112-114, 118-121, 126, 129, 156, 158, 169, 177, 179-183, 186, 191-195, 198, 200f., 210, 213, 222, 224, 233-237, 239-243, 246, 249, 255-260
Ireland 15f.
Italy 10, 15f., 57

Japan 15f., 19, 44, 98, 258

Kazakhstan 254
Korea, Republic of 258
Kyrgyzstan 254

Latin America 7
Latvia 96f.
legal system 103, 192
legalization 54, 64f., 72, 78f., 98, 111, 127, 148, 163, 169, 256, 259
liberalization 66, 71, 107, 109, 114, 117, 119, 133, 176, 178, 180f., 200f., 209, 211f., 254, 256, 258f.
Lithuania 96f., 254

Macedonia 4, 151, 154-158, 160-163, 168f., 173, 254
machinery 43, 66, 74, 124, 127, 129, 140, 159, 194, 198, 206, 229
macroeconomic conditions 43-45, 52, 66, 94-96, 104, 107, 109, 116-118, 120, 122, 128f., 133, 151, 154, 161f., 175f., 179f., 186, 192, 200f., 210, 212, 258, 260
Mafia 45f., 66
manufacturing → industry
Moldavia 112f.
monopoly 59, 66, 68f., 84, 88f., 98, 100f., 104, 116, 122, 126, 129, 133, 137, 145, 180, 222f., 255f.

Netherlands 15, 98f.
New Zealand 15
nomenclatura 42, 45, 53, 64, 66, 79, 89, 155f., 169, 178, 230, 232
Norway 15, 98

ownership 13, 28-31, 35f., 40f., 45-47, 60, 67, 69, 72, 75-77, 86, 95, 99f., 102, 107f., 111, 113f., 118f., 122, 131, 133-136, 141, 145-148, 150, 156, 158-161, 164-166, 170, 175-178, 182f., 185f., 192, 197, 199, 201, 218-222, 224f., 228, 231, 235f., 243, 246, 249, 253, 255

Poland 4f., 52f., 55f., 94f., 110, 113f., 116f., 131f., 143-145, 155, 175-181, 184f., 189-191, 200-202, 204-213, 253f.
policy towards new and small firms 1, 7, 18, 25-32, 56-59, 63-65, 69f., 85-89, 102, 107, 114, 116f., 124f., 127, 132f., 148, 157, 164, 169f., 191, 213f., 225, 234, 248f., 259-261
Portugal 95
privatization 1, 3f., 35, 40-43, 46, 52, 63-65, 69, 77, 95, 100, 102f., 107f., 112-114, 118f., 121f., 127, 129, 131-133, 143, 148, 151, 155f., 165, 175-183, 185-187, 189, 192, 195-197, 199, 201, 206, 209-214, 217-221, 225, 227, 229, 231, 235, 238, 240f., 253f.
profits 35, 42f., 57, 59, 74, 81, 86, 108, 114, 121, 127, 136f., 139, 141-143, 145, 147, 153, 182, 201, 220, 224, 256, 258, 260
property → ownership
property rights 29, 80, 87, 151, 175-179, 185, 219, 233, 255, 257

qualification 2, 8, 11, 13f., 21, 23, 28, 56f., 65, 72-74, 77, 85, 87, 90, 102, 116, 127, 129, 138f., 141, 152, 159, 185, 200, 211-213, 223, 228, 230f., 234, 236, 243-245, 250, 256, 258, 260

reform 65, 67, 72, 78, 212, 235
- economic 59, 66, 69-71, 96, 107, 116-118, 120, 122f., 125, 127, 129, 151f., 161, 178, 181, 183, 186, 189, 198, 200, 212, 221
- monetary 44, 96, 102f., 200
- political 35, 79, 104, 116, 121, 127, 132
regulation 25, 28f., 75, 114, 120, 122, 153, 157, 192, 222f., 233, 235, 256-258, 260
resources 2f., 8, 15, 20, 26-28, 31, 36, 41, 43, 47, 55f., 65f., 69, 76, 82, 100, 113, 121, 124, 148, 169, 177, 180, 185-187, 192, 194, 200, 209f., 212f., 222f., 225, 231, 238f., 256-259
Romania 4, 107-114, 117, 120, 178, 254
Russia 4, 12, 40, 52, 59-90, 94, 97, 99f., 103f., 144, 186

science parks 4, 72-90
second economy → underground economy
self-employment 9, 13f., 17, 20, 53, 98, 100, 118, 122, 154f., 168, 217, 222, 234, 236, 244-246, 250, 253
services 11-15, 17, 19, 28f., 31, 36, 38, 41, 47, 55f., 59-61, 64-67, 76f., 89, 99f., 109f., 118f., 123f., 127, 129, 133f., 148, 156f., 166-168, 178, 184f., 189, 191-194, 201, 211, 218, 223, 229-231, 234, 239-243, 249f., 254f., 259, 261
shadow economy → underground economy
Slovak Republic 117, 178, 254
Slovenia 4, 151, 154-158, 160-163, 166-169, 254
socialism → communism
state-owned enterprises (SOEs) 1, 3f., 35-44, 46, 53, 60, 62f., 65, 68, 75, 95, 98, 100-103, 107-109, 111, 113f., 116, 118f., 121, 123f., 129, 131f., 134-148, 150-152, 156, 158f., 161f., 164-166, 175, 178, 179-187, 198, 200, 206, 209, 222f., 235, 254, 257f.,
Sweden 10, 15-17, 27, 97-99
Switzerland 15

Tajikistan 254
tariffs 66, 258, 260
taxes 9, 15, 36, 39, 43-45, 47, 53f., 66, 68f., 102f., 111, 114, 127f., 181, 191, 194, 223, 234, 237, 257f.

tax reform 71, 102, 117, 119, 121, 128
technology diffusion 80, 83, 191, 213
top-down transformation 1, 3f., 35, 38f., 46, 114, 254, 260
trade
- policy 180
- sector 18, 29, 55, 59, 64f., 99f., 104, 107, 110-113, 118, 123f., 126, 129, 134, 156-158, 166-168, 178, 184, 189, 191, 193, 201, 211, 228-230, 240-242, 244, 249f., 254f., 261
- unions 138f., 141, 143, 145, 178
training → qualification
transaction costs 25, 45, 166, 257, 259
transportation 11, 13, 19, 25, 29, 59, 65, 99, 254
Turkmenistan 254

underground economy 30, 36, 54, 59, 63-65, 109f., 134, 155, 169, 220, 256f., 259
unemployment 1, 3, 10f., 13f., 18, 20, 26, 44, 95, 101, 110, 117, 119, 153-156, 162f., 168, 176, 178f., 181, 183f., 198, 212, 231, 243-246, 250, 254, 257, 260
United Kingdom 15-17, 19, 26f., 30, 57, 73, 75, 80, 83, 86, 88, 90, 98, 154
United States 1, 10f., 15-17, 19, 21, 24, 26-29, 45, 56, 85, 97-99, 189
unofficial economy → underground economy
Uzbekistan 254

wages 10, 13, 95, 109, 133, 138f., 142-144, 154, 184, 192, 194, 198, 200f., 210-212, 257
Western Europe 8, 27, 96f., 112, 128, 192, 234
World Bank 95f., 120, 176, 181, 186

Yugoslavia 151, 156f., 161, 163, 169